STUDIES IN MANUSCRIPT ILLUMINATION

NUMBER 6

STUDIES IN MANUSCRIPT ILLUMINATION

KURT WEITZMANN, *GENERAL EDITOR*

PUBLISHED FOR THE

DEPARTMENT OF ART AND ARCHAEOLOGY

PRINCETON UNIVERSITY

THE ILLUSTRATIONS
OF THE
LITURGICAL HOMILIES OF
GREGORY
NAZIANZENUS

BY GEORGE GALAVARIS

PRINCETON, NEW JERSEY

PRINCETON UNIVERSITY PRESS

1969

Printed in the United States of America
by Princeton University Press

This book has been composed
in Times Roman type

Frontispiece: Gregory Nazianzenus, from Codex Sinai gr. 339

TO MY PARENTS

PREFACE

A PAPER prepared for Professor Kurt Weitzmann in 1955 gave life to the idea of writing this book. Its growth was nurtured by the belief that a proper study of the group of monuments that illuminated manuscripts constitute could offer much new information to the art historian, the historian, and the theologian. That belief was accompanied by an awareness that many illuminated manuscripts remain unknown or incompletely studied. My intention has been to close at least one gap in their study by attempting to show the contribution that the illustrations of the Homilies of Gregory Nazianzenus have made to our knowledge of Middle Byzantine book illumination and the part that liturgy played in the art and thought of the time.

The writing of this book took me from Princeton to the Dumbarton Oaks Research Library and Collection of Harvard University (Washington, D.C.) where a two-year fellowship enabled me to write and revise a considerable part of the text. I traveled also to the Holy Mountain, to the Library of the Ecumenical Patriarchate at Constantinople, and several times to European libraries; but I have not been to Sinai, Jerusalem, or Moscow, where the only manuscripts I have not examined personally are housed. Material and data about these manuscripts were supplied to me by Professor Weitzmann and the Dumbarton Oaks Research Library and Collection. For comparative material I have used some photographs of other unpublished manuscripts which are deposited in the Department of Art and Archaeology of Princeton University.

It is a great pleasure to think of all the friends who have been encouraging and helpful through the years, and to record here my deeply felt obligation to them. I am grateful to every member of the faculty of the Department of Art and Archaeology of Princeton University. Professor Weitzmann has been an ever present help. He placed his notebooks at my disposal, provided me with photographs from his own collection, and secured other photographs from European libraries. He and Dr. J. Weitzmann-Fiedler have given me their help in other ways too many to enumerate; both have freely shared their immense knowledge with me, and made excellent suggestions for the revision of the manuscript. If Professor Weitzmann had not been the editor of this series of studies, I would have liked him to share with my parents the dedication of the present work as an indication of my appreciation for all he has done for me.

I should like to thank Professor E. Kitzinger, formerly Director of Studies at the Dumbarton Oaks Research Library and Collection, Professor S. Der Nersessian who read an early draft of the manuscript, and my colleagues Drs. E. Bickersteth, D. Hitchcock, and H. Lieb for many kindnesses.

For permission to study the original manuscripts and for help in various ways, I am greatly indebted to the following librarians, keepers of manuscripts and libraries: Drs. R. Hunt, W. O. Hassal and the Bodleian Library, Oxford; Professor T. J. Brown, Mr. G. Bonner and the British Museum, London; the late Mr. J. Porcher and the Bibliothèque Nationale, Paris; Professor S. Bassi and the Biblioteca Nazionale, Turin; Monsignor G. Galbiati and the Biblioteca Ambrosiana, Milan; the Librarian of the Biblioteca Laurenziana, Florence; Monsignor A. Albareda, Professor A. van Lantschoot and the Biblioteca Apostolica Vaticana; Mr. A. Photiades and the National Library, Athens; the librarians of the Holy Community of Mt. Athos; the Rev. P. Theodorides and the Ecumenical Patriarchal Library, Istanbul.

I want also to acknowledge the many courtesies of the Misses L. Keane (London) and S. Pilson (Montreal), and Mesdames J. Porter (Montreal) and E. Owen (Oxford). Finally I offer my sincere thanks to Princeton University Press and, in particular, to Miss H. Anderson. There are others who have helped me whose names I have omitted; I would like them to find here the expression of my gratitude.

Even with all this kind assistance I have doubtless made errors; I should be held responsible for them and for every imperfection in the work, while its merits should be ascribed to the help of my friends.

Montreal   G.G.
1967

CONTENTS

CONTENTS

ILLUSTRATIONS

TEXT FIGURES

PLATES

ABBREVIATIONS

AB	*The Art Bulletin*
Bandini	A. M. Bandinius, *Catalogus codicum manuscriptorum Bibliothecae Mediceae Laurentianae*, I, Florence 1764
Beckwith, *Constantinople*	J. Beckwith, *The Art of Constantinople*, London 1961
Bénéchévitch, *Catalogus*	V. N. Bénéchévitch, *Catalogus codicum manuscriptorum graecorum qui in monasterio Sanctae Catharinae in monte Sina asservantur*, I, St. Petersburg 1911
Bibl. Nat., *Byzance*	Bibliothèque Nationale, *Byzance et la France Médiéval*, Paris 1958
Bordier, *Description*	H. Bordier, *Description des peintures et autres ornements contenus dans les manuscrits grecs de la Bibliothèque Nationale*, Paris 1883
Brett, *Great Palace*	G. Brett *et al.*, *The Great Palace of the Byzantine Emperors*, Oxford 1947
Brightman, *Liturgies*	F. E. Brightman, *Liturgies Eastern and Western*, I, Oxford 1896
D.A.C.L.	F. Cabrol, H. Leclercq, *Dictionnaire d'archéologie chrétienne et de liturgie*, I-XV, Paris 1907-1953
Coll. Paleo. Vat., I (1905)	*Miniature della Bibbia, cod. vat. regin. greco 1 e del Salterio cod. vat. palat. greco 381* (Collezione paleografica vaticana, facs. I), Milan 1905
Coxe	H. O. Coxe, *Catalogi codicum manuscriptorum Bibliothecae Bodleianae*, I, III, Oxford 1853, 1854
Demus-Diez	O. Demus, E. Diez, *Byzantine Mosaics in Greece*, Cambridge, Mass. 1931
Der Nersessian, *Barlaam*	S. Der Nersessian, *L'illustration du roman de Barlaam et Joasaph*, Paris 1937
DeWald, *Vat. gr. 1927*	E. T. DeWald, *Vaticanus graecus 1927* (The Illustrations in the Manuscripts of the Septuagint, III, 1), Princeton 1941
DeWald, *Vat. gr. 752*	E. T. DeWald, *Vaticanus graecus 752* (The Illustrations in the Manuscripts of the Septuagint, III, 2), Princeton 1942
Diehl, *Manuel*	C. Diehl, *Manuel d'art byzantin*, 2nd ed., I-II, Paris 1925-1926
Ebersolt, *Miniature*	J. Ebersolt, *La miniature byzantine*, Paris-Brussels 1926
Ehrhard, *Hom. Literatur*	A. Ehrhard, *Überlieferung und Bestand der hagiographischen und homiletischen Literatur der griechischen Kirche* (Texte und Untersuchungen zur Geschichte der altchristlichen Literatur, 50, 51), I-II, Leipzig, 1936-1938
E.E.B.S.	Ἐπετηρὶς τῆς Ἑταιρείας Βυζαντινῶν Σπουδῶν
Eustratiades-Arcadios, *Catalogue Vatopedi*	S. Eustratiades, Arcadios, *Catalogue of the Greek manuscripts in the Library of the Monastery of Vatopedi on Mt. Athos*, Cambridge, Mass. 1924
Fleury, *Hellenism*	E. Fleury, *Hellénisme et christianisme. Saint Grégoire de Nazianze et son temps*, Paris 1930
Frantz, *AB* (1934)	M. A. Frantz, "Byzantine Illuminated Ornament," *Art Bulletin*, 16 (1934), pp. 43-76
Friend, *Evangelists*	A. M. Friend, "The Portraits of the Evangelists in Greek and Latin Manuscripts," *Art Studies*, 5 (1927)
Gallay, *La vie*	P. Gallay, *La vie de saint Grégoire de Nazianze*, Lyon 1943
Gardthausen, *Codices Sinaitici*	V. Gardthausen, *Catalogus codicum graecorum Sinaiticorum*, Oxford 1886
Grabar, *Ambros. 49-50*	A. Grabar, *Les miniatures du Grégoire de Nazianze de l'Ambrosienne* (Ambrosianus 49-50), Paris 1943
Grabar, *Empereur*	A. Grabar, *L'empereur dans L'art byzantin*, Paris 1936

ABBREVIATIONS (continued)

Grabar, *Min. Byz.*   A. Grabar, *Miniatures byzantines de la Bibliothèque Nationale*, Paris 1939

Il menologio   *Il menologio di Basilio II* (*Cod. vat. gr. 1613*) (Codices e Vaticanis selecti, VIII) (facsimile), Turin 1907

Kondakov, *Histoire*   N. P. Kondakov, *Histoire de l'art byzantin consideré principalement dans les miniatures*, II, Paris 1891

Koukoules, *Bios*   P. Koukoules, Βυζαντινῶν Βίος καὶ Πολιτισμός, I-V, Athens 1948-1952

Lambros   S. Lambros, *Catalogue of the Greek Manuscripts on Mt. Athos*, I-II, Cambridge 1895, 1900

Lazarev, *History*   B. N. Lazarev, *Istoria vizantiiskoi zhivopisi*, Moscow 1947-1948

Lefherz, *Studien*   F. Lefherz, *Studien zu Gregor von Nazianz, Mythologie, Überlieferung, Scholiasten*, Bonn 1958

Martin, *Ladder*   J. R. Martin, *The Illustrations of the Heavenly Ladder of John Climacus*, Princeton 1954

Millet, *Dalmatique*   G. Millet, *La Dalmatique du Vatican*, Paris 1945

Millet, *Mistra*   G. Millet, *Monuments byzantins de Mistra*, Paris 1910

Millet, *Recherches*   G. Millet, *Recherches sur l'iconographie de l'évangile*, Paris 1916

Morey, *AB* (1929)   C. R. Morey, "Notes on East Christian Miniatures," *Art Bulletin*, 11 (1929), pp. 5-103

Morey, *Freer Coll.*   C. R. Morey, *East Christian Paintings in the Freer Collection*, New York 1914

Omont, *Evangiles*   Bibliothèque Nationale, *Evangiles avec peintures byzantines du XIᵉ siècle*, I-II, Paris 1908

Omont, *Inventaire sommaire*   H. Omont, *Inventaire sommaire des manuscrits grecs de la Bibliothèque Nationale*, I-VII, Paris 1886-1898

Omont, *Min. gr.* (1929)   H. Omont, *Miniatures des plus anciens manuscrits grecs de la Bibliothèque Nationale du Ve au XIVᵉ siècle*, 2nd ed., Paris 1929

Ouspensky, *Octateuque*   F. I. Ouspensky, *L'octateuque de la Bibliothèque du Sérail à Constantinople* (Bulletin of the Russian Archaeological Institute at Constantinople, XII), Sofia 1907

Papadopoulos-Kerameus   A. Papadopoulos-Kerameus, Ἱεροσολυμιτικὴ Βιβλιοθήκη, I-IV, St. Petersburg 1891-1899

PG   J. P. Migne, *Patrologia cursus completus, series graeca*, 1-161, Paris 1857-1866

Plagnieux, *St. Grégoire*   J. Plagnieux, *St. Grégoire de Nazianze théologien*, Paris 1952

Pokrovskii, *Evangelie*   N. P. Pokrovskii, *Evangelie v pamiatnikakh ikonografii preimushchestvenno Vizantiiskikh i Russkikh*, St. Petersburg 1892

Sajdak, *Scholia*   J. Sajdak, *Historia critica scholiastarum et commentatorum Gregorii Nazianzeni* (Meletemata Patristica I), Cracow 1914

Schlumberger, *Epopée*   G. L. Schlumberger, *L'épopée byzantine à la fin du dixième siècle*, I-III, Paris 1896-1905

Schultz, *Torcello*   B. Schultz, *Die Kirchenbauten auf der Insel Torcello*, Berlin 1927

Schweinfurth (1943)   P. Schweinfurth, *Die byzantinische Form, ihr Wesen und ihre Wirkung*, Berlin 1943

Sinko, *Traditione*   T. Sinko, *De Traditione orationum Gregorii Nazianzeni*, pars prima (Meletemata Patristica II), Cracow 1917

Soteriou (1937)   G. Soteriou, Κειμήλια τοῦ Οἰκουμενικοῦ Πατριαρχείου Κωνσταντινουπόλεως, Athens 1937

ABBREVIATIONS (continued)

Spyridon-Eustradiades, *Catalogue Lavra*	Spyridon and S. Eustratiades, *Catalogue of the Greek Manuscripts in the Library of the Lavra on Mt. Athos* (Harvard Theological Studies, XII), Cambridge, Mass. 1925
Stornajolo, *Cosmas*	C. Stornajolo, *Le miniature della Topografia cristiana di cosma Indicopleuste; codice vaticano greco 699* (Codices e Vaticanis selecti, X) (facsimile), Milan 1908
Stornajolo, *Giacomo monaco*	C. Stornajolo, *Miniature delle omilie di Giacomo monaco (cod. vatic. gr. 1162) e dell'Evangeliario greco urbinate (cod. vatic. urbin. gr. 2)* (Codices e Vaticanis selecti, series minor, I), Rome 1910
Strzygowski, *Rep. f. Kunst.* (1888)	J. Strzygowski, "Die Monatscyclen der byzantinischen Kunst," *Repertorium für Kunstwissenschaft*, 11 (1888), pp. 23-46
Strzygowski, *Rep. f. Kunst.* (1890)	J. Strzygowski, "Eine trapezuntische Bilderhandschrift von Jahre 1346," *Repertorium für Kunstwissenschaft*, 13 (1890), pp. 241-263
Talbot Rice, *Byzantium*	D. Talbot Rice, *The Art of Byzantium*, London 1959
Tikkanen, *Farbengebung*	J. J. Tikkanen, *Studien über die Farbengebung in der mittelalterlichen Buchmalerei und der Renaissance*, Helsingfors 1933
Vogel-Gardthausen	M. Vogel, V. Gardthausen, *Die griechischen Schreiber des Mittelalters und der Renaissance*, Leipzig 1909
Weitzmann, *Buchmalerei*	K. Weitzmann, *Die byzantinische Buchmalerei des 9. und 10. Jahrhunderts*, Berlin 1935
Weitzmann, *Chronicles*	K. Weitzmann, "Illustrations for the Chronicles of Sozomenos, Theodoret, and Malalas," *Byzantion*, 16 (1942-1943), pp. 87-134
Weitzmann, *Joshua*	K. Weitzmann, *The Joshua Roll, A Work of the Macedonian Renaissance*, Princeton 1948
Weitzmann, *Lectionary Morgan 639*	K. Weitzmann, "The Constantinopolitan Lectionary, Morgan 639," *Studies in Art and Literature for Belle da Costa Greene*, Princeton 1954, pp. 358-373
Weitzmann, *Mythology*	K. Weitzmann, *Greek Mythology in Byzantine Art*, Princeton 1951
Weitzmann, *N.T. Mss Studies*	K. Weitzmann, "The Narrative and Liturgical Gospel Illustrations," *New Testament Manuscript Studies*, M. Parvis, A. Wigren eds., Chicago 1950, pp. 151-174
Weitzmann, *Semin. Kondak.* (1936)	K. Weitzmann, "Das Evangeliar im Skevophylakion zu Lawra," *Seminarium Kondakovianum*, 8 (1936), pp. 83-98
Weitzmann, *Roll*	K. Weitzmann, *Illustrations in Roll and Codex; a Study of the Origin and Method of Text Illustration . . .* , Princeton rev. ed. 1969

THE ILLUSTRATIONS
OF THE LITURGICAL HOMILIES OF
GREGORY NAZIANZENUS

INTRODUCTION

THE homilies of Gregory of Nazianzus have been considered heretofore only from a literary and theological point of view. Theologians have characterized the homilies as "homage to God, a work of beauty for the glory of the Logos,"[1] and have emphasized the fact that, like the work of the Church itself, they serve eternity, of which our earthly life is but a phase.

In these sermons Gregory communicates with the soul of mortal man as well as with God. At times he seems to retreat from this world of the incarnate soul, and at other times he expresses a profound feeling for the life on earth, nature, the beauties of the universe, and the activities of man. As he describes the splash of the waves or men's occupations in the spring, he creates a picture of unique freshness. Furthermore, he shows his compassion for human suffering. He does not remain indifferent to the ruins of terrestrial cities as did Plotinus; instead he hastens to the aid of his friends, helps the poor, and defends his compatriots.[2]

In the homilies two streams of thought often converge: Gregory feels the freshness of nature and of the world; at the same time he conveys an intense awareness of eternity and the presence of God. Since these two streams flow in his writings, they may also appear in the illustrations of the text. An examination of these illustrations will show whether or not the artists have captured Gregory's thoughts and presented, in a single illustrated book, religious and secular art normally found only in separate works. If they have, the actual contribution of the illustrations of Gregory's homilies to these two areas of art should be assessed. For the investigation of such problems, a comprehensive and systematic study, the importance of which has long been realized, of the extant illustrated manuscripts of the homilies must be undertaken.[3] The present work attempts that study.

Both the edifying nature and the literary qualities of Gregory's sermons—their power, their eloquence, the inventive imagination demonstrated in them, and the poetic and often passionate language—explain their popularity and the survival of more illustrated manuscripts of his homilies than of those by Basil the Great and Gregory of Nyssa, the other two members of the Cappadocian triad. Gregory's text offered greater opportunities to the illustrators. "Son éloquence chaude et brillante," says Kondakov, "riche en comparaisons imagées, pleine de formes classiques et de pensées élevées, charmait ses admirateurs comme ses disciples. De là l'immense quantité de copies des œuvres de cet orateur . . . de là aussi le grand nombre de miniatures qui ornent ses Homélies."[4] The personal interest of Emperor Constantine VII in the cult of Gregory may also explain the homilies' popularity, for, by removing Gregory's relics from Cappadocia to Constantinople and depositing them in both the

---

[1] Plagnieux, *St. Grégoire*, p. 259.
[2] *Ibid.*, p. 401.

[3] Weitzmann, *Mythology*, passim; *idem, Roll*, p. 199.
[4] Kondakov, *Histoire*, p. 57.

church of the Holy Apostles and the chapel of St. Anastasia, the Emperor revived interest in the Cappadocian Church Father.[5]

The illustrated manuscripts of the homilies of Gregory fall into three categories. The first category, in existence by the ninth century, consists of manuscripts containing a complete edition of all of his forty-five homilies. The best representatives of this category are the codd. Paris gr. 510, and Milan, Ambros. E. 49-50 inf.[6] The second category includes manuscripts, none dated earlier than the first half of the eleventh century, which contain only sixteen of the forty-five homilies, those that were to be read on certain feast days. Because these sixteen homilies were included in the readings of the liturgy, this edition has been called *liturgical*.[7] The manuscripts of this category may be subdivided into those which have as illustrations only frontispieces and title miniatures, and those which also have supplementary narrative miniatures.[8] The third category consists of the illustrated commentaries on the homilies. To it belong two illustrated manuscripts: the eleventh-century cod. Jerusalem, Taphou 44, containing the commentaries of George and Basil on the sixteen homilies,[9] and the twelfth- or thirteenth-century cod. A.N.I.8 in the University Library of Basel containing the commentaries of Elias of Crete.[10] A third codex dating from the late four-

[5] The letter of the Emperor Constantine VII concerning the transfer of Gregory's relics has been published by J. Sakkelion, Δελτίον τῆς Ἱστορικῆς καὶ Ἐθνολογικῆς Ἑταιρείας τῆς Ἑλλάδος, 2 (1885), pp. 264ff.; cf. Lefherz, *Studien*, p. 99. The Church commemorates the transfer of the relics on January 19. Stephen of Novgorod (c. 1350) mentioned that Gregory's hand was in the monastery of the Mother of God in Constantinople; see B. de Khitrovo, *Itinéraires russes en Orient*, Geneva 1889, p. 122. During the last years of the Empire the relics were placed in the church of Hagia Sophia. Later, nuns escaping the barbarians carried Gregory's relics to Rome and deposited them in the church of Santa Maria in Campo Martio. On June 11, 1580, Gregory XIII took the relics into the Vatican basilica. Gregory's head, however, is shown in the monastery of Vatopedi on Mt. Athos. See *Acta Sanctorum*, Maii, II, pp. 425ff.; E. Gedeon, Βυζαντινὸν Ἑορτολόγιον, Constantinople 1899, pp. 60-64; A. G. Paspates, Βυζαντιναὶ Μελέται, Constantinople 1877, pp. 368, 369; J. Ebersolt, *Sanctuaires de Byzance*, Paris 1921, pp. 33, 38, 91; Sajdak, *Scholia*, p. 281 n. 1. During the Macedonian period the interest in Gregory was great. He was compared to Demosthenes and a special liturgy was composed for him. See Sajdak, *Scholia*, pp. 255, 263; Ebersolt, *Miniature*, p. 38.

[6] Plates and description of the miniatures of the Paris manuscript in Omont, *Min. gr.* (1929), pp. 10ff.; for a discussion of the relationship between text and images see S. Der Nersessian, "The illus-

trations of the homilies of Gregory of Nazianzus, Paris gr. 510," *Dumbarton Oaks Papers*, 16 (1962), pp. 196-228; for the Milan manuscript see Grabar, *Ambros. 49-50*; and Weitzmann, *Buchmalerei*, p. 81.

[7] Cf. A. Michel, *Histoire de l'art*, I, Paris 1905, p. 243.

[8] Cf. *ibid.*, p. 244. It should be noted that there are a few codices containing sermons selected from the complete edition. These sermons, however, are not contained in the liturgical edition; their number varies and the study of the illustrations must be included in the study of the manuscripts containing the complete edition. The following manuscripts dating from the tenth and eleventh centuries are known: Athos, Vatopedi 121; London, Brit. Mus. Add. 22732; Paris gr. 515; Paris gr. 567; Sinai 347. See Eustratiades-Arcadios, *Catalogue Vatopedi*, p. 31; British Museum, *Catalogue of Additional Manuscripts, 1854-1860*, London 1875, p. 725; Bordier, *Description*, p. 116; Omont, *Inventaire sommaire*, I, pp. 68, 91; Gardthausen, *Codices sinaitici*, p. 75. The cod. London, Brit. Mus. Add. 49060, a new addition to the British Museum manuscripts, must be included here: see G. Bonner, "A New Patristic Manuscript," *The British Museum Quarterly*, 21 (1959), pp. 91, 92.

[9] Papadopoulos-Kerameus, I, p. 125; Sajdak, *Scholia*, p. 69.

[10] K. Escher, *Die Miniaturen in den Basler Bibliotheken, Museen und Archiven*, Basel 1917, p. 22,

teenth century, cod. Paris gr. 541, contains both the sixteen homilies of the liturgical edition and the commentary on them by Nicetas of Serrae.[11] Its three miniatures, however, illustrate the text of the homilies, not the commentary, and these illustrations must therefore be included in the second category.

Because the manuscripts of the first and third categories have their own problems and require separate analysis, the present study is confined exclusively to the illustrations of the liturgical edition.

---

pls. II, III; A. Xyngopoulos, " Ἰωάννης ὁ Χρυσόστομος Πηγὴ Σοφίας," Ἀρχαιολογικὴ Ἐφημερίς, 81-83

(1942-1944), p. 26 n. 1.
[11] Omont, *Inventaire sommaire*, I, p. 80.

I. THE AUTHOR AND THE TEXT

GREGORY of Nazianzus, known also as Gregory the Theologian, has been fortunate in his biographers, who have drawn their information about his life primarily from his own writings and particularly from his long autobiographical poem and letters.[1] Since special monographs have been devoted to these topics, neither the life of St. Gregory, nor a complete account of his works, nor even a discussion of theological and literary matters, are given here. Instead this chapter acquaints the reader with persons and events referred to in the texts of the homilies under discussion and provides the background necessary to the development of the study.

Gregory takes his appellation from Nazianzus, a small town in southwestern Cappadocia. He was supposedly born in the year A.D. 329/330 in Arianzus near Nazianzus. His studies in oratory took place primarily in Athens, where he went as "a beardless youth," and where he spent at least ten years. Himerius and Prohairesius, famous sophists of the time,[2] and Libanius, who taught in Athens in 353, may have been his teachers.[3] Leaving Athens in 356, Gregory went to Constantinople and from there to Nazianzus where, against his will, he was ordained a priest, probably on Christmas Day, A.D. 361.[4] He had hardly been ordained when, in a moment of "cowardice and weakness" (Or. I, 2) and feeling an exaggerated fear of the responsibilities of spiritual office, he fled to Pontus to live in solitude with Basil the Great. He returned, however, and the following year preached the first of his two Easter sermons in the church of Nazianzus. This first discourse is a short address stressing the duties of forgiveness and of devotion to God. Almost ten years later, in 372, the year of his ordination as bishop of the small frontier village of Sasima, Gregory delivered a sermon addressed to Gregory of Nyssa who had been sent by Basil the Great "ut ipsius afflictum ob consecrationem animum consolaretur," as the commentator says.[5]

Some of the orations discussed in this study were prompted by various events occurring during his episcopate in Sasima and Nazianzus. One of them was inspired by the disasters of 372. In that year there occurred an epidemic among the cattle, a drought, and a hail storm that devastated parts of Cappadocia. These disasters led the poverty-stricken inhabitants of Nazianzus to seek consolation from Gregory the Elder, Gregory's father. But Gregory the Elder remained silent. Gregory the Younger

---

[1] For a full account of Gregory's life, see the prefixed life to the Benedictine edition of the Works by Clémencet. The lives by Ullmann, Benoit, and Caillau are standard. The more recent bibliography is found in Gallay, *La vie*, pp. xiii-xx, whose account is followed here in general lines. See also K. Bones, Τὸ γενεαλογικὸν δένδρον Γρηγορίου Ναζιανζηνοῦ, Athens 1953.

[2] W. Schmid, O. Stählin, *W. von Christs Geschichte der griechischen Literatur*, II, 2, Munich 1924, p. 1001; Gallay, *La vie*, pp. 40ff.

[3] Gallay, *La vie*, pp. 50, 51; Fleury, *Hellenism*, p. 138.

[4] Gallay, *La vie*, p. 73; Fleury, *Hellenism*, p. 127.

[5] *PG*, 35, 817; Gallay, *La vie*, p. 115.

therefore undertook the task of delivering a sermon in which he related human sin to natural disasters.

It was probably in the following year that Gregory preached both a stirring extolment of Christian charity, his sermon on the Love of the Poor, and his magnificent panegyric on the Maccabees. Nothing is more moving than the picture of human suffering he presents in the former,[6] nor more compelling than the power of faith he so dramatically depicts in the latter.

Gregory's father died in the spring of 374. In the same year Gregory wrote to Julian the Tax Collector (who should not be confused with the Emperor Julian the Apostate),[7] to ask that the clergy and the poor be exempted from paying taxes. Julian demanded that Gregory deliver a sermon, and made compliance a condition of the exemption. Gregory acquiesced, producing an eloquent sermon dealing with the vanity of all earthly things, in which he exhorted every man to devote himself and his possessions to God.

In 375 he retreated to Seleucia, metropolis of Isauria. Four years later, in January 379, Gregory's dearest friend, Basil, died; but not until the year 382 (January 1) did Gregory pronounce the last farewell. The funeral oration expresses all the sadness and bleak despair he felt at the death of his most intimate friend. Basil's death was an experience which reinforced Gregory's growing inclination to retreat from the world of men and to await his admission to an eternal home.

However, this humble bishop who preferred not to rule even an obscure diocese was to become the patriarch of Constantinople. This was providential, for the Orthodox Christians of that city hoped that the Emperor Theodosius' rise to power would, in accordance with Nicene theology, bring about a needed unity of the faith that had been shaken by the Arian heresy.[8] Gregory journeyed to the capital of the empire where he helped to restore the Nicene faith to the Church. Early in his sojourn in Constantinople, Gregory delivered the following homilies in the chapel of St. Anastasia: on St. Athanasius in May 379, on Pentecost in June, and on St. Cyprian in October of the same year.[9] He delivered three more sermons at the end of the year 379 and the beginning of 380 on the Nativity, on Epiphany, and on Baptism.

In the spring of the year 381 the second Ecumenical Council met in Constantinople under the presidency of Meletius of Antioch. It was then that Gregory was elected and formally installed as patriarch of Constantinople. Shortly thereafter Meletius

---

[6] See A. Donders, "Eine soziale Predigt des christlichen Altertums," *Kirche und Kanzel*, 4 (1920), pp. 125-29. For the erroneous mediaeval tradition according to which this sermon was delivered at Basil's hospital in Caesarea see Gallay, *La vie*, p. 87, cf. Sajdak, *Scholia*, p. 173.

[7] The Byzantine commentators imply that such confusion existed in their own time. See Sajdak, *Scholia*, pp. 90, 169; Gallay, *La vie*, pp. 127, 128.

[8] For a detailed account of the activities of the various religious sects in Constantinople before and after Theodosius' rise to power, see Fleury, *Hellenism*, pp. 270ff.; Gallay, *La vie*, pp. 132ff. On the Church at the time of Theodosius, see G. Rauschen, *Jahrbücher der christlichen Kirche unter dem Kaiser Theodosius dem Grossen*, Freiburg in Breisgau 1897, esp. p. 77.

[9] Gallay, *La vie*, pp. 149ff.; Fleury, *Hellenism*, p. 294.

died suddenly and the old controversy about the occupation of the see of Antioch was revived; a solution of the crisis became pressing. The proposals made by Gregory, who now presided over the Council, were met with great opposition and were finally defeated. Since he had not been able to resolve the dispute, Gregory decided to resign as patriarch and return to his beloved solitude.[10] Before he left Constantinople he assembled the people and the Council in his church for the last time and delivered his farewell oration, an *apologia* for his life and struggle for the good of the people and the peace of the Church. His active life ended at this time, except for three further occasions: the homily delivered on St. Basil's death (1 January 382), the second sermon on Easter (9 April 383), and the homily on New Sunday (383).[11] His contemplative life was to continue until his last days in Arianzus, where the eloquence of his sermons assumed the form of moving sacred poems.[12]

The sermons mentioned in the brief biography above comprise the liturgical edition. The only known separate edition of the liturgical sermons, and indeed the earliest of the Greek editions, is that of M. Musuri, published in Venice in 1516. There is no satisfactory printed edition of Gregory's complete works in existence today.[13] The chief editions are the edition of Johannes Hervagius (Basel 1550), the Greek text of what was purported to be the *Opera omnia*; the Latin version of Leuvenklaius (Basel 1571), containing twenty sermons and selections of the commentaries of Elias and others; the Billy-Morel edition (Paris 1609-1611), accompanied by a Latin translation;[14] and the edition of the Benedictines of St. Maur, of which the first volume, containing the orations, was published in 1778, and the second volume, prepared by Clémencet, was edited by Caillau in Paris in 1840. The Benedictine edition was reprinted in Migne's *Patrologia Graeca* in 1885 with Jahn's notes upon Elias added, and is still in use.

English translation of ten of the liturgical homilies, unfortunately containing a number of inaccuracies, have been published in the series *Nicene and Post-Nicene Fathers*.[15] An accurate English translation of the funeral orations has appeared in the series *Fathers of the Church*.[16]

---

[10] Gregory gives a very moving account of his decision to resign in his autobiographical poem, *De vita sua*. See *PG*, 37, 1143ff.

[11] Gallay, *La vie*, pp. 214, 215, 224.

[12] For the poems see: M. Pellegrino, *La poesia di S. Gregorio Nazianzeno*, Milan 1933; De Jonge, *De. S. Gregorio Nazianzeno carminibus quae inscribi solent περὶ ἑαυτοῦ*, Amsterdam 1910.

[13] A full account of the older editions is to be found in C. Clémencet, D. Caillau, *Sancti patris nostri Gregorii Theologi, vulge Nazianzeni archiepiscopi Constantinopolitani, opera omnia quae extant*, I, Paris 1842, pp. 1ff.; *PG*, 36, pp. 10ff. See also: Schmid, Stählin, *op.cit.*, II, 2, pp. 1416ff.; Lefherz, *Studien*, pp. 86ff. (here more complete bibliography and discussion); J. Karmires, Ἡ ἐκκλησιολογία τοῦ Ἁγίου Γρηγορίου τοῦ Θεολόγου,

Athens 1960, pp. 53-54. Cf. D. Meehan, "Editions of St. Gregory of Nazianzus," *The Irish Theological Quarterly*, 18 (1951), pp. 203-27; G. Downey, "Patristic Studies: The Present State of Bibliography," *The Proceedings of the American Theological Library Association*, 1961, pp. 102-15. In this paper Downey has collected a vast amount of bibliographical matter and has presented it with a critical eye.

[14] De Billy's Latin translation of the *Opera omnia* was published by C. Fremy in Paris in 1569 and reprinted several times; see Meehan, *op.cit.*, p. 206.

[15] H. Wace, P. Schaff, *A Select Library of Nicene and Post-Nicene Fathers*, 2nd series, VII, Oxford-New York 1894, pp. 203ff.

[16] P. McCauley *et al.* trans., *Funeral Orations*

The Benedictine edition is therefore the only usable one containing all the homilies with which this study is concerned, even though it too possesses the shortcomings common to such texts: errors in punctuation, spelling, and readings, as well as errors in the Latin translation. Before World War II, T. Sinko prepared a new edition and announced that no important changes had been made in the text.[17] This edition has not yet been published.

There have been many discussions of the theological and literary problems inherent in the text. Theologians who have dealt with Gregory's sermons have noted that Gregory, in addition to adapting secular ideas and language to the Christian vocabulary, was greatly influenced by Hellenic thought.[18] Philologists have been able to show Gregory's indebtedness to Hellenism by pointing to his borrowings from the Athenian school of rhetoric.[19]

The results of these theological and literary investigations are significant to those studying the illustrations of the homilies because they may be applied to the criticism of the illustrations as well. The central question is whether or not the man who illustrated Gregory's homilies was indebted to both pagan and Christian illustrators in the same way that Gregory was indebted to pagan and Christian authors.

Why were these sixteen sermons chosen from among the forty-five to be read on certain feast days, and when was this selection made? Evidently the contents of these homilies account for their selection: they were the most appropriate to supplement the Gospel lections and to provide suitable readings for the great festivals of the Church and certain martyrs' days.

The evidence presented by Ehrhard, which I have undertaken to supplement in my investigation of the earliest known manuscripts of the homilies, indicates that the selection of these particular homilies was cumulative.[20] The scholarly reconstruction of this edition shows parallels to the creation of another liturgical book, the lectionary.

Probably a few homilies were selected quite early to be read, with the relevant

---

by St. Gregory Nazianzenus and St. Ambrose, New York 1953.

[17] Plagnieux, St. Grégoire, p. x; Gallay, La vie, p. x n. 2; T. Disdier, "Nouvelles études sur saint Grégoire de Nazianze," Echos d'Orient, 30 (1931), pp. 485-97; Meehan, op.cit., pp. 203-19; Lefherz, Studien, passim.

[18] For a discussion of the subject, see R. Gottwald, De Gregorio Nazianzeno platonico, Bratislava 1906; H. Pinault, Le platonisme de saint Grégoire de Nazianze, La Roche-sur-Yon 1925, pp. 34-39, 240-41; Fleury, Hellenism; Plagnieux, St. Grégoire (the more complete bibliography here); cf. F. X. Portman, Die göttliche Paidagogia bei Gregor von Nazianz (Kirchengeschichtliche Quellen und Studien III), St. Ottilien 1954.

[19] M. Guignet, St. Grégoire de Nazianze et la rhétorique, Paris 1911; N. Malin, Οἱ ἐπιτάφιοι λόγοι Γρηγορίου τοῦ Ναζιανζηνοῦ ἐν σχέσει πρὸς τὴν ῥητορείαν, Athens 1929; Sinko, Traditione; H. L. Davids, De Gnomologieën van sint Gregorius, Nijmegen 1940; B. Wyss, "Gregor von Nazianz, ein griechisch-christlicher Dichter des 4 Jahr.," Museum Helveticum, 6 (1949), pp. 177-210; J. Lercher, "Die Persönlichkeit des h. Gregorius von Nazianz und seine Stellung zur klassischen Bildung (nach seinen Briefen)," (Phil. diss. typewritten) Innsbruck 1949.

[20] Ehrhard, Hom. Literatur, I, 1, pp. 39-85; II, pp. 4ff. Cf. S. Salaville, "La formation du calendrier liturgique byzantin . . . ," Ephemerides Liturgicae, 50 (1936), pp. 312-23. For a list of the pericopes, see also C. R. Gregory, Textkritik des Neuen Testaments, I, Leipzig 1907, pp. 327-42.

Gospel lections, on the occasion of church festivals.[21] By the ninth century, as the cod. Paris gr. 514 illustrates,[22] some of the sixteen homilies had been chosen from the forty-five, and they were grouped at the beginning of a codex which contained homilies by other authors as well. Since these homilies refer both to the great festivals of the Church and to saints' days, their selection may have been made at the same time. This process of selection probably continued throughout the ninth century. After the choice of the desired number had been completed and established, a need arose for a separate edition, which was to be used in the various church services. The evidence is insufficient to date exactly the appearance of this particular kind of edition. The earliest extant dated or datable manuscripts are from the eleventh century, but the text of the liturgical edition probably first appeared during the tenth.

Soon after these sixteen homilies were singled out from among the forty-five, the order in which they had originally stood in the complete edition was changed. If they were to constitute suitable readings for the church feasts, the homilies had to follow the arrangement of the relevant Gospel lections as well as the sequence of the various feasts according to the Greek ecclesiastical year, which consists of two main parts: the "movable year," which begins on Easter and contains feasts that depend on Easter, and the "calendar year," which begins on September 1 and contains feasts that are observed on fixed dates.

The new order of the homilies is not the same in all manuscripts, but in the list given below I have adhered to the most common usage. In order to make the liturgical sequence clear, the day for which each homily was appointed is also indicated.[23] In cases where the connection between the content of the homily and the day on which it was read is not self-evident, the Gospel lection for the day is given to explain the relationship. The Greek titles of the homilies are given as they appear in the Migne edition.

1. Εἰς τὸ ἅγιον Πάσχα καὶ εἰς τὴν βραδυτῆτα
   —First homily *on Easter* (*PG*, 35, 396), read on Easter Sunday.

2. Εἰς τὸ ἅγιον Πάσχα
   —Second homily *on Easter* (*PG*, 36, 624), read on Monday after Easter.

3. Εἰς τὴν Καινὴν Κυριακήν
   —*On New Sunday* (*PG*, 36, 608), read on New Sunday, i.e. the first Sunday after Easter, commonly known as Thomas's Sunday.

---

[21] In the ninth-century typicon of Hagia Sophia in Constantinople only the sermon on Pentecost has been included as a reading of the day. See Ehrhard, *Hom. Literatur*, I, 1, p. 39, cf. pp. 85-86.

[22] Omont, *Inventaire sommaire*, I, p. 68; Lefherz, *Studien*, p. 133; cf. the uncial, ninth-century codex Scorial gr. 236, which contains five homilies of the liturgical edition grouped together; see Ehrhard, *Hom. Literatur*, II, pp. 4ff.

[23] For the dates of the reading of the homilies, see Ehrhard, *Hom. Literatur*, I, 1, pp. 25ff. Each sermon was divided into sections. Indications of these divisions are found in manuscripts such as ἀρχὴ πρώτης ἀναγνώσεως, δευτέρας, etc. The sections are read on the same day. This is especially true for monastic communities, where the reading of the sermon begins at Matins and continues in the refectory during the meal hours of the same day.

4. Εἰς τὴν Πεντηκοστήν

        —*On Pentecost* (*PG*, 36, 912), read on the day of Pentecost.

5. Εἰς τοὺς Μακκαβαίους

        —*On the Maccabees* (*PG*, 35, 912), read on August 1, the Maccabees' day.

6. Εἰς τὸν ἅγιον ἱερο-μάρτυρα Κυπριανόν

        —*On the Saint and Holy Martyr Cyprian* (*PG*, 35, 1169), read on October 2, St. Cyprian's day.

7. Εἰς τοὺς λόγους καὶ εἰς τὸν ἐξισωτὴν Ἰουλιανόν

        —*To Julian the Tax Collector* (*PG*, 35, 1044), read on December 21. One of the Gospel lections of this day is Matt. 18: 31-36, referring to the parable of the creditor and his debtor.

8. Εἰς τὰ Θεοφάνεια, ἤγουν γεννέθλια τοῦ Σωτῆρος

        —*On the Nativity* (*PG*, 36, 312), read on December 25.

9. Εἰς τὸν μέγαν Βασίλειον, ἐπίσκοπον Καισαρείας Καππα-δοκίας, ἐπιτάφιος

        —*Funeral oration on Basil the Great, Bishop of Cappadocia* (*PG*, 36, 493), read on January 1, St. Basil's day.

10. Εἰς τὰ ἅγια Φῶτα

        —*On Epiphany* (*PG*, 36, 336), read on January 6, feast of Christ's Baptism.

11. Εἰς τὸ ἅγιον Βάπτισμα

        —*On Baptism* (*PG*, 36, 360), read on January 7, St. John's day. The subject of this sermon is in fact a commentary on the Gospel lection which refers to the baptism of the people.

12. Εἰς Γρηγόριον Νύσσης, τὸν τοῦ μεγάλου Βασιλείου ἀδελφόν

        —*To Gregory of Nyssa, the Brother of Basil the Great* (*PG*, 35, 832), read on January 10, St. Gregory of Nyssa's day.

13. Εἰς τὸν μέγαν Ἀθανάσιον ἐπίσκοπον Ἀλεξανδρείας

        —*On Athanasius the Great, Bishop of Alexandria* (*PG*, 35, 1081), read on January 18, St. Athanasius' day.

14. Συντακτήριος εἰς τὴν τῶν ρν´ ἐπισκόπων παρουσίαν

        —*A Farewell Oration Delivered before 150 Bishops* (*PG*, 36, 1081), read on January 25, St. Gregory of Nazianzus' day.

15. Περὶ φιλοπτωχίας

        —*On the Love of the Poor* (*PG*, 35, 857), read on Sunday of the Apo-creo, a movable feast that comes fourteen days after the beginning of the Triodion. The Gospel

16. Εἰς τὸν πατέρα σιωπῶντα
διὰ τὴν πληγὴν τῆς χαλάζης

lection of this Sunday is
Matt. 25: 31-46 (". . . I was an
hungred, and ye gave me meat . . .").

—*To His Father, Who Kept Silent
about the Plague of Hail* (*PG*, 35,
933), read on Sunday of the week
of Tyrophagus, a movable feast
which follows the Apocreo. The
Gospel lection of the day is
Matt. 6: 14-21 ("Lay not up for
yourselves treasures upon
earth where moth and rust doth
corrupt . . .").

Ehrhard has shown that the homiletic literature found in the movable liturgical cycle of the ecclesiastical year is based on the *pericopes*, i.e. the readings from the Gospels. The list of Gregory's homilies cited above supports this observation. The homilies follow the arrangement of both the *pericopes* according to the movable year and the calendar feasts of saints. The *pericopes*, however, constitute a special liturgical book, the lectionary, which contains the lessons according to both years, as well as commemorations of saints which are added to the readings arranged according to the calendar year.[24] In other words, the lectionary contains the movable and the calendar feasts and obviously is the book upon which the arrangement of the homilies has been based. It must be pointed out, however, that in the lectionary, since the tenth century, the feasts are separated in two parts, whereas in the new liturgical edition of Gregory's selected homilies, the calendar feasts are incorporated into the movable year in chronological order.

Of the thirty-six illustrated manuscripts, six codices deviate from the order given in the list. The deviation is caused by the position of homilies 5 and 6, i.e. the homilies on the Maccabees and on St. Cyprian, which have become homilies 14 and 15 in the codd. Sinai 339, Sinai 346, and Oxford Roe 6. The new position of the two homilies is an irregularity that remains unexplained. The occurrence of homily 16, i.e. to His Silent Father, between homilies 4 and 5 in the cod. Milan, Ambros. G. 88 sup., probably is related to some anomaly. Moreover, in the cod. Oxford Roe 6, homily 7, i.e. to Julian the Tax Collector, is found between homilies 11 and 12, and in the cod. Paris gr. 533, the homily 16 is before homily 15. Perhaps an error by the scribes accounts for these two last deviations. Finally, the cod. Vat. gr. 463 presents another arrangement, also unexplained: the book opens with the homily on the Nativity and ends with the homily to Julian the Tax Collector. In this case, therefore, the sequence of the homilies runs from Christmas to December 21.

[24] For the ecclesiastical year and the text of the lectionary, see E. C. Colwell, D. W. Riddle, eds., *Prolegomena to the Study of the Lectionary Text of the Gospels* (*Studies in the Lectionary Text of the Greek New Testament*, I, II), Chicago 1933, 1936. E. P. F. Mercenier, *La prière des églises de rite byzantin*, II, 1, Amay-sur-Mense 1939, pp. xvff. For the ecclesiastical year and the calendar feasts, see Ehrhard, *Hom. Literatur*, I, 1, pp. 25ff.

II. THE ILLUSTRATED MANUSCRIPTS

THIRTY-SIX extant illuminated manuscripts of the liturgical edition are known to me, but not all of them contain pictures for all the sixteen homilies. Some manuscripts are very simple and their illustrations consist of an author portrait. Others limit their decoration to a few historiated initials.

Twenty of the manuscripts, however, are fully illustrated; that is, they have illuminations for all or most of the sixteen homilies (see text fig. 1). A discussion of these twenty manuscripts constitute the main subject of this study and the reader must acquire some familiarity with the material which is discussed in the following pages. This is particularly necessary because the plates are not arranged in the sequence of the text, but reproduce each manuscript as an entity and in chronological order, so that access to source material may be facilitated and so that the value of each manuscript may not be diminished for the scholar. To make possible, therefore, an over-all introduction of the material, the twenty main manuscripts are listed in the table, and their dating and illustrations are indicated. A complete list of all thirty-six manuscripts, details about their appearance, the physical relationship to the text of each illustration, the reasons for the suggested datings and the pertinent bibliography are found in the catalogue at the end of this book.

The format of the miniatures varies, and their placement is not uniform in all manuscripts. They may head the text of each of the sixteen homilies as *title* miniatures, either in full-page or strip format; in the latter case, the miniatures extend over one or both of the written columns of the text. According to other systems, the miniatures (either as title or as *supplementary*, narrative illustrations) have been placed in the margins, within the written columns, or only in the initial letters of the text. With the exception of the codd. Istanbul, Patr. 16, Vat. gr. 463, and Sinai 346, in which the illuminations have been systematically confined to the initials, and the cod. Athos, Vatopedi 107, which has only marginal miniatures, no particular system has been used exclusively in any of the main manuscripts. The codices may be distinguished, however, according to the predominating method of their illustration. In some manuscripts, full-page miniatures have been placed before the text of each homily. These are the codd. Oxford, Roe 6 and Paris gr. 543. In others, miniatures of a strip format are found above the title of the homily. These are Athos, Dionysiou 61; Florence, Plut. VII, 32; Milan, Ambros. G. 88; Oxford, Selden. B. 54; Paris gr. 550; Paris gr. 541; and Princeton 2. The cod. Oxford, Canon. gr. 103 should be included among them; the miniatures of this manuscript are not placed above the title but frame the title and consist of one or two horizontal strips and two vertical ones. The artists of still other manuscripts favor the column or the marginal system, or both, in addition to using the two systems mentioned above. The following manuscripts exemplify this category: Athos, Panteleimon 6; Jerusalem, Taphou 14; Moscow, Hist. Museum 146; Paris gr. 533; Paris, Coislin 239; Vat. gr. 1947; Sinai 339; Turin Univ. Lib., C. I. 6.

13

1. COMPARATIVE CHART OF ILLUSTRATIONS FOR THE HOMILIES IN THE 20 MANUSCRIPTS MOST FULLY ILLUSTRATED

Manuscripts	Frontispieces	1	2	3	4	5	6	7
Athos, Dionysiou 61 XI/XII c.	Dedication page	Anastasis	Vision of Habakkuk	Mamas (portrait and scene). Church-Synagogue. Teaching scene	Pentecost	—	Teaching scene and Cyprian. Justina, Christ and Cyprian	Julian the Tax Collector as a ruler. Gregory and scribe
Athos, Panteleimon 6 XI c.	—	Anastasis	Vision of Habakkuk	Mamas (portrait). Church-Synagogue. Teaching scene. Bucolic scenes	Pentecost	Maccabees, Eleazar, Solomone (portraits). Teaching scene	Cyprian (portrait)	Gregory and Julian the Tax Collector as writers. Scribe
Athos, Vatopedi 107 XI/XII c.	Cross and two angels	Anastasis	—	Doubting Thomas. Mamas (portrait). Bucolic scenes	Pentecost	Maccabees, Eleazar, Solomone (portraits)	Gregory, Cyprian and Justina (portraits)	Three Holy Children in the Fire, Daniel
Florence, Laur. Plut. VII, 32 XI/XII c.	—	—	Miniature flaked	Mamas (portrait and scene)	Pentecost	Maccabees, Eleazar, Solomone (scene)	Gregory and Cyprian conversing	Gregory and Julian the Tax Collector as writers
Istanbul, Patr. 16 XI c.	Author portrait	Anastasis	Author portrait	Mamas (portrait), Teaching scene	Pentecost	Maccabees, Eleazar, Solomone (portraits)	Cyprian and Justina (scene)	Teaching scene and Julian the Tax Collector
Jerusalem, Taphou 14 XI c.	Author portrait	Anastasis. Teaching scene	Vision of Habakkuk. Eosphoros. O.T. scenes	Mamas (scenes). Bucolic scenes	Pentecost	Maccabees, Eleazar, Solomone (scenes)	Teaching scene and Cyprian	Gregory and Julian the Tax Collector as writers
Milan, Ambros. G. 88 sup., XII c.	Teaching scene	Anastasis	Vision of Habakkuk	Author portrait	Pentecost	Maccabees. Eleazar, Solomone (portraits)	Gregory and Cyprian (portraits)	Author portrait
Moscow, Hist. Mus. 146, XI c.	—	Anastasis. Teaching scene	Vision of Habakkuk	Encaenia. Doubting Thomas. Mamas (scene)	Pentecost	Maccabees. Eleazar, Solomone (scene)	Cyprian (scene)	Julian the Tax Collector as money changer
Oxford, Canon. gr. 103, XI/XII c.	Author portrait	Anastasis. Teaching scene	—	—	Pentecost	Maccabees, Eleazar, Solomone, Christ (portraits)	Gregory and Cyprian (portraits)	Gregory and Julian the Tax Collector as writers
Oxford, Roe 6, XIII c.	Author portrait	Anastasis	Vision of Habakkuk. Teaching scene	Mamas (portrait)	Pentecost	Maccabees, Eleazar, Solomone (portraits)	Cyprian (portrait)	Portraits of martyrs
Oxford, Selden. B. 54, XI/XII c.	—	—	—	—	Pentecost	—	Gregory and Cyprian conversing	Gregory and Julian the Tax Collector as writers
Paris, gr. 533, XI c.	Teaching scene	Anastasis	Vision of Habakkuk	Bucolic scenes	Teaching scene	Teaching scene	Teaching scene	Teaching scene. Julian the Tax Collector as writer
Paris, gr. 543 XIV c.	—	Anastasis. Teaching scene	Vision of Habakkuk. Resurrection	Doubting Thomas. Encaenia	—	Maccabees. Eleazar, Solomone (scenes)	Cyprian (scenes). Author portrait	Julian the Tax Collector as money changer. Author portrait and martyrs
Paris, gr. 550 XII c.	Crucifixion. Basil, John Chrysostom, Nicholas of Myra. Author portrait	Anastasis. Author portrait	Vision of Habakkuk	Mamas (scenes). Teaching scene. Church-Synagogue. Baptism. (liturgical scene)	Pentecost	Maccabees. Eleazar, Solomone (portraits)	Cyprian and Justina (portraits)	Julian the Tax Collector giving the tax orders

8	9	10	11	12	13	14	15	16
Nativity	Koimesis of Basil. Painter at work	Christ's Baptism	—	Gregorys conversing. Gregorys in proskynesis and Christ	—	Gregory and Bishops	Gregory and the poor. Almsgiving	Gregory, his father and people. Teaching scene
Nativity. John the Baptist	Koimesis of Basil. Scenes of Basil's life. Mythological and Biblical scenes	Christ's Baptism. John the Baptist. Mythological scenes	Teaching scene	Proskynesis scene	Koimesis of Athanasius	Gregory and Bishops. Julian the Apostate (scene). Valens	Gregory and the poor	Gregory and his father
Virgin and Child	Teaching scene	Christ's Baptism	Christ baptizing Peter. Koimesis of Basil	Proskynesis scene	Koimesis of Athanasius. Distribution of bread to the poor	Teaching scene	—	Gregory and his father
Nativity. Teaching scene	Koimesis of Basil	Christ's Baptism. Teaching scene	Teaching scene	Proskynesis scene	Athanasius (portrait)	Gregory and Bishops	Teaching scene	Teaching scene
Nativity	Teaching scene	Christ's Baptism	Christ's Baptism	Proskynesis scene	Athanasius (portrait). Teaching scene	Gregory and Bishops	Almsgiving	Teaching scene
Nativity	Koimesis of Basil	Christ's Baptism	Teaching scene	Proskynesis scene	Teaching scene and Athanasius	Gregory and Bishops. Farewell scene	Gregory and the poor. Teaching scene	Gregory, his father and people
Nativity	Koimesis of Basil	Christ's Baptism	Baptism (liturgical scene)	Proskynesis scene and Christ	Gregory giving book to Athanasius	Gregory and Bishops	Gregory and the poor. Teaching scene	Author portrait
Nativity	Koimesis of Basil	Christ's Baptism	Baptism of people	Proskynesis scene and Sending of Letter (?)	—	Gregory and Bishops	Almsgiving	Sending of Letter
Nativity	Koimesis of Basil	Christ's Baptism	—	Proskynesis scene, Teaching scene	Gregory addressing Athanasius	—	—	Teaching scene
Nativity	Koimesis of Basil	Christ's Baptism	—	Teaching scene	Athanasius (portrait)	Teaching scene	Teaching scene	Teaching scene
—	Koimesis of Basil	Gregory, Christ, John the Baptist	Teaching scene	Proskynesis scene	Athanasius (portrait)	Gregory and Bishops	Teaching scene	Gregory, his father and people
—	Gregory and Basil (portraits)	Teaching scene, Christ meets John the Baptist. Christ's Baptism	Teaching scene	Proskynesis scene	Gregory giving scroll to Athanasius	Gregory and Bishops	Teaching scene	Teaching scene
Nativity. Genesis scenes. Panagia Blachernitissa (scene)	Koimesis of Basil	Christ's Baptism. Christ meets John the Baptist, John preaching	Baptism of people. Teaching scene	—	Koimesis of Athanasius. Teaching scene	Gregory and Emperor Theodosius. Gregory and Bishops	Teaching scene Gregory and the poor	Gregory, his father and people. Teaching scene
Nativity	Koimesis of Basil	Christ's Baptism	Baptism of people	Ecstatic Meeting of Gregorys	Koimesis of Athanasius. Gregory and Athanasius (portraits)	Gregory and Bishops	Almsgiving (scenes)	Gregory, his father and people

Manuscripts	Frontispieces	1	2	3	4	5	6	7
Paris, Coislin 239 XI c.	—	—	Vision of Habakkuk. O. and N.T. scenes	Church-Synagogue. Author portrait. Bucolic scenes. Mamas (portrait)	Pentecost. O.T. scenes	Maccabees, Eleazar, Solomone (portraits and scenes)	Teaching scene and Cyprian. Teaching scene and Justina, Cyprian (scenes)	Gregory and Julian the Tax Collector seated
Rome, Vat. gr. 463, *Anno* 1062	Author portrait	Anastasis	Habakkuk (portrait)	Christ seated	Pentecost	Maccabees and angel (scene)	Teaching scene	—
Rome, Vat. gr. 1947, XI c.	—	Miniature flaked	Vision of Habakkuk	Mamas (scene)	Pentecost	Maccabees, Eleazar, Solomone (scene)	Teaching scene and Cyprian	Gregory and Julian the Tax Collector seated
Sinai, gr. 339, XII c.	Author portrait	Anastasis	Vision of Habakkuk (two versions)	Teaching scene. Mamas (scene and portrait). Doubting Thomas. Encaenia	Pentecost	Maccabees, Eleazar, Solomone (portraits and scenes)	Gregory, Cyprian, Justina (portraits). Cyprian (scene)	Gregory and Julian the Tax Collector as writers. Julian as money changer. Gregory and scribes
Sinai gr. 346, XI c.	—	—	—	Teaching scene. Mamas (portrait)	Pentecost	—	Gregory and Cyprian. (portraits)	Julian the Tax Collector as writer. Gregory teaching
Turin, Univ. Lib. C. I. 6, XI c.	—	Anastasis	Author portrait	Doubting Thomas. Encaenia. Teaching scene	—	Maccabees, Eleazar, Solomone (scenes)	Koimesis of Cyprian. Cyprian scenes. Author portrait	Julian as money changer

8	9	10	11	12	13	14	15	16
vity	Koimesis of Basil	Christ's Baptism. Mythological (scenes)	Teaching scene	Proskynesis scene	Koimesis of Athanasius	Gregory and Bishops	Teaching scene	Gregory, his father and people
vity	Basil (portrait)	Christ's Baptism	Christ's Baptism	—	Athanasius (portrait)	Farewell scene	—	Author portrait
vity	Koimesis of Basil	Teaching scene (?)	Christ's Baptism	Proskynesis scene	Koimesis of Athanasius	Gregory and Bishops	Teaching scene	Gregory, his father and people
vity. gia hernitissa ne)	Koimesis of Basil	Christ's Baptism	Teaching scene	—	—	—	Gregory and the poor. Almsgiving	—
vity	Koimesis of Basil	Christ's Baptism	Christ's Baptism	Proskynesis scene and Basil	—	Teaching scene	Almsgiving	Gregory and his father
—	Ecstatic meeting of Peter and Paul. Basil's life (scenes)	—	—	—	—	—	—	—

17

III. FRONTISPIECES AND TITLE MINIATURES

MOST of the miniatures of the extensive cycle in the manuscripts of Gregory can be found elsewhere. In fact, only seventeen of the title and twelve of the supplementary miniatures were designed especially for his texts. The others occurred first in earlier texts, from which they migrated into Gregory's homilies. For example, when the homily deals with a Christian festival, the illustration has been copied from a Gospel book or lectionary. When the oration concerns the life of a saint, the illustrations have been taken from a menologion, i.e. the service book that contains the Lives of the Saints, so that the artist had no need to invent a new picture. In certain instances, however, migrated miniatures display elements that indicate that the artist adapted them to fit Gregory's text. Furthermore, at times the original miniatures contain elements borrowed from illustrations of other texts, or they are based on iconographic models which can be found elsewhere. The distinction, therefore, between *invented* and *migrated* miniatures is not rigid. Nevertheless, the distinction is necessary, for the structure of the manuscripts cannot be understood unless the iconographic groups found in the manuscripts are analyzed and studied separately with regard to the specific texts of their origin. Obviously, the question of the relationship or recension of the manuscripts cannot be settled until the iconographic cycles have been isolated and examined.

Criteria must be established to isolate the cycles and to determine if a miniature was originally made for Gregory's homilies or borrowed from another illustrated manuscript. A satisfactory method has been employed by K. Weitzmann in his *Illustrations in Roll and Codex*. First, the degree of correspondence between the picture and the text to which it is attached must be ascertained. When the homily is sufficiently explicit to account for the details of the picture, the miniature is presumed to have been invented for it. If, however, the homily alludes to a theme that can only be fully explained by a different text, the illustration is assumed to have been derived from that other text.

Before examining the relationship of the miniatures to the text of the homilies, the miniatures which are not text illustrations in the proper sense of the word must be discussed, i.e. the frontispieces and teaching scenes. The frontispieces occur at the beginning of the codex and contain the author portrait, the dedication page, and additional illustrations. The teaching scene is generally not intended to illustrate the text of a particular sermon, but designed for inclusion at the beginning of every homily.

18

A. THE AUTHOR PORTRAIT, THE DEDICATION PAGE, AND ADDITIONAL FRONTISPIECES

1. THE AUTHOR PORTRAIT

The portrait of the author is an independent unit and the iconographic types to which it may belong are interchangeable. Consequently it varies markedly in different manuscripts and cannot provide an answer to questions about the type used by the illustrator of the first manuscript of the liturgical edition of Gregory's homilies.

a. *The Seated Type*
–The Author Thinking

One of the early examples is the author portrait of the cod. Jerusalem, Taphou 14, fol. 2ᵛ (Fig. 98). In this full-page miniature, Gregory, wearing a monk's vestments, is represented in three-quarter view, seated, and facing right. He has just ceased writing in a codex on his lap, while his left hand supports his chin. He appears to be thinking. In front of him is a desk with a lectern on it, from which hangs a scroll. Both chair and desk are richly decorated.

The portraits in the codd. Florence, Laur. Plut. VII, 24, fol. 3ᵛ, and Vat. gr. 464, fol. 1ᵛ, are similar in most respects (Figs. 97, 470). In these miniatures, Gregory seems to be dressed as a bishop. In the miniature of the former manuscript, he touches with his left hand a codex placed on a lectern in front of him. His right hand rests on his knee and holds a pen. His countenance shows the intelligence and power that express themselves in his sermons. Above and to the right appears the blessing *dextera Domini* indicative of divine inspiration. This motif is lacking in the miniature of the Vatican codex, which is executed with a drawing technique in slight color washes. In his right hand the pensive author holds a scroll on which the beginning of his first sermon is written. The architectural setting of both miniatures contrasts with the neutral background of the miniature of the Jerusalem codex.

The appearance of the author portrait at the beginning of his works, as if to affirm their authority, occurs frequently in manuscripts of the Middle Ages, and the origin of the custom can be traced to pagan antiquity. In the Middle Byzantine period, the portrait of the seated, pensive author appears in representations of the evangelists and the apostles.[1] The portrait of Gregory is derived from an evangelist's portrait. Since there are no standard types for the four evangelists, and since the existing types are interchangeable, the specific evangelist used as the model for this seated portrait of Gregory cannot be identified. Only the pensive evangelist who has paused in his writing, for instance, Matthew in the twelfth-century Gospel book in Venice, cod. gr.

---

[1] See, for example, the seated, pensive St. Paul in the mid tenth-century codex, Oxford, Canon. gr. 110 (Acts and Epistles), fol. 176ᵛ, repro- duced in O. Pächt, *Byzantine Illumination*, Oxford 1952, p. 7, pl. 5a.

Z. 540, can be suggested as the ultimate source of the portrait in the Jerusalem manuscript,[2] or the contemplating evangelist, for instance, Mark in the eleventh-century Gospel in Vienna, cod. Nat. Lib. suppl. gr. 50, as the ultimate type of Gregory's portrait in the Florence and Vatican manuscripts discussed above.[3] The inspirational motif is an element that also often accompanies the evangelist in Byzantine art.[4]

—The Author Writing

A different portrait type appears in the cod. Princeton 2, whose full-page miniature preceding the text represents Gregory as a bishop in the act of writing his homilies (Fig. 256). The leaf containing this miniature, as Weitzmann has observed, was inserted at a later period, and had originally decorated another Gregory codex of larger proportions.[5] In front of Gregory is the usual table, with writing implements and a lectern on it. But the text on the lectern—the beginning of the first homily—and Gregory's name written on the gold ground were added by a later hand. The architectural setting in the background consists of a building with an open hall on the right and another building with a door, topped by an airy baldachin, on the left. A wavy line runs across the bottom of the picture, separating the water from the shore, along which small bushes are painted in grisaille. Such strips of water are frequently found in pictures of John and Prochoros where the locality is supposedly the Island of Patmos. The portrait of the cod. Vat. gr. 463, fol. 3[v], is similar, although there is no architectural background (Fig. 78).

Gregory appears as a busy writer in the miniatures of the codd. Oxford, Roe 6, fol. 1[v]; Oxford, Canon. gr. 103, fol. 2[v]; Istanbul, Patr. 16, fol. 2[v]; Paris gr. 541, fol. 0[v] (badly flaked and not illustrated). In the first three miniatures Gregory wears monk's vestments (Figs. 435, 275, 61). Only in the first has the figure of Gregory been placed against an architectural background, formed by two buildings, while in the third the neutrality of the background has been varied by the use of hanging drapery crowning the scene. Such drapery often appears in representations of the evangelists.[6] In the miniature of the cod. Oxford, Roe 6, the beginning of the homily on Resurrection by John Chrysostom is written on Gregory's scroll. Indeed, the text of Chrysostom's homily begins on fol. 1[r] but, in all probability, it is a later insertion. It seems probable that when this insertion was made a scribe added the beginning of the homily to Gregory's scroll, for there is no doubt that the script of the scroll is not contemporary with the script of the text in the homilies. Nor is there any doubt that the portrait

[2] Friend, *Evangelists*, pl. xiv, 144.

[3] *Ibid.*, pl. xiv, 142.

[4] O. Dalton, *Byzantine Art and Archaeology*, Oxford 1911, p. 455. Morey, *Freer Coll.*, p. 36 n. 2.

[5] K. Weitzmann, "A Codex with the Homilies of Gregory of Nazianzus," *Record of the Museum of Historic Art, Princeton University*, 1 (1942), p. 17.

[6] See an example in a twelfth-century Gospel book in the Walters Art Gallery, cod. 522, fol. 141[v]; The Walters Art Gallery, *Early Christian and Byzantine Art*, Baltimore 1947, p. 141, no. 715.

shows Gregory and not John Chrysostom, whose face is more ascetic than Gregory's, with bony cheeks and a thin, short beard.

In the miniature of the cod. Oxford, Canon. gr. 103, Gregory is seated on an elaborate high-backed chair, set against plain parchment rather than the usual gold background. He has a comparatively small head relieved by the golden light of a large nimbus. The lectern is supported by a fish, as in the miniature of the patriarchal codex, and a lamp hangs over it. Another interesting feature of the Oxford miniature is the depiction of the ground on which everything rests. It is fresh with tiny flowers, which spring up between the chair, the footstool, and the table, and are watered by a wavy blue line at the bottom. All this freshness gives an earthly quality to the hieratic and ascetic concept of the saint.

The author portrait of the cod. Sinai 339, fol. 4ᵛ, belongs to the same type of Gregory seated and writing (Fig. 377). Beneath a tripartite arch supported by knotted columns, Gregory, dressed as a monk, sits on a chair facing the right. On his left knee he supports a piece of parchment on which he is about to write his sermon. The decoration of his large nimbus, similar to those found in certain representations of evangelists,[7] is most impressive. Such ornamentation probably derives from enamel icons.[8] On a table placed before Gregory is a lectern supported by a stylized fish. Above, filling the right curve of the arch, is painted a bust of the Blessing Christ, from whom comes the inspiration to write. Gregory is within an architectural complex, topped by domes and saddled roofs. Through the drum of the central dome, so to speak, can be seen the apse of the church on which the Virgin is represented seated on a *thokos*, a backless throne, holding the Child Jesus in her lap. This representation is similar to those depicted in the apses of many Byzantine churches. The architectural complex which surrounds the figure of Gregory, and recalls the famous architectural frontispieces in the manuscripts of the homilies of James of Kokkinobaphos, is important because of its origin and its influence on Russian manuscripts. It has been the subject of much discussion. Kondakov interpreted it as a monastery.[9] Xyngopoulos has rejected this idea, and suggested that the miniature of the Sinai manuscript is, in fact, a development of two older types appearing in the homilies of Gregory.[10] One of these is a miniature in the cod. Paris gr. 510, showing the author flanked by gardens and a church; and the other is a miniature in the cod. Milan, Ambros. E. 49-50 inf., representing Gregory inside a basilica. As for the architectural form of the church itself, Xyngopoulos has shown that the whole structure is derived

[7] H. Gerstinger, *Die griechische Buchmalerei*, Vienna 1926, pl. XIX.

[8] See the enamel icon of the archangel Michael in San Marco's treasury in Venice; N. Kondakov, *Histoire et monuments des émaux byzantins*, Frankfort on the Main 1892, pl. 27; A. Grabar, *Byzantine Painting*, Geneva 1953, p. 186 (here a better reproduction).

[9] Kondakov's view is presented by A. J. Ne-krasov, "Les frontispieces architecturaux dans les manuscrits russes . . . ," *L'art byzantin chez les Slaves, Recueil T. Uspenskij*, II, 1, Paris 1923, p. 253 n. 2.

[10] A. Xyngopoulos, " Ἡ μικρογραφία ἐν ἀρχῇ τοῦ Σιναϊτικοῦ κώδικος 339," *E.E.B.S.*, 16 (1940), pp. 128-37; idem, " Ἡ προμετωπὶς τῶν κωδίκων Βατ. 1162," *ibid.*, 13 (1937), pp. 158-78.

from a similar composition found in the illustrated manuscripts of the homilies of James of Kokkinobaphos in Paris and the Vatican, as well as in the liturgical scrolls of Athens and Patmos. But he sees the Sinai frontispiece as "simply a degenerated form of a frontispiece which represented a five-domed church," which in its original form can be seen in the frontispiece of the twelfth-century roll in the National Library of Athens (Liturgy of Basil the Great). Xyngopoulos is right in rejecting Kondakov's interpretation. This architectural complex does not represent any specific building; it shows, however, how real architecture can be put to a decorative use.

The same writing type is found in the cod. Moscow, Hist. Museum 155, fol. 4^r, dating from the fifteenth century (Fig. 473). There is no architectural background and the inspirational motif is no longer a bust of Christ, but the *dextera Domini*. Christ as the source of inspiration, however, appears in the miniature of the author portrait of the cod. Athos, Pantocrator 31, fol. 4^v, dating from the twelfth century (Fig. 428). In this representation, Christ is leaning over Gregory's shoulder, whispering to him. The same motif of inspiration occurs in the author portrait of the miniature of the cod. Jerusalem, Sabas 258, fol. 1^v, also of a twelfth-century date (Fig. 429). Since this miniature is not well preserved, it is impossible to determine whether the leaning figure is Christ, or simply a personification of inspiration.

The type of author portrait which shows the subject writing is the most usual in the Middle Byzantine period. In addition to the representations of the evangelists, in which the iconographic model of the type is found,[11] this type appears in monastic treatises or in hagiographic writings.[12] Among the evangelists, Luke is always represented as a busy writer, and the miniatures depicting Gregory writing his homilies are ultimately derived from Luke portraits.

The inspirational motif also finds parallels in the portraits of the evangelists. There the motif appears either high above the author, as it does in the Sinai miniature, or leaning over the author, as it appears in the Jerusalem miniature. The latter form is rare in representations of evangelists in Byzantine art,[13] since figures derived from classical antiquity and personifying inspiration are usually represented standing in front of the author.[14] Customarily, the inspiring figure standing behind the author appears with the author portrait of John Chrysostom,[15] and by analogy has been

[11] Friend, *Evangelists*, pl. x, 105.

[12] For examples, see the portraits of John Climacus and Barlaam: Martin, *Ladder*, pl. VI, 18; Der Nersessian, *Barlaam*, pl. I, 1; for writing monks, see Weitzmann, *Buchmalerei*, pls. XL, 221; LXXXI, 501.

[13] At times John the Evangelist is shown with an angel behind him, as, for example, in the cod. London, Brit. Mus. Add. 37008, fol. 1^v.

[14] The best-known examples are Aratos and Urania (mosaic of Monnus); Dioscurides and Heuresis (Vienna cod. med. gr. 1, fol. 4^v); Rossano Gospels and others. See Friend, *Evangelists*, pl.

xv. Not only were seated authors accompanied by inspiring figures, but standing poets were accompanied by Muses. See G. Lippold, *Die Skulpturen des Vaticanischen Museums*, III, 1, Berlin 1936, pl. 30. J. Weitzmann-Fiedler, "Ein Evangelientyp mit Aposteln als Begleitfiguren," *Festschrift zum 70. Geburtstag von A. Goldschmidt*, Berlin 1935, pp. 30-34.

[15] Examples have been collected by A. Xyngopoulos, " Ἰωάννης ὁ Χρυσόστομος Πηγὴ Σοφίας," Ἀρχαιολογικὴ Ἐφημερίς, 81-83 (1942-1944), pp. 1-36. Here the inspiring figure is Paul, who guides John in the writing of his sermons on Paul's

22

applied to representations of Gregory, as in the miniature of the Pantocrator codex.

The fact that Gregory too is represented with the inspirational motif has hitherto been unknown. The obvious deduction from this evidence is that the association of the inspirational motif with a Father of the Church is not an isolated phenomenon but is another indication of the importance given to patristic writings and their authors in the Middle Byzantine period. The works of the Fathers, like those of the evangelists, were inspired from on high. However, while Peter the Apostle dictated the Gospel to Luke, and the commentary of his letters to John Chrysostom, Christ himself inspired Gregory of Nazianzus. Apparently in each case the choice of the inspiring figure depended on the content of the writings: Chrysostom wrote a commentary on Peter's letter, the authenticity of which was guaranteed by Peter; but Gregory wrote on the mysteries of the Divine, so Christ himself inspired him and guaranteed the truth of the content of Gregory's sermons.

b. *The Standing Type*

The author portrait of the frontispieces in the codd. Paris gr. 550, fol. 4ᵛ; Athos, Karakalou 24, fol. 3ᵛ; and Athos, Lavra B. 111, fol. 1ᵛ, is of a different iconographic type (Figs. 400, 452, 430). All three miniatures—the last two are the only illustrations in their respective codices—show Gregory as a bishop standing against a timeless background and holding a book. Attention should be drawn especially to the miniature of the Paris manuscript in which the artist has conveyed an intensity of feeling in Gregory's ascetic physiognomy and an expression of compassion in his deeply set eyes. Gregory's frontal posture and his gesture of blessing bring him into direct communication with the beholder. An abbreviated form of a standing portrait is the flaked bust of Gregory appearing above the left column on fol. 1ʳ of the cod. Milan, Ambros. I 120 Sup. Here, too, the author is shown in a bishop's vestment and holding a book (Fig. 451).

Standing author portraits, although less common in Byzantine art, are found in Gospel books[16] and, more commonly, in hagiographic writings and in menologia.[17] A menologion seems to be the most likely source for Gregory's standing portrait.

The author portrait is also occasionally found in homilies as a title miniature—for instance, in the codd. Vat. gr. 464, fols. 44ᵛ, 76ᵛ (homilies 9 and 8), and Paris gr. 543, fol. 87ᵛ (homily 6)—or as a marginal illustration, as in the codd. Athos, Pan-

---

[16] Friend, *Evangelists*, pls. I, III.

[17] One example of a standing author portrait in hagiographic writings is the portrait of Barlaam in cod. Paris gr. 1128; see Der Nersessian, *Barlaam*, p. 34, pls. XLV, XCIV, 377. In the menologion of the Bibliothèque Nationale in Paris, cod. gr. 580, each saint whose vita is contained in the text is represented by a portrait at the beginning of the codex; see Omont, *Min. gr.* (1929), pl. CII.

epistles. The figure standing behind David and inspiring him in composing the Psalms is another example. See H. Buchthal, *The Miniatures of the Paris Psalter*, London 1938, pl. XVI, 23; J. Strzygowski, *Die Miniaturen des serbischen Psalters der Königl. Hof-und Staatsbibliothek in München* (Denkschriften der kaiserlichen Akademie der Wissenschaften, philosophisch-historische Klasse, 52), Vienna 1906, pl. V, fig. 8.

teleimon 6, fol. 119ʳ (homily 9), and Paris, Coislin 239, fol. 22ʳ (homily 2) (Figs. 471, 472, 459, 154, 196), or as an illustration of the initial. The following codices contain initials historiated with a simple author portrait: Istanbul, Patr. 16, fol. 5ᵛ (homily 2); Paris gr. 550, fol. 5ʳ (homily 1); Milan, Ambros. G 88 sup., fols. 29ʳ, 48ʳ, 85ʳ (homilies 3, 16, 7); Vat. gr. 463, fols. 295ʳ, 391ʳ (homilies 16 and 6); Athos, Stavroniketa 15, fol. 205ʳ (homily 12) (Figs. 63, 401, 302, 304, 307, 87, 92, 433). Although initials illustrated with the portrait of the author are not unusual,[18] the presence of Gregory's portrait in some of the homilies points to the conclusion that initials historiated with the figure of the author form part of a system of illustration according to which the author portrait can be represented before each homily as a frontispiece, as a miniature heading the title, or, in reduced form, as an illustration of the initial letter of the homily. Such a system of illustration finds a parallel in the cod. Paris gr. 510 where, on fol. 424ᵛ, in the bottom strip of the miniature preceding the text of the homily on the Consecration of Eulalius, Gregory is depicted writing.[19] Occasional use has been made of the author portrait in combination with other iconographic elements for the creation of scenes which are discussed later.

The question that has to be answered now is whether or not these portraits present a real likeness of the saint. The artists have been consistent in depicting the same likeness, whose main characteristics are an ascetic face, a short, square beard, and a bald head. These details do not correspond to what is known of Gregory's personal appearance. Ullmann gives the following description of him: "Gregory was of middle height . . . his hair was thick and blanched by age, his short beard and conspicuous eyebrows were thicker. On his right eye he had a scar."[20] The portraits in the miniatures do not conform to this description. Further, the physiognomy of Gregory in the manuscripts of the homilies does not resemble that of the Gregory found in the manuscripts of the Sacra Parallela, although there the medallion-portraits are rather conventional.[21] In fact, the physiognomy of the saint finds parallels in the portraits of the evangelists, just as does the type of the author portrait. For instance, the portrait of Gregory in the Jerusalem manuscript resembles the portrait of the Evangelist John in the cod. Athos, Stavroniketa 43, with regard to iconographic type as well as physiognomy.[22] Such similarities can be traced in other manuscripts.[23] Friend has shown that the iconographic model for the figure of John in the Stavroniketa manuscript is simply the portrait of the pagan philosopher Zenon,[24] who must have been the ultimate model for Gregory's portrait.

[18] See another example in Lazarev, *History*, II, pl. 134b.

[19] Omont, *Min. gr.* (1929), pl. LV.

[20] The source of the description of Gregory's physiognomy by Ullmann is the cod. Vat. gr. 549, quoted in *Acta sanctorum*, Maii, II, p. 428. Cf. also Lefherz, *Studien*, pp. 97, 98.

[21] Cod. Paris gr. 923, fol. 53ᵛ. A publication of this manuscript is being prepared by K. Weitzmann.

[22] Friend, *Evangelists*, pl. VIII, 98.

[23] Cf. portraits in the codd. Vat. gr. 463 and Athos, Dionysiou 34; Florence, Laur. Plut. VII, 32 and Athos, Vatopedi 949; Princeton cod. 2 and Venice gr. Z. 540; Oxford, Canon. gr. 103 and Paris gr. 74. See Friend, *Evangelists*, pls. XIII, 131; XIV, 135, 147; Omont, *Evangelists*, II, pl. 142.

[24] Friend, *Evangelists*, pp. 142ff.

The study of these portraits has made clear the distinction of types according to posture, i.e. seated and standing, as well as according to clerical rank, i.e. Gregory as bishop and as monk. The depiction of Gregory as a monk can be considered an unhistorical rendering because Gregory earlier held the title of bishop of Sasima and later the title of patriarch of Constantinople. The artist's decision to represent him as a monk can only be ascribed to the direct influence of monasticism, which became very marked in the thought of Byzantium in the eleventh century and later.

2. THE DEDICATION PAGE

Only the cod. Athos, Dionysiou 61, fol. 1ᵛ, contains a dedication page (Fig. 355). Gregory stands in episcopal vestment giving a book to a young man, perhaps a prince, attired as a member of the imperial court. A bust of Christ is within an aureola above them. The two figures resemble similar representations of saints, who face one another as they receive the blessings of the Almighty.

The unknown prince with dark hair and large, expressive eyes wears a long tunic and a chlamys decorated with floral motifs. The decoration, purple color, and large borders indicate that the chlamys was produced in an imperial workshop.[25] The ivy leaves of the chlamys suggest the floral motifs which often decorate the imperial costume and which are described by the Emperor Constantine Porphyrogenitus.[26] During the Macedonian Renaissance, especially under the Emperor Basil II, imperial clothes were richly decorated with floral and zoomorphic motifs. The decoration of the prince's chlamys resembles one on a medallion in the Zwenigorodskoi collection,[27] and the ornamental border of his tunic recalls that of the Archangel Michael on the dedication page of the manuscript of John Chrysostom's homilies, cod. Paris, Coislin 79, fol. 2ᵛ, illustrated for the Emperor Nicephorus Botaniates between 1078 and 1081.[28] The similarities between the two dedication miniatures extend to the concept expressed in their scenes: Gregory presents his homilies to a prince and John Chrysostom offers his book to the emperor. In each case, the presentation is witnessed by a representative of the heavenly world, Christ in the former and the Archangel Michael in the latter.

3. ADDITIONAL FRONTISPIECES

Two additional frontispieces occur in the cod. Paris gr. 550. One, fol. 3ᵛ, shows a Crucifixion scene within a quatrefoil framed by another ornamental frame (Fig. 398). The dead Christ, in a loincloth, hangs with his head slightly inclined. The Virgin stands at the left, touching her chin with one hand, as if to hold back her tears,

[25] J. Ebersolt, *Les arts somptuaires de Byzance*, Paris 1923, p. 40.

[26] *Ibid.*, p. 71.

[27] N. Kondakov, *Histoire et monuments des émaux byzantins*, Frankfort on the Main 1892, pls. 9, 11. The collection is now in the Metropolitan Museum of Art, New York.

[28] Omont, *Min. gr.* (1929), pl. LXIV; Bibl. Nat., *Byzance*, no. 29, p. 18; cf. also the presentation picture in the Gospel book, cod. Paris gr. 74, fol. 61ᵛ: here Matthew presents the Gospel to the abbot of the monastery, Omont, *Evangiles*, I, pl. 56. For bibliography on cod. Paris gr. 74 see Bibl. Nat., *Byzance*, no. 21, pp. 13-14.

and lifting the other toward her son. On the other side of the crucified Christ, John, the beloved disciple, stands frontally. The golden background and the admirably well-balanced *contrapposto* of the figures lend a classical air to the miniature. The iconography of the scene follows Middle Byzantine representations of the Crucifixion depicting Christ dead on the cross.[29] This scene is one of the most important feast pictures, and occurs frequently. The position of the miniature and the metallic quality of its decoration, stressed by the ropelike ornament common in metal work,[30] indicate its source. This Crucifixion was probably copied from the silver cover of the liturgical book used by the illustrator as a model for the illustrations of Gregory's homilies. Byzantine liturgical books frequently have silver and gold covers with the Crucifixion on the front cover and the Descent into Hell on the back.[31] This usage reflected in the homilies of Gregory emphasizes the importance of liturgy and dogma in both the thought and art of the period.

The other frontispiece, fol. 4ʳ, is of a similar nature (Fig. 399). Beneath a cusped arch stands an ornamental cross on a stepped base; in the center of the cross is a large medallion containing a bust of St. Basil holding a closed book. The upper arm of the cross is flanked by two smaller medallions, the left one containing a bust of St. John Chrysostom, and the right another bishop, probably Nicholas of Myra,[32] with a short, white beard. Two date palms, schematically represented, flank the lower arm of the cross. The spandrels of the arch are decorated with a floral pattern and the background is gold. Two birds with spread wings rest on the border. This miniature is similar in decoration to a frontispiece of the cod. Sinai 418, fol. 2ʳ, containing the work of John Climacus.[33]

Since the images of the three Fathers often appear in frontispieces of liturgical books, the medallions of the three bishops may not have been chosen specifically for the manuscript of Gregory's homilies.[34] The inclusion of the three bishops can perhaps be explained by the diptychs of the κεκοιμημένων in the liturgy in which all three are mentioned.[35]

[29] For the iconography of the Crucifixion, see Millet, *Recherches*, pp. 396ff.; Demus-Diez, pp. 68ff. For a discussion of the dead Christ, see J. R. Martin, "The Dead Christ on the Cross in Byzantine Art," *Late Classical and Mediaeval Studies in Honor of A. M. Friend, Jr.*, ed. by K. Weitzmann, Princeton 1955, pp. 189ff.

[30] O. Wulff, *Altchristliche und byzantinische Kunst*, II, Berlin 1924, p. 601, fig. 511. It should be noted that the ropelike motif ornament appears in frescoes, see G. de Jerphanion, *Les églises rupestres de Cappadoce*, Album III, Paris 1934, pl. 147, 2.

[31] One known example of a gold book cover with such representations exists in the monastery of St. Catherine on Mt. Sinai; cf. also enamel plaque with the Crucifixion in the San Marco treasury in Venice. See E. C. Colwell and H. R. Willoughby, *The Four Gospels of Karahissar*, II, Chicago 1936, p. 409, pl. CXXIX.

[32] Cf. Rome, Lib. Vat. gr. 1 (Bible of Leo), fol. 3ʳ, *Coll. Paleo. Vat., I* (1905), pl. 5; Menologion of Basil II, *Il menologio*, p. 226; for bibliography see Talbot Rice, *Byzantium*, p. 319 and Beckwith, *Constantinople*, p. 94.

[33] Martin, *Ladder*, p. 87, pl. LVIII.

[34] A parallel example is found in the aristocratic psalter in Berlin, cod. Mus. Sem. christl. Archaeol. 3807, fol. 1ᵛ, dating from the eleventh or twelfth century; see G. Stuhlfauth, "A Greek Psalter with Byzantine Miniatures," *AB*, 15 (1933), 317ff., fig. 11.

[35] Brightmann, *Liturgies*, p. 502.

B. THE TEACHING SCENE

1. CHARACTERISTICS OF THE TEACHING SCENE

Gregory preaching to a group is the simplest illustration; it is also the most fundamental type of scene. In a few manuscripts the teaching scene is the opening miniature
(Figs. 234, 299), while in others it is placed in the body of the manuscript, next to
a particular homily. In the latter case, the teaching scene appears above the title of
each individual homily, or in the margins of the written column, or forms the initial
letter of the text. The teaching scene, however, was not intended for a particular
sermon, but for the beginning of every sermon. Evidence to substantiate this is found
in the cod. Milan, Ambros. E. 49-50, inf., containing the forty-five homilies of Gregory, and in the manuscripts of the liturgical edition. In the Milan codex, every homily
begins with an illustration presenting Gregory teaching a group of people, often ecclesiastics. The illustrators of Gregory's homilies may have found models in classical
teaching scenes, or in similar illustrations of the Old Testament.[36]

At times, however, the teaching scene does not appear alone, but is conflated with
the pictorial rendering of the subject of the sermon. There is little doubt that these
conflations, wherever they occur, are the result of a desire to clarify the subject of
Gregory's oration pictorially. These teaching scenes may include Gregory and his
audience, or only Gregory teaching and the subject of the sermon. Moreover, the
appearance of the conflations does not preclude the presence of a simple teaching
scene in the same homily, as is proven in the cod. Milan, Ambros. E. 49-50, inf. and
the manuscripts of the liturgical edition. In the former, a simple teaching scene is
placed at the beginning of the homily to Julian the Tax Collector. In addition, another
teaching scene, which includes the figure of Julian, appears in the margin to clarify
the subject of Gregory's sermon.[37] A further example occurs in the cod. Paris gr. 533,
where the illustrations of the same homily begin with a simple teaching scene, fol. 70^r
(Fig. 244); on fol. 77^v another teaching scene includes Julian (Fig. 245). The conflated teaching scenes of the manuscripts of the liturgical edition and the scenes of
the cod. Milan, Ambros. E. 49-50, inf. differ, however. In the latter, Julian is not
separated from the audience; he is distinguished only by his inscribed name and his
decorated tunic. In the former, the protagonist of the oration stands apart from the
audience and occupies an eminent position.

Obviously, it is not possible to disentangle the varieties of conflated teaching scenes
without considering at the same time the pictorial renderings of the subject matter of
each sermon. That investigation is undertaken in the second part of this chapter.
However, I present first a classification of teaching scenes according to format and
composition, and a discussion not only of the simple scenes but of those composite
scenes whose conflation is self-evident.

[36] See cod. Vat. gr. 747 (Octateuch), fol. 192^r—
Moses teaching the Israelites.

[37] Grabar, *Ambros. 49-50*, pl. XXI, 3.

27

2. TEACHING SCENES AS FRONTISPIECES

Only two manuscripts, the codd. Paris gr. 533, and Milan, Ambros. G. 88 sup., have teaching scenes as frontispieces. The miniature of the Paris manuscript, fol. 3ᵛ, represents Gregory in episcopal vestments seated on a gilt throne, blessing with one hand, holding a book with the other, and resting his feet on a jewel-studded footstool (Fig. 234). On either side of him a group of clerics holding scrolls listen to him while they write. Behind the figure of Gregory towers a baldachin supported by four colonettes painted in imitation of marble, and set in front of a screenlike edifice. The miniature of the Milan codex, fol. 3ᵛ, is similar to that of the Paris manuscript, but the groups of people differ and the architectural setting is less elaborate (Fig. 299).

Both of these frontispieces are good examples of what may be called a *hieratic teaching scene*. The over-all composition suggests the term hieratic since the seated teacher, flanked on either side by the audience, forms the axis and conveys the impression of solemnity. Teaching scenes placed in the body of the homilies are often of this type.

3. TEACHING SCENES IN THE HOMILIES

—Homily 1

In the lower register of fol. 23ᵛ of the cod. Paris gr. 543 Gregory appears, standing and holding a scroll (Fig. 454). On the right is a group of monks, and on the left Gregory's father stands in front of a building, presumably a church. While the illustration is a teaching scene, since Gregory is reading his sermon, the presence of his father identifies the homily as the one delivered in A.D. 362, on Gregory's return to Nazianzus where his father was a bishop. This sermon must therefore have been delivered in the presence of Gregory's father whose inclusion in the teaching scene reveals the illustrator's desire to adapt it to a specific homily. This practice occurs frequently throughout the manuscript.

The title miniature of the cod. Jerusalem, Taphou 14, fol. 3ʳ, is a conflation of a teaching scene and a pictorial representation of the subject matter of the sermon (Fig. 99). Such conflations also appear in other miniatures of this manuscript.

—Homily 2

A figure of the teaching Gregory combined with the subject of the sermon, the vision of the Prophet Habakkuk, forms the initial E of the homily in the codd. Sinai 339, fol. 9ᵛ, and Paris gr. 543, fol. 28ʳ (Figs. 379, 456). The teaching Gregory alone, however, forms the initial E in the codd. Oxford, Roe 6, fol. 4ʳ, and Turin, Univ. Lib. C. I. 6, fol. 3ʳ (Figs. 437, 20). In the first, the teacher is standing; in the second, he is seated. The seated position and the codex on the lectern recall the author portrait and suggest that this historiated initial presents a variant in which the writing Gregory of the initial is replaced by the teaching Gregory.

A different teaching scene depicting the teaching Gregory and the fallen Lucifer,

28

mentioned in the sermon, occurs in the codex Jerusalem, Taphou 14 along the bottom margin of fol. 9ʳ (Fig. 101). Here Gregory's figure is not conflated with the subject miniature of the entire sermon but with the illustration of a specific paragraph. The miniature, therefore, exemplifies another variety of illustration. In addition to the opening teaching scene, other teaching scenes inserted in the text serve to illustrate it in a narrative fashion. They usually include the teacher and his topic, but no audience. Many parallels of these scenes are found in the cod. Milan, Ambros. E. 49-50, inf., especially in the illustrations of the orations against Julian the Apostate, in which an explanatory text beside the miniatures specifies the occasion to which they refer.[38]

–Homily 3

The cod. Sinai 339 displays two varieties of teaching scenes for the third homily. A simple teaching scene, forming the initial E, fol. 42ᵛ, depicts Gregory of Nazianzus instructing a group of people who stand in front of a church (Fig. 380). On the upper part of the letter is a bust of Christ, leaning down from heaven and blessing his followers. This scene is a reduction of a title miniature, and reappears in a more reduced form (only the teacher reading his sermon remains) in the cod. Turin, Univ. Lib. C. I. 6, fol. 16ʳ (Fig. 27).

In addition to the teaching scene of the historiated initial, the cod. Sinai 339 contains another one, which refers to the concluding paragraphs of the sermon, in the title miniature conflated with a portrait of St. Mamas. No audience appears in this title miniature, but the inclusion of a simple teaching scene for this homily may account for the omission. Gregory may be serving as a witness in the title miniature of the Sinai manuscript, not as a teacher.

A conflated teaching scene including the audience, the teacher and the subject of his sermon (Church and Synagogue) appears in the title miniature of the cod. Athos, Panteleimon 6, fol. 30ʳ (Fig. 139). Gregory and his audience occupy the left part of the composition. A reduced form of this miniature, including all the elements, can be seen in the historiated initial E of the cod. Paris gr. 550, fol. 30ᵛ (Fig. 407).

–Homily 4

Only the cod. Paris gr. 533, fol. 35ᵛ, has preserved a simple teaching scene in this homily (Fig. 241). The illustration is a combination of the historiated initial and marginal systems. Gregory, holding an open scroll, on which is written the beginning of his sermon, forms the letter Π, while his audience stands on the opposite side of the column.

–Homily 5

The cod. Athos, Panteleimon 6, fol. 63ᵛ, contains a teaching scene forming a vignette (Fig. 145). The scene is divided into two parts by the column of the text,

---

[38] Grabar, *Ambros. 49-50*, pls. LXIX, 2, 3; LXXI, 1.

but is unified by the common ground on which the figures stand. Gregory, in episcopal vestments, is the main figure of the composition. Standing on the right, he addresses a group of people headed by a bishop. Since the main figure is at the side, this compositional scheme can be termed *lateral* as opposed to *centralized* or *hieratic*. Originally this marginal miniature was a column miniature which, when displaced from the text, lost frame and background. The same is true of the teaching scene found in the margins of the homily on fol. 47ʳ of the cod. Paris gr. 533 and of the other marginal scenes in this manuscript (Fig. 242). Here the figure of Gregory forms the initial T, and the audience is placed in the right margin.

–Homily 6

In the miniatures of the codd. Athos, Dionysiou 61, fol. 165ʳ; Jerusalem, Taphou 14, fol. 58ʳ; Paris, Coislin 239, fols. 46ᵛ, 50ʳ; Vat. gr. 1947, fol. 35ᵛ; Sinai 339, fol. 397ʳ, the teaching scene has been conflated with the subject of the sermon referring to St. Cyprian and in only the miniature of the last codex has the audience not been included (Figs. 373, 111, 214, 215, 127, 395).

Two other manuscripts have conflated the teaching scene with the subject of the sermon: codd. Florence, Laur. Plut. VII, 32, fol. 48ʳ and Oxford, Selden. B. 54, fol. 19ᵛ (Figs. 265, 289). The use of the type of the seated teacher, however, and the similar posture of the subject of the sermon creates a new pictorial theme. The most appropriate term for this is a "discussion group," and it is dealt with in another part of the study.

–Homily 7

The figure of the teaching Gregory standing on a pedestal forms the initial T of the homily's text in the cod. Paris gr. 533, fol. 70ʳ (Fig. 244). His audience, a group of laymen, stands opposite him in the right margin, so that the miniature has a lateral compositional theme.

–Homily 8

Only the cod. Florence, Laur. Plut. VII, 32, fol. 63ʳ has preserved a simple teaching scene in this homily (Fig. 267). Gregory and his audience are placed at either side of the homily's title. Gregory in his episcopal vestments occupies the left vertical bar, while the audience stands opposite him. Both he and his audience appear as columns which support the pictorial representation of the subject of the sermon, the Nativity.

–Homily 9

A teaching scene of lateral composition with a standing teacher appears in the lower register of the full-page miniature of the cod. Paris gr. 543, fol. 130ᵛ (Fig. 461). Gregory, standing by the door of a building with a gabled roof, delivers the funeral oration for Basil, his departed friend. His audience of bishops stands opposite him on the other side of the sarcophagus which occupies the center of the composition. A ciborium behind the marble sarcophagus and the architectural setting suggest the church in which the sermon is being delivered.

This and other scenes of the manuscript constitute the original format of the title miniature. The general format of this manuscript, which achieves a full-page miniature by superimposing two scenes, is common in Mediaeval book illumination.[39]

A sketchy marginal teaching scene appears in the cod. Athos, Vatopedi 107, fol. 188ʳ, while only the figure of the teaching Gregory remains in the initials E of the codd. Athos, Dionysiou 61, fol. 35ʳ; Sinai 339, fol. 109ʳ; and Athos, Stavroniketa 15, fol. 98ᵛ (Figs. 330, 363, 386, 432). In the last three codices the special type of illustrated initial in which the audience has not been included recalls similar historiated initials in Gospel books showing Christ teaching. The conventional scheme of a combined teaching scene, which included only the teacher and the subject, occurs in the miniature of the cod. Paris gr. 533, fol. 91ʳ (Fig. 248).

–Homily 10

The cod. Paris gr. 533 contains two marginal teaching scenes, one at the beginning and another in the course of the homily, fols. 146ʳ and 154ʳ (Figs. 246, 247). As in similar teaching scenes in this manuscript, Gregory occupies the left part while his audience stands in the opposite margin. There is a tendency to relate a teaching scene to the subject of the sermon, e.g. here Gregory points out the main miniature to his audience, and one of his listeners makes a corresponding gesture in the second teaching scene. This tendency is evident in other teaching scenes of the manuscript.

–Homily 11

The miniature of the cod. Sinai 339, fol. 217ʳ is a good example of a hieratic teaching scene (Fig. 390). Gregory, seated on a *thokos* against a gold background, faces the spectator. He is therefore more concerned with the invisible audience than with the audience shown in the picture; anyone at any time may thus become a member of his audience and find comfort and edification in his inspired sermons. The represented audience consists of bishops flanking Gregory like the complementary parts of a feast picture. The presence of bishops adds further significance to this teaching scene, for not only is the composition hieratic, but it also has a ceremonial aspect, and the scene undoubtedly reflects liturgical rites.

---

[39] A similar parallel is presented by the aristocratic psalter in Berlin, cod. Mus. Sem. christl. Archaeol. 3807, in which the full-page miniature is formed by two superimposed scenes; see Stuhlfauth, *op.cit.*, 311-26. There are also examples in which use has been made of more than two superimposed scenes in order to conform to the requirements of a full-page miniature. See, for example, the cod. Paris gr. 510, Omont, *Min. gr.* (1929), pl. xxiv, or the Gospels in Parma, Bibl. Pal., cod. 5, dating from the end of the eleventh century, reproduced in W. Felicetti-Libenfels, *Geschichte der byzantinischen Ikonenmalerei*, Lausanne 1956, pl. 13.

The bishops do not appear in the similar hieratic scenes depicted in the codd. Jerusalem, Taphou 14, fol. 186ʳ and Florence, Laur. Plut. VII, 32, fol. 120ʳ (Figs. 116, 269). In the miniature of the latter, a scribe, one of the group of people standing on Gregory's right, takes down the words of the teacher.

The cod. Paris, Coislin 239, fol. 130ᵛ contains a teaching scene representing Gregory sitting to the left and teaching two laymen who stand opposite him, forming a scene of lateral composition (Fig. 228). The teaching scene in the cod. Oxford, Selden. B. 54, fol. 67ᵛ, also lateral in composition, shows Gregory standing (Fig. 293).

In the title miniature of the cod. Athos, Panteleimon 6, fol. 178ʳ, Gregory is seated on the left with a deacon beside him, while three clerics, including a bishop, stand on the right (Fig. 172). The scheme of the miniature is thus neither centralized nor lateral, but, in manifesting some of the elements of both, it represents an intermediate phase. Once again the cod. Paris gr. 533, fol. 158ᵛ, provides an example of the marginal teaching scene (Fig. 249).

The cod. Paris gr. 543, fol. 213ᵛ (lower register), contains a teaching scene that is of special interest because of the difficulties in interpretation it presents (Fig. 465). Gregory of Nazianzus, dressed as a monk, is seated to the left. He holds a parchment on which he writes his sermon in the presence of three standing figures. Another monk is shown seated to the right. He has a nimbus, and holds a staff. His black beard suggests that he is younger than Gregory. From behind a lectern on which an open book is placed, he speaks to two figures who stand before him. The identification of this teaching monk is problematic. No other person is mentioned in the homily, which deals with the baptism of the people. In the fourth paragraph, Gregory, speaking about the Holy Trinity, says that there is nothing created in It, nothing accidental, "as I have heard one of the wise say."[40] The Byzantine commentators—Basil the Younger is one of them—have recognized in the cited passage a reference to Gregory Thaumaturgos. The possibility that the illustrator had in mind the commentator's interpretation, and included Gregory Thaumaturgos explaining the doctrine of the Trinity, cannot be excluded. Yet such an identification of the monk in the miniature does not seem plausible, nor can the scene be interpreted on the basis of the text of other homilies. If this monk is not a subject-illustration, a comparison of other teaching scenes in the same manuscript may clarify the thoughts of this particular illustrator with regard to teaching scenes. Only in the teaching scene of the first homily on Easter does an extra person, i.e. Gregory the Elder, appear. He, however, was present at the delivery of the sermon and the illustrator understandably considered his presence in the miniature necessary. It can be assumed that the problematic teaching scene presents a similar case, although the additional figure here cannot be merely a witness since he is speaking.

There are two men who might have been present at the delivery of this sermon,

40 *PG*, 36, 420.

which took place in Constantinople on January 7, 381. One of these is Evagrius of Pontus who, according to Socrates and Sozomenos,[41] had attended Gregory in Constantinople and became his archdeacon. It is known that Evagrius remained in Constantinople after the Council of 381, which was assembled in May of that year. The other possibility is St. Jerome, a few years younger than Gregory, who stayed in Constantinople until the end of 381.[42] Jerome had Gregory as his teacher and he left on record the pleasure with which he listened to and conversed with the bishop. Yet, neither of these two persons can satisfactorily be said to be the teaching monk of the Paris miniature, and his identity remains to be discovered.

–Homily 12

In the cod. Oxford, Roe 6, fol. 110ʳ, a teaching scene occupies an entire page, which is the usual format for this manuscript (Fig. 444). Gregory sits on the right with a scroll in his left hand and speaks to a man standing before him. This listener (the remnant of a larger audience), who has a very expressive face, bows slightly toward the seated teacher. Both figures are set against an architectural background.

Obviously this full-page miniature is an enlargement of a strip-like title miniature, for it is clear that the figures have been increased in height in order to fulfill the requirements of a full-page miniature. The architectural background which apparently existed in the model has not been enlarged in scale, but it has gained height by the addition of new elements. An analogous example is found in the full-page miniatures of the aristocratic psalters that were taken from column pictures of the Book of Kings.[43] Similar changes were made to adapt most of the miniatures in this codex.

In the cod. Oxford, Canon. gr. 103, fol. 192ʳ, figures of Gregory speaking and of Gregory of Nyssa appear (Fig. 284). Although this is a conventional scheme for a combined teaching scene without portraying the audience (the same scheme is used in the next homily in the same manuscript), the content of the homily introduces a different concept. So far, Gregory has been speaking of either feasts or saints long since dead. Now Gregory addresses Gregory of Nyssa, who is present, personally. This teaching scene, therefore, is to a certain extent a subject-illustration.

–Homily 13

In the lower register of the cod. Paris gr. 543, fol. 260ʳ, there is a hieratic teaching scene showing Gregory with a scroll in his hand, standing behind a sarcophagus

[41] *PG*, 67, 516; J. Bidez, G. C. Hansen eds., *Sozomenus Kirchengeschichte* (Die griechischen christlichen Schriftsteller der ersten Jahrhunderte, 50), Berlin 1960, p. 285.

[42] H. Wace, P. Schaff, *A Select Library of Nicene and Post-Nicene Fathers*, 2nd series, VII, Oxford-New York 1894, p. 198.

[43] Cf. David Anointed in the cod. Paris gr. 139, fol. 3ᵛ; Omont, *Min. gr.* (1929), pl. III; cod. Vat. gr. 333, fol. 22ᵛ (column picture); J. Lassus, "Les miniatures byzantines du Livre des Rois," *Mélanges d'archéologie et d'histoire*, 45 (1928), pl. II, 4.

(Fig. 466). The presence of the sarcophagus indicates that the conventional teaching scene has been replaced by one adapted to the content of the homily, making the miniature a more direct illustration of the homily's subject. Gregory delivers the eulogy of the departed bishop of Alexandria to two groups of bishops who flank the sarcophagus. Their postures and expressions differ, as does the treatment of their beards. The long beards recall figures of ascetics, while the short ones indicate comparative youth. The entire composition is framed by a tripartite arch supported by two knotted columns, and suggests the interior of the church in which the oration was delivered.

The teaching scene of Gregory seated in the title miniature of the cod. Jerusalem, Taphou 14, fol. 224ᵛ, is conflated with the subject of the homily (Fig. 118). The same conflation occurs in the initial A in the cod. Istanbul, Patr. 16, fol. 194ᵛ, where the illustrator has been faithful to the system of illustration followed throughout the manuscript and has not included the audience (Fig. 74).

Only the figures of Gregory and Athanasius, inserted in the decorative lay-out that includes the title of the homily, appear in the teaching scene illustrating this sermon in the cod. Oxford, Canon. gr. 103, fol. 197ʳ (Fig. 285). Gregory, standing to the left, holds a book and extends his left hand in a speaking gesture toward Athanasius, who stands facing the spectator and holding a book. Athanasius is portrayed, as in other representations, as an old, white-haired man. A similar conflation has occurred in the marginal miniature of the cod. Paris gr. 533, fol. 196ᵛ, which shows Gregory in the act of giving a scroll to Athanasius (Fig. 251). The scroll as an iconographic element has been used by the artist in other teaching scenes (cf. Figs. 248, 250).

–Homily 14

Also belonging to the tradition of the teaching scene are the miniatures of the codd. Athos, Dionysiou 61, fol. 130ʳ and Paris gr. 543, fol. 288ᵛ, lower register (Figs. 369, 467). In both cases Gregory is flanked by a group of standing bishops. In the miniature of the Athos codex, Gregory is enthroned under a ciborium set against an architectural background, while in the miniature of the Paris manuscript, Gregory stands on three steps.

The codd. Moscow, Hist. Museum 146, fol. 202ᵛ, Paris gr. 533, fol. 218ᵛ, and Athos, Vatopedi 107, fol. 208ᵛ, include marginal scenes showing Gregory standing and addressing a group of bishops, whereas the codd. Istanbul, Patr. 16, fol. 234ᵛ and Sinai 346, fol. 180ʳ, present teaching scenes in the historiated initials Π (Figs. 16, 252, 334, 75, 351).

In all these miniatures the presence of bishops illustrates the text of the homily addressed to the members of the Council of 381. Since the bishops are shown standing in the title miniatures and in the historiated initials as well, and are not seated as a representation of a council scene should require, these miniatures are basically teaching scenes adapted to the content of the homily.

–Homily 15

A hieratic teaching scene, whose axis is formed by the figure of Gregory, appears in the title miniatures of the codd. Florence, Laur. Plut. VII, 32, fol. 162ʳ, and Paris gr. 543, fol. 310ᵛ, upper register (Figs. 273, 468). In the first miniature, Gregory is seated and flanked by two groups of standing bishops. His figure not only balances the composition but dominates it and brings forth its hieratic qualities. In fact, Gregory resembles Christ teaching the apostles, for example, in the cod. Paris gr. 74, fols. 8ᵛ and 9ʳ.[44] In the Paris miniature, Gregory is represented as a monk standing with an open scroll and flanked by two listening groups consisting of clerics and laymen.[45]

Because the manuscript is poorly preserved, only the design can be detected in the miniature of the cod. Vat. gr. 1947, fol. 128ʳ (Fig. 136). Seated on the left in front of a building, Gregory addresses a group of people standing on the right. The teaching scene in the cod. Paris, Coislin 239, fol. 196ᵛ, is similar, but shows only four persons (Fig. 232).

The title miniature, again enlarged into a full-page miniature in the cod. Oxford, Roe 6, fol. 143ᵛ, represents the standing teacher in a lateral composition (Fig. 447). Gregory on the right addresses a group of people on the left. Both teacher and audience are set against an architectural background.

Another marginal teaching scene of lateral composition has been used by the illustrator of the cod. Paris gr. 533, fol. 251ʳ (Fig. 254). At the end of the text of the same homily, however, there is another marginal teaching scene, fol. 276ᵛ, representing, between the two written columns, a white-bearded monk holding a scroll and extending his hands (Fig. 255); below him to the left is a group of people obviously listening to him, while he points to a figure of Gregory dressed in bishop's vestments in the opposite margin. This scene does not belong to homily 15, or to any other, but to the text that follows it, which is a life of St. Gregory written by Gregory the Presbyter.[46] In fact, the illustrator of the Paris miniature had depicted Gregory the Presbyter giving an account of St. Gregory's life to the people.

As in other homilies, the teaching scene here has been conflated with the subject of the sermon. Examples of this fusion are found in the title miniature of the codd.

---

[44] Omont, *Evangiles*, I, pl. 12.

[45] That the figures with the long hats are clerics is proven by one miniature of the fourteenth-century Scylitzes manuscript in Madrid in which a group of people wearing the same hats is identified by an inscription as clerics (οἱ κληρικοί). See A. Xyngopoulos, " Ἰωάννης ὁ Χρυσόστομος Πηγὴ Σοφίας," Ἀρχαιολογικὴ Ἐφημερίς, 81-83 (1942-

1944), p. 11. The miniatures of this manuscript are reproduced in S. C. Estopañán, *Skyllitzes Matritensis*, I, Barcelona 1965.

[46] For the text of the *Vita* see *PG*, 35, 241-305, and for its author, H. G. Beck, *Kirche und theologische Literatur im byzantinischen Reich*, Munich 1959, p. 459.

Jerusalem, Taphou 14, fol. 265ᵛ; Milan, Ambros. G 88 sup., fol. 264ᵛ; and Athos, Panteleimon 6, fol. 257ʳ (Figs. 121, 315, 179). In these examples, the teaching scene is complete.

–Homily 16

A lateral composition is the main element of the teaching scene in the codd. Paris gr. 543, fol. 342ᵛ, and Florence, Laur. Plut. VII, 32, fol. 181ʳ, but in the former Gregory stands holding a scroll and in the latter he is seated (Figs. 469, 274). In both miniatures Gregory is opposite a group of people and in front of a building with a gabled roof. In addition to these elements, the miniature of the Paris manuscript, which more particularly recalls teaching scenes found in the cod. Milan, Ambros. E. 49-50, inf.,[47] contains, in the upper part, a segment of sky alluding to the subject of the sermon.

The same compositional scheme appears in the teaching scene of the cod. Oxford, Roe 6, fol. 175ᵛ, which occupies a full page and shows Gregory standing to the right in monk's attire addressing a group of people to the left (Fig. 450). This miniature, like others in the same manuscript, is an enlargement of a strip-like miniature, as the proportions of the figure and the architectural setting suggest.

In the miniature of the cod. Paris gr. 533, fol. 236ʳ, the teaching Gregory forms the initial T of the homily (Fig. 253). His audience, consisting of old, hooded monks, occupies the right margin. The hands of these persons are covered by their garments, an expression of their reverence for Gregory. There is neither background nor frame. The teaching scene applied to the historiated initial occurs once again in the codd. Athos, Dionysiou 61, fol. 172ᵛ and Istanbul, Patr. 16, fol. 261ʳ (Figs. 376, 77).

The preceding discussion of the teaching scene in the manuscripts of the liturgical edition has shown that a simple teaching scene existed at the beginning of each homily for, of the sixteen homilies, fourteen have preserved it. In the remaining two, the teaching scene has been conflated with the pictorial rendering of the subject of the sermon.

Variations in the composition and the format of the miniatures have also been indicated. Such distinctions aid in the understanding of each artist's approach to a general scene and his artistic transformation of it. In fact the use of the teaching scene parallels the use of the author portrait. The author portrait may appear as a frontispiece, the heading of a particular homily, within the body of the homily, in the margins, or forming the initial letter. The systematic illustration of the initial is of special interest because in manuscripts which follow this method of illustration the teaching scene is either alternated with the author portrait or combined with it.

In addition to the description of the composition, format, and physical relationship of the teaching scene to the text, a distinction may be made between simple and combined teaching scene. The combined scene is usually conflated with the subject of the

[47] Grabar, *Ambros. 49-50*, pls. XXXII, 2; XXXIII, 2; XXXVI, 3 etc.

sermon. The formation of these combined teaching scenes has nothing to do with the nature of the homily's subject, but seems to be the result of a tendency to reduce the original number of miniatures. This tendency offers an adequate explanation of the great number of extant combined teaching scenes and the comparatively few simple ones. The presence of the simple teaching scene in almost every homily has nonetheless demonstrated that the teaching scene is independent of the subject-illustration and that the former does not replace the latter, although it has done so to a certain degree in the codd. Paris gr. 533, Istanbul, Patr. 16, and Oxford, Roe 6. These have either followed the system of the historiated initial, or used the teaching scene as their main illustration.

C. THE INVENTED MINIATURES

The invented miniatures provide information about the character and relationships of the manuscripts. In Mediaeval book illumination it is usually possible to reconstruct an archetype from which other copies stem,[48] and such an archetype may be considered for the liturgical edition of Gregory's homilies. The following discussion attempts to show that all manuscripts belong to the same recension, and that there has been a single accepted tradition for the illustrations of the liturgical edition. Three of the manuscripts, the codd. Moscow, Hist. Museum 146, Sinai 339, and Paris gr. 543, which have many iconographic points in common with the other manuscripts, have more than one scene in each homily. Since scenes could have been added later, all illustrations should not necessarily be ascribed to their archetype. Nevertheless, in the illustrations of Gregory's homilies, the larger cycle suggests a fuller archetype from which the illustrators of the various copies have not chosen the same scenes. The following investigation of these problems considers the iconographic meanings of the miniatures of each homily, and groups the miniatures accordingly. An introductory account of the invented miniature, however, must precede the discussion of the illustrations of the homilies.

1. THE NATURE OF THE INVENTED MINIATURE

The content of an invented miniature is derived from the passage that it illustrates.[49] The dependence of the miniature upon its basic text varies; all the particular elements of the miniature arc not necessarily original, nor does their explanation always derive from the basic text alone. An invented miniature may contain borrowed elements, conventional concepts, adaptations of existing compositional schemes, and even conscious deviations from the text; occasionally it may not have a textual basis at all.

---

[48] The illustrated manuscripts of the romance *Barlaam and Joasaph* are a case in point, see Der

Nersessian, *Barlaam.*
[49] Weitzmann, *Roll*, pp. 130ff.

2. THE MINIATURES OF THE HOMILIES: ON NEW SUNDAY; ON ST. CYPRIAN; TO JULIAN THE TAX COLLECTOR; ON ST. BASIL; ON HOLY BAPTISM; TO ST. GREGORY OF NYSSA; ON ST. ATHANASIUS; THE FAREWELL ORATION; ON THE LOVE OF THE POOR; TO HIS SILENT FATHER

THE MINIATURES OF THE HOMILY ON NEW SUNDAY[50]

Of the two scenes forming the full-page miniature of the cod. Paris gr. 543, fol. 51ʳ, only the one in the lower register is discussed here (Fig. 457). This miniature schematically represents the interior of the sanctuary of a church, the walls of which have marble revetments and a decoration of acanthus leaves. Columns with Corinthian capitals support three arches; the central arch encloses the main scene. Gregory of Nazianzus, distinguished by his nimbus and physiognomy, kneels in front of an altar under a ciborium and examines (?) the altar's column. To the left of the ciborium there is a group of seven clerics, four of whom are bishops; to the right is a group of five deacons. Under each of the two side arches stands a table similar to the holy altar, but smaller. Probably the one to the left is the table of the prothesis and the one to the right, the table of the diaconicon. The same miniature recurs in the left margin of the codd. Sinai 339, fol. 42ʳ, Moscow, Hist. Museum 146, fol. 23ʳ, and Turin, Univ. Lib. C. I. 6, fol. 16ʳ (Figs. 380, 4, 28). Naturally these miniatures lost their frame and architectural setting as they were removed from the text. Moreover, the number of persons participating in the scene has been reduced to two: Gregory of Nazianzus who kneels in front of the altar and studies its column, and another figure standing behind him. This black-bearded figure, whose vestments identify him as a deacon, stands with arms crossed on his breast, looking out of the picture.

Because the homily has nothing to do with the feast of Pentecost, Kondakov is incorrect in suggesting that, in the miniature of the cod. Paris gr. 543, Gregory is saying the Pentecost mass;[51] consequently, his interpretation that the seven clerics symbolize the seven gifts of the Holy Spirit is also incorrect.[52]

The presence of this miniature is explained, not by the title of the homily, but by its opening sentence, which refers to the *encaenia*.[53] It is definitely a liturgical picture and therefore its detailed explanation can be found in one of the liturgical books, the euchologion, which contains the formulas particular to the celebration of the Liturgy and the administration of sacraments. The miniature refers to the church service used at the encaenia.

Strictly speaking, there is only one festival of encaenia in the ancient Church, the

---

[50] The "first" Sunday of the ecclesiastical year— in fact the first Sunday after Easter—is called New Sunday. For its meaning and significance see S. Zervos ed., *Pentekostarion*, Venice n.d., p. 30.

[51] Kondakov, *Histoire*, pp. 91, 92.
[52] *Ibid., loc.cit.*
[53] Ἐγκαίνια τιμᾶσθαι παλαιὸς νόμος. *PG*, 36, 608.

dedication of the church of the Holy Sepulcher in Jerusalem, instituted on September 13, 335, at the tricennalia of the Emperor Constantine, and described in the Life of Constantine by Eusebius. Black, who has studied the feast of the encaenia in the ancient Church, says that this feast is recorded as a purely ecclesiastical occasion commemorating the consecration, not of a particular church, but of the Church, or rather, of the Old Testament Temple which the Church succeeded.[54] The liturgical books of the Greek Orthodox Church, however, state that the ceremony of the feast of the encaenia is also the ceremony of the consecration of a particular church.[55]

It has been suggested that the delivery of the homily may be related to the transfer and deposit of the relics of St. Mamas in a new church near Nazianzus, and therefore the encaenia of which Gregory speaks in the opening paragraph of his oration may refer to this church.[56] If the illustrator had this in mind, the choice of the miniature was prompted by actual historical circumstances. The feast, however, of the encaenia is commemorated on the Sunday after Easter, on which day this homily is read, and it is possible that such a relationship inspired the subject of the miniature.

Whatever the case, according to the euchologion,[57] ceremonies employed in the consecration or the feast of the encaenia entail adorning the church, celebrating the eucharist with accompanying prayers, reading responses, and observing other pertinent rituals. Thereafter, the main rite is the anointing of the altar. Before the rite of the unction begins and after the upper part of the holy altar has been placed on the column, the bishop washes the column of the altar with a sponge. Then he takes a jar containing the oil for anointing, and while the deacon says, "πρόσχωμεν," the bishop pours the oil on the holy altar saying "alleluia" three times, and forms three crosses with it. Then with his hand he spreads the oil of these three crosses over the altar. He also makes crosses with the same oil on the column of the altar while reciting a psalm, and he continues to recite as he moves out to draw crosses with the oil on the columns of the church. After this ceremony, the covering of the table begins. Until this moment, there is no drapery on the altar, and the upper part of the table and the column which supports it are visible.

Clearly, the interpretation of the miniature under discussion is limited to two possibilities: the bishop is either washing the column with a sponge, or he is anointing it.

[54] M. Black, "The Festival of Encaenia Ecclesia in the Ancient Church with Special Reference to Palestine," *Journal of Ecclesiastical History*, 5 (1954), pp. 78-85.

[55] S. Zervos ed., *Euchologion*, Venice 1951. Cf. E. C. Harington, *Rite of Consecration of Churches*, London 1844, pp. 65ff. S. Salaville, *Cérémonial de la consécration d'une église selon le rite byzantin avec introduction et notes explicatives*, Vatican 1937; cf. K. E. Konstantinides, *Les reliques et la dédicace dans le rite byzantin jusqu'au début du moyen âge (VI-VIIe siècles)*, Strasbourg 1951

(Theol. diss.). Commentators on Gregory's sermons knew that encaenia was the consecration of a church. For example a commentator of the thirteenth century says that, encaenia is "ἐπὶ τοῦ ναοῦ μὲν ἡ πρώτη καθιέρωσις." See Sajdak, *Scholia*, p. 202.

[56] For a discussion of this problem, see A. Marava-Chadjinikolaou, Ὁ Ἅγιος Μάμας, Athens 1953, p. 59.

[57] S. Zervos ed., *Euchologion*, Venice 1951, pp. 288ff.

The second seems most probable, because the anointing is the more important part of the ceremony.

This scene is apparently unique. One parallel example occurs in the thirteenth-century Syriac lectionary in the British Museum (cod. Add. 7170, fol. 8ʳ) which, according to Jerphanion, represents the consecration of an altar.[58] Even if this interpretation were correct—and it is open to doubt—the Syriac miniature would present not the anointing of the altar, but its censing.

The importance of the miniature is obvious. It illustrates precisely a ceremony of the Middle Byzantine Church known from texts and from its survival in the present Greek Orthodox Church. Furthermore, it is an addition to other liturgical representations in Byzantine art, and is found only in the manuscripts of Gregory's homilies. Its presence in these homilies has a special significance because it emphasizes the liturgical aspect of the manuscripts and of their illustrations as well. Kondakov said that, from the point of view of iconography, it is difficult to find anything new in the Sinai manuscript.[59] This is no longer valid.

THE MINIATURE OF THE HOMILY ON ST. CYPRIAN

a. *Cyprian Bows to Gregory*

The charming miniature of the cod. Oxford, Canon. gr. 103, fol. 57ʳ, shows the two bishops forming part of a title frame that consists of three bars, one horizontal and two vertical, a composition used constantly in this manuscript (Fig. 279). Gregory appears in the left bar and Cyprian in the right. They are both vested as bishops and each holds a book. Gregory, with a large nimbus, faces the spectator, and Cyprian bows slightly toward Gregory. The creation of this miniature is certainly prompted by the title of the homily. But its compositional scheme, whose elements originated in the menologion, is used throughout the manuscript and Cyprian's posture may have no particular meaning; it is probably the result of the artist's attempt to create a relationship between the two figures.

The same iconographic elements form the initial M of the codd. Sinai 346, fol. 227ʳ, Paris gr. 533, fol. 58ʳ, and Milan, Ambros. G 88 sup., fol. 73ʳ (Figs. 353, 243, 306). Although the letter M is often historiated by two standing figures, the difference in the execution of that initial in these three codices is significant. In the first two, a scroll forms the middle part of the letter, and in the third the middle is a censer. Such a difference demonstrates the freedom each artist enjoyed in the use of compositional devices.

---

[58] G. de Jerphanion, *Les miniatures du manuscrit Syriac no. 559 de la Bibliothèque Vaticane*, Vatican 1940, p. 70, fig. 27. Other liturgical pictures, more common, show the celebration of mass.

Another example occurs in the eleventh-century psalter in Jerusalem, cod. Taphou 53, fol. 226ʳ; see Papadopoulos-Kerameus, I, p. 130.

[59] Kondakov, *Histoire*, p. 97.

b. *The Two Bishops Conversing*

Another iconographic type which has often been used in the illustrations of Gregory, and in other manuscripts as well, occurs in the codd. Florence, Laur. Plut. VII, 32, fol. 48ʳ, and Oxford, Selden. B. 54, fol. 19ᵛ (Figs. 265, 289). Seated and speaking to each other, the two bishops form a *discussion group*. In the first miniature the two bishops are represented against an architectural background, but in the second only a table with the writing implements on it is shown. Parallels of this latter element can be found in other representations of discussion groups.

c. *The Koimesis of St. Cyprian*

The cod. Turin, Univ. Lib. C. I. 6, fol. 37ᵛ, depicts the funeral of St. Cyprian in its title miniature (Fig. 44). This rendering can be justified only by the opening sentence alluding to the death of the saint. Since the sermon is a panegyric and not a funeral oration, the illustration is rather inappropriate. Moreover, from the point of view of iconography, it is unhistorical, because Cyprian was decapitated and his body did not receive a funeral after his martyrdom.

d. *Conflated Scenes*

At times certain manuscripts combine different iconographic traditions into a single scene. The customary combination is that of the teaching scene with the pictorial representation of the subject of the sermon. The following manuscripts present such scenes: Athos, Dionysiou 61, fol. 165ʳ; Jerusalem, Taphou 14, fol. 58ʳ; Paris, Coislin 239, fol. 46ᵛ; Vat. gr. 1947, fol. 35ᵛ (Figs. 373, 111, 214, 127). Gregory, dressed in episcopal vestments and holding a book, points out Cyprian, standing at the right of the scene, to a group of people at the left. Only the miniature of the Athos manuscript shows Gregory standing beneath a ciborium—a characteristic of teaching scenes— and an architectural background. A remnant of the latter element appears in the Vatican miniature. In the miniature of the cod. Paris, Coislin 239, the lack of space obliged the miniaturist to place the two gesticulating figures, representing Gregory's audience, outside the frame of the picture.

The elements of these miniatures—a simple teaching scene and the figure of Cyprian—are so closely related to Gregory's text that they can be explained only by means of it. Although in the first three miniatures Cyprian extends his right hand toward Gregory in a speaking gesture, in the Vatican miniature Cyprian bows slightly to the right. His attitude recalls that in the miniature of the cod. Oxford, Canon. gr. 103, fol. 57ʳ, discussed above, and it is possible that the illustrator of the Vatican manuscript was familiar with this iconographic type, which he then conflated with the teaching scene.

THE MINIATURES OF THE HOMILY TO JULIAN THE
TAX COLLECTOR

a. *Gregory and Julian the Writers*

The codex Sinai 339 contains three miniatures which illustrate this homily: a title miniature, one in the upper left margin, and one in the initial T, all on fol. 73ʳ (Fig. 383). The composition of the title miniature is simple and well-balanced. On the left, the author of the homilies sits on a high chair with a curved back and writes on a parchment which he holds in his left hand; his feet rest on a footstool. Opposite him, on the right side of the composition, Julian the Tax Collector is seated on a simple faldstool. He is represented as an old man dressed in a long garment and wearing a white cap. He too leans over and writes on a piece of parchment. Between the two writers are three scribes wearing long garments and white caps. Two of them are near Gregory and hold scrolls in their hands, while the third stands in front of Julian and holds an inkstand. This scene recurs in very reduced form in the historiated initial T of the same Sinai manuscript. The initial itself is formed by a figure of Gregory standing, while two scribes holding their scrolls are shown near the initial. Gregory's standing posture was dictated by the shape of the letter T. The representation of Gregory and Julian as writers, based on the title and the sixteenth paragraph of the homily,[60] and formed by an author portrait and a figure of the Tax Collector in the act of writing, recalls double portraits of letter writers found in the Octateuchs.[61]

Similar in iconography are the title miniatures of the codd. Jerusalem, Taphou 14, fol. 70ʳ, Florence Laur. Plut. VII, 32, fol. 56ʳ, and the reduced miniature of the cod. Oxford, Canon. gr. 103, fol. 69ʳ, although certain differences occur (Figs. 112, 266, 280). In the Jerusalem miniature, the figures that complete the composition are not between the writers, as in the Sinai miniature, but behind them; moreover, only one of the figures, the man who stands behind Gregory writing on a scroll, is a scribe. The illustrator of the Jerusalem codex also used this kind of arrangement in other miniatures. In the Florence manuscript one more element must be considered: the architectural setting, which may have existed in its model.

b. *Julian Collecting the Taxes*

The second illustration of this homily in the cod. Sinai 339, that of the upper left margin, is identical with the miniature of the cod. Moscow, Hist. Museum 146, which occupies the lower part of fol. 61ʳ, and is very similar to the miniatures of the codd.

---

[60] *PG*, 35, 1061.

[61] See cod. Vat. gr. 747, fols. 2ᵛ, 12ʳ; Seraglio, cod. 8, fol. 11ᵛ, reproduced in Ouspensky, *Octateuque*, pl. VII, 1. Further examples of two writers seated opposite each other may be found in representations of Eusebius and Carpianus in the Gospels (see cod. Parma, Pal. 5, fol. 11ᵛ, E. Martini, *Catalogo di manoscritti greci esistenti nelle bibl.*

italiane, I, 1, Milan 1893, p. 150), or in representations of evangelists (see fresco in the church of Panagia Mavriotissa in Kastoria, reproduced in S. Pelekanides, Καστοριά, Thessalonica 1953, pl. 65a). Cf. also a similar compositional scheme for other writers in general, such as John of Damascus and pupil in the Menologion of Basil, *Il menologio*, p. 213.

Paris gr. 543, fol. 102ᵛ, and Turin Univ. Lib. C. I. 6, fol. 47ʳ (Figs. 9, 460, 46). In all four miniatures the Tax Collector, dressed in his official costume and wearing a distinctive white cap, sits in front of a table. He holds a piece of parchment in his right hand while extending his left hand across the table in a gesture demanding or receiving the tribute. Behind him and beside a building stands a scribe, who writes on a piece of parchment. In the center of the picture and behind the table, another official dressed in a simple robe and wearing a similar cap holds in his right hand a pair of scales, while he extends his left hand toward a group of people standing to the right of the table. This group consists of four figures in the Paris miniature and three in the others. These poorly dressed people, who can be studied in detail in the Paris miniature, are portrayed in distinctive postures. One of them delivers his coins onto the table. The others stand by undecided, burdened with thoughts and worries, waiting for the final word of the Tax Collector. They are the debtors. In the background and to the right, in all four miniatures, is a rocky hill down which four more persons are coming to pay their tribute. In the Paris miniature one of these figures seems to be an official.

The minor differences between the miniatures pertain only to details of dress and furniture, which are subject to fashion, and to the architectural details of the building to the left of the composition. In the Paris miniature, Julian's robe is not striped as in the other miniatures, and he sits not on a faldstool but on a chair; moreover, the building has a gabled roof only, while in the other miniatures there are cupolas in addition to the gabled roof: two cupolas in the Moscow and Sinai miniatures, and one in the Turin.

The illustration of this homily with a taxation scene is suggested both by the title and by the contents of the homily. Gregory, mentioning the poor, the priests, and the philosophers presented to Julian for taxation, says: ". . . the only thing they possess is their bodies, yet not even those entirely; they have nothing to give to Caesar; everything is given to God: hymns and prayers, and vigilance, and tears. In order to die in the world and live in Christ they keep no possessions. So they may annihilate their flesh and liberate their soul from the body."[62] In the twelfth paragraph of the homily, Gregory turns to Julian and says: "You who are the registrar of our taxes, do your job in justice. Do not register my sermon of which little or no benefit comes, but enroll my people in justice, in sanctity, and in benevolence, taking into consideration nothing but the fact that our Lord was born during such an enrollment."[63] Gregory then gives an account of the enrollment for taxation of Mary and Joseph, which is, in fact, the subject of the Gospel lection (Luke 2: 1-5) read on the same day as Gregory's homily. Luke's account was illustrated rather early and possibly such a representation furnished the iconographic model for the miniature of the homily. Nevertheless, taking into consideration the fact that the two known instances illustrating the Gospel account—one found in the eleventh-century lectionary Athos, Dionysiou 587 and the

---

[62] *PG*, 35, 1061-64. All translations of the Greek texts are by the author unless stated otherwise.

[63] *PG*, 35, 1057.

other in the fourteenth-century mosaics of the Kahrie Camii[64]—do not closely resemble Julian's taxation scene, another suggestion regarding the iconographic model can be made: perhaps an actual taxation scene suggested the compositional scheme of the miniature.

c. *Julian Giving the Tax Orders to the Scribes*

The cod. Paris gr. 550, fol. 72[r], contains a title miniature which represents an entirely different action (Fig. 413). Julian is shown seated at a table, behind which stand six people in a single row. Their physiognomies are differentiated; they wear high hats similar to Julian's, and hold scrolls. The first of them is handing his scroll to Julian, who receives it by extending his hand in a rather restrained manner. The background is neutral. Clearly the standing figures are not the debtors, but the official scribes who probably give the tax orders to the Tax Collector.

This narrative composition of the miniature of the Paris manuscript seems to have been transformed into a hieratic one in the miniature of the cod. Athos, Dionysiou 61, fol. 28[v], which therefore may be considered a later substitute (Fig. 361). Its main characteristics are grim severity and stately dignity. There is something particularly delightful about the rigid and impressive figure of the Tax Collector, who occupies the very center of the composition between two groups of standing figures and sits behind a table on which rest writing implements. The first figure of the group on the right is a scribe who holds an inkstand in his left hand. The symmetrical arrangement of the group, the prominence of the seat, and the posture of Julian—intensified by the triangular voids between him and the flanking groups—make clear the ceremonial aspect of the composition. Julian is represented as a ruler attended by his scribe and his officials.[65] The ceremonial aspect and the ruler concept differentiate this miniature from those discussed so far, and while it suggests the use of a different model, it reveals the extent of the artists' inventiveness when they develop variations of the same theme.

d. *Gregory and the Martyrs*

In the cod. Paris gr. 543, fol. 102[v], there is a scene occupying the lower register of the full-page miniature (Fig. 460). Gregory as a busy writer sits in front of a building. Opposite him, on the right side of the picture, there is a group of figures. Each of the four figures in the first row, and presumably the others behind, whose heads only are visible, holds in his right hand a small cross, which is an attribute of martyrs.[66] Part of this miniature—the group of martyrs represented frontally in three

---

[64] P. A. Underwood, *The Kariye Djami*, I-III, New York 1966, II (The Mosaics), pl. 101. Cf. J. Lafontain-Dosogne, *Iconographie de la Vierge dans l'empire byzantin*, Brussels 1965.

[65] This ruler concept can be compared with the representation of a ruler on the west wall of the Dura Synagogue: A. R. Bellinger, F. E. Brown, A. Perkins, C. B. Welles, *The Excavations at Dura-Europos* (Final Report VIII, 1. C. H. Kraeling, *The Synagogue*), New Haven 1956, pl. LXV.

[66] For the cross as a symbol of martyrs, see G. de Jerphanion, "Les caracteristiques et les attributs des saints dans la peinture Cappadocienne," *La voix des monuments*, n.s. Rome-Paris 1938, p. 308.

rows—can be seen in the full-page miniature illustrating the same homily in the cod. Oxford, Roe 6, fol. 103ᵛ (Fig. 443).

In the sixteenth paragraph of the homily, Gregory states that Julian may record the taxes of the people, but he himself writes down the martyrs' offerings to God, which are more important.[67] The word martyr is used in a metaphorical sense, referring to those whose present life is a life of "martyrdom" for the sake of Christ. This meaning has been well understood by the illustrator of the Paris manuscript and, probably in order to interpret it pictorially, he does not use nimbi; the symbol of the cross is sufficient to suggest the "martyrdom" of a Christian life. The illustrator of the Oxford manuscript is less careful and, by depicting haloes around the heads of the represented figures, conveys the literal rather than the metaphorical meaning of the word martyr.

e. Conflated Scenes

Here too, as in the discussion of the illustrations of the preceding homilies, miniatures are found which have combined different scenes. The title miniature of the cod. Athos, Panteleimon 6, fol. 77ᵛ, has combined three scenes into one (Fig. 147). Gregory, dressed in bishop's vestments and holding a book, sits on a chair placed at the side of a table on which there are writing implements. Yet he is not writing his sermon but rather delivering it, for he extends his hand in a speaking gesture toward Julian, who sits across the table. Julian, in his usual dress, sits on a faldstool and rests his feet on a footstool; behind him there is a scribe from whom Julian has already received a scroll, probably a tax order, an action encountered in the cod. Paris gr. 550 (Fig. 413). Another figure stands behind Gregory. The arrangement of the two protagonists, seated opposite each other, and the posture of the figures standing near them resemble the composition of Julian and Gregory who are shown writing in the manuscript of Jerusalem (Fig. 112). In the Panteleimon miniature, however, Julian and Gregory are not merely writers. Three distinct elements are present, all fused into one scene: the teaching scene, the writers, and the collector of tax orders.

In the miniatures of the following codices there is only one type of combination, that of the teacher and the author: codd. Paris gr. 533, fol. 77ᵛ; Vat. gr. 1947, fol. 41ᵛ; Oxford, Selden. B. 54, fol. 25ᵛ; Paris, Coislin 239, fol. 57ʳ; and the initials of the manuscripts: Sinai 346, fol. 42ᵛ; Athos, Dionysiou 61, fol. 28ᵛ; Istanbul, Patr. 16, fol. 68ʳ (Figs. 245, 128, 290, 217, 345, 362, 68). The illustrator of the cod. Paris gr. 533 divides the scene into the two lateral margins as he has done in other instances. One margin is occupied by the seated Gregory and a group of people and the other by Julian writing at a table. The audience does not appear in the cod. Vat. gr. 1947, where, however, the arrangement of the main figures is similar and writing implements lie on the table. Traces of such a table, as well as the figure of the seated Julian, appear in the cod. Oxford, Selden. B. 54. The title miniature of the cod. Paris, Coislin 239,

[67] PG, 35, 1061.

contains an interesting detail: Julian sits under a canopy, which lends dignity to the scene and suggests the teaching scenes and the ceremonial quality of the miniatures of Athos, Dionysiou 61 (Figs. 369, 374).

In the historiated initials of the codd. Sinai 346, Athos, Dionysiou 61, and Istanbul, Patr. 16, the teaching Gregory forms the body of the letter while Julian appears in the margin opposite Gregory. In the marginal illustration of the cod. Sinai 346, which resembles the right side of the title miniature of the Jerusalem manuscript (Fig. 112), Julian, accompanied by one standing scribe, is shown seated. A standing scribe holding an inkpot, recalling the scribes of the title miniature of the cod. Sinai 339 (Fig. 383), is depicted in the Dionysiou miniature. But in all probability this figure is meant to represent Julian. The artist of the Patriarchal codex has also represented the Tax Collector standing and receiving from Gregory a scroll presumably containing the sermon composed at his request. The representation of Julian standing, rather than seated as in other miniatures of the same scene, probably derives from a confusion of the figure of Julian with those of the standing scribes.

THE MINIATURES OF THE FUNERAL ORATION
ON ST. BASIL

The illustrations of this homily belong to the same iconographic tradition, a Koimesis scene whose choice was undoubtedly motivated by the title of the oration.[68] It is represented, however, in two variants. The distinguishing characteristics of each variant are both the principal mourners and the composition. In the first variant, Gregory of Nyssa is included among the mourners, a fact that gives a distinct narrative aspect to the variant, as is shown below. In the second variant, Gregory of Nyssa is not represented and the solemn figure of Gregory of Nazianzus occupies the very center of the composition whose hieratic quality is the predominant element.

a. *Variant I*

The following codices have chosen this variant: Paris, gr. 543, fol. 130ʳ; Florence, Laur. Plut. VII, 32, fol. 70ʳ; Jerusalem, Taphou 14, fol. 114ʳ; Vat. gr., 1947, fol. 52ᵛ; Oxford, Canon. gr. 103, fol. 90ᵛ; Milan, Ambros. G 88 sup., fol. 105ʳ (Figs. 461, 268, 114, 130, 282, 309). The first of these miniatures is the most iconographically accurate. In the lower register, Gregory of Nazianzus is depicted delivering the funeral oration over a sarcophagus in the center of the miniature. His attentive listeners are bishops, who stand on the right. One of these bishops is nimbed, but the nimbus alone does not identify him. Although this scene can be considered a teaching scene, it is to a certain extent a subject-illustration, for the funeral sermon was in fact delivered

---

[68] Although there was a controversy among the Byzantine commentators on whether this was a funeral sermon or a panegyric (Basil the Younger, for example, favors the latter view), the manuscripts under discussion bear the same title and present it as a funeral sermon, see Sajdak, *Scholia*, p. 49; cf. p. 170.

over the tomb of St. Basil two years after his death.[69] The actual funeral of St. Basil is depicted in the miniature of the upper register. The dead bishop lies on a bier in the center flanked by two groups of bishops holding candles, an interesting narrative element which breaks the hieratic effect of the composition.[70] The same effect is achieved by the position of the baldachin over the head of the dead bishop; it is placed toward the left side of the composition rather than in the middle, as in other miniatures of this variant.

Gregory of Nazianzus has not been included among the mourners. Since he has already been represented in the lower miniature, it might be supposed that the artist omitted him here to avoid repetition. Yet this suggestion is unlikely, for instead of Gregory of Nazianzus, another bishop mourns and embraces Basil's feet, and thus seems to be the principal mourner. The second nimbed and black-haired bishop is seen in all miniatures of the manuscripts cited earlier which have used this variant. In fact, the physiognomy of this bishop can better be studied in these codices, especially in the miniature of the Jerusalem manuscript. He is Gregory of Nyssa, as is proven by comparisons with other representations of that saint,[71] and he must have attended St. Basil's funeral. This identification explains why Gregory of Nazianzus has not been included: he was not present at the funeral.

The accuracy of the illustrator of the Paris codex has not been observed by the illustrators of the other manuscripts. Instead, the two separate scenes have been conflated and the actual funeral scene includes both Gregorys. Most of the other elements have been preserved, although a few changes are noted. The group of mourners, composed exclusively of bishops in the Paris miniature, includes in others a variety of clerical ranks, especially deacons. This is shown clearly in the Florence and Jerusalem codices. In the latter manuscript the deacon heading the left group holds a censer and apparently a *pyxis* for the last communion of the departed. No groups of mourners at all appear in the reduced miniatures of the codd. Oxford, Canon. gr. 103 and Milan, Ambros. G 88 sup.; the latter retains only the three principal persons of the composition. Nor does the narrative element of the candle-bearers in the Paris miniature occur in other miniatures. In the Florence miniature, however, there are four candlesticks behind the bier; traces of them can also be seen in the Vatican miniature. Only this latter manuscript presents no architectural elements.

The cod. Florence, Laur. Plut. VII, 32 shows at each side of the composition, in the background, a ciborium attached to a building. Actually these structures should not be interpreted as separate buildings, but as the outside and the inside of a church.

---

[69] Sajdak, *Scholia*, p. 170.

[70] For the use of candles in funerals, see G. Dix, *The Shape of the Liturgy*, 2nd ed., London 1960, pp. 416, 417; Dix supports the view that the custom is of pagan origin.

[71] In the Ἑρμηνεία τῆς Ζωγραφικῆς Τέχνης of the monk Dionysius of Fourna, Agrapha (A. Papadopoulos-Kerameus ed., *Manuel d'iconographie*

chrétienne, St. Petersburg 1909, p. 154), Gregory of Nyssa is mentioned as γέρων ὀξυγένης and in some manuscripts (primarily menologia) he is represented as gray-haired. But cf. Gregory of Nyssa in the mosaics of Hosios Loukas (Demus-Diez, fig. 27), and in the frescoes of the Metropolis at Mistra (Millet, *Mistra*, pl. 86, 1). In these examples he is represented with a black beard.

This device, an attempt to render a building in perspective, is common in Mediaeval art. All the other miniatures discussed here, including the initial E of the cod. Milan, Ambros. G 88 sup., do not retain the ciborium over the bier but behind it. In addition, the Jerusalem miniature shows a canopied bookstand with a book on it to the left of the picture and a baptismal font under a canopy to the right.

A new element found only in the cod. Florence, Laur. Plut. VII, 32 is especially important. In the upper part of the gold background of this miniature, two angels carry the soul of St. Basil into heaven, indicated by an arc in the right corner of the miniature. This particular element is required by the text itself,[72] but it may betray the use of a particular model, such as a Koimesis of the Virgin that presents other similarities to St. Basil's Koimesis scene.[73] Attention is drawn to the mourners. Admittedly, the presence of two persons, one of whom leans over the head of the departed while the other mourns by his feet, is common in death scenes,[74] and therefore the position and posture of Gregory of Nazianzus and Gregory of Nyssa alone do not necessarily indicate the use of a scene representing the Koimesis of the Virgin as a model. But the physiognomic types of these two church fathers coincide with the types of the two apostles who occupy similar positions in the Koimesis of the Virgin scene, and thus the latter may possibly be a model for the former. In fact the black-haired Paul at the feet of Mary could easily become Gregory of Nyssa, while John with his white hair by the head of Mary could be changed into Gregory of Nazianzus. If that is the case, another insight has been obtained into the working method of the Byzantine artist, who, in approaching a particular picture, searches for relationships other than those offered by the compositions alone.

Some miniatures, although iconographically similar to those already discussed, do not depict Gregory of Nyssa; perhaps their small size accounts for the omission of the second bishop. These miniatures belong to the following codices: Oxford, Roe 6, fol. 38^r; Athos, Panteleimon 6, fol. 100^r; Oxford, Selden. B. 54, fol. 36^r; and Paris, Coislin 239, fol. 74^r (Figs. 441, 149, 291, 221). In the miniature of the first, only the second bishop on the extreme left of the large group of bishop mourners remains. In the miniature of the Panteleimon codex, the head of Gregory of Nazianzus can be seen behind the straight, marble sarcophagus on which the dead Basil lies; this representation is similar to that in the miniatures of the other manuscripts which follow the variant under discussion. Even more reduced is the title miniature of the cod. Oxford,

---

[72] *PG*, 36, 600, 601.

[73] For the iconography of the Dormition of the Virgin, see L. Wratislaw-Mitrović, N. Okunev, "La Dormition de la Sainte Vierge dans la peinture Médiéval orthodoxe," *Byzantinoslavica*, 3 (1931), pp. 134-80; J. Duhr, "La Dormition de Marie dans l'art chrétien," *Nouvelle revue théologique*, 72 (1950), pp. 134-57; E. M. Jones, "The Iconography of the Falling Asleep of the Mother of God in Byzantine Tradition," *Eastern Churches Quar-*

terly, 9 (1951), pp. 101-12.

[74] Three examples are cited here; the scene of Sarah's death in the Vatican Octateuch, cod. gr. 747, fol. 44^r; the Koimesis of the Virgin in Martorana, O. Demus, *The Mosaics of Norman Sicily*, London 1949, fig. 56; the Koimesis of Ephraim the Syrian, J. R. Martin, "The Death of Ephraim in Byzantine and Early Italian Painting," *AB*, 33 (1951), p. 220, fig. 8.

Selden. B. 54. Gregory, hardly visible, leans over Basil. The same rectangular sarcophagus with the body is represented in the cod. Paris, Coislin 239 with Gregory leaning over it. A mourning monk comes out of a portal to the right which balances another structure on the left. An old, white-bearded monk blowing on a censer hovers in the air between the two buildings.[75] Evidently the figure is placed there because of the lack of space elsewhere. The exclusive presence of monks recalls once again the death scenes of monks, which monastic art so often depicted.

Two more miniatures must be discussed here although they do not follow the same trend of composition utilized in the miniatures considered so far. The first miniature is in the cod. Moscow, Hist. Museum 146, fol. 81ʳ, and, like those discussed in the previous paragraph, does not include Gregory of Nyssa (Fig. 11). In composition, however, it differs from them, as it differs also from the miniatures of the second variant which is discussed below; Gregory of Nazianzus is shown neither behind the marble sarcophagus leaning over the head of Basil, nor standing in the center of the composition, as in the manuscripts of the second variant, but on the left side of the sarcophagus. This position recalls the miniature of the lower register of the cod. Paris gr. 543, with which this illustration shares other compositional similarities (Fig. 461). In both these miniatures Gregory stands at the left side of the sarcophagus, which is placed before a ciborium, and balances a group of mourners on the opposite side. In the Moscow miniature the mourners are monks, headed by a figure, perhaps a bishop, who swings a censer. This figure resembles in gesture the bishop who heads a group of mourners in the Paris miniature. Furthermore, in the Paris miniature, Gregory holds a scroll, whereas in the Moscow miniature he extends his hand in a speaking gesture. But these are minor differences.

More significant and more noticeable is the fact that in the Paris miniature the sarcophagus is empty, while in the Moscow miniature it contains Basil's body lying with the head toward the right side of the composition, recalling the historiated initial of the cod. Milan, Ambros. G. 88 sup. in which Basil's body has been shown in a similar manner (Fig. 309). This difference, which is fundamental since it changes the meaning of each scene, could be explained as a conflation of the two scenes. Instead of moving Gregory in the funeral scene as other illustrators had done, the artist of the Moscow miniature preferred to transfer Basil's body to the empty sarcophagus of the scene depicting the delivery of the sermon. The resultant miniature, although it is a Koimesis scene, resembles compositionally the scene of the delivery of the sermon. If this explanation does not seem arbitrary, the Moscow miniature reveals the artist's different approach to the miniature which he used as a model. His work deviates from

---

[75] Omont's interpretation of the scene is not correct. He says: ". . . deux (moines) sont debout à chaque extrémité du sarcophage; l'un examine le sang du saint en le faisant couler avec un tube dans un petit vase, l'autre porte à son nez le même vase, contenant le sang afin d'en reconnaître l'odeur, tandis que le troisième s'approche pour examiner la face du saint, mort d'une hémorragie provenant du foie." Omont, *Min. gr.* (1929), p. 54.

that of the miniatures created by other illustrators, but the deviation has occurred within the iconographic tradition common to all these manuscripts.

In the light of this explanation, the second miniature included here, that of the cod. Athos, Vatopedi 107, fol. 135ᵛ, may perhaps be interpreted as a reduced form of the Moscow miniature (Fig. 328). Gregory, holding a censer, stands to the left of the sarcophagus and leans over the head of Basil. On the opposite side and behind the sarcophagus stand three figures, a remnant of a larger group of mourners. There are two candlesticks behind the sarcophagus.

b. *Variant II*

The miniatures of the second variation also omit the figure of Gregory of Nyssa in their Koimesis scene. The figure of Gregory of Nazianzus in this case, however, is different, and this difference distinguishes Variant I from Variant II, which occurs in Athos, Dionysiou 61, fol. 35ʳ; Sinai 339, fol. 109ʳ; Paris gr. 550, fol. 94ᵛ; and Sinai 346, fol. 61ʳ (Figs. 363, 388, 415, 349).

In the first three miniatures the central part of the composition is occupied by the body of St. Basil on a bier, the mattress of which forms a sweeping curve. Gregory of Nazianzus stands in the middle of the composition. His actual posture shows slight variations from one miniature to another. In the first two miniatures he extends his right hand, as if he were speaking to the dead, perhaps in these words from the homily: "What am I doing here on earth, when my better half has been torn away? How much longer will my exile be prolonged?"[76] In the miniature of the Paris manuscript, however, Gregory rests his head against his hand, showing his resignation before the shadow of death and clearly expressing the text of the sermon. In all three miniatures, the bier is flanked by two groups of mourners; only in the Sinai miniature are the mourners exclusively bishops.

The differences in the treatment of background are also important. Whereas the Sinai miniature has a neutral background and the Dionysiou miniature includes only three candlesticks, the Paris miniature has many more interesting elements. Above Gregory a pair of angels, flying from either side of the picture, are ready to receive St. Basil's soul and carry it to heaven. In the upper corners of the composition, behind short balustrades, appear half-visible figures of two groups of mourners. All these elements are explained by the text; however, they, as well as the differences in the treatment of the background, may be derived from the model used by the illustrators. Undoubtedly this variant of the Koimesis of St. Basil scene is modeled after a representation of the Koimesis of the Virgin from which the miniaturists have chosen the figure of Christ and modeled the figure of Gregory of Nazianzus on him. Whereas the first two manuscripts have probably used an earlier version of a Koimesis of the Virgin

---

[76] *PG*, 36, 601, 604. The English translation is taken from P. MacCauley *et al.*, trans., *Funeral Orations by St. Gregory Nazianzenus and St. Ambrose*, New York 1953, p. 97.

scene with a neutral background,[77] the illustrator of the third manuscript—if the iconographic additions in the background are not due to his knowledge of the text—must have used a later version of a Koimesis of the Virgin scene that included all the elements of the background.[78]

Comparison of these three title miniatures with the corresponding miniature in the full edition of the homilies, the cod. Paris gr. 510, shows that there is no relation among them, and that the miniature of the full edition has a narrative character that is lost in the miniatures of the liturgical edition;[79] in the latter a hieratic concept predominates.

Evidently the small miniature of the cod. Sinai 346, containing only three figures, constitutes a reduced form of the miniatures already discussed. The historiated initial E, however, of the cod. Paris gr. 550 with only two figures—the dead Basil and Gregory of Nazianzus—presents an interesting variation: Gregory swings a censer. He therefore seems to replace the censing bishop of the title miniature of the same manuscript. Naturally the shape of the latter requires the depiction of Gregory at the left side of the bier, but the addition of the censer reveals the artist's ingenuity (Fig. 417).

c. Conflated Scenes

An interesting case of conflation occurs in the cod. Istanbul, Patr. 16, fol. 89^v, which remains faithful to one system of illustration, that of the historiated initial (Fig. 70). In the initial E, Gregory holding a scroll reads the funeral sermon over the dead Basil, whose body forms the middle horizontal bar of the letter. Obviously the funeral scene has been combined with the scene in which Gregory delivers the funeral sermon. The combination becomes evident when the scene is compared with the cod. Paris. gr. 543, fol. 130^v, in which the two episodes form separate scenes (Fig. 461).

A marginal, conflated teaching scene occurs in the cod. Paris gr. 533, fol. 91^r (Fig. 248). Gregory of Nazianzus on the left and Basil on the right appear in the margins on either side of the written column. No audience has been included. Gregory holds a scroll in his right hand, but no particular significance seems to be attached to it. The scroll has been used in three more scenes, two of which are teaching scenes, and it may simply be a peculiarity of this manuscript.

It cannot be determined whether the initial E of the cod. Athens, Nat. Lib. 2254, fol. 69^v, consisting of the figures of Gregory and the dead Basil, is a reduction of one

[77] See, for example, the Dormition of the Virgin in the lectionary of Nicephorus Phocas, fol. 134^v reproduced in Weitzmann, *Semin. Kondak.* (1936), pl. III, 1.

[78] See, for example, the Dormition of the Virgin in the twelfth-century Gospel book, cod. Brit. Mus. Harley 1810, fol. 174^r, reproduced in Mitrović, Ocunev, *op.cit.*, fig. 6. The relationship of such a model to the Paris miniature makes it clear that the view of the author of the catalogue of the Paris exposition 1958 (Bibl. Nat., *Byzance*, p. 25) to the effect that the persons appearing behind the balustrades in Basil's Koimesis scene are the Elect, is not correct.

[79] Omont, *Min. gr.* (1929), pl. XXXI.

of the variants or a conflation of two scenes (Fig. 260). The initial E's of the codd. Vat. gr. 463, fol. 22ʳ, and Turin, Univ. Lib. C. I. 6, fol. 89ᵛ (the latter is not reproduced), are conventionally historiated by the figure of Basil standing and teaching, probably a substitute for the teaching Gregory (Fig. 81).

THE MINIATURES OF THE HOMILY ON HOLY BAPTISM

In this homily, Gregory speaks extensively about the sacrament of Holy Baptism and urges his audience to receive it. The artist of the cod. Milan, Ambros. G 88 sup., fol. 176ᵛ, illustrates the homily by a miniature placed in the left margin before the opening sentence of the text (Fig. 311). The miniature portrays the rite of the sacrament of Holy Baptism. A nimbed bishop stands in the center and baptizes a group of people in a font on the right. A group of deacons is depicted on the left. The deacon heading this group holds a censer and a chrismatory in his veiled hands. Since the miniature has flaked in many parts, the identification of the bishop is uncertain (although he is probably Gregory of Nazianzus), and the number of figures in the font cannot be determined. Normally only one figure is shown in the font, but the inclusion of more is justified by the text of the twenty-seventh paragraph of the homily, where Gregory speaks of a baptism in which the poor will be baptized with the rich and the free man with the slave.[80]

The euchologion describes the office of the Holy Baptism and explains the details of this picture.[81] By comparing the miniature with the text of the euchologion, the actual moment of the ceremony can be determined. The officiating bishop, having censed the font and given the censer to be held, performs the actual baptism by placing his hand on the head of one person in the font. More probably, however, the miniature shows a phase before the actual performance of the baptism, that of the anointing. The bishop has dipped two fingers into the oil and makes the sign of the cross upon the brow of the person receiving baptism.

This miniature representing the performance of a sacrament is a rare liturgical picture in published material. Contrary to representations in Latin manuscripts where this liturgical scene is often depicted,[82] the baptism scene in the Greek manuscripts is related to the activities of the apostles or the lives of the martyrs.[83] In these cases it lacks the liturgical details of the miniature of the Milan manuscript.

---

[80] *PG*, 36, 396.

[81] S. Zervos ed., *Euchologion*, Venice 1951, pp. 94ff.

[82] The liturgical scene of baptism appears mainly in sacramentaries as, for example, in the sacramentary of bishop Warmundus (Ivrea, Kapitelbibliothek, cod. 86, fol. 61ʳ) reproduced in G. Ladner, "Die italienische Malerei im 11 Jahrhundert," *Jahrbuch der Kunsthistorischen Sammlungen in Wien*, 5 (1931), fig. 119.

[83] See examples in the cod. Paris gr. 510, fols. 87ᵛ, 426ᵛ, Omont, *Min. gr.* (1929), pls. XXX, LVI. The only other known examples containing liturgi-cal elements occur in the Vatican psalter, cod. gr. 752, fol. 193ʳ, and in the manuscript of the Chronicle of Scylitzes in Madrid, fols. 112ʳ, 134ᵛ. It should be borne in mind that the baptismal scenes in the latter manuscript are historical in that they show the baptism of rulers and, strictly speaking, are not liturgical. For reproductions of these miniatures, see De Wald, Vat. gr. 752, pl. XXXIV; Koukoules, *Bios*, IV, pl. B, 2, 3. A reproduction of all of the miniatures in the Scylitzes manuscript can be found in S. C. Estopañán, *Skyllitzes Matritensis*, I, Barcelona 1965.

A much reduced miniature appears in the cod. Paris gr. 550, fol. 34ᵛ (Fig. 408). A bishop, in this case definitely identified as Gregory, performs the rite of baptism. The miniature is in the left margin of the homily on New Sunday, but there is no reason to assume that this was its original position. Certainly the change is intentional. In the passage next to which the miniature is placed, Gregory speaks of a new way of life in which happiness supplants worry and hope supplants sadness. "And this is the way that man is renovated; and this is the way that the day of the encaenia is honored."[84] The artist apparently interpreted this renovation as baptism, through which the Christian "puts on Christ," becoming a new man, and thought it proper to choose and put here a miniature from the homily on Holy Baptism. However, in order to adapt the miniature to its new context, he had to show only one figure in the font instead of two.

THE MINIATURES OF THE HOMILY TO ST. GREGORY
OF NYSSA

Gregory of Nyssa visited Gregory of Nazianzus in order to persuade him to remain with his own flock because the burden of the episcopal duties, heavy though it might be, was not supported by human power but by the Grace of God. On this occasion Gregory of Nazianzus delivered a homily that is a hymn to friendship and a humble expression of love. At the end Gregory confirms before everyone, and especially his friend, his intent to undertake the guidance of the flock entrusted to him by God. The text, because of its very abstract content, must have presented great difficulties to the illustrators. The opening sentence of the homily demonstrates the artist's difficulties: "Nothing can be given in exchange for a faithful friend; nor can anything measure his goodness. A faithful friend is a stronghold, a fortress. More to be desired is he than gold, than much fine and precious stone. A garden enclosed is he; a spring shut up, a fountain sealed that opens occasionally and then becomes a common possession. A port of rejoicing is he."[85]

a. *The Two Bishops Conversing*

In the title miniature of the cod. Athos, Dionysiou 61, fol. 113ʳ, the two bishops are seated opposite each other (Fig. 366). Each holds a book and rests his feet on a footstool. The older, white-bearded Gregory of Nazianzus, sitting on the right, extends his right hand in a speaking gesture. Opposite him the black-haired and black-bearded bishop of Nyssa places his right hand on his breast in a gesture of respect. Behind each of the two seated friends stands a building. In the background there is another building with two gates, topped by an airy baldachin.

The tradition of the seated bishops has already been encountered in the discussion of another homily, but the present miniature is historical, inasmuch as the two bishops did meet and discuss the episcopal duties which form part of the subject of the sermon. A scene like this, however, could not explicitly illustrate the main subject of the sermon

[84] *PG*, 36, 616. [85] *PG*, 35, 832.

which concerned friendship based on the love of God and the care of the souls entrusted to the two bishops by God. The artist had to invent a new scene in order to render some of the ideas of the homily pictorially.

b. *Gregory of Nazianzus and Gregory of Nyssa in Proskynesis*

The iconographic tradition of the *proskynesis* is followed by the title miniatures of the codices: Jerusalem, Taphou 14, fol. 219ᵛ; Vat. gr. 1947, fol. 104ʳ; Oxford, Selden. B. 54, fol. 85ᵛ; Florence, Laur. Plut. VII, 32, fol. 145ʳ; Athos, Panteleimon 6, fol. 214ʳ; Paris, Coislin 239, fol. 158ᵛ; the marginal miniature of the cod. Athos, Vatopedi 107, fol. 203ᵛ; and by the historiated initials of the codd. Athos, Dionysiou 61, fol. 113ʳ; Milan, Ambros. G 88 sup., fol. 213ʳ; Sinai 346, fol. 152ᵛ; and Istanbul, Patr. 16, fol. 189ᵛ (Figs. 117, 133, 294, 271, 174, 229, 331, 367, 312, 350, 73).

In the miniature of the Jerusalem and Vatican codices, Gregory of Nazianzus stands on the left with raised hands (Figs. 117, 133). He bows to Gregory of Nyssa who stands on the right, bowing more deeply than his friend. Both are nimbed and wear episcopal vestments. Above them is the arc of heaven. Two buildings, one on either side, and plants growing between them form the setting of the picture. In the Vatican miniature only one building is depicted.

Literary sources confirm that bowing, called proskynesis, was one form of greeting.[86] If greater respect and honor were to be suggested, both the bowing of the head and the bending of the body would be more pronounced; the term used by the Byzantines in this case was "βαθεῖα προσκύνησις." Therefore Gregory of Nyssa bows lower than Gregory of Nazianzus. The pictorial rendering of the proskynesis, however, is not confined merely to a greeting scene, but embraces a deep liturgical concept which is clarified by the presence of the arc of heaven. In the last paragraph of the homily, Gregory places himself, and all those who guide the sheep of God, under the arc of heaven, or, as he says, "under the Father of Love, Love itself." The two bishops give themselves to this love and, at the same time, according to the text, they pray. Moreover, the miniature of the Jerusalem codex bears some resemblance to the ceremonial greeting of the deacon and the officiating priest at the opening of the liturgy.[87] Even Gregory's prayer in the last paragraph of the text is similar to the prayer in the liturgy pronounced by the priest after the ceremonial greeting and before the vesting.[88]

The smaller and simpler miniature of the cod. Oxford, Selden. B. 54, fol. 85ᵛ, lacks a setting, which is typical of this manuscript, and introduces an interesting new element: the hands of the two Fathers are veiled, a detail which intensifies the liturgical importance of the picture (Fig. 294). Like the apostles who approach the officiating

---

[86] Textual passages and a discussion of the subject are to be found in Koukoules, *Bios*, I, p. 108. For the proskynesis in ancient times and its imperial implications, see A. Alföldi, "Die Ausge-staltung des monarchischen Zeremoniells," *Mitt. Deut. Arch. Rome*, 49 (1934), pp. 49ff.

[87] Brightman, *Liturgies*, p. 353.

[88] *Ibid.*, p. 115.

Christ to receive the Holy Communion[89] or the angels who wait at the throne of the Almighty,[90] or even the physician saints, Cosmas and Damian, who receive their tools from heaven,[91] the two bishops stand with covered hands before the Father of Love to receive His guidance.

The title miniature of the cod. Florence, Plut. Laur. VII, 32, shows another degree of proskynesis (Fig. 271). Although Gregory of Nyssa on the right is in proskynesis, Gregory of Nazianzus is kneeling and bowing, i.e. in "προσκύνησις ἕως ἐδάφους." This change in the posture of Gregory of Nazianzus indicates a change in the meaning of the scene. He now pays greater tribute to his friend. Here the artist has not taken age into consideration—normally younger persons pay tribute to older persons—but has interpreted the text literally: Gregory of Nazianzus is delivering a sermon in praise of Gregory of Nyssa.

Another variant of the proskynesis scene appears in the miniature of the codd. Athos, Panteleimon 6, and Paris, Coislin 239, showing both bishops on their knees (Figs. 174, 229). The ideas of prayer and of submission to God to which the text refers have been more strongly expressed here. Like the Byzantine emperor who, in the mosaic of the lunette over the royal door in the church of St. Sophia, is prostrate before Christ,[92] or like Abraham who communicates with God in a similar manner,[93] the two bishops communicate with the God of peace and pray to him earnestly. Yet neither the hand of God, as might be expected in such cases, nor a bust of Christ appears in the sky above. Instead, golden light descends and radiates in the picture. This is perhaps derived from the sixth paragraph of the oration where Gregory speaks about the light of the blessed Trinity "which will make us clearer and purer. . . ."

From the formal point of view, the rather ambiguous attitude—running and kneeling at once—of the two bishops in the Panteleimon codex can be explained as an attempt to fill a space wider than that of the Coislin miniature. It may, however, have an artistic purpose. The artist may have sought to express the two friends' eagerness to meet each other and dramatize the scene accordingly.

In the marginal miniature of the cod. Athos, Vatopedi 107, the city of Nyssa has been included (Fig. 331). Since the meeting of the two friends did not occur in the city of Nyssa, such a representation is nonhistorical. Nevertheless, the illustrator has been consistent and in other miniatures has depicted the cities related to the persons

[89] See fresco in the church of Staro Nagoričino (c. 1317) reproduced in R. Hamann-MacLean, H. Hallensleben, *Die Monumentalmalerei in Serbien und Macedonien*, Giessen 1963, pl. 278. For the significance of receiving with veiled hands, cf. F. Cumont, *Les religions orientales dans le paganisme romain*, 4th ed., Paris 1929, pls. v, 3; vii, 2; viii, 1. See also representations of Cain and Abel praying to God with veiled hands in the cod. Vat. gr. 747, fol. 25ᵛ.

[90] An example of angels attending Christ with

veiled hands occurs in a thirteenth-century evangelarion in Kiev, cod. gr. 54, reproduced in Lazarev, *History*, ii, pl. 254a; also frescoes in St. Anargyroi Lemniotou in Kastoria, S. Pelekanides, Καστοριά, Thessalonica 1953, pls. 6, 7.

[91] For an example, see Menologion of Basil II, *Il menologio*, p. 152.

[92] T. Whittemore, *The Mosaics of St. Sophia at Istanbul*, Oxford 1933, pl. xii.

[93] See cod. Vat. gr. 747, fol. 38ᵛ.

or subject about which Gregory is speaking. The characteristics of these cities are a crenelated wall with ramparts or towers and, within the city, in addition to a schematic representation of houses, a church in the form of a basilica, or a five-domed church in the form of a cross in a square. Also interesting is the depiction of trees within the city, which reveals either the illustrator's feeling for the picturesque or the pictorial wealth of his models.

In the initials of the codd. Athos, Dionysiou 61, fol. 113^r, and Milan, Ambros. G 88 sup., fol. 213^v, the arc of heaven, or the bust of Christ appearing in the more complete scenes of proskynesis, has been replaced by a figure of Christ (Figs. 367, 312). This is a compositional device appropriate for the letter Φ, which the artist undertook to historiate. In the initial of the cod. Sinai 346, fol. 152^v, where the same compositional device appears, the third figure—added to what is fundamentally a proskynesis scene—is not Christ (Fig. 350). Instead the artist has chosen Basil the Great and, in order to give eminence to Gregory of Nazianzus, has placed him on the vertical bar of the letter, so that Gregory of Nyssa and Basil are in proskynesis. In all probability the final words of the title, the name of Basil, have dictated the choice, which is again an evidence of the freedom and inventiveness of the artist.

The artist of the cod. Istanbul, Patr. 16, innovates less. He prefers to historiate the initial with the two figures in proskynesis, following a more traditional form according to which a letter is formed by one or two figures (Fig. 73). This method recalls the compositional devices of the historiated initials of the homily on St. Cyprian (Figs. 353, 243, 306).

c. *Gregory of Nazianzus and Gregory of Nyssa in an Ecstatic Meeting*

Another illustration of this homily in the cod. Paris gr. 550, fol. 204^r, shows Gregory of Nazianzus and Gregory of Nyssa embracing each other ecstatically (Figs. 416, 421).[94] This simple, moving composition is made for Gregory's text and is another rendering of a meeting scene that is entirely different from the proskynesis scene already discussed, which once again shows the extent of the artists' inventiveness. The embrace and the kiss were the customary greeting after a long absence, and, in art, which very often expresses the events of everyday life, representations of this scene occur frequently.[95] Yet the ecstatic meeting of the two bishops depicted in the miniature of the Paris manuscript is not merely a greeting scene, because iconographically

[94] A. Grabar interprets the black-bearded figure as Basil (*Min. Byz.*, p. 7, pls. 53, 54). If this interpretation is correct, it must be suggested that the artist confused the words ἀδελφὸν Βασιλείου of the title and represented Basil instead of Gregory. If a representation of the Fathers in the lectionary, Dionysiou 587, fol. 126^r, is taken into consideration (K. Weitzmann, "The Mandylion and Constantine Porphyrogennetos," *Cahiers archéologiques*, 11 [1960], fig. 7), then Grabar is right. However, if a fresco in the Metropolis of Mistra is considered (Millet, *Mistra*, pl. 86, 1), the black-bearded figure in the miniature is undoubtedly Gregory of Nyssa. This seems to be an interpretation which is in accordance with the text of the homily after all.

[95] For parallel examples, see cod. Athos, Panteleimon 2, fol. 236^r, Lambros, II, p. 291; cod. Vat. gr. 747, fol. 94^v (Moses and Jeth meeting in the wilderness).

it is modeled on a meeting of the two greatest church "pillars," namely the Apostles Peter and Paul, and it may be of particular significance. The meeting of the two apostles, according to the *Acts of Peter and Paul*, took place in Rome. Peter, having heard of the coming of Paul, "rejoiced with great joy; and rising up, immediately went to him, and seeing each other, they wept with joy and long embracing each other, they bedewed each other with tears."[96] No illustrated *Acts of Peter and Paul* has been preserved. Its existence, nevertheless, cannot be doubted, for miniatures which have migrated from this apocryphal book are found in other texts, including the miniature in the cod. Turin, Univ. Lib. C. I. 6, fol. 82[r], which is discussed later.[97]

The modeling of the two friends' meeting after that of the two great apostles—the migrated miniature in the Turin manuscript justifies the association—may perhaps have significance, if the opening passage of the *Ecclesiastical History* attributed to the patriarch Germanus is taken into consideration. The History states clearly that the Church was founded by the apostles and was decorated by the Fathers.[98]

The scenes in the now missing miniatures of the codd. Sinai 339, and Paris gr. 543 are unknown. The inserted fol. 270[r] in the Sinai codex contains the end of the homily on Holy Baptism. On the verso of this folio a space has been left empty, probably for a title miniature which was never executed. The same is true of the cod. Paris gr. 543. The text of the homily begins with an ornamental headpiece, but the miniature preceding the text has been cut out.

d. *Conflated Scenes*

According to literary sources, another variant of the proskynesis was the simultaneous bowing of the head and crossing of the hands on the chest. This was common between children and parents, servants and masters. Such is the posture of Gregory of Nyssa in the small miniature of the cod. Oxford, Canon. gr. 103, fol. 192[r] (Fig. 284). A similar posture occurs elsewhere in the same manuscript (cf. Fig. 279), and it may not be of special significance. Yet its relation to the text of this particular homily and the existence of proskynesis scenes in other manuscripts leave no doubt that the artist conceived Gregory of Nyssa in the act of proskynesis. However, Gregory of Nazianzus, who stands opposite his friend, is in the act of speaking; in fact, his figure is derived from a teaching scene, which indicates that this miniature is a combination of a proskynesis and a teaching scene. Since Gregory of Nyssa was present when the sermon was delivered, the teaching scene pictured here is to a certain extent subject-illustration.

[96] A. Walker, trans., *The Apocryphal Acts of Peter and Paul* (Anti-Nicene Library, XVI), Edinburgh 1890, p. 260.

[97] Other examples: Athens, Nat. Lib. cod. 7, fol. 2[r] (an eleventh-century psalter); Palermo, Capella Palatina; see P. Buberl, *Die Miniaturenhandschriften der Nationalbibliothek in Athen* (Denk-

schriften der Wiener Akademie, philosophisch-historische Klasse, 60, 2), Vienna 1917, pl. XVII, 39; O. Demus, *The Mosaics of Norman Sicily*, London 1949, pl. 43a.

[98] *PG*, 98, 384; cf. O. Demus, *Byzantine Mosaic Decoration*, London 1949.

Another possible combination of two different scenes appears in the codd. Moscow, Hist. Museum 146, fol. 177ʳ, and Paris gr. 533, fol. 192ʳ (Figs. 14, 250). The miniature of the former is more complete than that of the latter, which is divided on either side of the written column and contains no architectural background. In both miniatures Gregory of Nazianzus and Gregory of Nyssa are depicted standing opposite each other. Gregory of Nazianzus gives a scroll to his friend, who receives it with covered hands. In the Moscow miniature Gregory of Nazianzus also has one of his hands veiled, while in the Paris miniature he extends one hand in a teaching gesture. The architectural background of the Moscow miniature presents, on either side of the composition, two towers topped by airy baldachins each carrying a different type of dome. The tower on the right has a colonnade as well. These towers are attached to a wall which forms the central part of the background.

The scroll in Gregory's hand has already been encountered as an iconographic element in three other miniatures—all teaching scenes—of the Paris manuscript. In the discussion of them no particular significance was attached to the scroll, but it was suggested that its presence might be a peculiarity of the Paris manuscript. In the miniature presently under discussion—which includes the concept of a teaching scene as well, because of Gregory's speaking gesture—the scroll assumes greater importance since it appears also in the Moscow miniature. Naturally the first possibility to be considered is whether these miniatures depict the Sending of a Letter. If so, the covering of the hands signifies the sacredness of the received scroll and the respect of the recipient for it. Comparisons, however, with traditional representations of the Sending of a Letter in other works show either the sender and the recipient of the letter seated, or only the recipient standing, and usually the hands of both are uncovered.[99] Obviously these details do not find exact parallels in the Moscow and Paris miniatures, which show both figures standing. It seems, therefore, unlikely that these two illustrations constitute a variation of the subject. The covering of the hands and the posture of Gregory of Nyssa in both miniatures, but especially in the Moscow miniature, recall corresponding compositional and iconographic elements found in a proskynesis scene such as the one in the cod. Oxford, Selden. B. 54. The derivation of these two miniatures from two scenes, one showing the sending of a letter and the other a proskynesis, seems more likely. How the combination of these two distinct scenes came about is a matter for speculation. The original artist either combined two scenes existing in the same homily in the archetype, or used iconographic elements originating in other homilies with the intention of modifying a proskynesis scene. Perhaps the reason for this modification may be sought not only in the artist's desire to create something new, but also in his intent to express something more than a simple meeting: the eagerness of the two friends to meet each other.

[99] See cod. Vat. gr. 747, fol. 12ʳ, cf. Ouspenski, *Octateuque*, pl. VIII, 9, 10; Princeton Univ. Lib. cod. Garrett 16, fols. 1ʳ and 2ʳ, reproduced in Martin, *Ladder*, pl. IX, 29, 30.

This homily does not bear the same title in all manuscripts. In some it is called a funeral oration, and in others a panegyric, and this distinction probably had a bearing on the choice of illustrations.[100]

a. *The Koimesis of St. Athanasius*

Once the illustrator had invented a suitable scene for one funeral oration, he could easily use it for any other oration of similar purpose without essential changes. This is the case with some of the illustrations of this homily. Many elements of the Koimesis of St. Athanasius are repetitions of those found in the illustrations of the homily on St. Basil.

The general composition of the miniatures of the codd. Paris gr. 550, fol. 209ᵛ, and Paris gr. 543, fol. 260ᵛ, was derived from the illustrations of the homily on St. Basil in the same codices (Figs. 424, 466). In the cod. Paris gr. 550, two groups of mourners bearing candles flank the bier of the deceased bishop of Alexandria. In the upper part of the composition, four angels are ready to receive and carry into heaven the soul of the bishop whose death has caused much weeping.[101] The angels are not mentioned in the text, but they are included here because they were in the model, St. Basil's Koimesis scene. The figure of Gregory, however, which was in the model, is not represented. This change is iconographically necessary, because nowhere in the text does Gregory mourn St. Athanasius. If he had been depicted, anachronism would have been the main feature of the miniature since Gregory was not present at the death of St. Athanasius. In the conventional funeral scene of the cod. Paris gr. 543, the mourners are separated into a group of monks and a group of bishops. The body of the bishop has been placed under a ciborium.

In contrast to the miniatures of the above two manuscripts, which have not represented Gregory in the scene, the codd. Moscow, Hist. Mus. 141, fol. 181ᵛ, Vat. gr. 1947, fol. 106ᵛ, and Athos, Panteleimon 6, fol. 219ʳ, have included him, and the anachronism occurs (Figs. 15, 134, 175). All three miniatures are related to the illustration of St. Basil's funeral found in the same manuscripts. But the illustrator of the Panteleimon codex has included also a ciborium like the one appearing in the cod. Paris gr. 543. The inclusion of Gregory in the funeral scene shows another aspect of the Byzantine artist's approach to a given picture and its model: in this case the artist is not concerned with adapting the model and making it conform to the new text. A certain degree of adaptation, however, is evident in the Moscow miniature which does not depict Gregory as a mourner. He is addressing the dead and therefore the idea of the delivery of the homily must be understood.

---

[100] Some manuscripts have the following title: λόγος ἐπιτάφιος τοῦ Ἁγίου Ἀθανασίου; others this: εἰς τὸν Ἅγιον Ἀθανάσιον ἀρχιεπίσκοπον Ἀλεξανδρείας. The Byzantine commentators also had two different conceptions of the sermon; for example

Nicetas of Heraclea says: ". . . οὐκ ἔστι δὲ ἐπιτάφιος, ὥς τινες οἴονται, ἀλλ' ἐγκώμιον," Sajdak, *Scholia*, p. 171.

[101] *PG*, 35, 1128.

The cod. Paris, Coislin 239, fol. 163ʳ, which is similar in composition to the miniature of the Panteleimon codex, has not included the figure of Gregory (Fig. 230). The miniature of the cod. Athos, Vatopedi 107, fol. 226ʳ, is a repetition of the miniature of the Koimesis of St. Basil (Fig. 335). Facing this miniature, fol. 227ʳ, the artist has depicted the city of Alexandria in his usual schematic fashion (Fig. 336).

b. *Conflated Scenes*

The cod. Jerusalem, Taphou 14, fol. 224ᵛ, has combined two distinct scenes into one (Fig. 118). The miniature shows Gregory on the left, seated on a faldstool; he rests his feet on a footstool, holds a book on his lap, and, turning his head toward a group of people standing behind him, points to St. Athanasius with his right hand. The bishop of Alexandria, seated opposite him and dressed in episcopal vestments, holds a piece of parchment. Between the two is a font which probably has no special meaning, but is a peculiarity of this manuscript, since it occurs in another miniature as well (cf. Fig. 114). The architectural setting—one building in the background and another in the foreground—achieves an interplay of space and dimension. The elements of this picture are not difficult to detect: a teaching scene and a portrait of St. Athanasius have been combined to create a new scene. The same combination appears in the initial A of the cod. Istanbul, Patr. 16, fol. 194ᵛ (Fig. 74). Athanasius seated forms the left arm of the letter, and the teaching Gregory forms the right.

An attempt to combine Gregory's author portrait with a figure of Athanasius resulted in a confusion in the miniature of the cod. Florence, Laur. Plut. VII, 32, fol. 26ʳ (Fig. 263). An author portrait of Gregory (the identification is certain for he is not only meditating but is about to continue writing on a piece of parchment) has been coupled with an incorrect inscription—Ἅγιος Ἀθανάσιος.[102]

The scenes representing Gregory addressing Athanasius in the cod. Oxford, Canon. gr. 103, fol. 197ʳ, and presenting him with a scroll in the cod. Paris gr. 533, fol. 196ᵛ, have been discussed in the chapter on the teaching scene (p. 34; Figs. 285, 251). It is evident that the artists have created these scenes by combining elements of a teaching scene with a standing portrait of St. Athanasius which could be found in menologia. Possibly the figures of the two bishops in the initial A of the cod. Paris gr. 550 were derived from similar scenes (Fig. 424), but the miniature of the cod. Milan, Ambros. G 88 sup., fol. 220ʳ, showing Gregory giving Athanasius a book of his homilies, is probably a deviation from the miniature found in the Oxford and Paris codices (Fig. 313).

In the cod. Vat. gr. 463, fol. 192ʳ, the figure of Athanasius forms the initial A (Fig. 85). He extends his hand as if teaching, which is impossible, since Athanasius does not deliver the sermon. The position of the hand may have been necessary for the

[102] In Byzantine manuscripts St. Athanasius appears with white hair, narrow forehead, and a beard not as broad as Gregory's; cf. codd. Jerusalem, Taphou 14, fol. 224ᵛ (Fig. 118); Vat. gr. 1156, fol. 295ʳ; Menologion of Basil II, *Il menologio*, p. 320.

formation of the horizontal bar of the letter A, but since the illustrator of this manuscript has used the same compositional scheme in another initial already discussed
(cf. Fig. 81), it may be that this initial is a substitute for a teaching Gregory.

THE MINIATURES OF THE FAREWELL ORATION

Obviously a miniature based only on the title of the homily would have to follow
a traditional concept of illustration exemplified in teaching scenes, such as Gregory
addressing the bishops. Yet this homily is not an ordinary address. The title and the
contents prove that this oration delivered at the Ecumenical Council of 381 is a farewell to an assembly of bishops or, to use a phrase that occurs in the eleventh paragraph of the text, "a council of elders."[103]

a. *The Council Scene*

A council scene appears in the illustrations of the codd. Jerusalem, Taphou 14, fol.
247[r]; Florence, Laur. Plut. VII, 32, fol. 149[r]; Oxford, Selden. B. 54, fol. 99[r]; Athos,
Panteleimon 6, fol. 240[v]; Paris, Coislin 239, fol. 182[r]; Oxford, Roe 6, fol. 115[v]; and
Vat. gr. 1947, fol. 119[r] (Figs. 119, 272, 296, 176, 231, 445, 135).

Members of such councils are usually represented seated and these miniatures
follow the tradition. With the exception of the codd. Vat. gr. 1947 and Oxford, Roe
6, in all these miniatures Gregory is seated at the center of the composition. In the
miniatures of the codd. Jerusalem, Taphou 14 and Florence, Laur. Plut. VII, 32,
which are the most complete, Gregory is shown in a three-quarter view. In the Jerusalem miniature, Gregory turns toward a group of nine seated bishops on the left who
correspond to a similar group of seven on the right. The bishops are arranged in a
semicircle around rectangular draped tables. In the Florence miniature the number
of bishops is the same on either side, but no tables stand in front of them, and the
artist has related the parts of the composition by showing Gregory extending both his
hands. The artists of these two miniatures have varied the facial expressions, the ages,
and the poses of the figures, achieving a rhythm which relieves the rigidity of the
composition.

Compared to these two illustrations, the miniatures of the other manuscripts cited
above are simpler. The miniatures of the codd. Oxford, Roe 6, and Vat. gr. 1947
present an interesting point (Figs. 445, 135). In the Oxford codex Gregory is represented in three-quarter view, sitting on the right holding his pallium with his left hand
and addressing a group of bishops seated opposite. This figure of Gregory closely
resembles the one in the miniature of the Florence manuscript (Fig. 272); the Oxford
miniature probably made use of the left half of such a council picture. The Vatican

[103] *PG*, 36, 472. For the Fathers of the Council, see N. Q. King, "The 150 Holy Fathers of the Council of Constantinople 381 A.D.," *Studia patristica*, I (Papers presented to the second international conference on Patristic Studies, held at Christ Church, Oxford 1955, ed. by K. Aland, F. L. Cross), Berlin 1957, pp. 635-41.

miniature displays essentially the same composition, except for the view of Gregory, who is shown in profile.

Only a few parallel examples of council pictures will be cited here.[104] The representation of the same council (A.D. 381) in the full edition of Gregory's homilies, cod. Paris gr. 510, fol. 355[r], is justly famous;[105] so is the representation of the seventh ecumenical council (A.D. 787) in the menologion of Basil II, cod. Vat. gr. 1613.[106] The codd. Athos Vatopedi 483[107] and Paris gr. 1242, fol. 5[v],[108] contain two more council pictures. The link connecting these examples is the compositional scheme. The Vatopedi miniature is of special interest, because at first glance the miniature shows what seems to be a table before the council members, recalling the miniature of the Jerusalem codex. However, it is actually a scroll. Councils taking place in the apse of a church could not have made use of tables; therefore their presence in the Jerusalem manuscript is difficult to explain.

Although council scenes have provided the iconographic models for the miniatures of this homily, the latter differ from the former in that Gregory is seated in the center of the composition and is addressing the group. In the earlier council scenes, the central seat remains empty; later the emperor appears but he does not speak.

The title miniature of the cod. Paris gr. 550, fol. 232[r], is another council picture (Fig. 425). Gregory and eight bishops are seated on benches arranged in a semicircle. The figure of Gregory, larger in scale, occupies the middle of the semicircle. A reduced version of the same miniature is repeated in the initial Π. This title miniature, although related iconographically to the miniatures discussed so far, differs from them in its compositional scheme. The artist of the cod. Paris gr. 550 has used the scheme of the Pentecost scene that appears in the same manuscript (cf. Fig. 410).

b. *The Farewell Scene*

In the last two paragraphs of the homily, Gregory bids farewell to the church of St. Anastasia, the congregation, the choir, his friends, and the city of Constantinople.[109] This part of the text is illustrated in the cod. Jerusalem, Taphou 14, fol. 265[r], by a column picture placed between the concluding lines of the sermon. Other instances in this manuscript of scenes illustrating a specific passage of the text and placed close to it are discussed later. The column miniature under discussion represents Gregory standing in a boat with a crew of two, bidding a last farewell to a group of bishops standing on a dock at the left of the picture (Fig. 120). The architectural setting suggests the city of Constantinople. Obviously the artist could not recreate pictorially

[104] For the iconography of the councils, see S. Salaville, "L'iconographie des 'sept conciles oecumeniques,' " *Echos d'Orient*, 25 (1926), pp. 144-76.

[105] Omont, *Min. gr.* (1929), pl. L.

[106] *Il menologio*, p. 108. Cf. Weitzmann, *Chron-* icles, pp. 87ff.

[107] Reproduced in K. Weitzmann, "The Psalter Vatopedi 761," *The Journal of the Walters Art Gallery*, 10 (1947), fig. 17.

[108] Omont, *Min. gr.* (1929), pl. CXXVI.

[109] *PG*, 36, 492.

the concluding part of the sermon, but he used Gregory's actual departure which, however, took place some time after the oration had been delivered.

A miniature with the same subject matter is found in the cod. Paris gr. 510, fol. 239ʳ.[110] Here Gregory, in a different attitude, is not in the boat but standing near it with the bishops at the right of the composition. The tower, the gate of the city, and the harbor are not shown in the Paris miniature.

The differences between the two miniatures, although not essential, suggest that the Jerusalem miniature is not a direct copy of the Paris miniature. Nevertheless, the facts that the farewell scene is part of a narrative cycle and that it is also found in the ninth-century cod. Paris gr. 510 pose the problem of whether or not certain scenes of the liturgical edition have been derived from narrative illustrations of the complete edition. The question cannot be answered at this point with the information we presently have.

c. *Conflated Scenes*

The cod. Milan, Ambros. G 88 sup., fol. 245ʳ, presents a council scene in the initial Π (Fig. 314). Gregory, however, is standing and not seated as in the council scenes. This posture cannot be taken as an adaptation required by the shape of the letter since seated figures have been applied to the letter Π in other instances. Instead it suggests that the figure was derived from a teaching scene.

At first glance the small scene forming the initial Π of the homily in the cod. Vat. gr. 463, fol. 230ʳ, seems to be a simple teaching scene (Fig. 86). Indeed the posture of Gregory recalls the teaching figures used constantly in the historiated initials of this manuscript. Closer examination, however, reveals that one of the clerics on the left is covering his face with his mantle, obviously to wipe his tears. A weeping figure among Gregory's audience adds another meaning to the teaching scene, that of farewell.

THE MINIATURES OF THE HOMILY ON THE LOVE OF THE POOR

a. *Gregory and the Poor*

"Just in front of your eyes," says Gregory, "a miserable and terrible sight exists. It seems incredible to all, unless they have seen it. Here are dead men who are yet alive, amputated in most parts of their bodies. They can no longer be recognized . . . ,"[111] and he continues to make a plea full of compassion and tenderness for the poor, which touches the hearts of his listeners and makes them aware of charity, the greatest of virtues.

Basil the Younger, a tenth-century scholiast, thought that this homily was delivered at the institution that Basil had established for the sick and the poor. This opinion,

---

[110] Omont, *Min. gr.* (1929), pl. XLI.   [111] *PG*, 35, 869.

which was current in the Middle Ages, is not accepted by modern scholarship for it has been shown that Basil's hospital had not been built when the sermon was delivered.[112] There can be no doubt, however, as the cited text shows, that Gregory's audience included poor and sick people, and others that were in pitiable condition, to whom he pointed while he preached. Therefore, a scene depicting Gregory with the poor constitutes a suitable illustration for this homily and focuses the attention of the beholder on the terrible sight that Gregory describes. Such an illustration is found in the following codices: Athos, Dionysiou 61, fol. 142ʳ; Sinai 339, fol. 341ᵛ; Paris gr. 543, fol. 310ᵛ (Figs. 370, 391, 468).

The Dionysiou miniature shows Gregory standing to the left of the picture under a canopy. He holds a book in his left hand and addresses a group of people to the right, the "brethren in Christ," as the inscription calls them. This group is composed of the poor and the compassionate who share their troubles. A cripple has managed to reach Gregory with the aid of his hand-crutch. He raises his left hand toward Gregory, as if "beseeching him, and kneeling down to him, and saying unto him, if thou wilt, thou canst make me clean."[113] The posture of this first figure recalls the posture of the leper of the Gospel, from which the above quotation comes, and the figure who follows him suggests another of Christ's miracles of healing. Bending over his stick, the man walks, or rather staggers, and seems to be looking at the ground as if searching for something: his lost sight. He is the blind man of the Gospel.[114] A third and older person, probably a cripple or one who suffers from old age and disease, walks slowly, leaning on a stick, toward Gregory. Behind these "poor and wretched ones"[115] is the crowd, Gregory's audience. In the case of Christ, the members of the crowd are the witnesses of Christ's healing power; they have brought the sufferers to be healed. An architectural setting forms the background of the picture.

In the similar miniature of the cod. Sinai 339, Gregory stands in front of a church, speaking to the poor (Fig. 391). A young man, a cripple on hand-crutches, heads the group of the poor; between him and the third man (the blind in this case), there stands a hunchback. These figures resemble the left part of the miniature in the Gospel book of Florence, cod. Laur. Plut. VI, 23, illustrating the following verse from Matthew; "And great multitudes came unto him, having with them those that were lame, blind, dumb, maimed and many others, and cast them down at Jesus' feet; and he healed them:" (15: 30).[116] The illustrator of the Sinai manuscript has repeated the scene of the title miniature in abbreviated form in the initial A of the text of the homily (Fig. 394).

In the scene in the lower part of the full-page miniature of the cod. Paris gr. 543, all the same people and their gestures can be recognized (Fig. 468). Gregory, attired

---

[112] Sajdak, *Scholia*, p. 173; Gallay, *La vie*, p. 87.

[113] Cf. illustration in the cod. Paris gr. 74, fol. 15ʳ, Omont, *Evangiles*, I, pl. 16, 1.

[114] Matt. 8: 2; cf. cod. Florence, Laur. Plut. VI, 23, fol. 18ᵛ; for bibliography, see H. Gerstinger,

Die griechische Buchmalerei, Vienna 1926, p. 34 n. 272.

[115] *PG*, 35, 869.

[116] Cod. Florence, Laur. Plut. VI, 23, fol. 31ʳ.

as a monk, holds a staff. The figures, lacking the lively quality and the moving, natural expression of those in the Sinai miniature, stand in calculated immobility, as if desiring to ensure the spectator's recognition of their grief. The eyebrows arched toward the center of their foreheads intensify the feeling of restrained sorrow and communicate their attempt to hold back tears of grief and pain.

The iconographic parallels mentioned in the course of the discussion of these miniatures show that iconographic models for these representations were found in Gospel scenes representing miracles of Christ.

b. *The Almsgiving*

The miniatures of the codd. Paris gr. 550, fol. 251ʳ, and Moscow, Hist. Museum 146, fol. 219ᵛ, depict the central theme of almsgiving (Figs. 426, 17). While the fuller miniature of the former occupies a third of the page, the latter, a frameless marginal miniature, probably incomplete, appears beside the ornamental band of the title of the homily.

In the upper part of the miniature of the Paris codex, Gregory is represented giving alms to the poor. He stands in the middle, balancing the composition which may have been modeled on a Gospel scene such as the one in the Gospel book of Florence, cod. Laur. Plut. VI, 23, fol. 31ʳ. Below this first scene are two others: the one at the left shows a monk giving alms; the one at the right depicts a young man with a bag in his left hand, also distributing alms. This last scene reappears in the Moscow manuscript, although the composition is reversed. Furthermore, the group receiving alms includes figures that recall those in the scene, found in the Paris manuscript, showing Gregory giving alms. These comparisons suggest that the creator of the Moscow miniature borrowed his compositional elements from two separate scenes found in a manuscript that also served as a model for the illustrator of the Paris manuscript.

Actually, in the text of the homily, no mention is made of Gregory giving alms, but, since Gregory speaks constantly about charity and the love of the poor, and admonishes men to care for them, the artist could easily visualize him setting an example by giving alms himself. Or he may have thought of Basil's institute where, according to the opinion discussed earlier (p. 63), the homily was delivered and Gregory administered to the poor and the sick.[117] Whatever the case, the artist visualized the very essence of the sermon, seeing, above all, its moral implications. In terms of everyday life, the implications were that the example set by Gregory ought to be followed by all, clerics and laymen alike. This simplification of the central theme of the sermon had to be expressed pictorially. The artist, therefore, set himself the task

---

[117] D. K. Dyobouniotes, "Νικήτα Ἡρακλείας ἑρμηνεία εἰς λόγους Γρηγορίου Ναζιανζοῦ," Θεολογία, 21 (1950), pp. 354-84, esp. pp. 355-56. A composition showing Gregory and Basil ministering to the sick in Basil's institution occurs in the ninth-century codex Paris gr. 510, fol. 149ʳ. See Omont, *Min. gr.* (1929), pl. xxxiv; cf. S. Der Nersessian, "The Illustrations of Gregory of Nazianzus, Paris gr. 510," *Dumbarton Oaks Papers*, 16 (1962), p. 267, fig. 7.

of creating variations on the central theme, i.e. two more scenes, whose presence in this homily is thus fully justified. Apart from the relationship of these two scenes to the essence of the sermon, another more direct relationship pertains to the second scene, the distribution of alms by a young man. In the thirty-ninth paragraph of the homily, Gregory states: "we respect the youth's perfection which was defined and enacted in the giving of what he had to the poor."[118] Here Gregory refers to the well-known episode of the young man mentioned in Matt. 19: 21. The miniature, however, was not created to illustrate the Biblical episode for, in the Gospel, the young man went away because he did not want to deprive himself of the things of this world and there is no illustration in the Gospels showing him in the act of almsgiving. Therefore the miniature was definitely invented for Gregory's text.

Another variant of the almsgiving scene, differing in its derivation from those discussed above, is found in the cod. Athos, Vatopedi 107, fol. 248^v (Fig. 337). This miniature, placed in the lower margin of the page, shows, on the left, Christ seated on a mattress in an attitude of benediction. In the center a man distributes food from a table, and on the extreme right three men, one with a stick, are seated on benches. Below this scene, on the left, another man distributes loaves of bread from a basket. A small figure leading another, probably a blind man, by a rope approaches the distributor to receive a loaf. The blind man is followed by two other people, one of whom leans on a stick. This miniature has been influenced by the composition of the scene depicting the Feeding of the Five Thousand, found in illustrated Gospel books, as comparisons show.[119] For instance, the man who in the Gospel scene carries a basket appears somewhat modified in the Vatopedi miniature. Similarly the figure of Christ who blesses the feeding of the multitude in the Gospel scene, blesses the feeding of the poor in the miniature of the homily. The relationship to the Gospel scene is also indicated by the inscription that serves as a commentary and which is taken from the Gospel of Matthew, 25: 34-40. The Feeding of the Five Thousand is not the only Gospel scene that has left its traces on the Vatopedi miniature. The motif of Christ seated on a mattress appears in the scene of the Last Supper,[120] and the group of three figures seated on big benches on the right side of the Vatopedi miniature recalls the episode of the Washing of the Feet included in scenes of the Last Supper. The choice of compositional elements from the two different scenes cannot be accidental. In making these choices, the illustrator must have considered Christ the prime example of the precept of charity and humility about which Gregory speaks.

It is doubtful that the initials of the codd. Athos, Dionysiou 61, fol. 142^r, Istanbul, Patr. 16, fol. 243^v, and Sinai 346, fol. 194^v, showing Gregory giving alms, are derived from an independent scene (Figs. 372, 76, 352). It is more probable that they are simply the result of the necessity of forming the horizontal bar of the letter A.

---

[118] *PG*, 35, 909.

[119] Cf. cod. Florence, Laur. Plut. VI, 23, fol. 30^r, reproduced in Millet, *Recherches*, fig. 650.

[120] Cf. cod. Paris gr. 74, fols. 195^r and 196^r, Omont, *Evangiles*, II, pls. 167, 2 and 168, 2.

c. Conflated Scenes

The miniature of the cod. Jerusalem, Taphou 14, fol. 265ʳ, mentioned in the chapter on the teaching scene (p. 36), shows Gregory standing in the center of the composition, with a group of listeners on the left to whom he points out "a horrible sight from which people shrink in horror";[121] i.e. a group of poor and wretched people who occupy the right side of the composition (Fig. 121). Not one person, as in the miniatures of the other manuscripts, but two persons with hand-crutches are near Gregory's feet. The others are standing. They are of varying ages, barefoot, ill-clad, and pitiable in appearance. Two of them are covered with sores, a reference to "the sickness of the flesh."[122] Their gestures interpret very well the lines of the text: "that is why needy and unclothed, they wander night and day, showing their sickness. . . ."[123] Evidently the illustrator of the Jerusalem manuscript combined the teaching scene with the subject of the homily. This combination in the title miniature has been adapted by the same artist for other homilies as well (cf. Figs. 99, 111, 118).

The same conflation appears in the miniature of the cod. Milan, Ambros. G 88 sup., fol. 264ʳ, except that Gregory is seated and the group of listeners on the right consists of bishops (Fig. 315). Here, too, the compositional scheme and the seated teacher have been used in another instance by the artist (cf. Fig. 299).

A conflated scene appears in the miniature of the cod. Athos, Panteleimon 6, fol. 257ʳ (Fig. 179). The basic theme is Gregory teaching about the poor, who are included in the picture. The figure of Gregory, seated on a throne to the right of the composition, and of the bishop standing beside him, are part of a larger teaching scene like the one in the cod. Florence, Laur. Plut. VII, 32, fol. 162ʳ, for which the term "hieratic teaching scene" has been suggested (Fig. 273). The poor, who are in front of Gregory, have been derived from the scene with which the discussion of this homily began.

The illustration of the cod. Oxford, Selden. B. 54, fol. 108ʳ, is basically a small teaching scene (Fig. 297). However, between Gregory, who sits on the left, and his audience opposite him, there is a table with writing implements on it. This iconographic element, found in discussion groups, has been used in two other instances in the same manuscript: a discussion group and a representation of two writers, and it may be a conventional element. It is also possible that the artist intended to convey the roles of both teacher and author.

THE MINIATURES OF THE HOMILY TO HIS SILENT FATHER

a. Gregory and his Father

The cod. Paris gr. 550, fol. 279ʳ, presents the following miniature (Fig. 427). To the extreme left, Gregory the Elder is seated on a chair with a high, curved back. He is nimbed, wrapped in a mantle, and holds his left hand to his mouth (an indication

[121] *PG*, 35, 869.   [122] *PG*, 35, 868, 869, 872.   [123] *PG*, 35, 872.

of silence) in accordance with the title and text of the homily. In front of him is Gregory of Nazianzus in bishop's vestments. He, too, is nimbed and, with arms crossed on his breast, is bowing slightly. This gesture expresses respect, and the artist may have read the text where, in the seventh paragraph, Gregory says that he respects great age. Behind Gregory of Nazianzus, on the extreme right of the composition, several people gesticulate toward heaven from where thick hail is falling. In the lower part of the composition there is another group of people, perhaps added merely to fill this part of the quatrefoil frame of the miniature. Such devices are not unusual in Mediaeval book illumination.[124]

The hailstorm and the protest of the people have also been depicted in the cod. Paris gr. 510, fol. 78[r],[125] but again a comparison shows that the miniature of the full edition is not related to that of the liturgical edition. The only existing similarity is the actual hailstorm. This, however, is a conventional element which appears elsewhere, as in the Octateuchs.[126]

A similar iconographic and compositional scheme appears in the miniatures of the codices Jerusalem, Taphou 14, fol. 292[r]; Paris gr. 543, fol. 342[v] (upper register); Vat. gr. 1947, fol. 22[v] (Figs. 122, 469, 125). A comparison of these miniatures with those of the Paris gr. 550 shows that in the first two the compositional arrangement is reversed, and that the lower group of people does not appear in any of the three. Furthermore, in the miniatures of the Jerusalem and Paris gr. 543 codices, Gregory does not bow to his father as in the miniature of the cod. Paris gr. 550, but points him out to the group of people on the left. This act, which is justified by many parts of the sermon, is not clearly suggested in the Vatican miniature where the illustrator has been unsuccessful in relating all parts of the composition. In the Jerusalem miniature both father and son are presented in bishops' garments, as they should be; in the Paris miniature both wear monks' attire. Moreover, the rendering of the details in the former miniature shows great care on the part of the illustrator, who felt it necessary to individualize the two Gregorys and to differentiate their ages as well as to indicate the father's grave silence. The indication of silence, an important iconographic element, has also been clearly presented by the illustrator of the Vatican manuscript. But, in the miniature of the cod. Paris gr. 543, Gregory the Elder holds a staff in his left hand, while his right hand rests on his knee; he makes no speaking gesture, and his silence is thus implied.

The illustrators of the codd. Athos, Dionysiou 61, fol. 172[v], Paris, Coislin 239, fol. 217[r], Oxford, Selden. B. 54, fol. 121[r], and Athos, Panteleimon 6, fol. 281[r], use miniatures similar to those discussed, but with certain modifications (Figs. 374, 233, 298, 180). In the Dionysiou miniature Gregory the Elder, dressed as a bishop, sits under a light canopy on the left of the picture and blesses his son who occupies the middle part of the composition. Buildings with arches and crenelated walls form the

[124] Weitzmann, *Roll*, pp. 165ff.
[125] Omont, *Min. gr.* (1929), pl. xxix.
[126] See, for example, cod. Vat. gr. 746, fol. 176[v].

background. This rendering, traditional and beautiful as it may be, is iconographically less correct than the miniatures of the manuscripts discussed above, because the father's silence—the reason for the delivery of the sermon—is not indicated. The architectural setting appears neither in the miniature of the Paris, nor in that of the Oxford codices. In the latter, because of space limitations, Gregory of Nazianzus stands behind his father rather than between him and the people. Gregory the Elder has his fingers over his mouth to indicate silence, and therefore the miniature is iconographically better than those of the Paris and Dionysiou manuscripts. In the Panteleimon miniature Gregory the Elder, in bishop's vestments, is seated in the middle of the composition on a throne, and is speaking. His son, standing behind him in front of a building, addresses a group of people on the right who are headed by another bishop, also speaking.

Lack of space and persistent use of similarly shaped headpieces has influenced the iconography of the cod. Oxford, Canon. gr. 103, fol. 264^r (Fig. 286), and the illustrator has reduced the miniature to a minimum. A seated Gregory is inserted in the left arm of the frame which includes the title. Opposite him, in the right arm, is a group of people. This seated Gregory looks older than he does in other miniatures of the same manuscript. Probably he is Gregory the Elder but, instead of holding his hand to his mouth, he makes a gesture of benediction. There are two possible explanations of this miniature. Either the illustrator had a model in which the silencing gesture of the old man had already been changed into a speaking gesture, or, having omitted Gregory of Nazianzus, who addressed the audience, he found it necessary to create a relationship between Gregory the Elder and the people by means of gestures.

The initial T in the cod. Sinai 346, fol. 237^r, formed by the figure of Gregory teaching and his seated father is derived from a title miniature (Fig. 354).

b. *The Sending of a Letter*

The illustrator of the cod. Moscow, Hist. Museum 146, fol. 244^v, has chosen to illustrate this homily with a miniature showing what may be titled The Sending of a Letter (Fig. 18). This miniature, placed in the left margin, depicts Gregory of Nazianzus standing and giving a scroll to his father, who sits on a thokos and rests his feet on a footstool. Their faces have flaked off, but the remaining beards and hair make identification certain. Gregory of Nazianzus has dark hair, and his father, an aged man, has white hair. Both wear bishops' vestments.

The traditional representation of this subject portrays the writer and the recipient of the letter seated. A variation of this scheme showing the author seated and the recipient standing appears in the Princeton codex of the *Heavenly Ladder* by John Climacus, Univ. Lib. Garrett MS 16, and presents the closest parallel to the Moscow miniature.[127] Despite this parallel, the explanation of the scene and its relation to the text of the homily present difficulties, for neither the text nor the historical facts

---

[127] Martin, *Ladder*, pl. IX, 29, 30.

associated with it contain any reference to a letter. If the scroll is supposed to contain the text of the sermon, then perhaps Gregory is offering his sermon to his father to indicate the fulfillment of the task that fell to him because of his father's silence and to betoken the respect and honor due Gregory the Elder.

D. THE MIGRATED MINIATURES

The text of the homilies cannot adequately explain the miniatures included in this section. They have been taken over from different texts, and the main problem is to define the relationship between Gregory's homilies and the illustrated texts from which the miniatures were taken. The discussion considers first the largest and most complex group of miniatures, those from the New Testament.

1. THE NEW TESTAMENT GROUP

The miniatures of this group illustrate homilies delivered on the occasion of various Church feasts. These sermons are discussed in their liturgical sequence: First Homily on Easter, on New Sunday, on Pentecost, on the Nativity, on Epiphany, on Holy Baptism.

THE MINIATURES OF THE FIRST HOMILY ON EASTER

The subject of the illustrations in most of the manuscripts is the Descent into Hell.[128] Although the theme is supported in its theological content by canonical passages used in Byzantine theology,[129] its pictorial rendering is based on the apocryphal gospel of Nicodemus.[130] The miniatures do not all belong to the same iconographic tradition, but rather three main iconographic types can be distinguished and classified according to the represented action of Christ: a) Christ Approaching Adam, b) Christ Dragging Adam, and c) Christ Showing His Wounds to Adam and Eve.

a. *Christ Approaching Adam*

The characteristic of this *narrative* type,[131] which dates from the pre-iconoclastic period, is that Christ strides from right to left, or vice versa, across the broken gates, nails, and bars of hell. He approaches and seizes Adam with his outstretched right

[128] On the iconography of the Descent into Hell, see G. Millet, "Anastasis," *E. Piot, Monuments et mémoires*, 2 (1895), pp. 204-14; Morey, *Freer Coll.*, pp. 57ff.; *idem, AB* (1929), pp. 57-58; Demus-Diez, pp. 69ff.; M. Soteriou, "Χρυσοκέντη-τον ἐπιγονάτιον τοῦ Βυζαντινοῦ Μουσείου Ἀθηνῶν ...," Πρακτικὰ τῆς Χριστιανικῆς Ἀρχαιολογικῆς Ἑταιρείας, 2 (1933), p. 115; Weitzmann, *Semin. Kondak.* (1936), pp. 87ff.; A. Xyngopoulos, "Ὁ Ὑμνολογικὸς εἰκονογραφικὸς τύπος τῆς εἰς Ἄδου Καθόδου," *E.E.B.S.*, 17 (1941), pp. 113ff.; J. Villete, *La résurrection du Christ dans l'art chrétien du IIe au VIIe siècle*, Paris 1957; K. Weitz-

mann, "Aristocratic Psalter and Lectionary," *The Record of the Art Museum, Princeton University*, 19 (1960), p. 99, hereinafter cited as *Aristocratic Psalter*. Cf. K. Weitzmann, "Zur byzantinischen Quelle des Wolfenbüttler Musterbuches," *Festschrift Hans R. Hahnloser* 1961, pp. 233ff.

[129] For an excellent theological discussion of the theme, see J. Karmires, Ἡ εἰς Ἄδου Κάθοδος, Athens 1939. Cf. J. A. Macculoch, *The Harrowing of Hell*, Edinburgh 1930.

[130] C. Tischendorf, *Evangelia apocrypha*, 2nd ed., Leipzig 1876, pp. 323ff.

[131] Weitzmann, *Aristocratic Psalter, loc.cit.*

70

arm and raises him from his sarcophagus. Christ holds the so-called patriarchal cross.[132]

The miniatures of the following codices belong to this type: Athos, Dionysiou 61, fol. 2[r] (title miniature and initial A); Moscow, Hist. Museum 146, fol. 1[v]; Athos, Panteleimon 6, fol. 2[r]; Sinai 339, fol. 5[r] (title miniature and initial A); Paris gr. 543, fol. 23[v]; Paris gr. 541, fol. 9[v] (full-page miniature, badly flaked and not illustrated); Athos, Vatopedi 107, fol. 4[v] (marginal miniature); and the initial A of the codd. Oxford, Canon. gr. 103, fol. 3[r]; Milan, Ambros. G 88 sup., fol. 4[r]; Vat. gr. 463, fol. 319[r]; Istanbul, Patr. 16, fol. 3[r]; Paris gr. 533, fol. 4[r]; Athens, Nat. Lib. 2554, fol. 1[r]; Athens, Nat. Lib. 213, fol. 1[r] (Figs. 356, 1, 137, 378, 454, 317, 276, 300, 88, 62, 235).

In the miniature of the cod. Athos, Dionysiou 61, Christ strides from right to left (Fig. 356). Characteristically, the setting consists of a landscape with two mountains. The same posture of Christ occurs in the initial A's of the codd. Sinai 339, and Oxford, Canon. gr. 103, which also include a small figure of an angel flying toward him (Figs. 378, 276). Angels flying over Christ's head are often encountered in representations of the Anastasis.[133] The angels appearing in the flaked miniature of the cod. Paris gr. 541 carry the symbols of the Passion, while Christ strides from left to right, as in the title miniatures of the codd. Moscow, Hist. Museum 146, and Sinai 339; the latter is distinguished by the absence of a landscape setting (Figs. 1, 378).

The cod. Paris gr. 543 includes more figures, a characteristic of Palaeologan art (Fig. 454). Christ's fluttering garment in the Moscow and Paris manuscripts stresses his vigorous movement, and the oval mandorla framing his figure indicates that he has passed through the frightening Valley of the Shadow of Death and emerged into the full light of Easter morning. This fluttering garment is reminiscent of early stages in the development of the type,[134] which did not undergo drastic iconographic changes, save those imposed by the fashion of the time such as the introduction of rays breaking through the mandorla, a Palaeologan motif.[135] John the Baptist on the left, heading the group of the just, points to Christ, which suggests John's sermon in hell mentioned in the apocryphal gospel.

b. *Christ Dragging Adam*

The representation showing Christ vigorously dragging Adam appears in the title miniatures of three manuscripts: Jerusalem, Taphou 14, fol. 3[r]; Oxford, Roe 6, fol. 2[r]; and Patmos, cod. 45, fol. 1[v] (Figs. 99, 436, 341). This last manuscript contains

[132] Examples of this type outside the manuscripts of the homilies occur in the mosaics of Daphni, the cod. Leningrad 21, and the lectionary Athos, Dionysiou 587, fol. 2[r]; see Morey, *AB* (1929), fig. 64; Demus-Diez, fig. 100.

[133] An example may be found in the lectionary of St. Giorgio dei Greci in Venice, fol. 46[r] (A. Xyngopoulos "Τὸ Ἱστορημένον Εὐαγγέλιον τοῦ Ἑλλην. Ἰνστ. Βενετίας," Θησαυρίσματα 1 [1962], pp. 63-88); cf. S. Beissel, *Geschichte der Evange-*

lienbücher in der ersten Hälfte des Mittelalters, Freiburg in Breisgau 1906, p. 44; Kondakov, *Histoire*, p. 145.

[134] Morey, *Freer Coll.*, pp. 57ff.

[135] Examples of the same motif may be seen in the frescoes of the Athos monasteries, for instance, on the south wall of the trapeza of Lavra. See G. Millet, *Monuments de l'Athos. La peinture*, Paris 1927, pl. 146, 2.

only the Anastasis miniature and is mentioned here for the sake of thoroughness. Moreover the same type forms the initial A of the homily in the cod. Milan, Ambros. 120 sup., fol. 1ʳ (not illustrated).

The figure of Christ forms the axis of the miniature in the cod. Jerusalem, Taphou 14 (Fig. 99). Christ, in an imposing position, holds the so-called patriarchal cross in his left hand, as if showing it to the spectator. With his right hand he drags Adam, who is stepping out of the sarcophagus. Behind the rising Eve a group of people, two of whom are the prophet-kings David and Solomon, stands in typical postures of reverence and worship. On the right a group of the just headed by John the Baptist emerges from another marble sarcophagus. At the extreme right of the miniature stands the figure of the teaching Gregory, mentioned in the discussion of the teaching scene.[136]

The earliest example of this iconographic type of the Anastasis appears in the mosaics of Hosios Loukas in Phocis, and in the Lavra lectionary cod. 1.[137] This type is significant because of its indebtedness to classical models. Weitzmann first pointed out that Hercules dragging Cerberus from the underworld inspired the compositional scheme of Christ dragging Adam, and termed the type, belonging to the series of new creations of the Macedonian Renaissance in the tenth century, the *renaissance* type.[138]

Compared to the miniature of the Jerusalem manuscript, the miniatures of the two other codices are simpler with regard to the persons participating in the scene. In the full-page miniature of the Patmos manuscript, the just have been omitted, and those present in the scene, besides Christ and Adam, are Eve and John the Baptist, who balance the prophet-kings (Fig. 341). This miniature offers in addition the element of landscape, which exists neither in the miniature of the Jerusalem manuscript nor in the flaked miniature of the cod. Oxford, Roe 6 (Fig. 436). In the latter, which occupies three-quarters of the page, the same figures are omitted as in the Patmos manuscript.

Before proceeding to the discussion of the third iconographic type, the possible sources of the miniatures of the first two types with reference to the homily of Gregory may be indicated. Since Gregory's sermon was read on Easter day, the illustrators probably borrowed the pictures from lectionaries in which both types occur as illustrations of the Gospel lections for Easter. This borrowing brings the relationship of the two liturgical books into sharp focus. So far in the discussion their relationship has been based on the texts and the sequence of the festival cycle. Now it is extended to the pictorial cycle as well. The lectionaries begin with the festival of Easter, and the liturgical homilies of Gregory begin with the first homily on Easter. In both cases the Anastasis is the introductory miniature.

[136] Supra, p. 28.

[137] Demus-Diez, pl. xiv; Weitzmann, *Semin. Kondak.* (1936), pls. ii, iv.

[138] Weitzmann, *Semin. Kondak.* (1936), pp. 88ff.; idem, *Aristocratic Psalter*, p. 91. Demus has suggested that the two types of the Anastasis under discussion correspond to two different phases of the story of the Descent into Hell recorded in the gospel of Nicodemus; Demus-Diez, p. 71. Xyngopoulos argues convincingly against such a suggestion; *op.cit., loc.cit.*

c. *Christ Showing His Wounds to Adam and Eve*

The miniature in the cod. Paris gr. 550, fol. 5^r, occupies three-quarters of the page and is divided into nine compartments by two vertical and two horizontal bands (Fig. 401). The central section of the second register, which is the largest, is devoted to the theme of the Descent into Hell. Christ, facing the spectator, steps into the realm of darkness. Extending his hands, he shows his wounds to the two groups of the resurrected: Adam and Eve on the left, and the prophet-kings and John the Baptist on the right. Four angels, depicted as half-length figures and with covered hands, descend toward Christ from the two lateral sections of the upper register. Between the flying angels are four archangels bearing the symbols of the Passion. Below the central panel, in the middle compartment of the lowest register, the dead arise from peculiarly undulating ground. Dressed in white shrouds, they extend their hands toward the central scene. The rising dead are flanked by two groups of people bearing candles. In the compartments on either side of Christ, the Three Marys are shown on the left, and the disciples headed by Peter on the right.

The central part of the composition, the Descent into Hell, which differs markedly from the types already mentioned, is depicted in the same way, but with the addition of the mandorla around the figure of Christ, in an eleventh-century lectionary in the monastery of Iviron on Mount Athos, cod. 1 (which contains feast pictures)[139] and in an early icon in Leningrad.[140] These are early examples of the type.

In an interesting article summarized below, Xyngopoulos has discussed these two examples and the miniature of the cod. Paris gr. 550.[141] He called this type of the Descent into Hell *hymnologic* and reached the following conclusions. 1) The main difference between this type and the others lies in the fact that Christ neither drags nor approaches Adam and Eve, but extends his hands from the high hill on which he stands and "invites" them. 2) The earlier examples of this type, the miniature of the lectionary of Iviron and the icon in Leningrad, are only portions of a larger composition which has been preserved in the miniature of the cod. Paris gr. 550. 3) Many elements of this composition are based on the *historical* type, inspired by the gospel of Nicodemus. Yet many of the panels around the central composition cannot be explained by the apocryphal gospels. Furthermore, this miniature and the text of Gregory's sermon are in no way related. 4) All the elements of this composition can be explained by the hymns of Easter Sunday, chiefly the canon of John of Damascus. 5) The purpose of the hymnologic type is to represent the idea of the resurrection and redemption of mankind brought about by Christ's Resurrection. 6) This type, as seen in the cod. Paris gr. 550, was inspired by the canon, and was originally created for Gregory's first sermon on Easter, in which interpretations of Christ's Resurrection are to be found.

---

[139] A. Xyngopoulos, Ἱστορημένα Εὐαγγέλια τῆς Μονῆς Ἰβήρων Ἁγίου Ὄρους, Athens 1932, pl. 1.
[140] Lazarev, *History*, II, pl. 200. Cf. M. Chatzidakis, "Εἰκόνες ἐπιστυλίου ἀπὸ τὸ Ἅγιον Ὄρος,"

Δελτίον Χριστιανικῆς Ἀρχαιολογικῆς Ἑταιρείας, per. 4, 4 (1966), pp. 397ff.
[141] Xyngopoulos, *op.cit.*, *loc.cit.*

Some of Xyngopoulos's conclusions provoke reservations. According to methodological principles, a miniature either has or has not a basic text sufficient to explain its genesis. Since the text of Gregory does not explain the miniature, the illustration was not invented for it. The question then must be raised whether or not the miniature necessarily presupposes the text of the canon.

—Jesus

"Let us cleanse our senses and we shall see in the unapproachable light of the Resurrection, Christ in a blaze of light, and we shall hear Him loudly saying, 'rejoice'. . . ."[142] According to Xyngopoulos the word "rejoice" in this passage causes the creation of the type of Christ in the miniature, because Christ "invites the dead to the light." This interpretation becomes all the more unlikely when the Leningrad icon is considered. There, Christ shows the palm of one hand and the back of the other. This gesture, which also appears in Last Judgement scenes,[143] is not an invitation but is made to show the wounds. Thus Christ emphasizes the human body which suffered on the cross and which is now glorified. The Church Fathers who venerate Christ's human nature and his sufferings on the cross often point out the importance of the resurrected body of Christ.[144]

Obviously this type of the Descent into Hell—a type which is eternal and rich in dogmatic elements—does not need the canon of John of Damascus to explain it, because it resulted from a gradual development of dogmatic elements that crept into Middle Byzantine art from an earlier period.[145]

—Archangels

"Let us celebrate together with archangels. . . ."[146] Xyngopoulos suggests that this verse accounts for the archangels in the miniature. He rightly says that the archangels are not mentioned in the apocryphal gospels,[147] although angels are mentioned indirectly. They may have their source in the canon, referring to archangels, or they may well be a liturgical addition not dependent on the canon, for they occur in the representations of the Anastasis as, for example, at Torcello.[148] This suggestion is supported by the fact that small figures of angels descending are also found in Anas-

---

[142] S. Zervos ed., *Pentekostarion*, Athens n.d., p. 2, hereinafter cited as *Pentekostarion*.

[143] Cf. icon in Sinai reproduced in G. and M. Soteriou, *Icônes du Mont Sinai*, I (planches), Athens 1956, pl. 151.

[144] Eustathius of Antioch, *PG*, 18, 693-94; Athanasius of Alexandria, *PG*, 26, 437, 440ff.; John Chrysostom, *PG*, 61, 55, 57; Andreas of Crete, *PG*, 97, 691; cf. J. Pierres, *Formula Sancti Johannis Damasceni* Ἡ τοῦ Κυρίου σάρξ ὄργανον τῆς Θεότητος *e Sancto Maximo Confessore enucleata*

et auctoritas Damasceni circa potentiam animae Christi, Rome 1940.

[145] Weitzmann, *Aristocratic Psalter*, pp. 98-107.

[146] *Pentekostarion*, p. 9.

[147] Xyngopoulos, *op.cit.*, p. 119 n. 1.

[148] Schultz, *Torcello*, pl. 26. See also fresco in the church of the Holy Trinity in Sopočani; R. Hamann-MacLean, H. Hallensleben, *Die Monumentalmalerei in Serbien und Macedonien*, Giessen 1963, pl. 124; for a color reproduction see V. Dourić, *Copočani*, Belgrade 1963, pl. XIX.

tasis representations and yet are not mentioned in the canon.[149] Finally, the symbols of the Passion are explained by neither the apocryphal gospel nor the canon, yet they have appeared in Anastasis scenes since the twelfth century.[150] Consequently these iconographic elements apparently do not find their textual source in the canon.

–The Three Marys and the Disciples[151]

"The women with the spices, going to the sepulcher of the Life-Giver very early in the morning, found an angel seated on the stone who addressed them and spoke to them thus: Why seek ye the Living One among the dead? Why mourn ye for the Incorruptible One as if He were in corruption? Go and say these things to His disciples."[152] This part of the canon, which does not explain the miniature either, was borrowed from the second Heothinon Gospel (Mark 16: 1-8), read on the same day the canon was chanted. For this reason it should not be assumed that the derivative text of the canon, rather than the text of the Gospel, provided the basis for the composition under discussion. Moreover, the Marys form a single scene with the disciples, that is, the Marys Reporting to the Disciples, for they bear no spices. This episode is described in the fourth Heothinon (Luke 24: 1-12).

If the Heothinon Gospel explains the miniature more satisfactorily, the question then becomes whether or not pictorial evidence of illustrated Heothina can also be furnished. To my knowledge two lectionaries have illustrated Heothina: the codd. Athos, Dionysiou 587[153] and Jerusalem, Anastaseos 1, the former including the illustrated Heothina at the end of the book. It is also known that the Heothina were represented in the church of the Holy Apostles in Constantinople because, in Mesarites' description, the sequence of the episodes beginning with the Marys at the Tomb follows that of the Heothina Gospels.[154] The scene of the Marys Reporting to the Disciples is included among these representations.[155]

[149] See n. 133.

[150] A few examples are cited here: A metal Gospel cover in the monastery of Grand Lavra, which in Kondakov's opinion dates from the eleventh century, although a twelfth-century date seems more likely. See N. P. Kondakov, *Pamiatniki Khristianskogo iskusstva na Afone*, St. Petersburg 1902, p. 198, pl. XXVII. A miniature of a lectionary in the Walters Art Gallery, cod. 535, fol. B2ʳ, Walters Art Gallery, *Early Christian and Byzantine Art*, Baltimore 1947, p. 147. The fresco of the Anastasis in the church of Peribleptos at Mistra, dating from the fourteenth century, is reproduced in Millet, *Mistra*, pl. 116, 3. An icon in Leningrad of a fourteenth- or fifteenth-century date in Lazarev, *History*, II, pl. 324. An icon in Ochrid, probably fourteenth-century, reproduced in W. Felicetti-Liebenfels, *Geschichte der byzantinischen Ikonenmalerei*, Lausanne 1956, pl. 81b. Frescoes in the monasteries of Mt. Athos, G.

Millet, *Monuments de l'Athos. La peinture*, Paris 1927, pl. 129, 1.

[151] Kondakov, *Histoire*, p. 95, saw a symbolic significance in these two side panels and interpreted them as the Church on earth represented by the figures of the Marys and the apostles.

[152] *Pentekostarion*, p. 5.

[153] K. Weitzmann, *Aus den Bibliotheken des Athos*, Hamburg 1963, pp. 73ff.

[154] A. Heisenberg, *Grabeskirche und Apostelkirche*, II, Leipzig 1908, pp. 59ff., 251ff. For the possible position of the episodes on the walls of the church see *ibid.*, fig. 3. For a new edition of Mesarites' description see G. Downey, "Nikolaos Mesarites, Description of the Church of the Holy Apostles at Constantinople," *Transactions of the American Philosophical Society* 47 (1957), pp. 855-924.

[155] Heisenberg, *op.cit.*, pp. 67, 292.

-The Raising of the Dead

"Those who were kept together bound in the realm of Hades because of Thy infinite mercy, O Christ, were led to light."[156] Long before this canon was composed, the following line was written in the apocryphal gospel: "This is marvelous, that He rose not alone, but raised up many other dead men."[157] Clearly the text of the canon is not needed to explain the picture. Furthermore, it is interesting to note that this episode is part of the larger scene of the Descent into Hell, as parallel examples, such as the Anastasis mosaic at Torcello, show.[158]

-The Candle-Bearers

"Let us go to the Christ, who is coming out of the tomb, bearing candles as if to a bridegroom, and let us celebrate. . . ."[159] This verse explains the representation of candle-bearers better than anything else, and it could be taken as evidence for an illustrated canon, where it was the only original element, all the other elements harking back to other texts. However, the addition of a liturgical motif like the candle-bearers does not necessarily require a text.

The liturgy of Holy Saturday makes a reference to the theme of the Descent into Hell through the chanted hymns and the celebration of the blessing of the Easter fire. In the early hours of Easter morning the yellow flame of a candle raised by the priest pierces the total darkness of the church, and its light is transmitted to the tapers borne by the congregation, passing from neighbor to neighbor. The church gradually becomes a sea of illumination, an image of the redeeming light brought by Christ to those that were blanketed by the impenetrable shadow of death.

This ceremony is celebrated all over the Orthodox world, but in early times the tapers were lit outside the main church at the atrium ($\dot{\alpha}\phi\dot{\eta}$ $\tau\hat{\omega}\nu$ $\lambda\alpha\mu\pi\dot{\alpha}\delta\omega\nu$ $\ddot{\epsilon}\xi\omega$) and the people holding them entered the church singing the hymn "Christ is resurrected."[160] This particular ceremony, the entrance with tapers from the atrium to the nave, offered the artist the motif seen in the Paris miniature. Taking into consideration the fact that the information about this particular rite is taken from the texts of the euchologia and surviving practices in the Greek Church, the importance of this miniature is easily appreciated. The artist, depending on the actual liturgy, rather than on any written text, illustrated a particular moment. A parallel example is the picture of the Elevation of the Cross, which illustrates the feast of the Cross celebrated on September 14.[161] This illustration could be explained by the Book of Ceremonies of the

[156] *Pentekostarion*, p. 3.

[157] M. R. James, *The Apocryphal New Testament*, Oxford 1953, pp. 119-20.

[158] Schultz, *Torcello*, pl. 26. The episode appears in places where the influence of the canon cannot be justified, such as the Vatican psalter cod. gr. 1927, fol. 8ʳ, see DeWald, *Vat. gr. 1927*, p. 5,

pl. IV. It occurs also in the cod. Vat. gr. 752, fol. 44ᵛ, see DeWald, *Vat. gr. 752*, p. 11, pl. XIX.

[159] *Pentekostarion*, p. 3.

[160] D. I. Pallas, " 'Αρχαιολογικὰ-λειτουργικά, 7. Ἡ λαμπαδηφορία κατὰ τὴν λειτουργίαν, " E.E.B.S., 20 (1950), pp. 307, 313.

[161] Weitzmann, *N. T. Mss Studies*, p. 163.

Emperor Constantine VII Porphyrogenitus, but it seems rather to be an invention since there is no evidence that the Book of Ceremonies was illustrated.

So far the following conclusions are clear: there is no convincing reason to assume that the miniatures were invented for the text of the canon; the Three Marys and Disciples were created for the Gospel of Luke (24: 1-12, fourth Heothinon); the archangels and the Raising of the Dead belong to the main composition, which is purely dogmatic in character; and the invention of the candle-bearers has a liturgical origin.

Leaving aside for the moment the problem of whether these candle-bearers were invented for Gregory's homily, the following question must be considered: from which source did the Descent into Hell and the flanking episodes pass into Gregory's homily?[162]

In the discussion of the various episodes of this iconographic type, it has been pointed out that the scene of the Descent into Hell existed in lectionaries, its flanking episodes in mosaics, and the Raising of the Dead in psalters and mosaics as well. For reasons stated earlier, a lectionary again seems to be the most probable source of the illustrations. If this is so, then another question arises: was it the artist of the lectionary or Gregory's illustrator who arranged the sequence of episodes? The problem is open to discussion and no definite answer can be offered since the lectionaries vary in their arrangement. Probably it was Gregory's illustrator who, perhaps under the influence of the canon as Xyngopoulos has suggested, placed the scene of the Marys and the Disciples deriving from the fourth Heothinon, next to the principal illustration of the Easter lection, i.e. the Descent into Hell. And it may well be that this arrangement was actually made by the illustrator of the cod. Paris gr. 550.

THE ANASTASIS MINIATURE OF THE COD. PARIS GR. 543

In the cod. Paris gr. 543, fol. 27ʳ (lower register), the second homily on Easter is illustrated in the following manner (Fig. 455). The center of the composition is dominated by the hill encompassing the cave of hell, the doors of which, with their keys, have been thrown down. An angel with upraised wings hovers over the mouth of the cave and is apparently chaining Satan.[163] On either side of the hill are two sarcophagi from each of which four half-naked persons arise. The position of their hands

[162] This is not the place to enter into a discussion of the origin of the type. Suffice it to say that a ninth-century date for the creation of the type, as suggested by Xyngopoulos, seems very probable. However, it must be pointed out that the argument in favor of that date should not be based on the earliest extant illustrated Gregory manuscript, as Xyngopoulos thought, but on the earliest marginal psalter which made use of the type, i.e. the Chloudov psalter, fols. 63ʳ and 82ʳ. For a discus-

sion of these two miniatures see E. O. Kosteckaia, "L'iconographie de la Résurrection du Christ d'après les miniatures de psautier Chloudov," *Seminarium Kondakovianum*, 2 (1928), p. 63, pl. VIII. Cf. J. J. Tikkanen, *Die Psalterillustration im Mittelalter*, Helsingfors 1895, p. 60.

[163] Bordier, *Description*, p. 188, thought that he had seen a sarcophagus within the cave and an angel lifting the body of a woman out of it in order to take her to heaven.

suggests that they are trying to cover their nudity, or shivering, or standing in trembling and fear.

Gregory's text does not explain the picture. Only passing allusions are made, as in his reference to Christ's Passion. "There were a great many miracles. God was crucified . . . the sun was darkened . . . and shone again. The earth was shaken . . . stones were smashed over stones, the dead rose up in the faith of the last and common resurrection. . . ."[164]

Grabar has interpreted the scene as the Last Judgment, but this explanation presents difficulties.[165] When Christ refers to his second coming on the Last Day (Matt. 25: 31-46), no mention is made of the angel. The illustrations of the relevant Gospel verses present either the Raising of the Dead or a complete Last Judgment scene.[166] On the other hand, no Last Judgment representation in which the angel chains Satan is known.

It is more plausible to interpret the miniature as part of an Anastasis scene according to textual and pictorial evidence. Indeed, in the gospel of Nicodemus both the angel and the Raising of the Dead find explanation. As pointed out earlier, the apocryphal gospel of the Descent into Hell states that after Christ had trampled Satan, he delivered him to the angels to be chained.[167] The chaining of Satan is often included in the Descent into Hell during the Palaeologan period. A well-known example is the fresco of the Peribleptos at Mistra.[168] In Mistra, however, as in other examples,[169] the raising of Adam, Eve, and others of the righteous is depicted, but not the raising of the common dead. Yet the resurrection of the common dead and that of Adam and Eve is included in the Anastasis scene in the mosaic of Torcello.[170]

THE MINIATURES OF THE HOMILY ON NEW SUNDAY

The codd. Moscow, Hist. Museum 146, Sinai 339, Turin, Univ. Lib. C. I. 6 and Paris gr. 543 illustrate this homily with miniatures depicting the Incredulity of Thomas,[171] and present two different iconographic traditions: Christ Grasping the Hand of Thomas, and Thomas Approaching Christ.

a. *Christ Grasping the Hand of Thomas*

This iconographic tradition has been followed by the illustrators of the codd. Moscow, Hist. Museum 146, fol. 23ᵛ; Sinai 339, fol. 42ᵛ; and Turin, Univ. Lib. C. I. 6, fol. 18ʳ, whose marginal miniatures are similar (Figs. 3, 380, 29). In the Moscow and

---

[164] *PG*, 36, 661.

[165] Grabar, *Min. Byz.*, p. 7, pl. 56.

[166] See cod. Paris gr. 74, fol. 51ᵛ reproduced in Omont, *Evangiles*, I, pl. 41. Also cod. Vienna Theol. gr. 154, fol. 235ᵛ; for bibliography on this codex, see H. Gerstinger, *Die griechische Buchmalerei*, Vienna 1926, p. 33 n. 270.

[167] C. Tischendorf, *Evangelia apocrypha*, Leipzig 1876, p. 329.

[168] Millet, *Mistra*, pl. 116, 3.

[169] See, for example, the lectionary in the Walters Art Gallery, cod. 535, fol. B2ʳ, supra, n. 150.

[170] Schultz, *Torcello*, pl. 26.

[171] Discussion of the iconography in Morey, *Freer Coll.*, pp. 58ff.; *idem, AB* (1929), pp. 58ff.; Millet, *Recherches*, pp. 577ff.; Demus-Diez, pp. 66ff.

Sinai miniatures which are more complete, the scene takes place against a large square portal, referring to the "closed doors" of the Gospel account. The apostles are arranged in two groups around the central figure of Christ. The right group is headed by Peter, the left by the doubting disciple, who is in profile.[172] The hieratic Christ grasps Thomas's hand to apply it to the scar of the wound, so that he may believe. In the Turin miniature only these two main figures appear.[173]

This type of Christ, which is not very common in Middle Byzantine times, had already been depicted in the Early Christian period and is of Palestinian origin.[174]

b. *Thomas Approaching Christ*

In the miniature of the cod. Paris gr. 543, fol. 51^v (upper register), the scene takes place against an architectural setting: a structure with a gate, a cupola over it, and two lateral houses with entrances (Fig. 457). The gabled roofs of the houses are joined to the cupola of the central one by hanging drapery. Christ stands in front of the central portal, through which he has miraculously passed. He has raised one arm; his other hand does not point to the wound in his side, as in the Middle Byzantine examples, but holds a scroll. Thomas extends his right hand, seeking the side of Christ, without, however, touching it. The reduced marginal miniature of the cod. Athos, Vatopedi 107, fol. 27^v, belongs to the same type (Fig. 318).

The type of Thomas Approaching Christ is more common than the other. Examples can be found in lectionaries, such as that of the Morgan Library, cod. 639, fol. 9^v, and that of Jerusalem, cod. Anastaseos 1, fol. 204^v.[175] There are, however, some interesting iconographic motifs in the Paris miniature which do not occur in the examples already mentioned. Thomas seems to be hesitant and the disciples behind him seem by their gestures to be urging him to proceed. Christ shrinks from Thomas, as if afraid that he will touch the wound. Millet has observed the existence of these details in Mesarites' description of the Doubting Thomas scene in the church of the Holy Apostles and has concluded that they reappear only in the thirteenth and fourteenth centuries.[176] In this respect Millet has found another example parallel to the cod. Paris gr. 543 in the thirteenth-century lectionary in Berlin, cod. gr. qu. 66, fol. 336^v.[177]

Both iconographic types of the Incredulity of Thomas are used in lectionaries illustrating the pericope for Thomas's Sunday (John 20: 19-31). Since Gregory's sermon

[172] The profile motif appears already in the cod. Leningrad 21, but it occurs more often in Late Byzantine and post-Byzantine times. See Morey, *AB* (1929), p. 58, fig. 65. Cf. S. Pelekanides, Καστοριά, Thessalonica 1953, pl. 208a.

[173] There is a close parallel in a miniature of the cod. Vienna Theol. gr. 154, fol. 154^r. Another example of the same iconographic tradition appears in the cod. Vat. syr. 559, fol. 163^v; see G. de Jerphanion, *Les miniatures du manuscrit syriaque no. 559 de la Bibliothèque Vaticane*, Vatican

1940, pl. XXI, 44. Cf. V. Gurewich, "Observations on the iconography of the Wound in Christ's side, with Special Reference to its Position," *Journal of the Warburg and Courtauld Inst.*, 20 (1957), pp. 358-62.

[174] Millet, *Recherches*, p. 577 n. 5.

[175] Weitzmann, *Lectionary Morgan 639*, fig. 293. Papadopoulos-Kerameus, III, p. 193.

[176] Millet, *Recherches*, p. 578. Cf. Heisenberg, *op.cit.*, II, pp. 74, 264.

[177] Millet, *Recherches*, p. 578.

was read on this day too, there is no doubt that this picture, which cannot be explained by the homily, was borrowed from the illustration of the lection for the day. The figured initial E of the cod. Vat. gr. 463, fol. 359ʳ, formed by the seated Christ, presents a problem, for its derivation from any specific scene cannot be established (Fig. 90).

THE MINIATURES OF THE HOMILY ON PENTECOST

Pentecost is the theme of the illustrations for this homily.[178] The theme has been rendered pictorially by representing the apostles nimbed and Peter and Paul prominently seated on a bench. The lines of the grouping are either semicircular or straight, and the Gregory miniatures can be classified accordingly. Since the semicircular arrangement is traditional, it is discussed first.

a. *The Apostles Arranged in a Semicircle*

The miniatures in which the semicircular arrangement is found belong to the following manuscripts: Moscow, Hist. Museum 146, fol. 29ᵛ; Oxford, Roe 6, fol. 22ᵛ; Sinai 339, fol. 54ʳ; Athos, Panteleimon 6, fol. 39ᵛ; Paris gr. 550, fol. 37ʳ; Florence, Laur. Plut. VII, 32, fol. 18ᵛ; Athos, Dionysiou 61, fol. 21ᵛ; Paris, Coislin 239, fol. 28ʳ; Vat. gr. 1947, fol. 16ᵛ; Oxford, Canon. gr. 103, fol. 35ʳ; Paris gr. 541, fol. 85ᵛ (flaked); Athens, Nat. Lib. 2554, fol. 25ᵛ; Istanbul, Patr. 16, fol. 33ʳ; Sinai 346, fol. 32ʳ; Vat. gr. 463, fol. 371ʳ (Figs. 6, 439, 382, 143, 410, 262, 359, 360, 203, 124, 277, 258, 65, 344, 91). The miniatures of the last four manuscripts form the initial Π of the homily.

The representation of Pentecost in semicircular form is derived from the Constantinopolitan tradition as it appears in the cod. Paris gr. 510.[179] In contrast to the ninth-century model, however, the miniatures under discussion represent another phase in the development toward greater simplification and hieratic concentration.[180] The architectural setting has been omitted. The semicircle is heightened to the proportions of an arched doorway in which the representatives of the peoples and tongues are placed, rather than in the foreground.

This type is found in all media and is the norm in lectionaries of the eleventh

[178] For the iconography of Pentecost in general see: A. Baumstark, "Il mosaico degli Apostoli nella chiesa abbaziale di Grottaferrata," *Oriens Christianus*, 4 (1904), pp. 121ff.; A. Grabar, "Le schema iconographique de la Pentecoste," *Seminarium Kondakovianum*, 2 (1928), pp. 223ff.; Morey, *AB* (1929), pp. 73ff.; Demus-Diez, p. 84.

[179] Despite the objections raised (see Baumstark, *op.cit.*, and *loc.cit.*), the picture of the cod. Paris gr. 510, was derived from a dome of the church of the Holy Apostles in Constantinople. Grabar, *op.cit.*, pl. xxv, 2, recognized the essential traits of an older prototype of the Pentecost scenes in the miniature of the Carolingian Bible of St. Paolo

fuori le mura, but his views are open to discussion.

[180] Soteriou (1937), p. 84, makes the distinction between the type of Pentecost in "classicizing manuscripts," as the cod. Paris gr. 510, and the schematic renderings of the eleventh- and twelfth-century Byzantine Pentecosts. He derives the former from pictures of ecumenical councils and the latter from a picture like the meeting of physicians in the Dioscurides manuscript of Vienna. Cf. A. v. Premerstein, K. Wessely, and J. Mantuani, *Dioscurides, Codex Aniciae Julianae picturis illustratus, nunc Vindob. Med. gr. I* (Codices Graeci et Latini, x) (facsimile), Leyden 1906, p. 2, fol. 2ᵛ; Beckwith, *Constantinople*, pp. 35ff. n. 50.

century and later. A typical example is furnished by the miniature of the cod. Athos, Dionysiou 587, fol. 36ᵛ, illustrating John 7: 37-39.

In this line of development, the miniature of the cod. Moscow, Hist. Museum 146, is more like the ninth-century model in that the semicircle, which probably encloses three figures, has not yet been heightened (Fig. 6). However, the miniature of the cod. Oxford, Roe 6, has retained more elements of this model (Fig. 439). In addition to the apostles and the representatives of the tongues and peoples, more figures preserved only in the underdrawing appear in the spandrels. Probably they are the people usually seen in the foreground in earlier and more complete representations, for instance, in cod. Paris gr. 510.[181]

The miniature of the cod. Sinai 339 shows four figures within the semicircular area as representatives of the peoples and tongues (Fig. 382).[182] The remaining miniatures in this group include only two representatives, and they appear within the semicircular area, as in the cod. Oxford, Roe 6.

Another interesting illustration occurs in the cod. Vat. gr. 1947, where the doorway has been widened so that the composition is adapted to the particular, bandlike format of the headpiece which is often used by the illustrator of this manuscript (Fig. 124). Special mention should be made of the figured initial Π of the cod. Sinai 346, for, instead of rays descending upon the apostles, a bust of Christ is depicted. His open arms form the top of the letter (Fig. 344).

b. *The Apostles Arranged in a Straight Line*

Only four manuscripts use the linear arrangement: the codd. Jerusalem, Taphou 14, fol. 35ʳ; Milan, Ambros. G 88 sup., fol. 36ᵛ; Oxford, Selden. B. 54, fol. 8ᵛ; and Athos, Vatopedi 107, fol. 35ʳ (Figs. 109, 303, 287, 320). The apostles are seated on a bench, with Peter and Paul in the center on either side of the doorway-like opening, and they receive the tongues of fire descending from a segment of sky. Five of the apostles (Luke, Matthew, Paul, John, and Mark) depicted in the Jerusalem miniature hold books; the others hold scrolls.[183]

Considerations of format may well account for such an arrangement and probably affected the grouping, although traces of the semicircular arrangement have survived in the arch and the two figures beneath it that appear in the Jerusalem and Vatopedi manuscripts. A parallel example of a similar transformation, also the result of spatial limitations, is found in the Pentecost mosaic in Grottaferrata.[184]

Spatial limitations certainly dictated the straight compositional scheme of the

[181] Omont, *Min. gr.* (1929), pl. XLIV.

[182] A close parallel is found in the cod. Istanbul, Patr. 3, reproduced in Soteriou (1937), pl. 55.

[183] Identification is based on their physiognomies. Cf. the mosaics at Cefalu, O. Demus, *The Mosaics of Norman Sicily*, London 1949, pls. 4a, b.

[184] Baumstark, *op.cit.*, p. 130, fig. 2. Another

example of a Pentecost scene arranged in a straight line because of lack of space occurs in the bottom margin of fol. 129ᵛ of Hamilton Psalter (Berlin, Mus. Kgl. Kupferstichkab. 78 A.9). Representations of the apostles side by side may have been used by the artists as models for such an arrangement. Cf. Schultz, *Torcello*, pl. 26.

marginal miniature of the cod. Athos, Vatopedi 107, fol. 35ʳ (Fig. 320). They may also have been the reason for depicting the representatives of the various nations, to whom the Gospel was preached, in the form of busts.

The miniature of the cod. Oxford, Selden. B. 54 is of special interest from the point of view of iconography (Fig. 287). The apostles are sitting or standing—it is not clear which—behind a curtain. This curtain is probably a schematic remnant of the walls which, in the original model, surrounded the scene. Grabar, in suggesting that the miniature of the Bible of St. Paolo fuori le mura better represents the essential traits of the original Pentecost miniature, said that the architectural setting was simplified by the Byzantines. It remained as an architectural background in the cod. Paris gr. 510, but, contrary to representations of the theme in the West, the walls remained alien to the Byzantine Pentecosts of the eleventh and twelfth centuries.[185] If my interpretation is correct, Grabar's conclusions should be reconsidered.

THE MINIATURES OF THE HOMILY ON THE NATIVITY

This homily is illustrated by a scene of the Nativity. Two of the manuscripts, the codd. Sinai 339, fol. 91ᵛ, and Paris gr. 543, fol. 117ᵛ, contain two supplementary miniatures of different subject matter, which are discussed later (p. 144).

The Nativity miniature is the conventional Nativity feast picture predominant in Byzantine art since the Middle Byzantine period.[186] Two iconographic types can be distinguished by considering the posture of the Virgin and the position of the manger in relation to her. In type I the Virgin is lying down and the manger is above her, almost parallel to her body, but in type II the half-seated, half-reclining Virgin is opposite the manger.

a. *Type I*

To this type belong the following miniatures: Athos, Panteleimon 6, fol. 89ᵛ; Paris gr. 541, fol. 163ᵛ; Moscow, Hist. Museum 146, fol. 71ʳ; Vat. gr. 1947, fol. 47ʳ; Paris, Coislin 239, fol. 65ᵛ; Paris gr. 550, fol. 83ʳ; Sinai 339, fol. 91ʳ (title miniature and initial); Athos, Dionysiou 61, fol. 70ʳ; Paris gr. 543, fol. 116ᵛ; and the initial X's of this homily in the codd. Sinai 346, fol. 51ʳ; Vat. gr. 463, fol. 4ʳ; Athos, Stavroniketa 15, fol. 87ʳ; Milan, Ambros. G 88 sup., fol. 95ʳ; and Athens, Nat. Lib. 2554, fol. 60ᵛ (Figs. 148, 10, 129, 219, 414, 384, 364, 462, 346, 80, 434, 308, 259).

In the miniatures of the codd. Athos, Panteleimon 6, and Paris gr. 541—the latter is not well preserved—the composition is dominated by a pyramid-like mountain near the top of which is depicted the conventional Nativity scene (Fig. 148). The Virgin

---

[185] The wall re-appears in later Byzantine representations of councils; see Millet, *Mistra*, pl. 77, 3.

[186] For bibliography on the Nativity, see M. Schmidt, *Die Darstellung der Geburt Christi in der bildenden Kunst*, Stuttgart 1890; Millet, *Recherches*, pp. 93-169; Demus-Diez, p. 49; K. Kalokyres, Ἡ Γέννησις τοῦ Χριστοῦ εἰς τὴν Βυζαντινὴν τέχνην τῆς Ἑλλάδος, Athens 1956.

lies with her head toward the right, supporting it with her left arm. The Child, in a rectangular manger next to her, faces the same direction. At the left in the Athos, and at the right in the Paris miniatures, Joseph, looking pensive, is seated on a rock lower on the mountain with his back turned to both the Infant and the mother.[187] The scene includes the Bathing of the Child in the foreground.[188]

Two complementary scenes are added to this main part of the composition: the Adoration of the Magi on the left, and the Annunciation to the Shepherds on the right. The old shepherd, dressed in a *melote*, a sheep's skin, and leaning on a stick, is a familiar figure in eleventh-century iconography.[189] The miniature of the cod. Moscow, Hist. Museum 146 is flaked and it is impossible to tell whether or not the Adoration of the Magi was included (Fig. 10). Certainly this episode has not been used in the otherwise similar miniatures of the codd. Vat. gr. 1947, and Paris, Coislin 239 (Figs. 129, 219). Moreover, in the Vatican miniature there are only two singing angels and in the Coislin miniature, despite the fact that the shepherd is there, the annunciating angel has been omitted because of the narrow space available. Furthermore, in the Coislin miniature, Joseph turns his head toward the mother of the Child.

The three scenes described here as one were originally treated separately in the sequence of the Gospel account.[190] In the course of time, however, and under the influence of the liturgy, these narrative episodes were regrouped and transformed into what is called a feast picture. This evolution took place when the text of the Gospel formed another book, the lectionary, in which the lections of the episodes were placed together. Those accounts (Matt. 1: 18, Luke 2: 1, Matt. 2: 1) formed the readings for Christmas Eve, and two of them, the Nativity and the Adoration, were also the lections for Christmas Day, the day when all three events were commemorated.[191] The regrouping of the texts was followed by the gradual combination of the three scenes into one. Weitzmann has pointed out this transformation and its derivation "from a system of reducing the scenes . . . and of elaborating those of liturgical significance."[192] Thus the combination became the typical illustration of the lections for Christmas, as seen in the lectionary of Nicephorus Phocas in Lavra.[193] In the eleventh century it was used also in the illustrations of the four Gospels. Since Gregory's homily

---

[187] For a possible theological significance of Joseph's action, see K. Weitzmann, *The Fresco Cycle of St. Maria di Castelseprio*, Princeton 1951, pp. 67ff.

[188] For a discussion of the scene of the Bathing of the Child, see Weitzmann, *op.cit.*, p. 54; *idem, Semin. Kondak.* (1936), pp. 90-91.

[189] Millet, *Recherches*, p. 127.

[190] The Annunciation to the Shepherds in a treatment independent of the Nativity episode, appeared in the mosaics of Gaza, in the column of San Marco, in cod. Laur. Plut. vi, 23; see Millet, *Recherches*, pp. 124-25. In cod. Paris gr. 74, reproduced in Omont, *Evangiles*, i, pl. 96, the

Nativity is represented with the Annunciation to the Shepherds, but the Adoration is still treated separately. Even in the so-called Menologion of Basil the episode of the Nativity and the Adoration appear separately; see *Il menologio*, pp. 271, 272.

[191] See Μηναῖον Δεκεμβρίου, Athens n.d., p. 229; E. Gedeon, Βυζαντινὸν Ἑορτολόγιον, Constantinople 1899, pp. 203-204.

[192] Weitzmann, *N. T. Mss Studies*, p. 159.

[193] Cf. Nativity in the lectionary of the Skevophylakion of Lavra, Weitzmann, *Semin. Kondak.* (1936), pl. ii, 2.

was part of the lections for December 25, the illustrations of the Christmas lections could easily be borrowed to illustrate it as well.

In the feast picture, as exemplified in the Panteleimon miniature, there is a hieratic concentration and the emphasis is on the most important scene, in this case the Nativity episode. This episode has kept a narrative character, for it is not conflated with the scene depicting the Adoration. The two episodes are still discrete. The Magi are coming from behind the mountain, whereas the mother, because of her posture and position, is not related to them and cannot receive their gifts for the Child.[194] This distinguishing of the two episodes despite the formal unification is characteristic of type I. In this respect the Panteleimon miniature finds its closest parallel in the twelfth- or thirteenth-century lectionary in Berlin, cod. Hamilton 246, fol. 50ʳ.[195]

An attempt to relate the two episodes is apparent in the miniatures of the cod. Paris gr. 550 (Fig. 414). The Virgin faces the right and her reclining position is less accentuated than in the Panteleimon miniature. The rectangular manger with the Child still parallels her body. Despite the fact that the Virgin is thus spatially and compositionally closer to the adoring Magi, she is still not related to them, since her eyes are turned in a different direction. Another interesting iconographic feature of this miniature is the posture of Joseph, who seems to turn toward her. He sits not on a rock but on a wooden saddle, an allusion both to the journey of Mary and Joseph to Bethlehem and to the place of Christ's birth.[196] Three shepherds hear the good tidings; one, who points to the angel, has been placed in the margin with his flock around him. At the top of the frame are two half-figures of angels with veiled hands, with a cross and a dove between them. A close parallel, also including the saddle, occurs in the lectionary of Lavra.[197]

The similar miniature of the cod. Sinai 339, which includes all three episodes, shows another attempt to relate the Nativity scene to the Adoration (Fig. 384). The Virgin has turned her head, which is resting on her right arm, toward the Magi. A more hieratic effect has been achieved by the addition of two other angels on the right, next to the angel who speaks to the shepherds. The additional figures balance the composition of the three angels on the left. In the similar miniature of the cod. Athos, Dionysiou 61, the Magi have not been included (Fig. 364).

In the miniature of the cod. Paris gr. 543, Joseph has been moved from the left to the right (Fig. 462). This change in composition frees the space he formerly occupied for the Magi, who now are in the foreground moving toward the Virgin. A desire to relate the two episodes is probably responsible for the change. Still, the Virgin does not look at the Magi, but at the midwife who pours water into a basin, which centers

---

[194] The Virgin usually receives the Magi seated, the Child either on her lap (cf. cod. Vat. gr. 1156, fol. 279ᵛ reproduced in Millet, *Recherches*, fig. 94), or in the manger (cod. Laur. Plut. VI, 23, fol. 8ᵛ, reproduced in Millet, *Recherches*, fig. 86).

[195] J. Ebersolt, "Miniatures byzantines de Berlin,"

Revue archéologique, 2 (1905), pp. 55ff., fig. 4; Weitzmann, *Buchmalerei*, p. 68 n. 404; here the more complete bibliography.

[196] Weitzmann, *Semin. Kondak.* (1936), p. 89 n. 30.

[197] Weitzmann, *Semin. Kondak.* (1936), pl. II, 2.

Mary's attention on the Bathing of the Child. The six angels, three on each side, add to the hieratic concept of the composition, creating an equilibrium of masses and lines. A similar example with Joseph at the right of the composition appears in an icon at the British Museum dating from the fourteenth century.[198]

In the initials mentioned above, only the Nativity scene is shown (Figs. 346, 80, 434, 308, 259), but the figure of the Virgin suggests the derivation of these illustrations from a complete title miniature of type I. Joseph's expressive profile in the initial of the cod. Sinai 339 deserves special mention.

b. *Type II*

The problem of relating the Nativity and Adoration scenes is successfully solved by the miniatures of type II, in which the two scenes are conflated. This conflation was achieved by a change in the posture of the Virgin, who is half-reclining, half-seated. The following miniatures belong to this type: Jerusalem, Taphou 14, fol. 81^r; Oxford, Roe 6, fol. 30^v; Oxford, Canon. gr. 103, fol. 79^v; Florence, Laur. Plut. VII, 32, fol. 63^r; and the initial X of this homily in the cod. Istanbul, Patr. 16, fol. 78^v (Figs. 113, 440, 281, 267, 69).

All three scenes are shown in the miniature of the cod. Jerusalem, Taphou 14, which is the most complete and the best preserved of those mentioned (Fig. 113). The half-seated, half-reclining Virgin links the two scenes for, although her body faces the Magi, her head is turned toward the Child. She also extends her right hand and touches the Child, a motif which betrays the derivation of the type. In the seated type she is often shown touching the Child with both hands, a gesture which, according to Millet, is of Syrian origin[199] and implies that she is either about to lift the Child's head[200] or to take him onto her lap to receive the gifts of the Magi.[201] Since in this type she is not completely seated, the birth episode has not yet been replaced by the receiving of the gifts from the adoring Magi. By this conflation, the Nativity feast picture achieves real unification.

Joseph, who has turned his back to the Child, sits on a wooden saddle. The old shepherd on the right stands between two young ones, looking directly at the annunciating angel. The closest parallel examples of this type occur in the codd. Vat. Urb. gr. 2, fol. 20^v, and Paris gr. 74, fol. 4^r.[202] The latter includes the Arrival of the Magi instead of the Adoration.

Slight variations of the same iconography are observed in the full-page miniature of the cod. Oxford, Roe 6 (Fig. 440). In this case the Virgin does not tend the Child. Another variation may be seen in the foreground: a preceding phase, the Testing of

---

[198] Lazarev, *History*, II, pl. 310. Other examples: Peribleptos at Mistra, Millet, *Mistra*, pl. 118, 1; cod. Paris gr. 54, fol. 13^v, Omont, *Min. gr.* (1929), pl. XCII, 1.

[199] Millet, *Recherches*, pp. 116, 146.

[200] See cod. Laur. Plut. VI, 23, fol. 6^v, Millet,

Recherches, p. 147, fig. 86.

[201] See examples in the cod. Vat. gr. 1613, *Il menologio*, p. 272.

[202] Stornajolo, *Giacomo monaco*, pl. 84. Millet, *Recherches*, fig. 100. Cf. Omont, *Evangiles*, I, pl. 6.

the Water, is represented, rather than the Bathing of the Child. The Child rests on the midwife's lap,[203] while an assistant pours the water. Joseph seems to turn his head to the Nativity scene proper, while a young shepherd on the other side points it out to an old shepherd, recalling the Nativity scene in the cod. Parma, Pal. 5.[204] Again the emphasis has been on the main episode, and the hieratic concentration of the picture is stressed by the four angels singing the Doxology.

The miniature of the Oxford manuscript is also interesting from a formal point of view. The proportions of the figures are elongated, and the small space between the various episodes gives the impression that the composition has been compressed from the sides to gain height. This was evidently the result of an attempt to fit a striplike title miniature into the format of a full page.

Although all three episodes have been included in the miniature of the cod. Oxford, Canon. gr. 103, their close relationship has been lost because of the layout of the illustration (Fig. 281). The Nativity is placed on the top bar of the frame which includes the title of the homily. The posture of the Virgin is similar to that in the miniatures discussed so far, although she appears more reclining than seated, probably because of the narrow space available. Here again, as in the Jerusalem miniature, the Virgin touches the Child. The Bathing of the Child has been retained in its original position below the birth episode; below it, in the lower part of the left lateral bar, the Three Magi are depicted, probably placed there because of the format. The seated Joseph is their pendant counterpart in the right lateral bar, and above him are two shepherds. The Nativity miniature of the cod. Florence, Laur. Plut. VII, 32 (a teaching scene below it has already been discussed) includes neither the Adoration nor the Annunciation to the Shepherds (Fig. 267).

As mentioned earlier only one historical initial, that of the cod. Istanbul, Patr. 16, belongs to type II (Fig. 69). A comparison of this initial X with those belonging to type I is very instructive, as it shows the ingenuity of the artist who tried to adapt a complete title miniature to an initial. In the initials of both types, the center of the letter is formed by the manger. In type I, some artists use the figure of the Virgin to form one of the upper arms of the letter, which her posture fits (Figs. 308, 259). Other artists ingeniously confine the Virgin and Child to the center and use flying angels to form the upper arms of the latter (Fig. 384). In the second type the posture of the Virgin lends itself to forming part of the upper and lower left arm of the letter; and for this reason type II is much more easily adapted to the initial. The other elements of the composition have been preserved in their original place and the letter is formed without the device of the flying angels.

In contrast to all those artists who illustrate the initial X's with a Nativity scene,

[203] The motif of the Child sitting on the midwife's lap is common in representations of the Nativity in the Middle Byzantine period. Another example may be found in cod. Iviron 5, fol. 8ᵛ;

see A. Xyngopoulos, Ἱστορημένα Εὐαγγέλια τῆς Μονῆς Ἰβήρων Ἁγίου Ὄρους, Athens 1932, pl. 17.
[204] Reproduced in Lazarev, *History*, I, pl. XXVI.

the illustrator of the cod. Turin, Univ. Lib. C. I. 6, fol. 55ᵛ, displays greater originality in his choice. The title miniature has been cut out, but the initial X has survived and is formed by four flying angels who hold a medallion with a bust of Christ-Emmanuel (Fig. 48). The composition is not a new invention. Yet the choice of this particular iconographic type clearly shows that the artist was aware of its theological connotations. He chose to open the text of the homily on the Nativity not with a conventional Nativity scene (he may have used such a composition in the title miniature) but with an illustration which declared the great event of the Incarnation: Emmanuel meaning "God with us." Once again this miniature is another example which bears witness to the inner connection that exists between word and image in Byzantine art, and to the role of the artist as well.

THE MINIATURES OF THE HOMILIES ON EPIPHANY AND HOLY BAPTISM

The themes of the illustrations chosen for these homilies refer to the events commemorated at the festivals on which the sermons were read. They focus on Christ's Baptism and the activities of John the Baptist.

a. *Scenes Treated Separately*
—Christ's Baptism

The illustration of the homily on Epiphany in cod. Jerusalem, Taphou 14, fol. 173ʳ, represents the feast picture of Christ's Baptism (Fig. 115). Christ is immersed in the river Jordan, with the water reaching his shoulders. He is turned slightly toward John, who stands in his usual posture, wearing the himation and the chlamys. On the right bank two angels stand in familiar poses and the personification of the Jordan holding an urn reclines at the feet of Christ. The river flows between two rocky mountains. On the left a tree completes the picture.

This is the typical Byzantine type of the Baptism feast picture as it was developed in the tenth and eleventh centuries and as it is exemplified in book illumination and monumental art of the Constantinopolitan area.[205] A miniature similar to that of the Jerusalem manuscript is found in the lectionary Athos, Panteleimon 2, fol. 221ᵛ.[206]

The variations of this standard feast picture are slight and concern primarily the number of angels and the inclusion or exclusion of the personification of the Jordan. The latter has been excluded in the small miniature of the cod. Paris, Coislin 239, fol. 120ʳ, which is otherwise similar to the Jerusalem miniature and finds a parallel in the lectionary Iviron cod. 1, fol. 254ʳ (Fig. 226).[207]

[205] On the iconography of the Baptism see: J. Strzygowski, *Ikonographie der Taufe Christi*, Munich 1885; O. Dalton, *Byzantine Art and Archaeology*, Oxford 1911, pp. 654ff.; Millet, *Recherches*, pp. 170ff.; G. de Jerphanion, "Epiphanie et Théophanie," *Voix des monuments*, Paris-Brussels 1930, pp. 165ff.; Demus-Diez, pp. 57ff.

[206] Millet, *Recherches*, fig. 132.

[207] Xyngopoulos, *op.cit.*, pl. 7.

In two iconographic details the miniature of the cod. Oxford, Roe 6, fol. 73ᵛ, differs from those in the Jerusalem and Coislin codices (Fig. 442). One of Christ's legs is placed in front of the other as if he were walking toward John, who is dressed not in the himation and chlamys but in a *tunica exomis*. Christ's posture is the same, but reversed, in the miniature of the cod. Moscow, Hist. Museum 146, fol. 133ᵛ, in which the hand of God and two flying angels have been included (Fig. 12). According to Millet this posture is common in the twelfth century,[208] but John's tunic, seen in the Oxford manuscript, is an old element appearing in early representations of the type Millet has called "Hellenistic."[209] Both details find parallels in miniatures of the Middle Byzantine period.[210] It should be pointed out that a similar type of John, appearing, however, in the scene of the people's baptism, occurs in the lectionary of Dionysiou 587, fol. 137ʳ.[211] John wearing the *tunica exomis* is found also in the title miniature of the homily on Epiphany in cod. Paris gr. 550, fol. 153ʳ, and in the initial Π of the same homily in cod. Sinai 339, fol. 197ᵛ (Figs. 422, 387). In the title miniature of the Paris codex, the story of Christ's Baptism is told with simplicity. The absence of a landscape is characteristic. In the initials Π and Χ of both homilies in the same manuscript, and in the initial Χ of the cod. Sinai 339, fol. 217ʳ, John is dressed in the ancient costume (Figs. 422, 423, 393). A similar type of John is also chosen for the historiated initial Π in the cod. Athos, Dionysiou 61, fol. 77ʳ (Fig. 368).

A new iconographic motif is introduced with the cross that stands in the river which Christ blesses, in the miniature of the cod. Vat. gr. 1947, fol. 87ᵛ, illustrating the homily on Epiphany (Fig. 132). This iconographic element is related to the Palestinian literary tradition, according to which a cross was erected at the place of Christ's Baptism in the Jordan.[212] A parallel example can be seen in the eleventh-century lectionary of S. Giorgio dei Greci in Venice, fol. 362ʳ.

The initials Π of the homily on Epiphany in the codd. Oxford, Canon. gr. 103, fol. 146ʳ, Milan, Ambros. G 88 sup., fol. 163ʳ, and Π and Χ of both homilies in the codd. Vat. gr. 463, fols. 107ʳ and 127ʳ, Sinai 346, fols. 112ᵛ and 123ʳ, and Istanbul, Patr. 16, fols. 144ᵛ and 156ᵛ, are derived from title miniatures which depict John wearing the ancient costume (Figs. 283, 310, 82, 83, 347, 348, 71, 72). The initials of the Vatican miniatures present an interesting iconographic motif (Figs. 82, 83). John stands on the right, which means that these figured initials are derived from scenes that had adopted this arrangement; an example can be seen in the eleventh-century Vatican lectionary cod. gr. 1156.[213] In the marginal drawing of the cod. Athos, Vatopedi 107, fol. 93ᵛ, John appears in the usual posture (Fig. 326).

[208] Millet, *Recherches*, p. 182.

[209] Millet, *Recherches*, pp. 170, 182, 183.

[210] The closest parallel is the miniature of the cod. Paris gr. 74, fol. 6ʳ, reproduced in Omont, *Evangiles*, I, pl. 9, 1.

[211] Other examples of the same type of John are found in cod. Vienna Theol. gr. 154, fols. 145ʳ, 221ᵛ, 222ʳ.

[212] The pilgrims specified that the cross was of metal and that it was placed on a marble column. Texts and discussion in Jerphanion, *op.cit.*, pp. 169ff.

[213] Millet, *Recherches*, fig. 141 and p. 179 for a discussion of the motif and examples.

The miniatures underwent only minor compositional adaptations in their transformation from headpieces to initials. The central composition, i.e. Christ being baptized by John, could easily be adjusted to the shape of the Π. Some artists depicted both participants on the same level, so that John's arm would form the horizontal bar of the letter (Fig. 71). Other artists kept John's diagonal gesture (Fig. 347); still others used the two figures only for the vertical bars (Figs. 283, 310). The use of gestures for the formation of parts of a letter is common.[214]

As was the case with the initial X in the homily on the Nativity, flying angels here again form the upper arms of that letter. The formation of the lower part shows the minor compositional adaptations that each artist introduced. In two cases, John and Christ have kept their original positions (Figs. 423, 72). While the artist of the cod. Paris gr. 550 is satisfied with the portrayal of the two participants (probably because more detailed miniatures already existed in the headpieces of this manuscript), the artist of the Patriarchal manuscript attempts to include all the iconographic elements extant in the model. He therefore depicts the personification of the Jordan below John. This attempt is evident in other initials of the same manuscript already discussed (Fig. 69), and it reveals the artist's awareness of the fact that the system of decorating the initials is the only one that can be applied to this manuscript, and his desire to be as complete as possible.

In two other cases, both principal figures are on the same level and placed diagonally so that their heads form the center of the letter (Figs. 83, 348). Right above them, in the former example, and still within the body of the letter, the artist has chosen to present the Holy Spirit in the shape of a dove.

A treatment of landscape differing from that in the title miniatures discussed above, and a different iconographic type of John as well, appear in the Baptism scene of the upper register of the miniature in the cod. Paris gr. 543, fol. 197ᵛ (Fig. 464). The composition of the Baptism includes the main participants with three angels instead of two. The water of the river, however, does not form a dome around the body of Christ. Instead, the rocky, hard, zigzag banks of the Jordan are distinctly separated, and the straight horizon of the water is most conspicuous. John wears what the Evangelists Mark and Matthew call "a robe of camel's hair and a leather girdle about his loins" (Mark 1: 6, Matt. 3: 4). The treatment of the landscape setting and the figure of John find close parallels in works of Palaeologan times, such as in the Baptistery of St. Mark in Venice.[215]

---

[214] See, for example, the letter E whose horizontal bar is often formed by the extended hand of Gregory or other teachers; cf. Sinai 339, fol. 42ᵛ (Fig. 380).

[215] The straight horizon of the water and the type of John dressed in camel's hair do not appear for the first time in the Palaeologan period. For instance the straight horizon appears in cod. Vat. Urb. gr. 2, Millet, *Recherches*, fig. 139. A close parallel to the posture and dress of John is found in the Capella Palatina, Palermo, see O. Demus, *The Mosaics of Norman Sicily*, London 1949, pl. 19a.

–Christ Meeting John

This episode, described in the Gospel of Matthew (3: 13-15), is depicted in the lower left register of the miniature of the cod. Paris gr. 543, fol. 197ᵛ (Fig. 464). John, wearing the same robe of camel's hair that he does in the miniature of the upper register, bows slightly before Christ, who with a cruciform nimbus advances slowly toward him, extending his right arm in a gesture of benediction. Christ's movement has been superbly rendered by the artist and contrasts the rigid angularity of the ascetic John. The meeting takes place in a rocky landscape. This scene finds its closest parallels in illustrated lectionaries such as the codd. Athos, Dionysiou 6, fol. 241ᵛ, and Panteleimon 2, fol. 221ʳ.[216]

–John Preaching to the People

In the same cod. Paris gr. 543, and the lower register (right half) of the full-page miniature, fol. 197ᵛ, the episode of John Preaching to the People is depicted.[217] The artist has represented John as in the previous scene, but holding a staff bearing a cross on it. In the group of people standing opposite John, the artist has attempted to differentiate the figures by varying their postures. The closest parallel is again to be found in the lectionary of Dionysiou 587, fol. 8ʳ, and in the Gospel book Paris gr. 74, fol. 64ᵛ.[218]

–John Baptizing the People

Mark (1: 4, 5) gives the most detailed account of this episode, which illustrates the homily on Baptism in the codd. Paris gr. 543, fol. 213ᵛ, and Paris gr. 550, fol. 166ᵛ (Figs. 465, 423). The miniature of the latter is simpler than that of the former and lacks a landscape background. Instead it shows five angels flying down toward the people who are being baptized. The angels do not appear in the miniature of the cod. Paris gr. 543, which also differs in the number of figures participating in the scene, in the type of John, and in the treatment of the landscape. The closest parallel to these miniatures is the representation of this episode in the lectionary of Dionysiou 587, fol. 137ʳ. The scene is also illustrated in Gospel books.

Although parallels to the scenes discussed above are found in lectionaries and narrative Gospels, the lectionary constitutes the most plausible source for the illustrations of the homilies. Not only can it be demonstrated that the Gospels were definitely influenced by the lectionary, but the fact that the two homilies were read on the festival of Epiphany, and on the following day dedicated to St. John the Baptist, argues for the dependence of their illustrations on a lectionary. The argument in favor of a lec-

---

[216] The Panteleimon miniature is reproduced in K. Weitzmann, *Aus den Bibliotheken des Athos*, Hamburg 1963, pp. 81-83.

[217] The episode of John Preaching to the People occurs in all four Gospels: Matt. 3: 1-6; Mark 1: 4-7; Luke 3: 3-11; John 1: 15-18. The most complete account is given by Matthew.

[218] Omont, *Evangiles*, I, pl. 58.

90

tionary can be strengthened further by the following observations. Only the Gospels of Matthew and John mention all four episodes. There, however, the sequence of the episodes is this: John Preaching, John Baptizing the People, John Bearing Witness or Meeting Christ, and the Baptism of Christ.[219] The same sequence is observed in the extant illustrations for these Gospels.[220] This sequence does not agree with the order of the illustrations in the manuscript of the homilies. Admittedly, there is no reason why the scenes of the upper register in the two homilies on Christ's Baptism and the Baptism of the People should follow the order in which they occur in the Gospel. These are the principal miniatures and should be placed on top, no matter what their source. The illustrator of the cod. Paris gr. 543 was consistent in this respect throughout the manuscript.

The same explanation, however, cannot be offered for the order of the miniatures of the lower register. If the artist did derive the lower register miniatures from an illustrated Gospel book, why did he reverse their order, presenting first the Meeting of Christ and then the Preaching of John? This difficulty can be overcome if the use of a lectionary is accepted. The first lection for the day of the feast of Epiphany refers to Christ's Baptism and this is the principal illustration appearing in lectionaries.[221] The lection concerning the Meeting of Christ and John follows the Baptism and this order has also been observed in the lectionary illustrations. For example, in the lectionary of Athos, Dionysiou 587, fol. 141ᵛ, the principal miniature is the Baptism, while the Meeting appears as a secondary miniature in the margin. If the illustrations of the lections for Epiphany are accepted as possible sources for the miniatures of the homilies, the reversed order can be explained: the artist borrowed both miniatures from the same page of a lectionary and kept their original order. Since the second miniature was much smaller than the first, an empty space was left on the lower register, which he filled by borrowing an illustration from the lection of the Eve of Epiphany, referring to John's preaching.[222]

—Christ Baptizing Peter

In the lower corner of the left margin of the cod. Athos, Vatopedi 107, fol. 105ᵛ, the homily on Holy Baptism is illustrated by Christ baptizing a nimbed figure in a font, identified by an inscription as Peter the Apostle, while two other nimbed figures watch the scene (Fig. 327).

According to the canonical Gospels, Christ never baptized his disciples in a font,

[219] Matt. 3; John 1: 15-34; cf. Mark 1: 3-9; Luke 3: 3-22.

[220] See cod. Florence, Laur. Plut. VI, 23, fols. 7ᵛ, 8ʳ; cf. cod. Paris gr. 74 in Omont, *Evangiles*, I, pls. 8, 9, 58; II, pls. 99, 143-45.

[221] The lection of the Matins of January 6 is Mark 1: 9-11; the lection of the liturgy is Matt. 3: 13-17; see M. Saliveros ed., Τὸ Θεῖον καὶ Ἱερὸν Εὐαγγέλιον, Athens 1899, p. 214.

[222] The lection of the first hour is Matt. 3: 1-6; and that of the third hour is Mark 1: 1-5. See Saliveros, *op.cit.*, p. 212. For illustrations of these episodes in lectionaries, cf. cod. Dionysiou 587, fols. 141ᵛ and 137ʳ, K. Weitzmann, "Byzantine Miniature and Icon Painting in the Eleventh Century," *Proceedings of the XIIIth Inter. Congress of Byzantine Studies, Oxford 1966*, London 1967, pl. 3.

but in the chronicle of Hippolytus of Thebes, Pope of Rome, it is stated that only Peter was baptized by Christ.[223] No evidence has been produced so far to show that the chronicle of Hippolytus was illustrated and there is no reason to assume that this miniature was originally made for it. It seems more likely that the illustrator used as his model a miniature like the one in the lectionary Athos, Dionysiou 587, fol. 13^r, which shows Christ baptizing a person in a font while three disciples stand by and a fourth stands behind Him.[224] The artist of the Vatopedi miniature either misunderstood this model, or adapted it, aware perhaps of the tradition that survived in Hippolytus. Thus the illustrator conceived the Baptism of the People of which the homily speaks as prefigured in the Baptism of the apostles.[225]

b. *Conflated Scenes*

The miniature of the cod. Florence, Laur. Plut. VII, 32, fol. 110^v, extending over both columns, contains the figure of Gregory—already discussed in the chapter on the teaching scene—and a Baptism scene (Fig. 270). Christ blesses the water, in which stands a marble column surmounted by a cross. An interesting iconographic motif is the personification of the Jordan riding a dolphin.[226] On the right is a swimming figure, while a boy has thrown off his garment and is about to jump into the water. This miniature is apparently formed by a conflation of two scenes, the Baptism of the People and the Baptism of Christ. The closest parallel which stems from a similar conflation and also includes the cross is found in the thirteenth-century lectionary cod. Paris syr. 355.[227]

A similar Baptism scene appears in the miniature of the cod. Sinai 339, fol. 197^v, which illustrates the homily on Epiphany (Fig. 389). John is again dressed in the ancient tunic, but the Baptism is conflated with another scene, that of the disciples Andrew and John, half concealed behind the rock, bearing testimony to Christ's Baptism. That scene belonged originally to another which illustrated John 1: 35.[228] A separate treatment of each episode occurs in Gospel books and also in lectionaries, wherein the closest parallels are found.[229]

[223] F. Diekamp, *Hippolytos von Theben*, Munich 1898, p. 27.

[224] The miniature in the Dionysiou lectionary is a literal illustration of John 3: 22. Historically speaking, however, this illustration is not accurate, for it contradicts John 4: 1-2, according to which "Jesus himself baptized not, but his disciples." Another illustration depicting Christ baptizing a person in a font occurs in the Hamilton Psalter, fol. 121^r, in Berlin.

[225] For the Baptism of the Apostles, cf. E. Kantorowicz, "The Baptism of the Apostles," *Dumbarton Oaks Papers*, 9-10 (1956), pp. 203-51.

[226] The Jordan riding a dolphin is not a common iconographic motif. More usual is the motif of a personification of the sea riding a dolphin or other charger; cf. the frescoes of Gračanica and Vatopedi reproduced in Millet, *Recherches*, figs. 172, 180.

[227] Millet, *Recherches*, fig. 144.

[228] In John 1: 35, the disciples are not named. It was John Chrysostom who named one of them as Andrew. See *PG*, 59, 117; cf. Millet, *Recherches*, p. 190.

[229] See cod. Florence, Laur. Plut. VI, 23, reproduced in Millet, *Recherches*, fig. 157; also cod. Dionysiou 587 fol. 8^r. Further examples may be seen in cod. Vat. gr. 1613, *Il menologio*, p. 299, in the mosaics of Daphni, Demus-Diez, pl. XL.

Not only is the scene of the two disciples conflated with the representation of the Baptism, but it is also found combined with the Baptism of the People. This threefold conflation occurs in the cod. Athos, Dionysiou 61, fol. 77ʳ (Fig. 365). The closest parallel depicting the same three events conflated occurs in the Gospel book Vat. Urb. gr. 2, which was influenced by a lectionary.[230]

The two disciples also appear in the miniature of the cod. Moscow, Hist. Museum 146, fol. 145ʳ (Fig. 13). Here the scene to which they belong has been conflated with the Baptism of the People. John stands on the left bank of the Jordan and a group of Israelites on the right bank. Some people are diving into the water while others are swimming. On the left lower side, a mother is preparing her small child for immersion, while on the opposite bank another woman seems to be helping a boy to dress. Below them another boy, seated on the ground, is taking off or putting on his shoes. These very charming details imbue this religious picture with the spirit of a genre scene. At the roots of the tree behind John, however, there is an axe which belongs to the episode of John preaching (Luke 3: 9). This episode is the theme of the lection for January 5 (Eve of Epiphany), an illustration of which is found in the lectionary Dionysiou 587, fol. 138ʳ. The Moscow miniature is therefore the result of the conflation of three distinct scenes.

Again three scenes conflated into one are found in the miniature of the cod. Paris gr. 533, fol. 146ʳ, that illustrates the homily on Epiphany (Fig. 246). In this case the Meeting of John and Christ is associated with the scene showing the two disciples— now represented as Andrew and Peter—and with the Baptism of the People. No other example is known to me in which the representation of the two disciples is conflated with the Meeting scene.

The same manuscript includes a second miniature on fol. 154ʳ, illustrating the same homily and presenting another conflation, which occurs also in the miniature of the cod. Athos, Panteleimon 6, fol. 161ʳ, illustrating the homily on Holy Baptism (Figs. 247, 173). The main theme is the Baptism scene in its usual depiction. The only difference here lies in the absence of the personification of the Jordan. The axe at the root of the tree from the episode of John preaching is present. A similarly conflated scene appears in the twelfth-century Evangelarion no. 3 of the Patriarchal Library in Istanbul, fol. 3ᵛ.[231]

The parallel examples indicate that the nature of the various combinations in the miniatures discussed probably presupposes a lectionary and that, in fact, such conflations occurred in lectionaries, or in Gospel books influenced by lectionaries. It follows from this reasoning that a lectionary must have been the source of the miniatures for these sermons.

[230] Millet, *Recherches*, fig. 139. In this example there are three disciples pictured to correspond to the three angels. See *ibid.*, p. 190 n. 3.

[231] Soteriou (1937), pl. 56. This example includes the personification of the Jordan. Further examples: mosaics of Hosios Loukas; cod. Paris gr. 54; mosaic of the Baptistery of San Marco in Venice; see Millet, *Recherches*, figs. 140, 149, 150.

In addition to the feast pictures already discussed, other themes have been chosen to illustrate the first homily on Easter and the homilies on Easter and New Sunday. One of these themes, the Deesis, is liturgical, while the other, the personification of Church and Synagogue, is an allegorical representation of a liturgical concept. It is convenient to discuss the illustrations of the two themes separately.

a. *The Deesis*

The cod. Athos, Stavroniketa 15, fol. 1ʳ, contains an illustration at the head of the first homily on Easter, which consists of eight small medallions inserted in the square decorative frame enclosing the title of the sermon (Fig. 431). The three top medallions show Christ flanked by the Virgin and John the Baptist, thus forming a Deesis.[232] The Deesis or *trimorphon* represents God the Son with the "blessed among women" and the man about whom it was written that "among those born of women there is none greater."[233] The Mother of God and St. John intercede for mankind, *pro ecclesia*, before the Supreme Judge.

The Deesis often does not constitute a mere trimorphon, but it may include, in the ivories for instance,[234] apostles and saints, and church fathers. The miniature under discussion presents a similar case in that the five additional medallions represent church fathers. Four of the Fathers can be identified from their inscriptions. Below Mary is Gregory of Nazianzus. Gregory Thaumaturgos, John Chrysostom, and Gregory of Nyssa are in the lower part of the frame. The bust in the fifth medallion, now flaked, perhaps represented Basil the Great. Therefore, the miniature as a whole, like the ivories, represents the intercessory supplication offered up before Christ by the Virgin, John the Baptist, and the church fathers.

As an expression of intercession, the Deesis theme, which is derived from the liturgy, was not created for any specific liturgical book. On the contrary, since it could be used alone in any medium, it could appear in any liturgical book.[235] Its frequent position at the beginning of books can be explained by the nature of the theme, the prayer of

---

[232] For bibliography and discussion of the iconography of the Deesis, see T. Whitemore, *The Mosaics of St. Sophia at Istanbul* (Fourth preliminary report), Oxford 1952, pp. 23ff.; C. Osieczkowska, "La mosaïque de la porte royale à Ste. Sophie de Constantinople et la litanie de tous les saints," *Byzantion*, 9 (1934), pp. 41-83. Cf. G. Soteriou, "Χριστιανικὴ καὶ Βυζαντινὴ Εἰκονογραφία," Θεολογία, 26 (1956), p. 10; E. Kantorowicz, "Ivories and Litanies," *Journal of Warburg and Courtauld Inst.*, 5 (1942), pp. 56-84; O. Pächt, "The 'Avignon Diptych' and its Eastern Ancestry," *De Artibus Opuscula XL, Essays in Honor of E. Panofsky*, New York 1961, pp. 402-21.

[233] Whitemore, *op.cit.*, p. 24.

[234] Kantorowicz, *op.cit.*, p. 70, pls. 18, 19.

[235] Cf. aristocratic psalter in Berlin, Univ. Mus. fol. 2ʳ; see G. Stuhlfauth, "A Greek Psalter with Byzantine Miniatures," *AB*, 15 (1923), pp. 311-26, fig. 8; cf. also cod. Sinai gr. 418, fol. 290ʳ, reproduced in Martin, *Ladder*, pl. LXXVI, 216. In addition to the manuscripts and ivories, representations of the Deesis appear in other media and objects, such as the reliquary of the Holy Cross at Limburg on the Lahn; see M. Ross, "Basil the Proedros, Patron of the Arts," *Archaeology*, 11 (1958), pp. 271, 272; for a color reproduction, see Talbot Rice, *Byzantium*, pl. X, p. 318, no. 124 (here the more complete bibliography).

intercession. In lectionaries, it is placed at the beginning of the lection for Easter which opens the ecclesiastical year. Two characteristic examples are the twelfth-century lectionaries of the National Library of Athens, cod. 2645, fol. 1ʳ, and the Sinai cod. 208, fol. 1ᵛ.

The manuscripts of Gregory's homilies, like the lectionaries, placed the Deesis miniature at the top of the opening page where the sermon on Easter begins. In other words, the Deesis scene is another example showing the relationship between the two liturgical books. Thus the Deesis miniature, like the Anastasis discussed earlier, becomes another introductory miniature in the lectionaries and likewise in the homilies of Gregory.

The small miniature of the cod. Oxford, Selden. B. 54, fol. 62ʳ, doubtless was derived from a Deesis scene which had found a place in the homilies of Gregory (Fig. 292). The miniature illustrates the homily on Epiphany and not that on Easter, but it has not been misplaced for, in fact, an adaptation of the original Deesis has occurred: the place of the Virgin Mary has been taken by Gregory of Nazianzus. Thus the standing Christ, who holds a Gospel and pronounces a benediction, is flanked on the right by Gregory and on the left by John the Baptist. These two complementary figures are represented in three-quarter view and in an attitude of prayer. The concept of intercessory supplication is retained, but the presence of Gregory instead of Mary has given a particular character to this miniature and transformed it into an illustration of Gregory's homilies in general, if not of a specific homily.

b. *The Personification of Church and Synagogue*

The theme of Church and Synagogue was used to illustrate the homily on New Sunday in the following manuscripts: Athos, Panteleimon 6; Paris, Coislin 239; Athos, Dionysiou 61; London, Brit. Mus. Add. 24381 (another manuscript of Gregory's homilies now mentioned for the first time); Paris gr. 550 (Figs. 139, 195, 358, 94, 407).

In the title miniature of the cod. Athos, Panteleimon 6, fol. 30ʳ, there is another scene in addition to the teaching Gregory (Fig. 139). In the center of the composition, an angel guides a woman toward a church, the cupola of which towers up to the border of the picture. On the extreme right a second angel leads another woman out of the picture in the opposite direction.[236]

In the similar miniature of the cod. Paris, Coislin 239, fol. 22ʳ, the angel who guides the woman flies above her, while the woman herself carries a model of a church in her hand, a symbol that identifies her as the Church (Fig. 195). Obviously the woman being led away personifies the Synagogue. The flying angel is a clue in the search for

---

[236] It is interesting to note that in a manuscript of the complete edition of the homilies of Gregory, the cod. Athos, Iviron 27, there is a small, different miniature illustrating this homily; it shows a square structure, on top of which is a three-aisled basilica. Evidently the basilica is the Church surmounting the Synagogue. For a reproduction of this miniature, see Weitzmann, *Buchmalerei*, pl. xviii, 100.

sources for this composition. It occurs in the scene of the Crucifixion in the cod. Paris gr. 74, fol. 59ʳ, where, however, the personified Church holds a chalice rather than a model of a church.[237]

The miniatures of the Panteleimon and Coislin manuscripts are repeated at the top of two tower-like structures in the background of the title miniature of the cod. Athos, Dionysiou 61, fol. 17ʳ (Fig. 358).[238] The Church, holding a vessel from which flames emerge, enters from the right, led by an angel. The parable of the Wise and Foolish Virgins, to which the Church and the Synagogue have been related ideologically and pictorially,[239] may explain the vessel with flames as an attribute of the Church. It seems probable that the theme was modeled on the representations of this parable in which the angel plays the role of guide.[240]

A similar scene appears in the cod. London, Brit. Mus. Add. 24381, fol. 2ʳ (Fig. 94). On the left an angel takes the Church into an enclosure adorned with crosses and crowned by a baldachin. This enclosure is to be understood as the altar-screen. The Church is nimbed, wears a crown, and holds a jar. On the right another angel pushes away the nimbed but uncrowned Synagogue, who is thus distinguished from the crowned Church. The Synagogue stands outside the altar-screen; a piece of drapery crowns the scene.

In a similar but much reduced miniature that forms the initial E in the cod. Paris gr. 550, fol. 30ʳ, there is another modification because of the size of the miniature (Fig. 407). The angel has not been included and thus the motif has been changed into a representation of the Church pushing out the Synagogue, which appears in Crucifixion scenes. This time the closer parallel occurs in the thirteenth-century Syriac lectionary, Brit. Mus. Add. 7170, fol. 151ʳ, where the scene is presented in its entirety.[241]

Gregory's sermon does not explain the miniatures. It only alludes to the old dispensation, succeeded by a new life, which was derived from Christ's death and resurrection.[242] However, this theme of Church and Synagogue is always found elsewhere as part of a Crucifixion representation as parallel examples have shown, a relationship

[237] Omont, *Evangiles*, I, pl. 51. See J. D. Stefănescu, *L'illustration des liturgies dans l'art de Byzance et de l'Orient*, Brussels 1936, p. 81.

[238] In the miniature of the cod. Dionysiou 61, fol. 17ʳ, a fusion of three scenes has occurred. The two scenes of the foreground are discussed later.

[239] Cf. I. Nordström, *Virtues and Vices on the 14th Century Corbels in the Choir of Uppsala Cathedral*, Stockholm 1956, p. 112.

[240] See cod. Paris gr. sup. 27, fol. 59ʳ, Omont, *Min. gr.* (1929), pl. xcix, 6. In this example, the foolish virgins, pushed by an angel, are represented holding candles. However, in a representation of the parable in cod. Walters Art Gallery 539, fol. 124ʳ (Gospels dated A.D. 1262), the virgins hold lighted vessels like the one which the Church

holds in the miniature of the homily.

[241] G. de Jerphanion, *Les miniatures du manuscrit Syriac de la Bibliothèque Vaticane*, Vatican 1940, fig. 46. The motif of the crowned Church is common and the examples may be multiplied by including works of monumental art. In general see Millet, *Recherches*, p. 450, fig. 430. An earlier example is in the church of Panagia Mavriotissa, in Castoria, dated in the eleventh or twelfth century, see S. Pelekanides, Καστοριά, Thessalonica 1953, pl. 71a. J. D. Stefănescu (*L'illustration des Liturgies dans l'art de Byzance et de l'Orient*, Brussels 1936, p. 81) erroneously stated that the two personifications of Early Christian times reappeared in the sixteenth century, depicted at either side of the cross.

[242] *PG*, 36, 608ff.

derived from the liturgy and not from the Gospel. One of the hymns of the *Triodion* states that Christ's Church was watered like the garden of Eden by the blood that flowed from Christ's side, and that Grace had come to take the place of the shadow of the law.[243] Consequently the theme of Church and Synagogue is an allegorical pictorialization of a liturgical idea.

Weber, the first to dedicate a monograph to this subject, added more examples to those collected by Kondakov, and expressed the opinion that the occurrence of the theme in Byzantium was the result of Western influences, since there is a scarcity of examples in Byzantium, whereas many are to be found in the West.[244] Redin, and later Haseloff, protested strongly against the theory of a Western origin.[245] Their main arguments against Weber's hypothesis were that the motif of the angel leading the two personifications does not appear in the West and that examples in the East are widely dispersed.[246]

More recently Jerphanion expressed a compromise view.[247] He accepted the Western origin of the theme, but suggested its adaptation and transformation in Constantinople by the end of the eleventh century.

The examples offered by the study of the present manuscripts can now be added to those cited by these scholars. The miniatures of Gregory do not solve the problem of whether the theme is purely a Byzantine invention or a Western adaptation. Since the subject is found independently in another kind of important liturgical book, the hypothesis becomes more plausible that the theme is an autonomous Byzantine invention deriving from the theology of the Fathers and created under the liturgical influence of the Middle Byzantine Church.[248] Whatever its origin, since the theme is an allegorical pictorialization of a liturgical concept, it seems probable that it found its place first in a lectionary, from which it spread to other books such as psalters,[249] Gospels, and Gregory's homilies.

The feast of the Encaenia celebrates the consecration of the Church and commemo-

---

[243] " Ἡ ζωηφόρος σου πλευρά, ὡς ἐξ Ἐδέμ, πηγὴ ἀναβλύζουσα τὴν Ἐκκλησίαν σου Χριστὲ ὡς λογικὸν ποτίζει Παράδεισον, ἐντεῦθεν μερίζουσα, ὡς εἰς ἀρχὰς εἰς τέσσαρα εὐαγγέλια . . . ," see M. Saliveros ed., Τριώδιον, Athens n.d., p. 411. Cf. "Παρῆλθεν ἡ σκιὰ τοῦ Νόμου τῆς Χάριτος ἐλθούσης," N. Glykeus ed., Ἀνθολόγιον τοῦ ὅλου ἐνιαυτοῦ, Venice 1832, p. 669.

[244] P. Weber, *Geistliches Schauspiel und kirchliche Kunst, Ikonographie der Kirche und Synagoge*, Stuttgart 1894.

[245] H. Sauerland, A. Haseloff, *Der Psalter Erzbischof Egberts von Trier*, Trier 1901, pp. 181ff.

[246] In Western iconography the Synagogue standing by the cross is blind.

[247] Jerphanion, *op.cit.*, pp. 101ff.

[248] Another example supporting this suggestion occurs outside the manuscripts of the homilies. In the Crucifixion scene depicted in an altarpiece in

Berlin, dating from the first half of the twelfth century, there is the following representation: on top of edifices an angel urges on the Church, who holds a chalice while another angel urges on the Synagogue, whose crown is falling. The composition recalls the miniature of the cod. Athos, Dionysiou 61. Moreover, the personifications in the altarpiece are accompanied by inscriptions clearly indicating that the creator of this work was a Latin who copied a Byzantine model depicting the theme of Church and Synagogue. See B. Degenhart, "Deutsche Mittelalterliche Zeichnungen in der Bibliotheca Comunale von Siena," *Scritti di storia dell'arte in onore di L. Venturi*, I, Rome 1956, pp. 175-89.

[249] J. Strzygowski, *Die Miniaturen des serbischen Psalters* (Denkschriften der kaiserlichen Akademie der Wissenschaften, philosophisch-historische Klasse, 52), Vienna 1906, pl. x, 24.

rates Christ's Resurrection, which the Orthodox Church observes not only annually but on the eighth day after Easter as well. Gregory, in his homily read on that day, speaks of the new life that the Resurrection has opened to every Christian. In a general way, therefore, the whole concept of the feast and of the oration may have inspired the illustrator in his choice of subject. But in a more particular way he must have had in mind allusions to the subject in the sermon and in the hymns of the day which stress the "side [of Christ] that was pierced by lance," "the life-giving side," "the side that shone with divine fire." Guided by these allusions he borrowed the picture from a Crucifixion scene in a lectionary. The existing lectionaries with representations of this scene are, however, Syriac. Obviously then, the miniatures of Gregory's homilies attain a special importance as reflections of a lost Constantinopolitan lectionary in which the theme of Church and Synagogue was depicted.

THE IMPACT OF THE LECTIONARY ON GREGORY'S ILLUSTRATIONS

In the preceding paragraphs the direct sources of each miniature have been discussed separately, and in every case the possibility of a lectionary model seems the most likely. The Deesis miniature, which does not necessarily imply a lectionary model, was a special case. Apart from the fact that in the manuscripts of the homilies the cycle of the great feasts is closely related to the lectionary, a strong argument in favor of the lectionary is the liturgical affinity of the two books; i.e. the fact that the sixteen homilies have been selected to supply supplementary readings to the Gospel lections and that both the lectionary and the homilies of Gregory follow the same arrangement. This affinity caused the artists of the latter book to seek illustrations in those of the former. The Anastasis, the opening miniature in both books, is a case in point. So is the miniature of the Incredulity of Thomas in the codd. Sinai 339, Moscow, Hist. Museum 146, Turin, Univ. Lib. C. I. 6, and Paris gr. 543, an episode not even mentioned in the homily, but accompanying it because the homily was read on Thomas's Sunday. Possibly similar is the case of the narrative miniatures of the Baptism cycle in the cod. Paris gr. 543, or the conflated miniatures of the same cycle in other manuscripts. Moreover, the best parallel examples were found in lectionaries, or in Gospel books which were influenced by lectionaries. Had the artist chosen a Gospel book as a source of the homilies' illustrations, he would have had to search through many different pages in order to find the proper miniatures, as has been shown in the discussion of the cycles. This would certainly have been inconvenient, since the miniatures in the Gospel book do not follow the order of the homilies he intended to illustrate. Instead, it was natural and easier for the artist to use a book which not only contained the illustrations he wanted, but arranged them in the desired order as well. The lectionary was such a book.

Yet, this pattern represents no occasional transfer of pictures from one book to another, made because of the liturgical affinity of the two books and for the artist's convenience only. The relationship of the lectionary and Gregory's homilies and the effect of the former on the illustrations of the latter are not isolated phenomena.[250] The liturgical psalter which, after the lectionary, is the most important liturgical book, can be cited as a parallel example and is further evidence of the importance of the lectionary in Byzantine liturgy and art. The homilies, the psalter, and many other books that came under the influence of the lectionary, bear witness and constitute the particular expression of a trend which underscores the dominating force of the liturgy in Byzantine art.

If the lectionary origin is accepted, an attempt must be made to qualify the lectionaries that were used as models for the manuscripts of the homilies. These lectionaries contained the following feast pictures: Anastasis, the Incredulity of Thomas, Pentecost, Nativity, and Baptism (cf. Text fig. 1). They were, therefore, of the kind that Weitzmann, for methodological convenience, has called a *feast* lectionary. Two well-known examples are the lectionary of the skevophylakion of Lavra and the cod. Leningrad 21. Other particular traits of the lectionaries reflected in the illustrations of Gregory's homilies can be indicated. One lectionary—mirrored in the Jerusalem manuscript, for one—used the Macedonian Renaissance type of the Anastasis and the half-seated, half-reclining Virgin in the Nativity scene. Another lectionary, exemplified by the codd. Sinai 339 and Paris gr. 543—to mention only two examples— contained the old type of the Anastasis and the reclining Virgin in the Nativity. Finally, mention should be made of the lectionary reflected in the cod. Paris gr. 550, which is important for the Anastasis miniature and the classical trend characterizing its style.

2. THE MENOLOGION GROUP

Gregory speaks of the lives of St. Mamas, St. Cyprian, St. Athanasius, and the seven Maccabees in the homilies which he delivered on their feast days, but his texts do not sufficiently explain the miniatures that accompany them. Nor can a scene of an episode of Gregory's own life be explained by his "Farewell" oration in which the miniature is now found. The illustrations presuppose more complete texts, namely biographies of saints, which eventually were collected in a special book, the menologion. The illustrations of this book form the main source for the miniatures discussed here, which are, therefore, called the Menologion Group.[251]

[250] For the problem of the lectionary, its illustrations, and its influence on other books, see Weitzmann, *Semin. Kondak.* (1936), pp. 83ff.; *idem, N.T. Mss Studies*, pp. 153ff.; *idem, Lectionary Morgan 639*, pp. 358ff.; *idem*, "Ein kaiserliches Lektionar einer byzantinischen Hofschule," *Festschrift Karl Swodoba*, Vienna 1959, pp. 309-19; *idem*, "Zur byzantinischen Quelle des Wolfenbüttler Musterbuches," *Festschrift Hans R. Hahnloser*, 1961, pp. 223-50.

[251] For the illustrations of the menologion see in general S. Der Nersessian, "The Illustrations of the Metaphrastian Menologium," *Late Classical and Medieval Studies in Honor of A. M. Friend, Jr.,* ed. by K. Weitzmann, Princeton 1955, pp. 222ff.; P. Mijović, "Une classification iconographique de ménologes enluminés," *Actes du XIIe congrès inter. des études byzantines, Ochride 1961,* III, Belgrade 1964, pp. 271ff.; K. Weitzmann, "Byzantine Miniature and Icon Painting in the Eleventh

Gregory ends his homily with a reference to St. Mamas, in whose church the sermon was delivered: ". . . One of these [martyrs] is my wreath. This is to say the famous Mamas, the shepherd and the martyr. Mamas used to milk the hinds who jostled one another to reach him so that the righteous could be fed with their milk."[252]

a. *Mamas While Milking is Sought by a Soldier*

The codd. Jerusalem, Taphou 14, fol. 27ʳ, and Vat. gr. 1947, fol. 13ʳ, contain similar miniatures (Figs. 104, 123). In the former, Mamas, sitting on a faldstool in front of a cave, is milking a hind. A soldier walks toward Mamas from the left, carrying a spear in his right hand and a round shield on his left arm. A long sword is swung over his shoulder and his mantle flutters in the breeze. To the right of the picture two ibexes are grazing on the rocky cliff forming the background. In the Vatican miniature there are differences: Mamas wears a long tunic, the cave is not clearly indicated, and the attitude of the soldier is slightly different. He seems to be standing and extending his arms toward the saint. The milking scene appears also in the margins of fol. 53ʳ of the cod. Sinai 339, and of fol. 29ᵛ of the cod. Moscow, Hist. Museum 146 (in these two miniatures another hind stands next to the one being milked), and in the initial E in the cod. Paris gr. 550, fol. 30ʳ (Figs. 381, 5, 409). The pictorial rendering of the cave in the Sinai codex is more successful than in the Jerusalem manuscript, primarily because in the former the cave does not look like a door opened in the rocks.

The milking episode can be explained by Gregory's text, cited earlier; in fact the illustrators of the Moscow and Sinai manuscripts have placed this miniature next to the relevant passage. The text, however, offers no explanation for the other part of the Jerusalem and Vatican miniatures, which means that the originality of the entire illustration can justly be doubted. Marava in her study on St. Mamas put forward the theory that the soldier appears in order to indicate the military character of the saint.[253] This suggestion cannot be accepted because the whole scene is a narrative one and there can be no doubt that the soldier is walking toward Mamas.

The natural place to look for an explanation is in a *Vita* of St. Mamas. Indeed, in the Latin translation of the now lost Greek *Vita* written by Symeon Metaphrastes in the tenth century,[254] it is mentioned that when Mamas was in the mountains, "Alex-

---

Century," *Proceedings of the XIIIth Inter. Congress of Byzantine Studies, Oxford 1966*, London 1967, pp. 214ff.

[252] *PG*, 36, 620.

[253] A. Marava-Chatzinikolaou, Ὁ Ἅγιος Μάμας, Athens 1953, pp. 88, 89.

[254] The oldest extant manuscript of St. Mamas' *Vita* is in Latin and has been published by Dele-

haye, who dates it in the tenth century. The extant Greek versions of the *Vita* are much later, but they all go back to the same archetype, best represented in the Latin translation. For a detailed discussion of the extant manuscripts of the *Vita* of St. Mamas and their evaluation, see Marava, *op.cit.*, pp. 5ff.

ander . . . tunc creatus praeses Cappadociae . . . , mittit quosdam equites ad eum adducerent."[255] After the meeting of the *equites* with the saint, the following episode occurs: "Interim autem ad martyrem accedunt, ut consueverant, feminae animantes, ut unaquaeque suo lacte mulgeretur."[256] These passages explain fully the representation, which must be seen as an integrated whole and not as two isolated episodes, and prove that the title miniature of the Jerusalem codex was originally invented for an illustrated *Vita* of St. Mamas. Although the text mentions *equites*, a soldier could easily take the place of the horseman in the textual or in the pictorial tradition. Even though no illustrated *Vita* of St. Mamas has been found, its onetime existence is certain, because scenes that must have been invented for a *Vita*, such as the martyrdom scene, appear in synaxaria, i.e. the books which contain brief notes about saints.[257]

b. *Mamas Communicating with God*

The cod. Paris gr. 550 mentioned above represents St. Mamas in its title miniature praying to a bust of Christ, depicted above him (Fig. 409). The saint is dressed as a shepherd, wearing laced sandals and a short tunic tied with a girdle. A small shepherd's bag hangs from his right shoulder. Two stags and a hind stand in front of him.

This miniature forms part of a narrative tradition which is not explained by Gregory's text but by the Metaphrastian *Vita*. The Latin translation of the *Vita* states that when Mamas was brought to the mountains by the angels he communicated with God whose voice he heard and from whom he received a staff.[258] Evidently then, the miniature of the Paris manuscript has preserved the communication of Mamas with God, but not the receiving of the staff. In the *Vita* this episode precedes that of the sending of the messengers by Alexander, the governor of Cappadocia.

c. *Mamas as a Shepherd*
—*Mamas Standing*

Another pictorial tradition of St. Mamas is represented by the illustration of the cod. Oxford, Roe 6, fol. 18ʳ, showing St. Mamas in shepherd's attire, standing in a frontal position with his flock around him (Fig. 438).

This type differs fundamentally from the two scenes discussed previously. The scene is no longer specifically narrative, but represents Mamas the shepherd, i.e. the portrait of the saint. Portraits of saints are the most common type of illustration in the menologia or synaxaria and therefore it seems most logical to search in these books for similar representations of St. Mamas. Indeed, in the Vatican lectionary cod. gr. 1156, fol. 243ʳ, a similar standing figure of St. Mamas appears, and another in the menologion in Oxford, cod. Cromwell 26, p. 60.[259] Since the figure of St. Mamas is found in both menologia and lectionaries, the direct source of the miniature cannot be determined.

[255] *PG*, 116, 571. [256] *PG*, 115, 571. [258] *PG*, 115, 570. [259] See Coxe, I, p. 454.
[257] *Il menologio*, p. 5.

—Mamas Seated

In the title miniature of the cod. Sinai 339, fol. 42^v, the shepherd Mamas holds his staff and sits between two hills (Fig. 380). His posture shows quite clearly that this representation contains no narrative elements. It is a frontispiece which can be compared to the frontispiece in psalters representing David playing the harp.[260] Yet it is not a simple frontispiece, for it includes the teaching Gregory as well.

Gregory's text suffices to explain this frontispiece. Yet, since the illustration of the narrative episode of Mamas Milking the Hinds, found in this manuscript as well, is derived from the narrative part of a *Vita*, the invention of this frontispiece cannot be strongly supported. Its derivation from the frontispiece of a *Vita* seems more probable.

A similar concept is evident in the illustrations of two other manuscripts, the codd. Athos, Panteleimon 6, fol. 38^v, and Paris, Coislin 239, fol. 27^v, placed opposite the passage referring to St. Mamas (Figs. 142, 202). The former is in the margin, while the latter is in the column of the text. The two miniatures are similar. They represent Mamas seated on a hillock watching his flock of stags and does, and they may be derived from the frontispiece of a synaxarion.

d. *Conflated Scenes*

The miniature of the codd. Athos, Dionysiou 61, fol. 17^r, and Florence, Laur. Plut. VII, 32, fol. 14^v, depict St. Mamas standing with his flock around him (Figs. 358, 261). In the former miniature, St. Mamas is dressed as a shepherd, while in the latter his costume may be military, although the poor condition of the miniature prevents accurate identification. In addition to the standing figure of the saint and his flock, the Milking scene appears on the left of the Dionysiou miniature, in which only the underdrawing is visible,[261] and on the right of the Laurentian miniature. Evidently these miniatures present a combination of a narrative scene and a standing figure.

Among the marginal miniatures illustrating the pastoral passage of this homily, the cod. Paris gr. 533, fol. 34^r (top), contains a composition showing, in front of a building, a shepherd who seems to shear the wool of a struggling lamb (Fig. 237). His two goats and one sheep stand among three trees to the right. Marava interpreted the shepherd as St. Mamas.[262] Although the scene recalls the Milking episode as depicted in the Dionysiou and Sinai codices, it certainly does not represent the same subject matter. If indeed the shepherd is St. Mamas—and this is open to serious doubt—it must be admitted that a change has occurred in the process of copying, perhaps the result of a conflation of the Milking scene with one of the pastoral episodes properly speaking. A consideration of this possible conflation is attempted later in the discussion of the bucolic miniatures (p. 151).

---

[260] See psalter in the Ambrosian Library at Milan, cod. M. 54 sup., fol. 111^r, H. Buchthal, *The Miniatures of the Paris Psalter*, London 1938, pl. XVI, fig. 22.

[261] Marava (*op.cit.*, p. 88), following O. Wulff,

refers to the cod. Athos, Dionysiou 61 as cod. 63, and interprets the bowing figure of St. Mamas to the left of the composition as St. Mamas calling the hinds.

[262] *Ibid.*, p. 90.

In the codd. Istanbul, Patr. 16, fol. 27ʳ, and Sinai 346, fol. 27ʳ, the initial E of the homily is formed by a standing figure of St. Mamas combined with a portrait of the author in the former and Gregory teaching in the latter (Figs. 64, 343). A seated figure of St. Mamas, however, appears in the cod. Athos, Vatopedi 107, fol. 28ʳ, conflated with bucolic scenes (Fig. 319).

The conclusion can be drawn from the preceding discussion that two pictorial traditions are evident in the manuscripts of Gregory's homilies: an extensive pictorial cycle of St. Mamas's life and the tradition of synaxaria illustrated with portraits of saints.

THE MINIATURES OF THE HOMILY ON ST. CYPRIAN

a. *Narrative Scenes*

–*Cyprian the Magician Invoking the Demons against Justina*

In the upper register of the full-page miniature in the cod. Paris gr. 543, fol. 87ᵛ, Cyprian the magician is represented as seated in front of a house and reading a book (Fig. 459). A black, winged devil with whom he seems to be conversing stands in a font in front of him. Another devil flies toward the other side of the picture, while a third flies from the structure which occupies the right part of the composition toward the font. St. Justina, appearing at the window of a building on the right, extends her hand as if addressing someone. An image of the Virgin is depicted on the pediment above the door of the house. The same scene, reduced to the figure of Cyprian and one demon, appears in the historiated initials O and E of the cod. Turin, Univ. Lib. C. I. 6, fols. 42ᵛ and 43ʳ (not illustrated), that form part of the relevant textual passage. More abbreviated scenes, probably referring to the life of Cyprian and Justina, may have adorned the initials on fols. 43ʳ-46ᵛ in the same manuscript, which have been cut out. In other instances also the illustrator of this codex has followed the system of physically relating the miniature to the relevant text.

–*Martyrdom*

The portrait of the seated author, already discussed, appears in the lower register of the full-page miniature of the cod. Paris gr. 543, fol. 87ᵛ (Fig. 459). The old, white-bearded Gregory, dressed in monk's attire and holding an open scroll, sits in front of a building. On the right of the picture the martyrdom of St. Cyprian is represented. A rocky, schematic hill forms the background.

The title of the homily refers to St. Cyprian, but gives no explanation for the two scenes. The eighth paragraph of the text of the homily states that Cyprian has dealt with demons, while the ninth paragraph asserts that there was "a young virgin, modest and of noble family," for whose conquest Cyprian made use of demons.[263] Gregory goes on to say, "the tempter approached the lover and told him of his defeat: the lover felt contempt for him."[264] This may have suggested the arriving and departing demons

[263] *PG*, 35, 1177. [264] *Ibid.*, 1181.

in the miniature and may explain the one who stands in front of Cyprian. The extended hands of Justina may be explained by the passage "she prayed to the Virgin Mary."[265]

Nevertheless, these passages leave certain details of the miniatures unexplained. The passage alluding to Cyprian's conversation with the demons is very general. The name of the virgin who converted Cyprian to Christianity is never given, and nowhere is she mentioned as a saint or martyr, and therefore her nimbus in the miniature is not suggested by the text of the homily.

The natural place to look for an explanation is in an account of St. Cyprian's life found in a menologion. In fact, the life of St. Cyprian by Symeon Metaphrastes provides the important missing details. According to the twelfth paragraph, Cyprian consulted the magic books containing recipes and summoned one of the evil spirits.[266] Then follows a passage referring to Cyprian's relations with the demons, after which it is stated that the virgin was called Justina and that she was martyred. The house in which Justina appears, another important detail, seems to have a specific iconographic meaning; it plays a significant role in the life of St. Cyprian. According to the account in the *Vita*, the first demon filled the house with magic that was intended to cause Justina to yield to Cyprian's desires.[267]

Since the text of the *Vita* is more explicit, there is no doubt that the pictures in the cod. Paris gr. 543 were originally invented for it. Although no illustrated life of St. Cyprian is known, it must have existed, since its *disjecta membra* are found in another important manuscript containing the complete edition of the homilies of Gregory, the cod. Paris gr. 510, fol. 332[v].[268] Because of the date of this manuscript, the lost *Vita* it reflects must have been pre-Metaphrastian. Its miniature, although not the same as that in the cod. Paris gr. 543, probably is a variant of the same iconographic tradition. Both contain scenes of Cyprian conversing with the demons at the basin, the flying demons, and the praying Justina. In the cod. Paris gr. 510, however, Justina prays before a ciborium and a bust of Christ replaces that of the Virgin Mary, who is mentioned in the text. The martyrdom scene also differs in the two manuscripts. In the miniatures of both codices Cyprian bows his head, but in the ninth-century codex, the executioner is just removing the sword from its sheath while in the fourteenth-century manuscript, the executioner is about to strike off the bishop's head. Moreover, in the latter codex Cyprian's hands are under his garment, while in the former they are tied behind his body. This element appears in the beheading scene in the cod. Paris, Coislin 239, fol. 54[r], the composition of which is a reversal of that of the Paris gr. 543 (Fig. 218). The illustrator of the Coislin manuscript has inserted the miniature in the text-column—a system of illustration which will be encountered again—which physically relates the miniature to the relevant text.

The martyrdom scene appears also in the codd. Moscow, Hist. Museum 146, fol. 50[v], and Sinai 339, fol. 397[r], the latter a reduced version of the former (Figs. 8, 397). In the Moscow miniature the place of martyrdom is located in an imposing landscape

[265] *Loc.cit.*
[266] *PG*, 115, 857ff.
[267] *Ibid.*, 857ff.
[268] Omont, *Min. gr.* (1929), pl. XLVII.

outside the city, which is marked by an elegant city-gate, depicted at the far left of the miniature, and slender trees growing behind the walls. The figure of Cyprian resembles the one in cod. Paris gr. 543, but the executioner is different; the posture of his right arm recalls that of the executioner in cod. Paris gr. 510. These two miniatures may form a variant of the iconographic tradition exemplified by the cod. Paris gr. 510, although this cannot be proved because of the lack of comparative material in other manuscripts. If indeed all these miniatures depicting the Martyrdom of St. Cyprian belong to the same iconographic cycle, it is reasonable to assume that they ultimately reflect a pre-Metaphrastian *Vita*.

–Cyprian Before Decius

The cod. Paris, Coislin 239, fol. 53[r], contains a third scene from a narrative part of St. Cyprian's *Vita*, the episode of Cyprian Before Decius (Fig. 216). This illustration shows Cyprian being brought by an attendant to Decius, the Roman emperor, who sits on a folding chair in front of a baldachin.

In this case, Gregory's text suffices to explain the episode,[269] and it would be reasonable to assume that the illustration is an invention. Such an assumption may be countered by the fact that this episode also occurs in the *Vita*, where previously discussed episodes occurred, and for which pictorial evidence was found in the menologia.

–Cyprian Revealing the Location of His Relics

Although the provenance of the scenes discussed so far is certain, the source of this new scene is problematical. On fol. 55[r] of the cod. Paris, Coislin 239 a miniature is inserted in the column of the text, showing a woman lying in bed and St. Cyprian appearing to her (Fig. 220). On the left is a building from the roof of which hangs a piece of drapery.

This miniature illustrates a passage in the homily according to which Cyprian, after his martyrdom, appeared in a dream to a faithful Christian woman and revealed to her the whereabouts of his body.[270] No account of this episode is given in the extant version of the *Vita* of St. Cyprian and, since the homily fully explains it, it might be considered an invention for the text at hand. Here the question arises whether Gregory's text is the basic text, or whether the episode was borrowed from a version of a *Vita* now lost.

This problem is far from simple since it concerns only the text and since, to my knowledge, no other illustration of this episode appears elsewhere. It is generally agreed that Gregory delivered a eulogy on Cyprian, the bishop of Carthage, but confused his life with that of Cyprian of Antioch.[271] Scholars have tried to explain this

[269] *PG*, 35, 1185.

[270] *Ibid.*, 1189.

[271] For bibliography, see H. Delehaye, "Cyprien d'Antioch et Cyprien de Carthage," *Analecta Bol-* *landiana*, 39 (1921), pp. 314-32. See also a recent discussion in L. Krestan, A. Hermann, "Cyprian," *Reallexikon für Antike und Christentum*, III (1956), 467-77.

confusion by assuming that the panegyric was not prepared but improvised on delivery. Serious objections to this assumption were raised by Delehaye, who suggested that, since Gregory was a careful orator, the confusion perhaps existed in the source from which Gregory drew his information.[272] In order to solve the problem, Delehaye undertook a study of the texts. He concluded that Symeon Metaphrastes left out part of the story and that the fusion of the historical and non-historical elements in the panegyric could be explained by the existence of a biography of the martyr in which they were fused and from which they were derived. To prove this, Delehaye presented passages referring to St. Cyprian from the thirteenth chapter of the *Peristephanon* of the poet Prudentius and compared them with the relevant passages in Gregory. This comparison showed that in all probability both the poet and the orator made use of the same source, a biography in which the historical and the legendary elements were combined. This version of St. Cyprian's *Vita* is not extant.

It is not known whether this lost text contained the episode of the dream. If it did, it may be assumed that the picture which now accompanies Gregory's text was originally invented for it and that the two other miniatures of the cycle in the same manuscript came also from the same pre-Metaphrastian *Vita*.

b. *Standing Figures*
—Cyprian and Justina

In the cod. Sinai 339, fol. 397^r, in which the Martyrdom scene was found, there is a title miniature showing Cyprian in bishop's vestments extending his right hand in benediction toward the teaching Gregory to his right (Fig. 395). Next to Cyprian, Justina in a frontal position, wearing a maphorion over her head and a mantle, holds a martyr's cross. Gregory does not appear in the title miniature of the cod. Paris gr. 550, fol. 59^v, and therefore Cyprian and Justina are represented standing side by side facing the spectator (Fig. 412). The initial M's of these two miniatures repeat the title miniatures in a reduced form (Fig. 396). Moreover, the two saints appear in the initial M of the cod. Athos, Dionysiou 61, fol. 165^r, and in the marginal miniature of the cod. Athos, Vatopedi 107, fol. 59^v (Figs. 375, 323). In the latter miniature the hand of God appears between the two saints.

The initials are of special interest as they reveal the individuality of each artist and his freedom in the composition. In contrast to the composition of historiated initial M's elsewhere (cf. Fig. 306), the artist of the Sinai codex did not need to invent compositional devices, because the three figures could easily form the letter M. Symmetry has been achieved by placing the two bishops on the lateral bars of the letter while the figure of Justina, reduced in scale because of the shape of the letter, forms the middle bar. The artist of the cod. Paris gr. 550 invented a cross standing on a base and used it to form the middle bar of the letter M, thereby emphasizing

[272] Delehaye, *op.cit.*, pp. 314ff.

the martyrdom of the two saints. The artist of the Dionysiou manuscript preferred to use a third figure for the middle bar, just as did the Sinai artist. In this case, however, the third figure is Christ Emmanuel. The length of this middle bar, adequate for the figure of a child, probably dictated the type of Christ used.

The title miniatures in the codd. Sinai 339 and Paris gr. 550 reveal the pictorial traditions of the menologion, or of lectionaries which contain commemorations of saints. In fact a similar picture of the two martyrs standing side by side appears in the eleventh-century menologion of Vienna, cod. Hist. gr. 6, fol. 3ᵛ.[273] This tradition is even more evident in the Sinai codex, which includes the Martyrdom scene in addition to the portraits, and thus reflects a system of illustration which finds its best parallels in menologia.[274] In the Paris manuscript, however, there is no other scene that would have confirmed the direct derivation of the miniature from a book of the Lives of Saints. In this case there are alternative solutions to the problem of its migration into Gregory's text: the miniature may have been taken into the homily of Gregory directly from a book containing the fuller text of the Lives of Saints, or it may have been adopted through an intermediary lectionary.

−Cyprian

Some illustrators have chosen to represent only the standing figure of Cyprian. Thus, in the miniature of the cod. Athos, Panteleimon 6, fol. 64ʳ, he is shown standing frontally and holding a book (Fig. 146), and in the cod. Oxford, Roe 6, fol. 167ᵛ, he occupies the whole page, the background being formed by a building on either side (Fig. 449). Two historiated initials, E and K, in the cod. Turin, Univ. Lib. C. I. 6, fols. 39ʳ and 39ᵛ (not illustrated), placed in this homily and showing Cyprian standing, belong in this category.

c. Conflated Scenes

The figure of Cyprian, derived from a menologion, has been added to a simple teaching scene in the following manuscripts: Athos, Dionysiou 61, fol. 165ʳ; Jerusalem, Taphou 14, fol. 58ʳ; Paris, Coislin 239, fol. 46ᵛ; Vat. gr. 1947, fol. 35ᵛ (Figs. 373, 111, 214, 127). The Coislin manuscript contains another miniature which must be considered here. It is a column miniature, fol. 50ʳ, and represents Gregory in the middle speaking to a group of people, on the left, concerning Justina, who stands to

[273] Reproduced in W. Felicetti-Liebenfels, *Geschichte der byzantinischen Ikonenmalerei*, Lausanne 1956, pl. 14; see also the lectionary cod. Vat. gr. 1156, fol. 255ᵛ.

[274] In menologia, where the biographies are much longer than in synaxaria, both the portrait of the martyr and his martyrdom are frequently represented. Indeed, the portrait of Cyprian and his martyrdom are depicted in the Moscow meno-

logion (cod. 358, fol. 175ʳ), while the martyrdom of Cyprian in the presence of Justina is represented in the so-called Menologion of Basil II. See S. Der Nersessian, "The Illustrations of the Metaphrastian Menologion," *Late Classical and Mediaeval Studies in Honor of A. M. Friend, Jr.*, ed. by K. Weitzmann, Princeton 1955, p. 224 n. 17, 25; *Il menologio*, p. 80.

the right (Fig. 215). Justina with her martyr's cross and mantle resembles representations of her found in menologia and lectionaries. Obviously the miniature is formed by a simple teaching scene and a figure taken over from a menologion.

In the historiated initial M of the homily in the cod. Istanbul, Patr. 16, fol. 56ʳ, a narrative scene is combined with standing figures, and the special importance of the illustration lies in the fact that it adds another new scene (Fig. 67). The lateral vertical bars of the letter are formed by the familiar standing figures of Cyprian and Justina who, their extended hands forming the middle diagonal bars, hold scrolls above red flames. Clearly the scene showing Cyprian burning his magic books, of which the Metaphrastian *Vita* speaks, has been combined with the standing figures found in menologia and lectionaries.

The pictorial tradition of the menologion is evident in another conflated scene appearing in the initial M of the cod. Turin, Univ. Lib. C. I. 6, fol. 37ʳ, depicting the martyrdom of St. Cyprian in the presence of Justina who is shown in the act of receiving the martyr's head (Fig. 43). Evidently this representation constitutes a conflation of two different traditions just as they appeared in two separate scenes in the cod. Sinai 339: the beheading of St. Cyprian and the standing portrait (Figs. 397, 395). This combination, however, had occurred in the menologia, as is proved by a miniature in the so-called menologion of Basil, previously mentioned. It is obvious then that the illustrator of Gregory borrowed his miniature either directly or indirectly from such a book. The fact that Justina does not simply witness the scene, but participates in it, proves once again the inventiveness of the illustrator and his ingenuity in adapting a borrowed scene to the form of a given initial.

Another miniature, in which various elements are combined, should be included here, although the combination is of a different nature. The miniature appearing in the cod. London, Brit. Mus. Add. 24381, fol. 52ʳ, shows Christ enthroned and flanked by Gregory and Cyprian who are turned toward him in an attitude of prayer (Fig. 96). Justina stands in prayer at the right. The figure of the latter, taken from a larger scene (cf., for instance, the miniature of the cod. Paris gr. 543, Fig. 459), has been combined with standing figures modeled on a Deesis scene. The use of the Deesis scene as a model emphasizes again the liturgical aspect of the illustrations of Gregory.

As in the miniatures of St. Mamas, the manuscripts of Gregory's homilies reflect an extensive narrative cycle of the life of St. Cyprian as well as the current tradition of the standing portraits found in the synaxaria. With regard to the narrative pictorial cycle of the saint's life, a further distinction can be made between the manuscripts in which detailed illustrations have been preserved and those which show an abbreviated cycle. The abbreviated cycle does not seem to be the work of Gregory's illustrator; the abbreviation probably occurred within the tradition of the menologion. This implies that some artists borrowed their miniatures directly from the extensive cycle, while others borrowed them directly from the abbreviated cycle.

THE MINIATURES OF THE HOMILY ON ST. ATHANASIUS

The illustrator of the cod. Oxford, Roe 6, fol. 128ʳ, has chosen a frontal half-figure of St. Athanasius to illustrate Gregory's panegyric of him (Fig. 446). A small but complete standing figure of the bishop of Alexandria is depicted at the top of the initial A in the cod. Oxford, Selden. B. 54, fol. 88ᵛ, as an illustration of the same homily (Fig. 295).

Both the miniatures have their source in a menologion or synaxarion, where standing figures of Athanasius are found. The use of these figures (Figs. 285, 251) for the formation of scenes has been discussed earlier (pp. 34, 60).

THE MINIATURES OF THE HOMILY ON THE MACCABEES

The illustrations for this homily consist either of narrative scenes or of standing figures and medallions, and the manuscripts can be classified accordingly. The narrative scenes have been used by the illustrators of the codd. Moscow, Hist. Museum 146; Sinai 339; Paris gr. 543; Turin, Univ. Lib. C. I. 6; Florence, Laur. Plut. VII, 32; Vat. gr. 1947; Jerusalem, Taphou 14; Athos, Vatopedi 107 (Figs. 7, 392, 458, 37, 38, 40, 41, 264, 126, 110, 322). The supplementary illustrations of the cod. Paris, Coislin 239 are included here because they are narrative scenes that belong to the same cycle (Figs. 207-213).

a. *Narrative Scenes*
—Scenes Treated Separately

The Moscow, Sinai, Paris gr. 543 and Turin codices contain the greatest number of scenes referring to the martyrdom of the seven Maccabees, of their mother Solomone and of Eleazar, their teacher (Figs. 7, 392, 458, 37). In each of the four manuscripts six scenes form the title miniature. In the first two, each scene is framed separately. In the others, the frames have been eliminated.

The first scene (top left) of the miniatures of the codices Moscow, Hist. Museum 146, fol. 40ᵛ, and Sinai 339, fol. 381ᵛ, shows an executioner pushing Eleazar into the fire. The same scene appears in the cod. Paris gr. 543, fol. 74ᵛ, with the figure of one of the Maccabees already in the fire. The title miniature of the cod. Turin, Univ. Lib. C. I. 6, fol. 29ʳ, does not contain a corresponding scene, but the historiated initial X on the same folio depicts the Decapitation of Eleazar in a conventional manner (Fig. 38). The second scene (moving to the right) in the Moscow and Sinai manuscripts and a similar one in the Turin and Paris codices, represents two of the Maccabees, each on a separate wheel, operated by executioners, below which are instruments of torture. The third scene of the Moscow and Sinai codices, and a similar one in the Turin (left foreground) and Paris manuscripts (left side of the lower register), shows one of the Maccabees already in a pit, with another about to be thrown in after him. The fourth scene in the Sinai codex, identical to one in the Moscow miniature and similar to those in the Turin (upper right corner) and Paris (center of the lower register) codices, shows Solomone admonishing one of her sons, who is in the fire. In the Paris miniature, however, the youth is standing or walking in the fire. The Turin codex repeats this fourth scene in the course of the homily as an illustration of the initials Ω, Λ and Κ on fols. 30ᵛ, 31ᵛ, and 36ʳ next to passages referring to Solomone (Figs. 40, 41). Of these the historiated initial Λ deserves special mention. Recalling the first years of one of the future martyrs, the artist represents Solomone instructing one of her sons in his first steps. The fifth scene depicted in the Moscow and Sinai manuscripts represents one of the Maccabees, half nude and with hands bound, being led by one of the executioners. This scene has no counterpart in either the Paris or the Turin manuscripts. The last scene of the codd. Moscow and Sinai, which also has no parallel in the other two manuscripts, shows one of the executioners breaking one of the youth's legs.

The cod. Paris gr. 543 includes another scene that has no counterpart in the other manuscripts. One of the victims is tied to a pole and two executioners are piercing his sides with iron hooks.

Two more episodes are added in the Turin manuscript. In the lower corner of the miniature, an executioner beheads one of the Maccabees, another already having been decapitated. This decapitation appears in some psalters of the so-called monastic recension. Usually their heads are piled one on top of the other, the pile dominating the composition.[275] The second scene of the Turin manuscript occupies the upper left corner of the miniature. It is not well preserved and identification is uncertain. It probably depicted the tongue of one of the Maccabees being cut out.

The scenes of the supplementary miniatures of the cod. Paris, Coislin 239—all placed within the written column—are as follows: Eleazar Brought to King Antiochus, fol. 38ʳ; the Scourging of Eleazar before Antiochus, fol. 39ᵛ (the Scourging of Eleazar is paralleled in the cod. Paris gr. 510, fol. 340ʳ);[276] Antiochus and the Seven Maccabees, fol. 40ʳ; Antiochus Ordering the Eldest of the Maccabees to be Brought Forward, fol. 41ᵛ; the Admonition of the Seven Youths by Their Mother Solomone, fol. 43ᵛ; Solomone in a Furnace, fol. 44ᵛ; Antiochus Speaking to a Group of Israelites, fol. 45ᵛ (Figs. 207-13).

Of special interest is the initial T of the cod. Vat. gr. 463, fol. 411ʳ, which shows the seven brothers in a furnace being comforted by an angel, who holds two wreaths which allude to martyrdom (Fig. 93). This scene is patterned after a similar representation of the Three Holy Children in the Fire.[277]

---

[275] Some examples: London, Theodore Psalter, fol. 106ᵛ; Barberini (Vat. Barb. gr. 372), fol. 132ᵛ; Chloudov Psalter (Moscow, Hist. Mus. gr. 129), fol. 79ʳ, see N. P. Kondakov, *Miniatiury Grecheskoi rukopisi IX veka iz sobraniia A. I. Khludova*, Moscow 1878; psalter of the Monastery of Pantocrator on Mt. Athos, cod. 61, fol. 110ʳ, see Lambros, I, p. 99, S. Dufrenne, *L'illustration*

des psautiers grecs du moyen âge, Paris 1966, fig. 55. In these examples the decapitation takes place before Antiochus. Cf. R. L. McGrath, "The Martyrdom of the Maccabees on the Brescia Casket," *AB*, 47 (1965), p. 259 n. 28.

[276] Omont, *Min. gr.* (1929), pl. XLVIII.

[277] See cod. Vat. gr. 1927, fol. 280ʳ, DeWald, *Vat. gr.* 1927, pl. LXX.

—Conflated Scenes

In the light of the individual illustrations described above, the miniatures of the remaining manuscripts—which are the codd. Florence, Laur. Plut. VII, 32, Vat. gr. 1947, Jerusalem, Taphou 14, and Athos, Vatopedi 107—seem to be conflations of several episodes.

The cod. Florence, Laur. Plut, VII, 32, fol. 40ʳ, at the beginning of the sermon and above the text column, represents at the left the seated Antiochus wearing a crown and an imperial chlamys (Fig. 264). He addresses the seven Maccabees at the right. Among them is the figure of Solomone. Eleazar, whose figure belongs in a separate scene, has probably been included here too. Perhaps the same conflation occurred in the cod. Vat. gr. 1947, fol. 30ʳ, whose miniature is not well preserved (Fig. 126). A similar conflated miniature, which includes the seven Maccabees with Solomone and Eleazar in front of Antiochus, is used in the Regina Bible, cod. Vat. gr. reg. 1, fol. 450ʳ, as an illustration of the Fourth Book of the Maccabees.[278]

A martyrdom scene occupies the center of the title miniature in the cod. Jerusalem, Taphou 14, fol. 47ʳ (Fig. 110). One of the victims is placed on top of a wheel of torture, turned by means of ropes and pulled by an executioner on either side. Another youth has already been killed and his body lies underneath the wheel. To the left of the miniature is King Antiochus, who is portrayed as a middle-aged man with dark hair and beard. He wears a garment with decorated borders, a mantle, and has a crown on his nimbed head. He is seated, giving orders to the executioners. On the right the foremost figure is Eleazar, who is represented as an old man with a nimbus raising his hand in benediction. Next to him stands Solomone with her nimbed head covered and her left hand raised. Her five other sons stand behind her to the right. Clearly in addition to the conflation of the martyrdom of two of the members, two other scenes have been conflated in this composition: the figure of Eleazar is drawn from one that shows him before Antiochus, and the Maccabees before Antiochus comes from yet another (cf. Figs. 207, 209).

An illustration in the cod. Athos, Vatopedi 107, fol. 48ʳ, seems also to be a conflation (Fig. 322). The seven Maccabees, Eleazar, and Solomone are all in the fire. Solomone on the extreme right has raised her hands in an attitude of prayer.

In the text, Gregory speaks about the tortures of the Maccabees and their martyrdom, praises their mother, hails their suffering, and places them among the many of God's witnesses whose days were ended by the hand of an executioner. These comments are too general to explain the pictures. Sufficient details to explain them appear in the Fourth Book of the Maccabees in the Greek Old Testament (5: 1ff.).[279] The obvious conclusion is that the miniatures of the homily were originally made for that

[278] *Coll. Paleo. Vat.*, I (1905), pl. 16.

[279] This non-canonical book gives the fullest account of the martyrdom of Eleazar, the seven Maccabees, and their mother, which took place at Antioch under Antiochus IV, King of Syria (c. 175-164 B.C.). See R. H. Charles, ed., *The Apocrypha and Pseudepigrapha of the Old Testament in English*, II, Oxford 1913, pp. 653-65, 671.

book. Illustrated Books of the Maccabees certainly existed in the East,[280] and proof of this is furnished by the miniature of the Regina Bible, and by the miniatures which migrated to other manuscripts, including the cod. Paris gr. 510, and the monastic psalters.

In describing and comparing the miniatures of these codices, including the cod. Paris gr. 510, the existence of similar scenes has been noted. In addition to these, others were found which illustrate episodes not occurring in all manuscripts. All the miniatures, then, must belong to the same recension and must be excerpts from a fuller cycle. This conclusion permits a tentative reconstruction of at least parts of the Fourth Book of the Maccabees. Before that reconstruction is attempted, the question must be raised whether these scenes came directly from the Fourth Book of the Maccabees or from a menologion. It is raised because the text of the Fourth Book of the Maccabees is also used in menologia.[281] The little comparative material with scenes available has been described and does not lead to an answer. In addition to this difficulty, another one arises because some menologia contain the *Vita* of the Maccabees, and others do not. The Maccabees are not included, for instance, among the lives of the martyrs collected by Symeon Metaphrastes, but they are included in the menologion Paris gr. 1528, in which (fol. 131ᵛ) their pictures also appear. This inconsistency among collectors of *Vitae* may be explained by the comments of Nicetas, the eleventh-century bishop of Heraclea, concerning Gregory's sermon. He states that many doubted whether the Maccabees should be included among the martyrs since they had not died for Christ, and that Gregory dispersed these doubts in his sermon;[282] but apparently these doubts were not entirely eliminated.

A solution of the problem cannot be found. A preference for the menologion as an intermediary source seems logical for the following reasons: A menologion has been used for the miniatures referring to the lives of the saints discussed so far. Portraits of saints and representations of their martyrdom appear in menologia, as shown in discussion of the illustrations of other homilies. (A similar case is presented by the Sinai, Turin, and Coislin manuscripts which, in addition to the martyrdom scenes, include portraits of the martyrs.) Finally, the miniatures of the Coislin manuscript support the menologion tradition. Although this codex has retained scenes from a detailed cycle, the representations are banal and consist of types commonly used in menologia or synaxaria. This is clear in the scene of Solomone's death where, instead of depicting her self-immolation on the pyre on which her sons' bodies were burned, the miniature departs from the text and shows her in an oven, which is often found in representations of martyrdom scenes (Fig. 212).[283] Similarly, the initial X of the

---

[280] In the West an illustrated book of Maccabees has been preserved in Leyden (Lib. Bibl. der Univer., Perizoni 17), see A. Goldschmidt, *Die deutsche Buchmalerei*, I, Berlin 1928, p. 59, pls. 72, 73; cf. R. L. McGrath, "The Martyrdom of the Maccabees on the Brescia Casket," *AB*, 47 (1965), pp. 257-61.

[281] Ehrhard, *Hom. Literatur*, II, p. 615.

[282] See Sajdak, *Scholia*, p. 168. Cf. T. Sinko, "De Gregorii Nazianzeni laudibus Macchabaeorum," *Eos*, 13 (1907), pp. 1-29.

[283] Cf. *Il menologio*, pp. 155, 156, 183, 251, 255, 309.

Turin manuscript, fol. 29ʳ, may be invoked as a conventional representation of a beheading scene, common in menologia or synaxaria (Fig. 38).

b. *Portrait Types*

Both the initial letter T of the cod. Sinai 339, fol. 381ʳ, and the headpiece of the cod. Paris, Coislin 239, fol. 37ʳ, are formed by the medallions of Eleazar, Solomone, and her sons (Figs. 392, 206). The Coislin miniaturist has added a medallion of Gregory to balance the composition. In both cases, the medallions, as reduced forms of standing figures, may have come from a frontispiece in a menologion. If so, it can be assumed that the martyrdom scenes in both manuscripts have also come from a menologion.

A combination of standing figures and medallions appears in the miniature of the cod. Oxford, Canon. gr. 103, fol. 47ʳ (Fig. 278). They are all placed within the rectangular frame of the title. At the top in the center a medallion of Christ is flanked by those of Eleazar and Solomone. Evidently a Deesis scene was used as a model. Below, in the lateral parts of the frame, are four standing figures of the Maccabees; the busts of the other three, placed within medallions, are in the lower part of the frame.

As well as in these manuscripts, standing figures have been used in the codd. Oxford, Roe 6, fol. 159ʳ, London, Brit. Mus. Add. 24381, fol. 41ʳ, and Paris gr. 550, fol. 49ʳ, all three of which have similar miniatures (Figs. 448, 95, 411). The full-page miniature of the first manuscript contains the dominant figures of Eleazar and Solomone. In a row in front of them the seven martyrs are depicted on a smaller scale. The figures of the mother and the teacher must originally have been on either side of the children, as in the miniatures of the Paris and London manuscripts. This is a traditional compositional scheme.[284] However, the formal requirements of the full-page miniature, and the problem of filling the upper part of the illustration dictated the compositional change. The size of the miniatures also accounts for the compositional difference between the London and Paris manuscripts. The longer strip of the former required the arrangement of the children in one row, while in the smaller miniature of the latter the children are arranged in two rows. In the codd. Oxford, Selden. B. 54, fol. 14ʳ, and Athos, Panteleimon 6, fol. 53ʳ, the figures stand in one row. In the latter the figures of Eleazar and Solomone are not included (Figs. 288, 144). The one-row arrangement recalls the illustration of the same homily in the cod. Milan, Ambros. E. 49-50. inf., fol. 354ʳ.[285] There, however, the row is headed by Eleazar and Solomone. Their figures are not entirely frontal, for they turn slightly toward the teaching Gregory, and they consequently lack the iconic concept and the immediate reference to the spectator found in the miniatures now under discussion. This iconic concept is characteristic of the portrait types in menologia.

The initial T of the codd. Milan, Ambros. G 88 sup., fol. 63ʳ, and Istanbul, Patr.

[284] See representation of Leah's children in cod. Vat. gr. 746, fol. 99ᵛ.

[285] Grabar, *Ambros. 49-50*, pl. xxix.

16, fol. 45ʳ (Figs. 305, 66), and several initials throughout the homily in the cod. Turin, Univ. Lib. C. I. 6, fols. 29ʳ, 29ᵛ, 30ʳ, 34ʳ, 34ᵛ, historiated either with a group of portraits or with individual figures, belong to this discussion. Two of the initials in the Turin manuscript need special mention. One, the letter Θ, fol. 30ʳ, shows that the artist has not only successfully adapted two standing figures to the shape of the letter, but has ingeniously illustrated the word θυσίαν, to which the initial belongs, by presenting Eleazar and Solomone offering a "sacrifice" (Fig. 39). The other, the initial T, fol. 34ᵛ, illustrates the concept of the word ἀγών, which follows the initial, with two small angels touching Eleazar's head as if to place a crown on it (Fig. 42). The illustration of individual words occurs often in this manuscript and must be taken as an expression, not merely of a decorative tendency on the part of the artist but, of his awareness of the value and concept of the image in the Byzantine world.

These miniatures of portrait types represent the menologion tradition and are borrowed either directly from a menologion or from a lectionary influenced by a menologion, for standing figures appear in lectionaries as well.[286] No images of the Maccabees are known in either of these books. They must have existed, however, as their representation in the sticherarion of the monastery of Koutloumousi, cod. 412, fol. 155ʳ, which may have been derived from one or the other of these books, shows.

c. Reconstruction of Certain Parts of the Illustration of the Fourth Book of the Maccabees

The scenes are presented here in the sequence of the Fourth Book of the Maccabees and their corresponding illustrations in the manuscripts of the homilies respectively. This parallelism of text and pictures provides an insight into the density of the illustrations of the Fourth Book of the Maccabees. The miniatures begin with the fifth chapter.

1. 5: 4. "And when many had been taken by force, one man first from among the company was brought before Antiochus, a Hebrew whose name was Eleazar . . . ," cod. Paris, Coislin 239, fol. 38ʳ (Fig. 207).

2. 6: 3, 4. "Then binding his [Eleazar's] arms on either side they scourged him . . . ," codd. Paris, Coislin 239, fol. 39ᵛ, and Paris gr. 510, fol. 340ʳ (Fig. 208).[287] The miniature of Eleazar in the codex Paris, Coislin 239 is iconographically superior because he is pictured tied as the text states.

3. 6: 24. "So, they, seeing him [Eleazar] thus triumphant over the tortures and

---

[286] The standing figures of the Maccabees in Santa Maria Antiqua are so different that they cannot be related to the figures of the Maccabees appearing in Gregory's homilies. See W. de Grüneisen, *Sainte Marie Antique*, Rome 1911, pl. IC.XVII; J. Wilpert, *Die römischen Mosaiken und Malereien*, Freiburg 1916, II, pp. 653ff.; IV, pl. 133.

[287] Omont, *Min. gr.* (1929), pl. XLVIII. This plate contains all the scenes to which we refer during the discussion. The translations are from R. H. Charles, ed., *The Apocrypha and Pseudepigrapha of the Old Testament in English*, II, Oxford 1913, pp. 666ff.

unmoved even by the pity of his executioners, dragged him to the fire," codd. Moscow, Hist. Museum 146, fol. 40ᵛ, Sinai 339, fol. 381ᵛ, and Paris gr. 543, fol. 74ᵛ (Figs. 7, 392, 458).

4. 8: 3. "And under these orders of the tyrant seven brethren together with their aged mother were brought prisoners before him," codd. Florence, Laur. Plut. VII, 32, fol. 40ʳ, and Vat. gr. 1947, fol. 30ʳ (Figs. 264, 126). These miniatures are in poor condition, but it is clear that Eleazar has been included, which means that the illustrators have conflated two scenes, the second of which refers to chapter 5: 4 (scene 1).

5. 8: 4. Antiochus speaks to the seven youths, cod. Paris, Coislin 239, fol. 40ʳ (Fig. 209).

6. 9: 11. "So by his orders the scourgers brought forward the eldest of them and stripped him of his garment . . . ," cod. Paris, Coislin 239, fol. 41ᵛ (Fig. 210).

7. 9: 11, 12. ". . . and bound his [the eldest Maccabee's] hands and arms on either side with thongs. But when they had scourged him till they were weary . . . ," cod. Paris gr. 510 (third of the top register).

8. 9: 12, 13. ". . . they cast him upon the wheel," codd. Moscow, Hist. Museum 146, Sinai 339, Paris gr. 543, Turin, Univ. Lib. C. I. 6, and Paris gr. 510 (Figs. 7, 392, 458, 37).

9. 9: 26-28. ". . . the guards brought forward the second in age of the sons, and grappling him with sharp-clawed hands of iron, rent away all the flesh from his cheeks, and tore off the skin from his head," cod. Paris gr. 510 (second of top register).

10. 10: 6, 7. There follows the martyrdom of the third youth. "And they dislocated his hands and his feet with their dislocating engines, and wrenched his limbs out of their sockets and unstrung them; and they twisted round his fingers, and his arms, and his legs, and his elbow-joints," codd. Moscow, Hist. Museum 146 (sixth scene), Sinai 339 (Figs. 7, 392).

11. 10: 17, 18. "When he heard this the bloodthirsty, murderous, and utterly abominable Antiochus bade them cut out his tongue," (this refers to the fourth Maccabee) cod. Turin, Univ. Lib. C. I. 6 (Fig. 37).

12. 11:9. "As he [the fifth Maccabee] spake thus the guards bound him and brought him before the catapult," codd. Moscow, Hist. Museum 146 and Sinai 339 (Figs. 7, 392).

13. 11: 10, 11. ". . . they tied him [the fifth Maccabee] thereto on his knees, and, fastening them therewith iron cramps, they wrenched his loins over the rolling 'wedge' so that he was completely curled back like a scorpion and every joint was disjointed. And thus in grievous strait for breath and anguish of body . . . ," probably in cod. Paris gr. 510 (second of the bottom register).

14. 11: 17, 18. ". . . they brought him [the sixth Maccabee] to the wheel, and with care they stretched him out and dislocated the bones of his back and set fire

under him." One of the wheels in the codd. Moscow, Hist. Museum 146, Sinai 339, Paris gr. 543, and Turin, Univ. Lib. C. I. 6, must refer to this scene (Figs. 7, 392, 458, 37). Whether the wheel in the Jerusalem manuscript refers to the sixth, or another of the Maccabees, is not known (Fig. 110). In this last codex a conflation of the scenes 1, 4, and 5 has obviously occurred.

15. 11: 19, 20. "And they made sharp skewers red-hot and ran them into his back, and piercing through his sides they burned away his entrails also," cod. Paris gr. 543. There is confusion here: the youth is represented on a catapult, but the text specifies a wheel (Fig. 458).

16. 12: 1. "And when this one [the sixth Maccabee] also died a blessed death, being cast in the cauldron . . . ," codd. Moscow, Hist. Museum 146, Sinai 339, Paris gr. 543, Turin, Univ. Lib. C. I. 6 (Figs. 7, 392, 458, 37).

17 and 18. 12:7. "But the mother, speaking in the Hebrew tongue . . . encouraged the boy [the seventh Maccabee]. . . ." v. 20. "And with this prayer he cast himself into the red-hot brazier, and so gave up the ghost." The actual leaping into the fire is depicted in the cod. Paris gr. 510 (first from left to right in the bottom register). A conflation, however, of verses 7 and 20 may explain the scenes of the codd. Moscow, Hist. Museum 146, Sinai 339, Paris gr. 543, and Turin, Univ. Lib. C. I. 6, in which one of the Maccabees is in the fire, and Solomone seems to be speaking to him. There is still another possible explanation. In chapter 15: 14, it is stated that Solomone was looking "at the racking and roasting of each" of the sons. That is perhaps what she is doing in the scenes mentioned above.

19. 15: 20. ". . . the flesh of one son being severed after the flesh of another, and hand after hand being cut off, and head after head being flayed, and corpse cast upon corpse . . . ," cod. Turin, Univ. Lib. C. I. 6 (Fig. 37).

20. 16. Solomone is exhorting her sons, cod. Paris, Coislin 239, fol. 43ᵛ (Fig. 211).

21. 17: 1. Solomone "cast herself on the pyre . . . ," codd. Paris, Coislin 239, fol. 44ᵛ (Fig. 212), and Paris gr. 510; the latter presents the more original version. Solomone in the fire praying is depicted in the cod. Athos, Vatopedi 107, fol. 48ʳ (Fig. 322).

22. 18: 1. "For when the tyrant Antiochus saw the heroism of their virtue, and their endurance under the tortures, he publicly held up their endurance . . . ," cod. Paris, Coislin 239, fol. 45ᵛ (Fig. 213).

In this reconstruction, attention must be drawn to the conflation of certain episodes and the absence of others. Particularly, no scene was found corresponding to any of the tortures of the fourth Maccabee in the Moscow, Sinai, and Paris gr. 543 miniatures; nor did the last codex include a representation of the martyrdom of the fifth. Yet each miniature of these manuscripts contains seven scenes, which means that the martyrdom of one of the Maccabees is represented in two scenes. It is likely that the omission and the resulting substitution are due to mere confusion caused by the similarities of the tortures.

The attempted reconstruction of a part, at least, of the Fourth Book of the Maccabees is obviously important. The miniatures of Gregory's homilies become the main evidence for the existence of a densely illustrated book of the Maccabees. That book would have been illustrated line by line, and the mere examination of the pictures would have sufficed to communicate the story of the seven youths to the reader.

To summarize: the miniatures of Gregory's homily in all probability reflect a *Vita* of the Maccabees as their intermediary source. The *Vita*, because of the cod. Paris gr. 510, has to be dated sometime before the middle of the ninth century. As far as the standing figures are concerned, the Gregory miniatures possibly reflect the tradition of a lectionary.

A MINIATURE OF THE FAREWELL ORATION

Other illustrations chosen for this homily have already been discussed. One of these compositions represents Gregory delivering his farewell oration to the bishops of the Ecumenical Council of 381. The scene has been selected by the illustrator of the cod. Paris gr. 543 and is placed on the lower register of the full-page miniature on fol. 288ᵛ preceding the text of the homily. The miniature of the upper register shows on the left a group of clerics headed by Gregory of Nazianzus who, dressed in a simple brown tunic and mantle, is being given a staff by the Emperor Theodosius (Fig. 467). The emperor, wearing the imperial costume with the loros as it was developed in the last period of the Empire[288] and a Palaeologan crown, holds a scroll and stands in front of his throne on a cushion. Behind him stand four bodyguards, one of whom holds a sword, and a group of high officials distinguished by their high, bulbous white caps. Nothing in the text explains the picture.

A similar picture exists in the cod. Paris gr. 510, fol. 239ʳ,[289] and has been discussed by Weitzmann and Der Nersessian.[290] Weitzmann correctly observed that there was not the slightest relationship between the scene and the text of the homily. He suggested that the composition represented the recognition of Meletius, bishop of Antioch, by the Emperor Theodosius at the palace before the Council met, an event described by Theodoret in his *Historia ecclesiastica* (v, 7) and for which the scene was presumably invented.

Der Nersessian has proposed another explanation according to which Gregory converses with the Emperor and submits to him his resignation from the see of Constantinople. This event, which took place after the farewell address had been delivered,

---

[288] Cf. G. Galavaris, "The Symbolism of the Imperial Costume as Displayed on Byzantine Coinage," *Museum Notes* (ANS), 8 (1958), pp. 99-117.

[289] Omont, *Min. gr.* (1929), pl. XLI.

[290] Weitzmann, *Chronicles*, pp. 122ff.; S. Der Nersessian, "The Illustrations of the Homilies of Gregory of Nazianzus, Paris gr. 510," *Dumbarton Oaks Papers*, 16 (1962), p. 215.

is mentioned by Gregory himself in his autobiographical poem, *De vita sua* and has been included in Gregory's biography written by Gregory the Presbyter.

Considering the fact that the *Vita* was illustrated, as certain miniatures in the cod. Paris gr. 510 show,[291] this interpretation could be applied convincingly to the illustration of the cod. Paris gr. 543. There is, however, one difficulty caused by the staff which, as a symbol of authority, would suggest rather that the scene represented the election of Gregory as patriarch of Constantinople, mentioned by Sozomenus (VII, 7).[292] If this were the case, the original source of the miniature would have been one of the chronicles which, as Weitzmann has shown, were illustrated.

Yet, the explanation of the staff is not so important, for it may have been part of a conventional ceremony, or even an addition by the artist of the cod. Paris gr. 543, who represented Gregory holding a staff in another illustration as well, that on fol. 310ᵛ (Fig. 468). Whether or not the artist knew the correct meaning of the scene cannot be ascertained, for he probably took the scene from a manuscript of the full edition and not from an illustrated *Vita* of Gregory in which the illustration originated. When the miniature passed into Gregory's homily it lost its direct relation to the text for which it was invented.

3. THE OLD TESTAMENT GROUP
THE GENESIS SCENES

In the homily on the Nativity, Gregory speaks about the mind and senses. He tells how these two distinct elements were given to man by the Creator, and how God breathed the spirit of life into the material body. In the same homily Gregory continues to paraphrase the third and fourth chapters of the book of Genesis.[293]

For this account, the artist of the cod. Paris gr. 543 took illustrations from a book of Genesis. They occupy the lower register of the full-page miniature on fol. 116ᵛ, preceding the text of the sermon, and the left margin of the same folio (Fig. 462). The main miniature contains two distinct scenes. In the one on the right, God leans over Adam, who lies on his back, and gives him life by touching his left hand. At the same time, God's left hand gestures as if to breathe the spirit of life into him. Omont's interpretation that the scene represents the creation of Eve does not seem likely,[294] although it could be related to the event.

A comparison with the extant recensions of the books of Genesis reveals that this representation contains close similarities to a miniature in the Carolingian Bible of Tours, which belongs to the Cotton recension according to Köhler.[295] The main

[291] Der Nersessian, *op.cit.*, *loc.cit.*

[292] J. Bidez, G. H. Hansen eds., *Sozomenus Kirchengeschichte* (Die griechischen christlichen Schriftsteller der ersten Jahrhunderte, 50), Berlin 1960, pp. 309, 310. Cf. also *De ceremoniis*, Bonn 1879, pp. 564, 565; L. Bréhier, "L'investiture des patriarches de Constantinople au moyen âge,"

Miscellanea G. Mercatti, III, *Studi e Testi*, 123 (1940), pp. 368-72.

[293] *PG*, 36, 316, 324, 325.

[294] Omont, *Min. gr.* (1929), p. 57.

[295] W. Köhler, *Die Schule von Tours*, I, 1, Berlin 1930, pp. 186ff.; cf. Weitzmann, *Roll*, p. 193.

characteristic of this recension is the full-length figure of Christ-Logos.[296] The figure of Christ, however, is not a proof that the Paris miniature is a member of the Cotton family of manuscripts, since the figure of Christ also appears in Genesis scenes, such as those of the chapel of St. Demetrius in Dečani, dating from the fourteenth century, which are not related to this recension.[297] In addition to the figure of Christ-Logos, other similarities are apparent, including the motif of quickening Adam by touch. Indeed this motif is found in the Grandval Bible in London (Brit. Mus. cod. Add. 10546, fol. 5ᵛ), which does belong to the Cotton recension.[298] In that miniature, however, the relation of the Creator to the figure of Adam differs in detail from the scene in the Paris miniature. It is not possible to ascertain how the differences originated. Perhaps lack of space forced the illustrator of the Paris manuscript to place the Creator next to Adam. Another possibility is that the scene in the Paris miniature is a conflation of two scenes: the Quickening of Adam and the Creation of Eve. This conflation is possible since, in the scene of Eve's creation in the Vivian Bible, fol. 10ᵛ, the two figures are related in the same way that they are in the scene of the Paris miniature.[299] Nevertheless, it is conceivable that the differences may have occurred within the Cotton recension in the course of copying.[300]

The scene to the left in the Paris miniature showing Adam and Eve in Paradise Called by the Creator-Logos, parallels a scene on fol. 5ᵛ of the Grandval Bible.[301] Therefore, the assignment of both scenes to a Cotton recension of the book of Genesis can no longer be doubted.

The marginal Genesis miniature is almost completely flaked and only the outlines of Adam and Eve seated on a rock can be distinguished (Fig. 462). The figure sitting to the right, probably Adam, has his right hand on his chin, a pensive posture that would suggest an episode after the Fall. No seated figures, however, seem to exist in any of the extant Cotton recension manuscripts. Is this a scene which appeared in

[296] K. Weitzmann, "Observations on the Cotton Genesis," *Late Classical and Mediaeval Studies in Honor of A. M. Friend, Jr.*, ed. by K. Weitzmann, Princeton 1955, pp. 112ff. (here the older bibliography); cf. G. Bonner, "The Cotton Genesis," *The British Museum Quarterly*, XXVI (1963), pp. 22-26. In the mosaics of San Marco in Venice, which copy the miniatures of the Cotton Genesis, the scenes of the Animation and the Shaping of Adam occur, see J. J. Tikkanen, *Die Genesismosaiken von S. Marco in Venedig*, Helsingfors 1899, pl. I; cf. O. Demus, *Die Mosaiken von S. Marco in Venedig 1100-1300*, Baden bei Wien 1935, pl. 27.

[297] V. R. Petković, *La peinture serbe du moyen âge*, I-II, Belgrade 1930, 1934, figs. 95, 96, pls. CXXXII, CXXXIII, CXLIII.

[298] Köhler, *op.cit.*, pl. I, 50.

[299] *Ibid.*, pl. I, 70.

[300] A compositional scheme similar to that in the Paris miniature appears in a miniature showing the Creation of Adam, which is now in the marginal psalters, although originally it was in a Genesis book. For example, a miniature in the Barberini Psalter (Cod. Vat. Barb. gr. 372, fol. 201ᵛ; cf. also London, Brit. Mus. Add. 19352, fol. 162ʳ) shows the Logos bending over Adam and quickening him by touch; at the same time, the Creator appears as if breathing the spirit of life into him. Both motifs appear in the Paris miniature under discussion; here Christ touches Adam's hand, but in the psalter miniature he touches Adam's eye. On the basis of one miniature alone, it is impossible to decide whether or not the psalter miniature belongs to a Genesis of the Cotton recension and thereby to prove that its compositional scheme is a modification which occurred within the recension.

[301] Köhler, *op.cit.*, pl. I, 50.

the archetype of the Cotton recension and was not included in the extant manuscripts?[302] A somewhat similar scene, with some major differences, appears in the Octateuchs as an illustration of the episode "Unto Adam also and to his wife did the Lord God make coats of skins, and clothed them" (Gen. 3: 21).[303] In the flaked miniature of the Paris manuscript, no traces of "coats of skins" can be seen, and any relation to the Octateuchs recension seems unlikely. Even if it were related to the Octateuchs, it would be difficult to accept two scenes from the Cotton and one from another recension. The derivation of the marginal miniature from the same Cotton recension seems more plausible.

In any case, the certain migration of two scenes from a Cotton recension into the Gregory manuscript is of special importance, for it indicates that the Cotton Genesis recension existed also in Constantinople, where the two scenes were copied by the illustrator of Gregory's homilies.

THE SO-CALLED VISION OF HABAKKUK

The miniatures included here are title illustrations of the second homily on Easter, which opens: " 'I shall stand upon my watch today,' said the wonderful Habakkuk, 'since the authority and the contemplation have been given to me by the spirit.' I shall stand with Habakkuk and I shall observe and see what the vision will be, and I shall be told. And I stood and saw. Lo, a man riding on the clouds. He was very tall; his countenance was like the countenance of an angel. His garment was like the luster of lightning that passes by. He lifted his hand toward the east and spoke in a loud voice. His voice was like the voice of a trumpet; round about Him there was a multitude of the heavenly host. He spoke and said: 'salvation was granted to the world today. . . .' "[304]

Prompted by this opening paragraph the artists illustrated the homily with compositions representing Theophanies suitable to convey the meaning of the Resurrection, the glorification of Christ, of which Gregory speaks. Relevant to the "man riding on the clouds" two types of vision can be distinguished and the illustrations can be grouped accordingly: the vision of Christ, and the vision of Christ as an angel.

a. *The Vision of Christ*

The cod. Sinai 339, fol. 9ᵛ, as is usual with this manuscript, includes more than one miniature: a title, a marginal scene, and a historiated initial (Fig. 379). The youthful Christ-Emmanuel is depicted in the center of the title miniature seated on an arc of heaven within a mandorla carried by the four *zodia*, the Angel, Lion, Calf, and

---

[302] Seated figures appear in the ivory caskets published by A. Goldschmidt-K. Weitzmann, *Die byzantinischen Elfenbeinskulpturen*, Berlin 1934, I, pl. Ld. It is not certain that these ivories belong to the Cotton recension; it does seem that the

artists who decorated the caskets were acquainted with more than one iconographic tradition.

[303] Cf. illustration of this passage in cod. Vat. gr. 747, fol. 24ᵛ.

[304] *PG*, 36, 624.

Eagle.[305] Christ holds a codex in his left hand and extends his right hand in benediction. Below, Gregory is on the left of the miniature and the youthful Habakkuk holding a scroll on the right. Both have their heads turned toward the vision. This arrangement of the figures not only balances the composition and adds a hieratic effect, but emphasizes the role of Gregory, who, looking upward, appears not as a teacher but as a visionary. The figures of the two visionaries are repeated in the initial E, where the teaching Gregory is seated and the vision has been replaced by a bust of Christ leaning out of a segment of sky.[306]

If an explanation of the miniature is sought in the cited text of Gregory it will be realized that picture and text do not agree at all. The four apocalyptic animals cannot be explained by the text. Furthermore, the text implies a standing figure and not a seated one, for the impression that "he was very tall" could not have been created from a seated position. There can be no doubt that the picture was originally made for a more complete text. After all, Gregory quotes from another text, as the word φησίν clearly indicates. If this source could be located, it would be possible to discover the original source of the illustration.

The obvious place to look for the borrowed text and possibly the migrated picture is the book of the prophet Habakkuk. In the opening sentence of the second chapter, "I will stand upon my watch . . . ," the phrase that has passed into Gregory's text can be recognized and thus the assumption that the text is borrowed from the Book of Habakkuk finds some justification. But the vision described in the third chapter is general and does not correspond to the one illustrated in the Sinai miniature.

The same chapter contains the prayer of Habakkuk which was incorporated into the psalms. With the text, an illustration, originally invented for the prophet, migrated to the psalters, where Habakkuk is portrayed holding a scroll containing the prayer. The borrowing did not end here. The illustration passed into the homilies of Gregory as well. Indeed a representation of Habakkuk similar to the one in the Sinai miniature, which is found in the thirteenth-century Hamilton Psalter in Berlin,[307] proves that the figure of Habakkuk in the Sinai miniature has migrated into Gregory's text from either a psalter or a prophet book.

Still, the vision must be explained. In the miniatures which illustrate the prayer in the psalters, the depicted vision is either a bust of Christ or a hand of God,[308] whereas in the extant illuminated book of the Prophets there is no vision at all. The natural hypothesis would be to assume that there was not an established tradition concerning the illustration of the vision of Habakkuk and that the representation of any prophet's vision could be used for Habakkuk as well. This hypothesis can be substantiated by

[305] Cf. Millet, *Dalmatique*, pp. 51, 61.

[306] For similar initials in other manuscripts, cf. Lazarev, *History*, II, pl. 137b.

[307] Cod. Mus. Kgl. Kupferstichkab. 78, A. 9, fol. 251ᵛ; see P. Wescher, *Beschreibendes Verzeichnis der Miniaturen-Handschriften und Einzelblätter des Kupferstichkabinetts*, Leipzig 1931, pp. 95ff.

[308] See Theodore Psalter, cod. Brit. Mus. Add. 19352, fol. 198ʳ.

the mosaics of Hosios David in Thessalonica, where two prophets share the same vision, that of Ezekiel. One of them is Habakkuk who observes and "watches with his large ecstatic eyes to see what He will say."[309]

Apparently the same assumption can be made with regard to the illustrations of the homily of Gregory. The illustrators found other visions and used them as the visions of both Habakkuk and Gregory, either unchanged, or adapted to Gregory's text.

Actually, the vision in the title miniature of the Sinai manuscript is the vision of Ezekiel without any adaptation[310] as it appears in the church of Hosios David in Thessalonica and in the miniature of the twelfth-century Gospel book in Venice, cod. Marc. gr. Z. 540, which illustrates the Prologue to the four Gospels.[311] The inclusion of the figure of Gregory in the Sinai miniature and his participation in the vision is required by the text of the homily.

Christ in glory is the vision of both Habakkuk and Gregory in the title miniature of the cod. Paris gr. 550, fol. 8ᵛ (Fig. 402). This differs from that of the Sinai minia-ture in that it represents Christ as Pantocrator seated on a throne surrounded by a mandorla of light under an arch. The four apocalyptic animals no longer appear. Instead, Christ is flanked by a choir of angels and archangels. The figure of the prophet, youthful in this case and pointing with excitement to the figure of Christ, has a parallel in a figure in a thirteenth-century New Testament psalter in Berlin, cod. Lib. Staat. Octavo 13, fol. 247ᵛ.[312] The vision employed by the illustrator of the Paris manuscript is that of the Prophet Isaiah (6: 1-3) as it appears in the codd. Paris gr. 1208, fol. 162ʳ, and Vat. gr. 1162, fol. 119ᵛ.[313] The slight adaptations do not conceal the model. The arch above the figure of Christ and the arrangements of the heavenly army on either side prove that the vision of Isaiah could be transferred to both Habakkuk and Gregory.

The codd. Athos, Panteleimon 6, fol. 5ᵛ, Paris, Coislin 239, fol. 6ʳ, and Oxford, Roe 6, fol. 4ʳ, are similarly illustrated (Figs. 138, 181, 182, 437). Within the title miniature of the Panteleimon codex, Christ-Pantocrator, with his right hand extended in benediction, appears seated in a glory (Fig. 138). Six archangels support the man-

---

[309] A. Xyngopoulos, "Τὸ Καθολικὸν τῆς Μονῆς τοῦ Λατόμου ἐν Θεσσαλονίκῃ," Ἀρχαιολογικὸν Δελ-τίον, 12 (1929), pp. 142ff.; C. R. Morey, "A Note on the Date of the Mosaic of H. David, Salonica," Byzantion, 7 (1934), pp. 339ff.; S. Pelekanides, Παλαιοχριστιανικὰ Μνημεῖα Θεσσαλονίκης, Thessa-lonica 1949, pl. 12; A. M. Ammann, La pittura sacra Bizantina, Rome 1957, pp. 23, 24. For a color reproduction see W. F. Volbach, Frühchrist-liche Kunst, Munich 1958, pp. 134, 135, complete bibliography on p. 70.

[310] For representations of the vision of Ezekiel in art, see W. Neuss, Das Buch Ezechiel in Theo-logie und Kunst, Munich 1912. Cf. L. Bréhier, "Les visions apocalyptiques dans l'art byzantin," Arta și Archeologia, 4 (1930), pp. 1-12.

[311] Reproduced in Lazarev, History, II, pl. 157a. We discuss this miniature in our study on The Illustrated Prologues to the Gospels, which is in preparation.

[312] For the manuscript in general, see E. C. Col-well and H. R. Willoughby, The Four Gospels of Karahissar, II, Chicago 1936, pp. 4 and passim.

[313] H. Omont, "Miniatures des homélies sur la Vierge du moine Jacques," Bulletin de la Société française de reproductions de manuscrits à pein-tures, 11 (1927), pl. XXI; a better reproduction in A. Grabar, Byzantine Painting, Geneva 1953, fig. on p. 183; for bibliography, see Bibl. Nat., Byzance, pp. 22, 23, Stornajolo, Giacomo mo-naco, pl. 52.

dorla which consists of three distinct circles. Outside the title miniature and above the initial letter E of the homily, the prophet Habakkuk is represented, as the inscription above it indicates. He is pictured as an old man standing in front of a building, turning his head toward the vision. His raised left hand indicates wonder and fear, which can be explained only by the relevant verses of the prayer in the Book of Habakkuk (3: 1, 16). The title miniature of the Coislin manuscript shows only the vision. Here Christ is the youthful, eternally beautiful Emmanuel (Fig. 181). The figure of the prophet, trying to walk away because of his fear, forms the initial letter E of the homily in the same manuscript (Fig. 182).

In the Oxford miniature the angels who carry the glory in which Christ-Pantocrator sits have been reduced to two, and the prophet is now included in the title miniature (Fig. 437). Habakkuk stands to the left under an arch and, turning his head slightly toward the heavenly vision, pronounces a benediction. In his left hand he holds a scroll on which the beginning of the sermon is written. The figure of Gregory has not been included in these three miniatures, probably because of spatial limitations.

Here again the iconographic elements of the composition have been taken from their original source without alteration. A figure of Habakkuk, somewhat similar to that in the Athos miniature, appears in the Athens psalter, cod. 15, fol. 240ʳ.[314] The miniatures of both the homily and the psalter show the element of fear, indicating that the standing Habakkuk is a migrated picture that came into the text of Gregory either from a psalter or from a prophet book. Furthermore, the scroll which Habakkuk holds in the Oxford miniature betrays, more than anything else, the provenance of the figure from an illustrated canticle. In fact, a similar figure of Habakkuk appears in the eleventh-century psalter, cod. Vat. gr. 752, fol. 465ʳ.[315] It should be pointed out also that the vision in the miniature of the Panteleimon codex is identical to the one in the Florence Gospel (cod. Laur. Plut. VI, 23, fol. 50ʳ) which illustrates the teaching of Christ on his coming in glory.

The title miniature of the cod. Jerusalem, Taphou 14, fol. 6ʳ, has to a certain extent been adapted to the text of Gregory (Fig. 100). The two visionaries are on the left, while the vision is on the right in the upper part of the miniature. The figure of Gregory is derived from a teaching scene and, here again, the Jerusalem artist remains faithful to his principle in combining the teacher and the subject of the sermon. In this case, however, the figure of Gregory is required by the text. The prophet, an old man, looks toward the vision. The contrapposto and the raised hand express his wonder, whereas his flowing garment seems to indicate the stormy soul of a visionary. The depiction of the vision itself reveals a greater amount of adaptation to the text of the homily. Christ appears standing, not seated, within a mandorla of light between two angels; he thus conforms to the phrase in the text, "He was very tall." The mandorla has two distinct

[314] A. Delatte, *Les manuscrits à miniatures et à ornements des bibliothèques d'Athènes*, Liège 1926, pl. XXXII, b. The manuscript has been dated in both the twelfth and fourteenth centuries. The latter date seems to be the most plausible.
[315] DeWald, *Vat. gr. 752*, pl. IV.

circles. Christ is in the inner circle, from which rays of light emanate. There is no scenic or architectural background.

b. *The Vision of Christ as an Angel*

The cod. Athos, Dionysiou 61, fol. 4ʳ, contains a title miniature in which the two visionaries occupy the sides of the composition (Fig. 357). They are set against two mountains that, sloping toward the center, form between them a space which is occupied by the vision, showing an angel seated on an arc of heaven. The cipher IC-XC identifies him with certainty as Christ. A throng of angels carry the mandorla. Were Christ not winged, the vision would resemble the one used by the illustrator of the Panteleimon codex, the migration of which has been proved (Fig. 138). The addition of the wings and the consequent change of Christ into an angel-Christ may have been an adaptation to the phrase, "His countenance was like the countenance of an angel." It is not merely an adaptation, however, because in Byzantine art there is a type of Christ represented as an angel based on Biblical and patristic texts. In Isaiah (9: 6) the Messiah is referred to as μεγάλης βουλῆς ἄγγελος—the messenger of great counsel; and in Malachi (3: 1) as ἄγγελος τῆς διαθήκης—the messenger of the covenant. The idea passed into the writings of Christian theologians who interpreted the term ἄγγελος as a reference to the mission of the Logos in the world.[316] This type of *Christos-Angelos* is depicted often in Byzantine art, primarily in frescoes in Yugoslavia, and the monasteries of Athos.[317] It seems possible that the Dionysiou miniature is one of the earliest representations of Christ as an angel with his name inscribed. No such inscription appears next to the angel in the miniatures discussed below, but by analogy to the Dionysiou illustration, He may also be considered *Christos-Angelos*.

In the marginal illustration of the cod. Sinai 339, fol. 9ᵛ, as well as the two figures resembling those in the title miniature of the same manuscript, the *Christos-Angelos* of the vision appears standing within a mandorla around which are archangels with scepters (Fig. 379). If Christ were not winged, the vision would be like the one in the Jerusalem manuscript. In other words, the standing posture is here too an adaptation to the text of the homily. The archangels that surround *Christos-Angelos* have not been shown in the similar miniatures of the codd. Moscow, Hist. Museum 146, fol. 4ᵛ, Paris gr. 533, fol. 7ʳ, and Athos, Karakalou 24, fol. 6ᵛ. In the first the figure of the prophet Habakkuk stands between the written columns holding a scroll, and in the third he has not been included at all (Figs. 2, 236, 453).

[316] For a discussion of the theme in patristic thought see J. Barbel, *Christos-Angelos*, Bonn 1941; cf. J. Meyendorff, "L'iconographie de la Sagesse Divine dans la tradition byzantine," *Cahiers archéologiques*, 10 (1959), pp. 226-69.

[317] For examples, see A. M. Ammann, "Slawische Christus-Engel Darstellungen," *Orientalia Christiana Periodica*, 6 (1940), pp. 467-94; Millet, *Dalmatique*, p. 72 n. 1; G. Soteriou, Ἅγιον Ὄρος,

Athens n.d., p. 133, fig. 30; J. D. Stefănescu, *L'art byzantin et l'art lombard en Transylvanie*, Paris 1938, pp. 123, 143. The wings of Jesus are also cited in the secret prayer which is recited by the priest while he waves the ἀήρ over the eucharistic elements: "cover us, O Saviour, with the shadow of Thy wings. . . ." For a brief discussion, see G. Soteriou, "Χριστιανικὴ καὶ Βυζαντινὴ εἰκονογραφία," Θεολογία, 26 (1955), p. 7.

The miniature of the cod. Paris gr. 543, fol. 27ʳ, is of special interest because of its close conformity to Gregory's text (Fig. 455). The scene of the lower register depicting the resurrection of the dead is thematically allied to the miniature of the upper register since the resurrection of the dead, which has been discussed earlier (pp. 77, 78), is part of God's plan of salvation. In the miniature of the upper register, the *Christos-Angelos* of the vision, raising his right hand and holding a scroll with his left, is shown in a vivid walking posture, which illustrates literally the quick passing "like the luster of lightning" of the text. The impression of vividness is intensified by gesturing angels in the throng surrounding the central angel and included within the same mandorla of light. On the right, Habakkuk, holding an open scroll, seems to be trying to escape the supernatural experience which dominates the barren, rocky landscape. Gregory, standing on the opposite side, looks toward the vision with wonder, but also with greater certainty as if observing something that he knows well. A similar figure of Habakkuk is found in the Serbian psalter, fol. 194ʳ.[318]

The vision showing Christ as an angel has been depicted in the cod. Paris gr. 510, fol. 285ʳ,[319] but the differences between the miniature of the full edition and those of the liturgical edition are noteworthy. The latter miniatures are distinguished by the extent of their adaptation to the text of the homily and especially by their representation of the heavenly host surrounding Christ, which conforms to the "round about him" of the text. Furthermore, in all of them, the figure of Habakkuk differs from his figure in the miniature of the full edition.

In addition to the manuscripts mentioned in this discussion, two other codices consistent with their system of illustration contain figured initials which must have been derived from larger scenes whose type cannot be specified because of the abbreviated form of the historiated initials. The cod. Milan, Ambros. G. 88 sup., fol. 7ʳ, has, in the initial letter E, the figure of Habakkuk and an angel flying from above with a labarum (Fig. 301). The codd. Vat. gr. 463, fol. 324ʳ, and Athens 2554, fol. 3ʳ, show only the figure of Habakkuk in the initial E (Figs. 89, 257).

Evidently more than one pictorial tradition of the vision of Habakkuk existed. The artists found themselves free to choose from different representations of Theophanies and used them without alterations, or adapted them. The use of the models and the process of adaptation reveal each artist's ingenuity and freedom, which is also expressed in the choice of different types of Christ. Each type reveals a different aspect of Christ: Christ-Pantocrator, the transcendental God, the God of the Old and New Testament; Christ-Emmanuel, Son of God, the Anointed of the Holy Spirit, "the Resurrection and the Life"; and the third type, the *Christos-Angelos*, expressing the eternal wisdom of God. Wisdom, Salvation, and Judgment are the messages of these miniatures, which illustrate the sermon read on the first day after Easter.[320]

[318] J. Strzygowski, *Die Miniaturen des serbischen Psalters* (Denkschriften der kaiserlichen Akademie der Wissenschaften, philosophisch-historische Klasse, 52), Vienna 1906, pl. XLVIII, 113.

[319] Omont, *Min. gr.* (1929), pl. XLIII.

[320] Millet, *Dalmatique*, pp. 75ff.

IV. THE SUPPLEMENTARY ILLUSTRATIONS

IN THE introduction to this study it was stated that certain manuscripts have, in addition to the title miniatures, supplementary illustrations, i.e. miniatures inserted in the text of some of the homilies referring to a specific narrative part of the text. These manuscripts are Jerusalem, Taphou 14 (hom. 1, 3, 14); Athos, Panteleimon 6 and Paris, Coislin 239 (hom. 2, 3, 9); Paris gr. 533 (hom. 3); Sinai 339 and Paris gr. 543 (hom. 8). The miniatures do not appear as title miniatures in other manuscripts of the homilies, but they constitute a separate group that supplements the main illustrations of the cited homilies. Furthermore, the historiated initials of the cod. Turin, Univ. Lib. C. I. 6, referring to specific passages in the text of various homilies, as well as those initials and marginal miniatures of the same and other manuscripts which are merely decorative and unrelated to any textual passage, must be included in this part of the study.

Prior to the discussion proper of the various groups of these miniatures, the kind and nature of the illustrations should be defined. They are of two kinds; those which are inserted within the written column and are exclusively narrative scenes; and those which appear beside the written column or form an initial letter and are either narrative scenes or simple figures which often imply other narrative scenes. The column and marginal miniatures of the codd. Athos, Panteleimon 6, and Paris, Coislin 239 actually bear inscriptions identifying the represented subject matter. In addition to these inscriptions, the Coislin manuscript makes use of a commentary text, and, in certain cases, the miniatures are not illustrations of the text proper, but of the commentary. In other words they are "commentary illustrations."

Neither kind of illustration—the column or the marginal—appears here for the first time; both have a tradition in the history of book illumination. The marginal text illustrations, especially, existed before the sixth century; as Weitzmann has observed, this system had reached an advanced state in the Rabula Gospels.[1] In the Middle Byzantine period, this system of illustration found great favor in manuscripts in which great numbers of scenes from various sources had to be collected. The illustrated "Sacra Parallela" of John of Damascus (cod. Paris gr. 923), the marginal psalters of the ninth and eleventh centuries, lectionaries (cod. Morgan 639), and the complete edition of the homilies of Gregory of Nazianzus (cod. Milan, Ambros. E. 49-50, inf.) provide the necessary setting within which the supplementary illustrations of the manuscripts must be considered.

In these examples of marginal illustration, the selected miniatures form many cycles. Similarly, the miniatures of the manuscripts under discussion were not all made for Gregory's text; instead, each manuscript accumulated a great number of miniatures from different sources. The subject matter of some of these miniatures had also been

---

[1] Weitzmann, *Roll*, pp. 116ff.

chosen by illustrators of the earlier complete editions of Gregory's homilies, especially the illustrator of the Milan codex. This and the fact that the marginal system of illustration was used by the same illustrator of the complete edition raise another aspect of the question, referring to a possible relationship of the two editions, posed in the first part of this study: do the manuscripts of the liturgical edition depend on the full edition, as far as their supplementary illustrations are concerned, or is this an illustration made afresh by a new choice of miniatures, selected directly from various other sources. The comparisons which are made in the course of the following discussion provide the answer.

The supplementary miniatures of the manuscripts of the liturgical edition can, with regard to iconography and their relationship to the text, be categorized as religious, mythological, "historical," bucolic and decorative.

A. THE RELIGIOUS MINIATURES

1. INVENTED MINIATURES

a. *Scenes Referring to St. Basil's Life*

In the homily on St. Basil, Gregory, having given an account of the early life of Basil, proceeds to narrate the story of Basil's persecution during the reign of the Arian Emperor Valens. In the forty-eighth paragraph, Gregory says: "Who does not know the prefect of those days? It was before this man . . . that our noble champion [Basil] was brought. Rather he entered his court as though summoned to a banquet and not to a judgement. How can I give an adequate account either of the insolence of the prefect or of the wisdom with which Basil met his attack?"[2]

The illustrator of the cod. Athos, Panteleimon 6, fol. 134^v has placed the following miniature within the column on the right as an illustration of the passage (Fig. 153). St. Basil appears in the center, urged by a soldier toward the prefect, who is seated on the left in front of a building. There is another building on the right and an inscription in the background clarifies the subject.

The next paragraph of the same homily continues to describe the prefect's questioning of and threats to Basil.[3] Within the lines of this passage a picture is inserted, fol. 135^r, similar to the one discussed above (Fig. 157). The only differences are that the building on the right no longer appears, and a slight variation has occurred in the pose of the attendant who is pushing Basil, probably to express the threats mentioned in the text.

Both these passages are also illustrated by similar but simpler pictures in the cod. Paris, Coislin 239, fol. 100^v (Figs. 222, 224), in which neither an architectural back-

[2] *PG*, 36, 557. The translation of this passage and of others from the same homily, which follow, have been taken from P. McCauley and other trans., *Funeral Orations by St. Gregory Nazianzenus and St. Ambrose*, New York 1953, pp. 67ff.

[3] *PG*, 36, 560.

ground nor the attendant appears. The use of similar scenes to illustrate two phases of one episode indicates a great density of picture-narration.

Gregory tells his audience that the prefect was disappointed with his conversation with Basil, and that he went to report the events to the Emperor Valens.[4] A small column picture in the Coislin manuscript, fol. 101^v, illustrates this passage (Fig. 225). In the miniature Valens is coming out of his palace and is gesturing expressively to the prefect.

The next events from Basil's life that Gregory narrates are Basil's exile and the miraculous healing of the emperor's son.[5] These two episodes, illustrated only in the Panteleimon codex, fol. 138^r, appear in two superimposed column pictures (Fig. 158). The smaller one at the top represents a boat in which a crew of five pulls the oars; in the extreme left of the boat appears the nimbed figure of the black-bearded Basil. In the center of the miniature below, the son of the emperor appears to be sleeping. Behind the bed on which the ailing boy lies, Basil stands in a three-quarter pose, blessing him. Basil's eyes are directed towards Valens who, in imperial attire, emerges from a building on the right. On the left another building with a gabled roof completes the architectural background of the miniature. The composition of this second miniature, which is completely different from the illustrations of the same episode found in the cod. Paris gr. 510, recalls the Gospel miniatures showing Christ's miracles, on which it was probably modeled.[6]

Divine manifestations on Basil's behalf did not end with the healing of Valens' son. "The same thing was said to have occurred also in the case of the prefect not long afterwards. An attack of sickness caused him likewise to humble himself beneath the hands of the saint. For men of sense a stroke of calamity really becomes a source of instruction, and affliction is often a greater blessing than prosperity."[7] The text goes on to describe how the prefect was healed by Basil. This passage is illustrated by a small, framed, marginal miniature in the Panteleimon codex, fol. 138^v (Fig. 159). The suffering prefect lies on a bed; Basil stands behind him. To the left is a small building which completes the scene.

As well as having the gift of healing, Basil protected the weak and persecuted. Gregory tells that a judge was trying to force a widow to marry him. In order to escape the judge's attentions, the woman took refuge in the sanctuary of a church and there she was protected by Basil from the demands of the judge and his friends.[8] An illuminated initial H (not illustrated) in the relevant passage in the cod. Turin, Univ. Lib. C. I. 6, fol. 89^v, represents Basil and the woman. This episode from Basil's life, illustrated in the cod. Paris gr. 510 as well, is also quoted by John of Damascus in his Sacra Parallela, and a ninth-century manuscript containing this work in Paris (cod.

[4] *Ibid.*, 561.
[5] *Ibid.*, 564.
[6] Cf. Omont, *Min. gr.* (1929), pl. xxxi and cod.

Paris gr. 74, fol. 16^v, Omont, *Evangiles*, i, pl. 17, 2.
[7] *PG*, 36, 565.   [8] *Ibid.*, 568.

gr. 923, fol. 300ʳ) illustrates it with two scenes.⁹ Unfortunately the Turin initial is too abbreviated to allow comparison with either the illustrations of the full edition or of the Sacra Parallela.

As a result of this interest in the weak and persecuted, Basil was taken to the judge and again questioned.¹⁰ The Panteleimon manuscript, fol. 140ʳ, repeats the picture of fol. 135ʳ (Fig. 160). In the margin outside this miniature, a fire, a saw, two iron hooks that scratch the flesh, and perhaps a cauldron are shown. No actual reference to these instruments occurs in the paragraph; instead they are mentioned in the forty-ninth paragraph describing the first trial of Basil during which he was threatened by the prefect with confiscation of his belongings, exile, tortures, and finally death. Basil's response to these threats was: "Fire and sword and wild beasts and tongues that tear the flesh are a source of delight to us rather than of terror."¹¹ Therefore the instruments of torture should have accompanied the miniature for the forty-ninth paragraph; that is to say, the miniature of fol. 135ʳ. The apparent misplacement probably resulted from the similarity of the column miniatures.

During the second questioning of Basil, the prefect became greatly angered by Basil's persistence in not yielding or compromising and he ordered Basil's mantle torn from his back. Basil answered, "I will strip myself to my tunic as well, if you so desire."¹² The Coislin manuscript, fol. 104ᵛ, illustrates this passage with a miniature showing Basil, the prefect, and the attendant trying to remove Basil's mantle instead of taking him to the prefect as shown in the Athos manuscript (Fig. 227). This attitude becomes even clearer in the cod. Paris gr. 510, fol. 104ʳ, where the posture of the attendant differs from that in the Coislin miniature.¹³

The behavior of the prefect was more than the people of Caesarea could tolerate. Gregory gives a lively description of what followed. They took torches, stones, and clubs as weapons against the prefect, but Basil saved the prefect from their wrath.¹⁴ The Panteleimon codex, fol. 140ᵛ, contains a column miniature representing, in the center, the prefect seated in front of a building (Fig. 161). At either side a group of people with weapons on their shoulders gesticulate angrily. In the similar miniature of the Coislin manuscript, fol. 105ʳ, one of the groups of gesticulating people has been omitted (Fig. 223). The same episode is also illustrated in the cod. Paris gr. 510, fol. 104ʳ, fused, however, with the previous scene.¹⁵

No further discussion is needed to show that all these miniatures referring to episodes in St. Basil's life are derived from the text of Gregory. Nothing is left unexplained save the figure of the attendant, which is only implied by the text. The attendant, however, is a conventional figure, often appearing in similar scenes in Mediaeval book illumination.

---

⁹ Omont, *Min. gr.* (1929), pl. xxxi; Bibl. Nat., *Byzance*, pp. 34-37, pl. xxii.
¹⁰ *PG*, 36, 568.
¹¹ *Loc.cit.*

¹² *Loc.cit.*
¹³ Omont, *Min. gr.* (1929), pl. xxxi.
¹⁴ *PG*, 36, 569.
¹⁵ Omont, *Min. gr.* (1929), pl. xxxi.

Among the invented scenes referring to Basil's life, two more found in the Panteleimon codex, fols. 115ʳ, 105ʳ, should be included (Figs. 152, 151). Although the elements of the first miniature are not original, they are so well integrated with Gregory's text that they can only be explained by it. In the text, Gregory refers to his own and Basil's early youth in Athens at which time they built up "the structure of knowledge" in order to offer it later to the service of God. Gregory states: "Such were the things with both of us. And after having supported the strongly built chamber, as Pindar said, with golden columns, we marched onwards. God and our affection were our coadjutors."[16] This chamber with the golden columns is rendered pictorially as a ciborium from which candles hang, Gregory and Basil standing on either side of it. The ciborium may simply be a literal rendering of the text, but since it customarily indicates the altar of a church, it could allude to the Church as well as to the structure of knowledge that was offered to it for the sake of God. The two figures of the Fathers ultimately go back to representations in menologia or lectionaries, such as those found in the cod. Vat. gr. 1156, fol. 283ʳ and fol. 295ᵛ.

The second miniature, fol. 105ʳ, refers to the seventh paragraph of the same homily (Fig. 151). There Gregory, speaking about Basil's family, mentions the persecution and the life in the desert which was forced upon them. During that period, they fed on milk of hinds which were miraculously guided to them. Next to this passage a frameless, marginal miniature shows a group of hinds. This direct illustration of the text is sufficiently explained by it and a fuller illustration is found in the cod. Paris gr. 510, fol. 104ʳ.[17] Since illustrations of hinds appear in other manuscripts as well, for instance, the Psalter Leningrad gr. 214 (1074-81),[18] it is possible that illustrations of such animals may ultimately go back to illustrated animal treatises.

b. *The Fallen Heosphoros*

In the second sermon on Easter, Gregory speaks about Christ's redemptive work, and closes the fifth paragraph as follows: "the brilliant Heosphoros, because of his arrogance, became dark and took his name thereafter from this quality. Even the rebellious powers that were under him, by escaping the Good, became the creators of Evil and causes of evil to us."[19]

A marginal illustration of this passage appears in the cod. Jerusalem, Taphou 14, fol. 9ʳ (Fig. 101). On the right Gregory is teaching and in front of him on the left is a winged figure either falling or already fallen. This figure is apparently the Heosphoros of the text. His arms are stretched above his wings, his feet are extended upward, with the right leg slightly bent at the knee, and he wears only a loincloth. This nudity, unusual in such illustrations, combined with the detailed rendering of form, creates a sculpturesque effect, betraying the representation's classical ancestry.

---

[16] *PG*, 36, 521.
[17] Omont, *Min. gr.* (1929), pl. XXXI.

[18] Lazarev, *History*, II, pl. 136b.
[19] *PG*, 36, 629.

Gregory's text refers to the fall of the angels, and especially to the name of Lucifer, but the reference is not explicit. More explicit, and of earlier date, are the words of Christ as they are recorded in the Gospel of Luke: "I beheld Satan as lightning fall from heaven" (10: 18); but even Christ alluded to Isaiah 14 and Ezekiel 28 which are the *loci classici* regarding the fall of the angels. "How are thou fallen from heaven, O Lucifer, son of the morning!" says Isaiah, "how art thou cut down to the ground, which didst weaken the nations!"[20]

It would be natural to assume that the illustration of the Fallen Heosphoros was borrowed either from the Book of Isaiah or from one of the Gospels. To my knowledge, only the Gospels have this passage illustrated with the theme of the fall of angels, which is more popular in the West than in the East. In the cod. Paris gr. 74, fol. 131[r] and in a Slavonic Gospel, Brit. Mus. Add. 34677, fol. 169[v], to mention only two examples,[21] one sees a nimbed archangel holding a staff and a globe, standing on an arc of heaven from which a nimbed figure casts devils down into a pit. The devils are rendered in the Mediaeval fashion—black and with tails—but these characteristics have nothing in common with the Jerusalem miniature. Clearly then this rendering of Lucifer is not derived from them nor has it any relation to them. The two concepts are so different that a transformation from one to the other seems impossible. On the contrary the miniature under discussion was created for the passage of the homily it illustrates, adapted, however, from a classical antecedent, as the figure of the fallen angel indicates. The representations of two different myths may have served as models for the Gregory miniature. One is the story of Phaethon, the other, the story of Icarus. The one common point connecting their stories with that of the fallen angels is their disobedience to their fathers. Yet it seems more likely that the Icarus myth rather than the Phaethon myth served as the model for the Jerusalem miniature, chiefly because Icarus had wings.[22]

The story of Icarus occurs in the so-called Apollodorus' *Bibliotheke* and in Ovid's *Ars amatoria* adapted from Greek sources.[23] Illustrations of this story appear in Pompeian frescoes. A figure of Icarus, in one instance falling and in another already fallen, comes close to our type.[24] A similar figure probably existed in a *Bibliotheke* of Apollodorus, known in the Middle Byzantine period and indisputably illustrated, and was

[20] In general see *The Catholic Encyclopedia*, I, p. 479; IX, p. 410.

[21] Omont, *Evangiles*, II, pl. 115. B. Filov, *Les miniatures de l'évangile du roi Jean Alexandre à Londres*, Sofia 1934, pl. 81, fig. 221.

[22] The type of Phaethon appearing in a series of Roman sarcophagi, which illustrate the story of his fall, is different from that of Icarus and from the figure depicted in the Jerusalem miniature. Phaethon differs in the position of the legs and in the absence of wings, although the floating cloak could easily have been changed into a pair

of wings. See C. Robert, *Die antiken Sarkophag-reliefs*, III, Berlin 1904, p. 340, pls. CX, CXI.

[23] For the date and sources of Apollodorus, see M. Van der Valk, "On Apollodori *Bibliotheca*," *Revue des études grècques*, 71 (1958), pp. 100-68. For Ovid's literary models, see G. L. Lafaye, *Le Métamorphoses d'Ovide et leurs modèles grecs*, Paris 1904, pp. 187ff.

[24] P. H. Blanckenhagen, "Narration in Hellenistic and Roman Art," *American Journal of Archaeology*, 61 (1957), p. 82, fig. 11.

used as a model for the Heosphoros miniature of the Gregory manuscript. The addition of a loincloth was an adaptation by the illustrator.

So Heosphoros, the "fallen son of the morning," and the fallen Icarus probably have been related, with respect to their pictorial type and their meaning. If this is accepted, the Heosphoros miniature is another example to be added to those showing the adaptation of classical compositional schemes by the Mediaeval miniaturists investigated by Weitzmann.[25]

2. MIGRATED MINIATURES

a. *The Old Testament Group*

In delivering Basil's eulogy, Gregory compares his friend's good deeds with those of patriarchs and prophets. These witnesses extend from Adam to the Prophet Elijah and the Three Holy Children in the Fire, following more or less the sequence of the Biblical books. In the same way, in the second homily on Easter, Gregory emphasizes the importance of the mystery of Christ's Resurrection and the redemption of mankind through Christ by referring frequently to the story of man under the law and alluding to various important events of the Old Testament. In both homilies these passages are illustrated in two ways. In some cases the painter satisfied himself with the portrait figure of the witness, but in other cases he added pictures with scenes instead of simple figures.

—Miniatures from the Octateuchs

Gregory begins his comparisons of Basil to the Biblical figures by stating: "Adam was deemed worthy of the hand of God and the delights of Paradise and the first legislation . . . he did not keep the command."[26] The cod. Athos, Panteleimon 6, fol. 151^v, contains a framed miniature on the left margin showing Adam standing in the garden of Eden in an attitude of prayer (Fig. 162). Outside the picture, in the upper right hand corner, is an arc of heaven.

The place to look for a source of this miniature would be the Book of Genesis. There a complete account of the events related to the Creation and the Fall of Man is given. Moreover, in the illustrations of these events in the Vatican Octateuch, cod. gr. 747, fol. 21^r, there appears a figure of Adam similar to the one found in the Panteleimon miniature. In these two miniatures, Adam is still in the realm of bliss preceding the Fall. There is one difference however: the Adam of the Panteleimon miniature is clothed—a fact that contradicts the statement of Genesis. The clothing was probably added by the illustrator of the Panteleimon codex and might be explained as an attempt to express better the idea of "patriarchal witness."

---

[25] Weitzmann, *Roll*, pp. 173ff.; cf. *idem*, "The Survival of Mythological Representations in Early Christian and Byzantine Art . . . ," *Dumbarton* *Oaks Papers*, 14 (1960), pp. 45-68.
[26] *PG*, 36, 592.

Gregory in his second sermon on Easter says "God placed [Adam] in Paradise, . . . but Adam transgressed the given law. . . ."[27] This passage is illustrated by a marginal miniature in the cod. Jerusalem, Taphou 14, fol. 11ʳ, showing Adam nude, seated in a pensive pose among the trees of Paradise (Fig. 102). Frontal busts of Adam included in circular medallions appear in the cod. Milan, Ambros. E. 49-50 inf.,[28] but they bear no relation to the Jerusalem miniature which is a scene, not a bust. A scene with Adam in a pensive pose appears in cod. Paris gr. 510, fol. 52ᵛ.[29] This cannot be related to the Jerusalem miniature either because, in the full edition, the miniature illustrates the first sermon on Peace, which has not been included in the liturgical edition and, more important, the two scenes in the two editions differ from one another.

In the miniature of the full edition, Adam sits with Eve and the two figures form a scene which comes after the Expulsion, whereas in the Jerusalem miniature Adam is alone; furthermore, his figure must have been taken from a scene which comes after the Fall but before the Expulsion, because he is still in the Garden of Eden. These observations help locate the Jerusalem picture directly in a Book of Genesis. In fact, such a scene is found in a miniature of the Vatican Octateuch (cod. Vat. gr. 747, fol. 24ᵛ), illustrating verses 14-21 of the third chapter in two scenes. The Adam of the second scene, although a mirror image, is similar to the Adam of the Jerusalem miniature. The first man has just heard the tragic words of his Creator: "For dust thou art, and unto dust shalt thou return" (Gen. 3: 19). He knows what awaits him now; this is man contemplating his fate.

In the same homily Gregory, meditating on the events described in Genesis pertaining to Adam's transgression and Fall, speaks of death that came upon the first man and mankind as a result of sin. These lines are illustrated by a marginal frameless miniature in the cod. Jerusalem Taphou 14, fol. 11ʳ, depicting a seated young person who contemplates or mourns over the body of an old bearded man. The body is not on a bier but lies stretched on the ground (Fig. 102). Obviously the scene represents the death of the first man and of man in general. The composition is conventional and since death scenes occur in a variety of examples, to indicate a specific model would be hazardous. The artist could have borrowed any death scene from an Octateuch or a monastic treatise such as the Heavenly Ladder by John Climacus,[30] and adapted it to a new context by eliminating any unnecessary elements.

Similarly, it cannot be determined with any degree of accuracy whether or not a historiated initial Z in the cod. Turin, Univ. Lib. C. I. 6, fol. 18ᵛ, depicting Eve's Temptation, is related to the same cycle of miniatures in the Octateuchs (Fig. 31). This initial is found in the homily on New Sunday and illustrates the following passage

[27] *PG*, 36, 632, 633.

[28] Grabar, *Ambros. 49-50*, pls. xxxiv, 1; xxxviii, 5.

[29] Omont, *Min. gr.* (1929), pl. xxiv.

[30] Cf. death scenes in the cod. Vat. gr. 746, fols. 63ᵛ and 84ʳ. I owe this reference to Mrs. D. Mouriki, whom I thank; cf. also cod. Vat. gr. 1754, fols. 16ʳ and 16ᵛ, Martin, *Ladder*, pl. ciii, 271, civ, 272.

of the sixth paragraph: ". . . don't let yourself be defeated by a desire for beauty, don't let your eyes take you away . . . but remember Eve . . . the sweet temptation. . . ."[31] And indeed the illustrator depicts Eve seated by the Tree of Knowledge conversing with the serpent, which coils around it. The shape of the letter is especially demanding, and if the artist has borrowed this miniature from a Book of Genesis, he had to transform it to such an extent that its model cannot be determined with accuracy.

Continuing to compare Basil to the Old Testament figures, Gregory refers to Enos— who should not be confused with Enoch[32]—saying: "Enos had hoped to invoke the name of the Lord."[33] In the cod. Athos, Panteleimon 6, fol. 151[v], a marginal, frameless miniature shows the figure of Enos standing and praying beneath an arc of heaven (Fig. 162). This figure differs from the conventional frontal medallions appearing in the cod. Milan, Ambros. E. 49-50 inf.[34] Gregory's passage is taken almost verbatim from the Book of Genesis. There is no evidence to show that this passage was illustrated, so it might well be an invention of the illustrator of Gregory's homilies, who adapted the praying Adam to represent the praying Enos. Adaptations of similar kinds occur in the psalters.[35]

Later in the same homily Gregory mentions the translation of Enoch. In the Panteleimon manuscript on fol. 152[r], a frameless, marginal miniature shows Enoch being taken into heaven by an angel (Fig. 163). Gregory's passage is the same as that found in Genesis 5: 24, yet the illustrations for each are not the same. Nowhere does there occur a translation of Enoch similar to that in the Panteleimon manuscript. In the Octateuchs and in the Vatican Cosmas Indicopleustes, cod. Vat. gr. 699, fol. 56[r], there is a miniature that presents Enoch standing, blessing, and holding a scroll.[36] A small personification of Death is seated on a stool by him. Death turns its head away from Enoch, thus indicating Enoch's escape from death. Since it seems that no translation of Enoch was represented, the only possible solution with reference to the miniature of the Panteleimon codex is that Gregory's illustrator adapted a model which represented the Translation of a Saint. The miniature of the *Metastasis* of St. John as it appears in the cod. Paris gr. 510, fol. 32[v], seems to be the closest parallel.[37]

Next, Gregory compares Basil to Noah. The Panteleimon manuscript on fol. 152[r] illustrates this passage with a standing figure of Noah, who points to the ark at the right of the miniature (Fig. 163). The ark, resting on a podium, is a tall, thin structure with a door and a sloping roof.

A bust of Noah within a medallion is found in the cod. Milan, Ambros. E. 49-50

---

[31] *PG*, 36, 613.

[32] Cf. Gen. 4: 26; 5: 9-11; 5: 18-24.

[33] *PG*, 36, 592.

[34] Grabar, *Ambros. 49-50*, pl. XXXIV, 4. Cf. Gen. 4: 26.

[35] Cf. in psalters, prophet figures represented praying—a posture not required from the point of view of iconography. See cod. Vat. gr. 752, fol. 469[r], DeWald, *Vat. gr. 752*, pl. LV; also cod. Paris gr. 139, fol. 431[v], H. Buchthal, *The Miniatures of the Paris Psalter*, London 1938, pl. XII.

[36] See cod. Vat. gr. 746, fol. 48[v], and Stornajolo, *Cosmas*, pl. 19.

[37] Omont, *Min. gr.* (1929), pl. XXII (third register). For the problem of the ascension of Henoch, see J. Danielou, "L'ascension d'Henoch," *Irénikon*, 28 (1955), pp. 257-67.

inf.,[38] but it does not form a scene and therefore cannot be related to the Panteleimon miniature, whose source must be sought elsewhere. Its original location, in fact, was in an Octateuch, as is shown by a similar miniature including a standing figure of Noah and a building at his left resembling the ark, which appears in the Vatican Octateuch (cod. gr. 747, fol. 28ᵛ). In that scene Noah is commanded to build the ark, but the structure by his side is probably a temple. It is probable that the artist of the Panteleimon miniature misunderstood the scene and erroneously called a temple an ark.

Gregory continues his comparison and mentions Abraham and his sacrifice.[39] Beside this pasage in the Panteleimon codex, fol. 152ʳ, there are two miniatures, both marginal and frameless (Fig. 163). The miniature above shows Abraham just about to sacrifice Isaac. The patriach's head is turned to the left, looking up to an arc of heaven from which rays of light descend. A tree and a ram complete the picture. In the miniature below, Isaac carries wood for the sacrificial fire burning in front of him.

The fact that these miniatures are complete scenes precludes the possibility of any direct relationship with the medallions in the cod. Milan, Ambros. E. 49-50, inf.[40] Nor can such a relationship be supported by the historiated initial T in the cod. Turin, Univ. Lib. C. I. 6, fol. 21ᵛ, showing a portrait of Abraham as a supplementary illustration of the homily on Pentecost, since the Turin illustrator, favoring the system of the historiated initial, has accepted its limitations, which involve in most cases great reduction of larger scenes (Fig. 35). The Turin initial is placed beside the following passage: "I mean Abraham who excelled himself in the patriarchate."[41] Perhaps the idea of glory, implied in this sentence, inspired the use of what seem to be palm branches framing the figure of Abraham.

The Sacrifice of Abraham occurs also in the cod. Paris gr. 510, fol. 174ᵛ, illustrating, however, the homily on God which is one of the four theological orations not contained in the liturgical edition.[42] Since no other miniature of this particular cycle seems to have been taken directly from the full edition, it is highly unlikely that the miniature under discussion presents a different case. If, then, a direct relationship between the miniatures of the liturgical edition and those of the complete edition cannot be confirmed, the origins of the former miniatures must be sought elsewhere. In fact, the two Panteleimon miniatures find their best parallels in the Octateuchs.[43]

Jacob with his ladder is the next person to whom Gregory compares Basil.[44] Indeed, on fol. 152ᵛ, of the Panteleimon codex, there is a marginal, frameless miniature representing a standing figure of Jacob pointing to the ladder which two angels are ascending (Fig. 164). In his comparison, Gregory refers to two different episodes of Jacob's

[38] Grabar, *Ambros. 49-50*, pl. xxxiv, 4.
[39] *PG*, 36, 592.
[40] Grabar, *Ambros. 49-50*, pls. xxxiv, 4; xlviii, 1; lvi, 1.
[41] *PG*, 36, 434.
[42] Omont, *Min. gr.* (1929), pl. xxxvii.

[43] Cf. Sacrifice of Abraham in cod. Vat. gr. 747, fol. 43ᵛ, and Isaac carrying the wood in the Octateuch of the Seraglio, cod. 8, fol. 87ᵛ, reproduced in Ouspensky, *Octateuque*, pl. xiv, 47.
[44] *PG*, 36, 592.

story. The text of those episodes and their illustrations are found in two distinct scenes in the Vatican Octateuch (cod. gr. 747, fols. 50ʳ and 53ᵛ). A comparison of the two miniatures with the miniature of Gregory's homily shows that Gregory's illustrator borrowed from the two scenes the elements appropriate to form the miniature found in the Panteleimon manuscript, and that he has not used the cod. Paris gr. 510 whose miniature (fol. 174ᵛ), depicting Jacob's Dream and illustrating the theological oration on God,[45] does not contain all those elements.

Next in the series of comparisons comes Joseph and the feeding of his hungry brothers.[46] The same manuscript contains a marginal miniature on fol. 153ʳ with a scene depicting Joseph seated on the left dressed in imperial loros, while in front of him stand four of his brothers, among them Benjamin (Fig. 165). Although the cod. Paris gr. 510 includes an extensive cycle describing the story of Joseph, fol. 69ᵛ,[47] the scene of the Panteleimon miniature does not appear there. Actually the picture of Joseph recognizing his brethren, headed by Benjamin, found in the Octateuch of Smyrna, fol. 46ʳ,[48] most closely resembles the Panteleimon miniature, in which, however, the number of brothers has been reduced and the bodyguard has been omitted. An Octateuch, therefore, is once again the source of the illustration in the Panteleimon codex.

The Genesis cycle does not end here. In the second homily on Easter, Gregory mentions Lot's wife and her metamorphosis into a pillar of salt.[49] The illustrator of the cod. Paris, Coislin 239, fol. 15ʳ, has depicted Lot's wife in the margin (Fig. 187). This picture, with the text for which it was originally created, is to be found in the cod. Vat. gr. 747, fol. 40ʳ, and even more clearly in the other Vatican Octateuch, cod. gr. 746, fol. 76ʳ. In both pictures Lot's wife stands in the middle, as if separating two worlds. With her left hand she points to a world dominated by flying angels, while her head is inclined toward the world of fire and destruction. The illustrator of Gregory's homily chose only the frozen figure of Lot's wife because she alone was alluded to in the text.

In the seventy-second paragraph of the homily on St. Basil, Gregory continues to compare Basil to the great figures of the Old Testament. He states: "Moses was great. Aaron was Moses's brother. . . . What was best with Joshua? Leadership and the conquest of the Holy Land."[50] The illustrator of the Panteleimon manuscript employs a standing figure of each of the patriarchs mentioned by Gregory. The first two, Moses and Aaron, appear in the margins of fol. 153ʳ (Fig. 165). The last one, Joshua, appears in the margin of fol. 153ᵛ (Fig. 166).

These three patriarchs are the protagonists in Moses' second book, Exodus. Since they are single frontal figures, it is impossible to determine where they originated. One

[45] Omont, *Min. gr.* (1929), pl. XXXVII.
[46] *PG*, 36, 593.
[47] Omont, *Min. gr.* (1929), pl. XXVI.
[48] D. C. Hesseling, *Miniatures de l'octateuque*

grec de Smyrne (Codices Graeci et Latini, suppl. VI) (facsimile), Leyden 1909, p. 45, fig. 136.
[49] *PG*, 36, 648.
[50] *PG*, 36, 593.

thing is certain: they have no relationship to the busts of Moses and Aaron and the standing figure of Joshua in the cod. Milan, Ambros. E. 49-50 inf., because they are altogether different.[51] Possibly the figures in the Panteleimon manuscript were at the beginning of the Book of Exodus like portraits of authors,[52] or they may have been taken from a specific scene. Scenes showing Moses and Aaron in frontal position are not rare in the Octateuchs. A scene showing Moses and Aaron before the Ark of the Covenant found in the Octateuch of Seraglio, cod. 8 fol. 333ʳ, or 351ᵛ [53] seems a probable source of these figures, because of the similarities in posture of Moses and Aaron to those of the manuscripts under discussion, and because Gregory alludes to the Ark of the Covenant when he speaks about Moses and Aaron. It may then be assumed that the artist who decided to make use of supplementary illustrations was aware of the text and chose the figures from the related scene.

Joshua's figure presents a similar case. He is shown carrying a sword and a sheath. The text of Gregory is not sufficient to explain the miniature since it gives only a few general facts concerning Joshua, i.e. "leadership, distribution of land and conquest of the Holy Land."[54] The scene showing Joshua meeting the angel in the Book of Joshua is the only one in which he appears holding a sword.[55] There, he brandishes it, a fact which makes no sense. If the figure in the Gregory miniature is not related to this scene, it must have come from a Bible the illustrations of which consisted of standing figures.

In the second homily on Easter, Gregory refers again to Moses, and to the brazen serpent that symbolizes Christ's Crucifixion as "breathless, dead still in the shape of a serpent hung up. . . ."[56] Two miniatures illustrate this passage in the Coislin manuscript. In the margin of fol. 11ᵛ, Moses is represented looking toward the sky (Fig. 184). The other miniature, fol. 18ʳ, inserted in the column of the text, shows Moses lifting up the brazen serpent, while a figure, already bitten by the snakes, sits on a rock (Fig. 190). The explanatory text of the miniatures appears in the Book of Exodus and their pictorial representations are found in the Octateuchs. While the figure of Moses may have come from any scene showing him communicating with God (e.g. the cod. Vat. gr. 747, fol. 95ʳ), the miniature of the brazen serpent has an

[51] Grabar, *Ambros. 49-50*, pls. xxvi, 1; xxv, 2; cf. also Moses and Aaron in other homilies in the same codex, *ibid.*, pl. xiv.

[52] See the Old Testament codex, Paris syr. 341, containing standing figures; H. Omont, "Peintures de l'ancien Testament dans un manuscrit syriaque," *E. Piot, Monuments et mémoires*, 17 (1909), pp. 85-98, pls. vii-ix, especially the figures of the Prophet Zephaniah, whose posture is similar to that of the figure under discussion. The same kind of Bible illustration was used by the illustrator of the Vatican Cosmas, cod. gr. 699.

See Stornajolo, *Cosmas*, pl. 31. Cf. also pictures of prophets in front of their books in cod. Oxford, New College, 44, a manuscript which dates from the thirteenth century, reproduced in O. Pächt, *Byzantine Illumination*, Oxford 1952, p. 9, fig. 10.

[53] See Ouspensky, *Octateuque*, pls. xxvi, 161; xxvii, 170.

[54] *PG*, 36, 593.

[55] See cod. Athos, Vatopedi 602, fol. 350ᵛ reproduced in Weitzmann, *Joshua*, pl. iv, 15. Cf. cod. Vat. gr. 747, fol. 220ʳ, *ibid.*, pl. iv, 14.

[56] *PG*, 36, 653.

exact parallel in the codd. Vat. gr. 747, fol. 172ᵛ, and Seraglio 8, to mention two examples.[57]

One other miniature comes from the Book of Exodus. Gregory in his sermon on Pentecost refers to the seven lamps of Solomon's Temple. This passage is illustrated in the manuscript of Paris, Coislin 239, fol. 30ʳ (Fig. 204). The same candelabrum, however, can be seen in the Vatican Octateuch cod. gr. 747, fol. 106ᵛ.

—Miniatures from the Book of Kings

In his sermon of St. Basil, Gregory continues to compare Basil to figures of the Old Testament, and in the seventy-third paragraph he states: ". . . and Samuel among those who invoked God's name, and among kings David of eternal memory . . . Solomon asked God for a magnanimous heart. . . ."[58]

Three standing figures of David, Solomon, and Samuel are in the margin of fol. 154ʳ of the cod. Athos, Panteleimon 6, (Fig. 167). The same passage is illustrated in the codex Milan, Ambros. E. 49-50 inf., fol. 276ʳ with a medallion bust of David, and the standing figures of Solomon and Samuel[59] that differ from those in the Athos manuscript, which were certainly invented originally from the First Book of Kings. An extant twelfth-century manuscript of the Book of Kings, cod. Vat. gr. 333, richly but unevenly illustrated, contains no portraits.[60] Therefore, it cannot be determined with any certainty whether the portraits in the manuscripts of the homilies were taken from scenes of the Book of Kings, or whether they existed independently in the same book. It is probable, however, that they came from a book whose illustrations consisted only of standing figures like those in the Syriac Bible mentioned above.[61]

Concerning the figures of David and Solomon, there is another possibility. Since both are authors of separate books, there must have been an author portrait at the beginning of their respective works, such as David's portraits in illustrated psalters. In fact, David's portrait found in the tenth-century psalter in Oxford, cod. Auct. D. IV, I, fol. 15ᵛ,[62] has striking similarities to the figure of David in the Athos manuscript of the homilies. Yet it is possible that neither David nor Solomon were borrowed directly from the sources already mentioned, but rather from a synaxarion of a lectionary, in which such standing figures are common.

The next person to whom Gregory compares Basil is the Prophet Elijah, to whose Ascension he refers.[63] A miniature on fol. 154ᵛ of the Panteleimon manuscript, showing the prophet ascending and tossing his mantle to Elisha, who eagerly grasps at it, illustrates this passage (Fig. 168). Elijah and Elisha are also shown in a miniature of the cod. Milan, Ambros. E. 49-50, inf. illustrating another homily, but they are

[57] Ouspensky, *Octateuque*, pl. xxviii, 173.

[58] *PG*, 36, 596ff.

[59] Grabar, *Ambros. 49-50*, pls. xxvi, 2, 3; xxv, 3.

[60] J. Lassus, "Les miniatures byzantines du Livre des Rois," *Mélanges d'archéologie et d'histoire*,

45 (1928), pp. 38ff.

[61] Supra, n. 52.

[62] Weitzmann, *Buchmalerei*, pl. lxviii, 405.

[63] *PG*, 36, 596.

of different iconography.[64] Once again the passage in the homily is not sufficient to explain the miniature, and the Fourth Book of Kings (2: 11-14) must be consulted so that the miniature may be fully explained. Furthermore, the existence of a similar picture in the Book of Kings, cod. Vat. gr. 333,[65] proves that the miniature was originally invented for the text of the Fourth Book of Kings. From there, the miniatures migrated to the manuscripts of Gregory's liturgical homilies, as well as to the full edition, cod. Paris gr. 510 (fol. 264ᵛ), and to other manuscripts.[66] There is no reason, however, to assume that the Panteleimon miniature is directly related to that in the cod. Paris gr. 510.

The tradition of the standing figure is exemplified by the initial K in the cod. Turin, Univ. Lib. C. I. 6, fol. 22ʳ formed by the Prophet Elijah holding a scroll (Fig. 36). This initial, whose direct source cannot be specified, is placed next to a passage referring to the prophet in the homily on Pentecost.[67] Originally there were other miniatures on this folio, probably containing more scenes, which have been cut out.

A relationship to a particular recension cannot be established on the basis of a single scene. Nevertheless, it seems likely that the miniatures represent two types of books: one illustrated extensively with scenes, the other with standing figures.

—A Miniature from a Psalter

In the cod. Turin, Univ. Lib. C. I. 6, fol. 18ʳ, there is a figured initial A in the text of the homily on New Sunday (Fig. 30). The initial is formed by a seated figure of a young saint playing the harp. His mantle flutters in the breeze. No mention of any harpist is made in the text, the last paragraph of which refers to St. Mamas. Since St. Mamas was not a harpist, the presence of the harp argues for the identification of the figure as David, and thus a psalter may be suggested as the source of the miniature. Indeed a similar figure of David as a harpist appears in the psalter of the British Museum.[68] Why was David chosen as an illustration of this homily? His figure is suggested by the quotations from Psalms 149: 1, 137: 4 which Gregory used in the first paragraph of his sermon.

—Miniatures from the Books of the Prophets

In the homily on Pentecost, Gregory mentions the Prophet Joel, who appears in the margin of fol. 34ᵛ of the cod. Paris, Coislin 239 (Fig. 205). He is standing in an almost three-quarter posture, as if walking, and holds a scroll in his left hand. It should be pointed out that a standing figure of Joel appears also in the cod. Milan, Ambros. E. 49-50, inf., illustrating another homily.[69] This figure is different from the one in the Paris manuscript; the latter comes from a book of the prophets, as is shown by a

---

[64] Grabar, *Ambros. 49-50*, pl. XLVII, 2.
[65] Lassus, *op.cit.*, p. 64, pl. VI.
[66] Omont, *Min. gr.* (1929), pl. XLII; Weitzmann, *Roll*, p. 198.

[67] *PG*, 36, 433.
[68] H. Buchthal, *The Miniatures of the Paris Psalter*, London 1938, pl. XVI, fig. 19.
[69] Grabar, *Ambros. 49-50*, pl. V, 2.

comparison with a similar figure of Joel found in the Vatican manuscript of the prophets (cod. Chigi gr. R. VIII, 54, fol. 19^v).[70]

Traces of the Book of Daniel are evident in the narrative illustrations when Gregory compares the faith of Basil to the faith of the Three Holy Children in the Fire. The cod. Athos, Panteleimon 6, contains a miniature showing the three youths burning in the furnace on fol. 154^v, next to the relevant passage in the homily (Fig. 168). The youths are being comforted by an angel who cools the fire by spreading his mighty wings. In the marginal miniature of the cod. Athos, Vatopedi 107, fol. 72^r, illustrating the same subject, there is no angel, but rather a bust of Christ to whom the Prophet Daniel prays (Fig. 324). The identification of Daniel is possible because of an inscription placed next to him.

No account of the story of the Three Children in the Fire is given in Gregory's text. Their story forms part of the third chapter of the Book of Daniel, where all the necessary details are found. Although no illustrated text of Daniel is now known, there can be no doubt that it was illustrated. Daniel's text and its pictures have migrated to other works, such as the Sacra Parallela (cod. Paris gr. 923, fol. 373^v) and psalters.[71] Whether this miniature came into the manuscript of the homilies directly from a book of prophets, or via another manuscript—a psalter—cannot be determined.

b. *The New Testament Group*
—Miniatures from the Gospels

In his second homily on Easter Gregory briefly mentions such persons as John the Baptist, Simon who carried the cross of Christ, Joseph of Arimathaea, and the women who shed tears during the Passion of Christ, but who rejoiced when they realized that Christ was not among the dead.

Illustrations of these passages, which cannot be explained on the basis of Gregory's incidental references, appear in the margins of the text in the cod. Paris, Coislin 239. A figure of John the Baptist standing in a frontal position and holding a cross has been depicted on fol. 15^v (Fig. 188). This figure has no relation to the bust of John in the cod. Milan, Ambros. E. 49-50, inf.[72] and has probably come from a synaxarion of a lectionary, as is suggested by a similar figure appearing in the lectionary cod. Vat. gr. 1156, fol. 253^v where it illustrates John's conception, celebrated on September 23. The same applies to the figures of John in the cod. Athos, Panteleimon 6, fols. 90^v, 155^r and 173^r (Figs. 150, 169, 171).

On fol. 18^v of the Paris manuscript there is a miniature showing Simon of Cyrene— identified by inscription—carrying the cross of Christ (Fig. 192). The basic text of this miniature is found in the Gospels (Matt. 27: 32; Mark 15: 21; Luke 23: 26)

[70] A. Muñoz, *I codici greci miniati delle minori biblioteche di Roma*, Rome 1905, pl. I. Cf. Joel standing and holding a book in the cod. Vat. gr. 699, fol. 68^v, Stornajolo, *Cosmas*, pl. 31.

[71] See, for example, the cod. Vat. gr. 752, fol. 473^r, DeWald, *Vat. gr. 752*, pl. LVI.

[72] Grabar, *Ambros. 49-50*, pls. XXXVIII, 1; XLVIII, 2.

and a similar picture appears in a twelfth-century Gospel book of Athens, Nat. Lib. cod. 93, fol. 84ʳ.[73]

On the same folio of the Paris manuscript, there is a column miniature representing Pilate sitting at the right and speaking to Joseph of Arimathaea (Fig. 191). Joseph is nimbed and, standing before Pilate with his arms crossed, he bows slightly. The miniature can only be explained through the full text of the Gospels and illustrates the moment when Joseph of Arimathaea went to Pilate and begged for the body of Jesus (Matt. 27: 57-59; Mark 15: 43, 45; Luke 23: 50-52; John 19: 38). Once again a similar picture found in the same Athens Gospel, fol. 65ʳ [74] proves the migration of the scene into the homily of Gregory. It must be pointed out, however, that this Gospel book has emphasized the Passion cycle in its illustrations, thus revealing the influence of a lectionary, for there are lectionaries, such as the cod. Morgan 639, that, in narrative scenes taken over from the Gospels, stress the Passion episodes from the Life of Christ. This observation would indicate that the two Passion scenes under discussion may have existed in a lectionary as well, from which they possibly migrated directly into the Paris manuscript.

Another column picture in the Paris manuscript, fol. 19ʳ, shows the two Marys at Christ's tomb, on which an angel sits speaking to them (Fig. 193). The episode of the two Marys mentioned by Matthew (28: 1) is illustrated also in lectionaries, for example, the cod. Athos, Dionysiou 587, fols. 113ᵛ and 168ᵛ.

In the twenty-fifth paragraph of the same homily, Gregory, referring to the Prophet Isaiah—who prophesied the coming of Christ—quotes the following passage from the Book of Isaiah (63: 1ff.). "Who is this that cometh from Edom, with dyed garments?" A standing figure of Isaiah illustrates this passage on fol. 19ᵛ in the Coislin manuscript, left margin (Fig. 194). The prophet points to a frontal figure of Christ in the right margin, whose presence makes very unlikely the direct relation of the prophet's figure to any of those appearing in the cod. Milan, Ambros. E. 49-50 inf., where Christ does not appear.[75]

There is no evidence to show that such a scene appeared in the Book of Isaiah. In fact, both figures have come from a Gospel book, as a comparison of parallel examples found in the Gospels of Rossano and Sinope proves.[76] Figures of prophets accompany the Gospel scenes in both manuscripts and verify the fact that the New Testament is the fulfillment of the Old. More specifically, the figure of Isaiah pointing to Christ above him appears in almost every extant folio of these Gospels. Possibly the artist of the Coislin manuscript has used the same source for another supplementary, marginal illustration of the second homily on Easter fol. 13ʳ, representing Isaiah (Fig. 185).

[73] P. Buberl, *Die Miniaturhandschriften der Nationalbibliothek in Athen* (Denkschriften der Wiener Akademie, 60), Vienna 1917, pp. 16, 17.
[74] Buberl, *op.cit.*, p. 17.
[75] Grabar, *Ambros. 49-50*, pls. XI, 2; XXXVI, 2;

XL, 5.
[76] A. Muñoz, *Il codice purpureo di Rossano e il frammento Sinopense*, Rome 1907, pls. I-II, IV, VI. A. Grabar, *Les peintures de l'évangéliaire de Sinope*, Paris 1948.

—Miniatures from the Book of Acts and Epistles

In the same second sermon on Easter, Gregory quotes Paul: "Stand, therefore, having your loins girt about with truth."[77] Paul's figure appears in the margin of fol. 16ʳ in the cod. Paris, Coislin 239 (Fig. 189). The appropriate place for such a figure would have been either in an edition of Paul's letters or a Book of Acts. In the former, Paul should have been represented as the author of the letters or as the teacher of their content. In fact, a standing figure of Paul, a bust of him, or a teaching scene appears at the beginning of each letter in an illustrated book of the Acts of the Apostles and Epistles in the Walters Art Gallery in Baltimore, cod. 533, dated between the twelfth and fourteenth centuries;[78] Paul's figure on fol. 133ᵛ is the same as that appearing in the Coislin manuscript.

Undoubtedly this picture has migrated to Gregory's text from an illustrated book of Epistles. A parallel example showing a definite migration from an illustrated book of Epistles is found in the cod. Milan, Ambros. E. 49-50, inf., fol. 278ʳ.[79]

Gregory alludes briefly to the Stoning of Stephen at the end of his sermon on St. Basil.[80] The Panteleimon codex illustrates the scene with a miniature placed in the left margin, next to the text, fol. 155ᵛ (Fig. 170). This miniature was never completed. On the left, in front of a building Paul is seated on a folding stool. In the center of the composition a Jew is carrying stones to throw at Stephen, who is kneeling below an arc of heaven from which rays of light descend. Only the nimbi have been filled with gold. The remaining parts are still in the preliminary drawing stage.

A miniature depicting the Stoning of Stephen, but illustrating another homily, appears in the cod. Milan, Ambros. E. 49-50, inf., fol. 175ʳ.[81] This miniature not only differs in the postures of the figures, but is less complete than the Panteleimon miniature from the point of view of iconography. The iconographic completeness of the latter miniature precludes any direct relationship to the former, for it presupposes a fuller model as its source.

The episode of the Stoning of Stephen is mentioned in the seventh chapter of the Acts of the Apostles (vv. 58-60) for which the miniature of the Panteleimon manuscript was originally invented. Of the extant illustrated books of Acts, one in Paris (Bibl. Nat., cod. gr. 102) contains one miniature, fol. 7ᵛ, so similar to the one in the homily that there can be no doubt that the Gregory miniature migrated from an illustrated book of the Acts.

—A Miniature from the Apocryphal Acts of Peter and Paul

The cod. Turin, Univ. Lib. C. I. 6, fol. 82ᵛ, has a historiated initial E in the homily on St. Basil, formed by the figures of two saints embracing each other (Fig. 56). It

---

[77] *PG*, 36, 649. Cf. Eph. 6: 14.

[78] This manuscript was previously in the monastery of Iviron on Mt. Athos, cod. 24; see Walters Art Gallery, *Early Christian and Byzantine Art*,

Baltimore 1947, p. 142, pl. xcvii.

[79] Grabar, *Ambros. 49-50*, pl. xxvi, 4.

[80] *PG*, 36, 597.

[81] Grabar, *Ambros. 49-50*, pl. xvii, 2.

may be suggested that this is a representation of an ecstatic meeting of Gregory of Nazianzus and Gregory of Nyssa. This interpretation cannot be valid, because neither of the two figures wears a pallium. In fact, the miniature depicts an ecstatic meeting of the Apostles Peter and Paul.

The text of the homily makes no mention of such meeting and it does not explain the miniature. As indicated in another case, this miniature has migrated from a book of the Apocryphal Acts of Peter and Paul.[82] The reason for its migration into the homily on St. Basil is given in the seventeenth paragraph, to which the initial under discussion belongs. In this paragraph Gregory speaks of his friendship with Basil, which grew stronger after they met again in Athens. The illustrator found the best parallel of this friendship in the lives of Peter and Paul, whose ecstatic meeting became a symbol of friendship and the love which unites, and prefigured, so to speak, the friendship and love of the apostles' successors within the body of the Church. The miniature, which actually represented the meeting of Peter and Paul, was thus appropriate to illustrate the idea of friendship between Gregory and Basil.

c. *The Menologion Group*

Another miniature not deriving from a Biblical book, but referring to one of the church fathers, must be included among the group of the religious miniatures. Gregory, referring to the mystery of the Holy Trinity in his second homily on Easter, says: "The Holy Trinity had been thought of in the best way by one of our predecessors."[83]

In the left margin of fol. 8ʳ in the cod. Paris, Coislin 239, next to the quoted passage, there is a standing bishop (Fig. 183). He has a rather square white beard, a nimbus, and holds a book in his left hand. His right hand makes the gesture of benediction. The cited text does not mention a bishop and identification would be impossible had not the illustrator added the following commentary: Ἀθανάσιον λέγει τὸν ἐπίσκοπον Ἀλεξανδρείας.

This miniature, evidently, was created not to illustrate the text, but to explain it. It replaces a commentary and identifies the author of the quotation as Athanasius, the bishop of Alexandria. Weitzmann introduced the term, "commentary illustrations," with specific reference to the illustrations of the monastic psalters.[84] This miniature offers another example of that kind of illustration in another variety of liturgical book.

The original source of this portrait would have been a menologion.[85] When the menologion influenced the second part of the lectionary, Athanasius' standing figure migrated there.[86] On the basis of a single miniature, it is not possible to determine

---

[82] See supra, p. 57. For the illustrations of the *Apocryphal Acts of Peter and Paul*, see J. Myslivec, *Dve Studie Zdejin Byzantskeho Umeni*, Prague 1948, pp. 107ff.

[83] *PG*, 36, 628ff.

[84] Weitzmann, *Roll*, p. 118.

[85] See cod. Vat. gr. 1613, *Il menologio*, p. 329. Cf. cod. Brit. Mus. 19352 (Theodore Psalter), fol. 15ʳ.

[86] See an example in the lectionary cod. Vat. gr. 1156, fol. 295ʳ.

whether the miniature migrated directly into the text of Gregory from a frontispiece of a menologion, or through another intermediary source.

d. *A Miniature from a Theotokarion* (?)

At the end of the first paragraph of the homily on the Nativity, Gregory speaks about the rejoicing of heaven and earth at the birth of the Saviour. He states: "Christ appeared in flesh, rejoice. . . . Christ was born by a Virgin: women be virgins so that you may become mothers of Christ. Who does not adore Him, Who was from the beginning?"[87] The initials of Christ's name in the codd. Sinai 339, fol. 91ᵛ and Paris gr. 543, fol. 117ᵛ are formed by an icon of the Panagia Blachernitissa. Next to the initial, in the margin, are women worshipers, five in the former miniature and two in the latter (Figs. 385, 463). An image of the Panagia Blachernitissa without the worshipers is also found in the cod. Athos, Vatopedi 107, fol. 277ᵛ (Fig. 339). It has been placed, however, at the end of the codex and not in a particular homily, thus it has no direct relation to any narrative part of the text.

The worshiped icon cannot be explained by the cited text; in fact, the scene was not made for Gregory's text at all. This is not the place to discuss the miraculous icon of the Blachernae church, the development of its type, and its theological content,[88] but only to mention that the Panagia Blachernitissa adored by saints does appear in the illustrations of the *Akathistos Hymnos*.[89] The suggestion of any relationship between these examples and the two miniatures under discussion must be made with great caution, since in them the Virgin of Blachernae is a whole figure and not a portable icon. Whenever a portable icon has been depicted in the illustrations of the Akathistos, the Virgin is of the Hodegetria type.[90] A closer parallel is offered by a miniature of a psalter in the Benaki Museum at Athens, cod. 1, fol. 194ʳ, in which, three kneeling women are included among the worshipers of the Blachernitissa icon.[91] The accompanying text is a prayer to the Virgin, which suggests that the original textual source of the miniature is not the psalter but perhaps a Theotokarion.[92] This, however, cannot be proved, since no illustrated Theotokaria have survived. Thus it

[87] *PG*, 36, 313.

[88] For brief discussions on the iconography of the Panagia Blachernitissa, see C. C. Cecchelli, *Mater Christi*, I, Rome 1946, pp. 213, 223. A. Vloberg, "Les types iconographiques de la Mère de Dieu dans l'art byzantin," *Maria*, 2 (1952), pp. 403ff. G. Soteriou, "Χριστιανικὴ καὶ Βυζαντινὴ εἰκονογραφία," *Θεολογία*, 27 (1956), pp. 5ff.

[89] Examples are found in the monasteries of the Holy Mountain and in those of Moldavia. See G. Millet, *Les monuments d'Athos. La peinture*, Paris 1927, pls. 147, 1, 2; J. D. Stefănescu, *L'illustration des liturgies dans l'art de Byzance*

et de l'Orient, Brussels 1936, pl. CXXVIII. On the illustrations of the *Akathistos Hymn*, cf. J. Myslivic, "Ikonografie Akathistu Panny Marie," *Seminarium Kondakovianum*, 5 (1932), pp. 97ff.

[90] Examples are to be seen in the top frieze of the trapeza of the monastery of Grand Lavra, see Millet, *op.cit.*, pl. 147, 1.

[91] The manuscript is unpublished. I am indebted to Dr. M. Chatzidakis, Director of the Benaki Museum, for permitting me to study it.

[92] See another related prayer in S. Eustradiades, Θεοτοκάριον, Chennevieres-sur-Marne 1931, p. 157.

cannot be determined whether the miniatures of Gregory's homily migrated directly from their hypothetical original source or through an intermediary.

The choice of the Blachernitissa icon as an illustration of a passage referring to Christ's Incarnation is of great importance because it clarifies the real meaning of this representation. It clearly shows that the artist was aware of the fact that this type of the Virgin was not merely related to the icon of the Blachernae church, but that it embodied the meaning and connotations of the doctrine of the Incarnation.

B. THE MYTHOLOGICAL MINIATURES

Two of the manuscripts, the codd. Athos, Panteleimon 6, and Paris, Coislin 239, include mythological miniatures in the text of the homily on Epiphany. The former contains eleven mythological scenes and the latter ten, all of which have been published and discussed by Weitzmann.[93] For the sake of thoroughness, his results are summarized here.

These miniatures cannot be fully explained on the basis of Gregory's brief mythological allusions. Originally, the miniatures belonged to a commentary on four of the homilies written by Nonnos, usually called Pseudo-Nonnos, from which they migrated into the text of Gregory. The text of Pseudo-Nonnos and its illustrations are found in two other manuscripts of the homilies: the codd. Jerusalem, Taphou 14, and Vat. gr. 1947. In these codices the Pseudo-Nonnos text forms a separate entity, placed at the end of the text of the homilies.

The miniatures of Pseudo-Nonnos belonging to these four manuscripts have been divided by Weitzmann into two categories:[94] miniatures that can be traced from a classical pictorial tradition and that have mythological subject matter, and miniatures that are Byzantine inventions, representing primarily cults and oracles. The basic text of the first category is not the commentaries of Pseudo-Nonnos, but a mythological treatise of the Classical period. Weitzmann suggested that such a book might have been the so-called *Bibliotheke* of Apollodorus, which had survived the breakdown of the pagan world and was still known and available to the Byzantine writers. It was from such a text, according to Weitzmann, that the miniatures migrated into the Pseudo-Nonnos text sometime between the ninth and eleventh centuries when the Pseudo-Nonnos commentaries were first illustrated.[95] But the *Bibliotheke* of Apollodorus is not the ultimate source of the miniatures. The archetype of the miniatures is older than the Hadrianic period and is a compilation based on older texts of the same kind. Therefore, the illustrations were originally made, not for the Apollodorus handbook, but for its model.

[93] Weitzmann, *Mythology*, see index for figures. Cf. *idem, Ancient Book Illumination*, Cambridge, Mass. 1959, pp. 95ff.

[94] *Ibid.*, pp. 74ff.

[95] *Ibid.*, p. 92.

C. THE "HISTORICAL" MINIATURES

In the third paragraph of his Farewell oration, Gregory, speaking of those who forgot God's will, says: ". . . the first who was with Christ, like a maniac arose against Christ . . . and hated Christ and instead of the sacred books, he re-established the godless sacrifices. . . . But the Lord had mercy on us and delivered him to the hands of the ungodly. He sent him to the Persians. . . . There, not long after, his soul was delivered to Hades. . . . The second was not better than the first . . . he was named after Christ but he was a pseudo-Christian and he was a burden and a shame to the Christians. . . ."[96]

Next to this paragraph, the cod. Athos, Panteleimon 6, fol. 242^v, has two marginal illustrations in preliminary drawing only (Fig. 177). The top one represents a nimbed figure, apparently a saint, who is mounted on a horse and has just pierced a fallen figure with a spear. The latter holds a shield in his left hand, while his right hand is upraised. An inscription identifies him as Julian the Apostate.

The miniature below this shows a prostrate figure wearing a crown, with his hands covered by a mantle. He is enclosed in a semicircular structure and identified by inscriptions as Valens the Arian. This miniature accompanied by the same inscription appears in another manuscript of Gregory's homilies, the cod. Athos, Iviron 271, fol. 252^v (Fig. 178).

A comparison with the text of Gregory shows that not even the names of these two emperors are mentioned; there are only vague allusions to them. The obvious conclusion is that the origin of the miniatures can be traced to another text. In fact, their origin can be established with the help of the representation of Julian's death. In this scene, according to legend, Julian is killed by St. Mercurius. Gregory's sermon does not, however, indicate that Gregory knew Julian's killer. In the second sermon against Julian the Apostate, Gregory refers to the murder as having been committed by a discontented soldier, by a barbarian who followed the army, or by one of the Saracens.[97] Therefore, the text explaining this miniature must be sought outside of Gregory's works.

In connection with the story of St. Mercurius, Binon, who has collected literary sources referring to the death of Julian,[98] has shown that early historians were not certain about the cause of his death, which is shrouded in mystery. The earliest sources explaining the miniature are the chronicles of Sozomenos and Malalas. Sozomenos gives an explicit report (VI, 1-2): "After darkness and mist had spread around, a horseman riding at a gallop transfixed the emperor with the lance and inflicted upon him a mortal wound."[99] Then he lists the various opinions about the identification of the killer. Commenting on the opinion of Libanius, he states: "He [Libanius] indi-

---

[96] *PG*, 36, 461.   [97] *PG*, 35, 680.

[98] S. Binon, *Essai sur le cycle de Saint Mercure*, Paris 1937, pp. 14, 25ff.

[99] The translation of this passage and those that follow has been taken from Weitzmann, *Chronicles*, p. 115.

cates that the slayer of Julian was a Christian and this is probably the truth. It is not unlikely that one of the soldiers in the Roman army conceived the idea. . . ." The agreement between the miniature and this description is perfect, the nimbus adding weight to the argument for a Christian.

A similar picture with more details, such as the inclusion of the horse from which the emperor has fallen, appears in cod. Paris gr. 510, fol. 409ᵛ (lower register).[100] There the killer has been identified as St. Mercurius. Weitzmann, who deals in detail with this miniature and the others which belong to the same cycle, has suggested that it was originally made for the text of Sozomenos, which presupposes that the text was illustrated.[101] Then, Weitzmann continues, it migrated into the Malalas text in which the murderer was identified as Mercurius. Binon and Weitzmann have observed that the episode occurs also in the Chronicle Paschale and that of John Nikiou (seventh to eighth century).[102] The illustrations of both were copied from the chronicle of Malalas. The real question, however, is whether this miniature migrated to the Panteleimon manuscript directly from one of these chronicles or through the cod. Paris gr. 510. In view of the fact that other miniatures (discussed below) originating in chronicles have not migrated into the manuscripts of the homilies of the liturgical edition through the cod. Paris gr. 510, it seems unlikely that a single miniature of the historical cycle was derived from the full edition.

The derivation of the miniature placed below the one already discussed, and also that of the cod. Athos, Iviron 271—both representing the Emperor Valens—is very problematic. The difficulty arises from the fact that Valens' posture is unexplained. Furthermore, the miniature may or may not be part of a larger scene. It may be assumed that the original source of this miniature is the same as that of the miniature depicting Julian's death, i.e. a chronicle.

All earlier and later chroniclers have devoted much space to the Arian emperor and his persecutions. A full account is given by Sozomenos and a shorter one by Malalas.[103] Episodes of Valens' persecutions are illustrated in Paris gr. 510, fol. 104ʳ and in the Cappadocian churches.[104] Yet none of these accounts offers a satisfactory explanation of the miniature. They do not even contain an allusion which might help identify the scene. Could the semicircular structure be considered a schematic representation of a church in which the emperor prays?[105] None of the chroniclers mention that the emperor prayed in a church. Sozomenos and Theodoret mention a visit by

[100] Omont, *Min. gr.* (1929), pl. LIV.

[101] Weitzmann, *Chronicles*, pp. 114ff.

[102] Binon, *op.cit.*, p. 23; Weitzmann, *Chronicles*, p. 116.

[103] Sozomenus, *Historia ecclesiastica*, VI, 6; J. Bidez, G. C. Hansen eds., *Sozomenus Kirchengeschichte* (Die griechischen christlichen Schriftsteller der ersten Jahrhunderte, 50), Berlin 1960, p. 244. Malalas, *Chronographia*, ed. Bonn, pp. 342ff.

[104] Omont, *Min. gr.* (1929), pl. XXXI; Weitzmann, *Chronicles*, pp. 117ff. G. de Jerphanion, "Histoire de saint Basil dans les peintures cappadociennes . . . ," *Byzantion*, 6 (1931), pp. 535ff.

[105] The prostrate posture is often assumed by persons in prayer as an expression of submission, as a figure of David inscribed ΔΑΥΙΔ ΕΥΧΟΜΕΝΟC in the Chloudov Psalter (Moscow, Hist. Mus. gr. 129, fol. 25ʳ) illustrates.

Valens to the church of St. Basil where he presented gifts on the holy altar.[106] Does the presentation of gifts imply prayer? If so it would mean that the picture was taken from Sozomenos, where the episode of Julian's death was found. Or must the prostrate attitude of the emperor be interpreted as a gesture of repentance, inspired by his refusal to be baptized and the resultant death of his son Galates?[107] The text of Theodoret implies this interpretation, but does not state explicitly that the emperor fell to the ground in repentance.

These suggestions, however, seem most improbable. There is a more convincing explanation: the figure of Valens resembles the figures of Arios and Nestorios found in a miniature in the lectionary of the Morgan library, cod. 639, fol. 42[r].[108] There Arios and Nestorios are in *anathema*, i.e. they are lying under a curse. The prostrate posture of Valens would imply a similar explanation. Another example supporting this interpretation comes from the menologion of Basil II. It shows a similar prostrate figure in the illustration of the seventh council under Constantine and Irene against the iconoclasts.[109] The text in the miniature specifically states: "they condemn in written form every heresy and the leaders of heresies."[110]

Another anathema scene, this time referring to Arios and thus eliminating any doubt about interpretation, appears in the same Panteleimon manuscript as a marginal illustration of the homily on St. Basil, fol. 123[r]. Gregory, speaking of Basil, mentions Arios, and next to this passage there is a miniature, of which only the frame and the name Arios, have been preserved (Fig. 155). How Arios was actually represented cannot be determined. The frame presents the same semicircular structure in which the prostrate figure of Valens was depicted. It is reasonable, then, to assume that Arios was shown in the same posture and that therefore, as in the Morgan lectionary, he was in anathema. Such a figure may have migrated from any of the chronicles mentioning the story of Arios' condemnation, and Sozomenos again seems a likely source.[111]

In the same homily Gregory describes Basil's sufferings under the persecution of Valens, who "arrived with a large army."[112] A frameless marginal miniature in the Panteleimon codex, fol. 132[r], illustrates the sentence (Fig. 156). The miniature shows an emperor on a horse, holding a spear, and leading a group of horsemen. A second

[106] Sozomenus, *loc.cit.*; Theodoret, *Historia ecclesiastica*, IV, 19, L. Parmentier, F. Scheidweiter, eds., *Theodoret Kirchengeschichte* (Die griechischen christlichen Schriftsteller der ersten Jahrhunderte, 44), Berlin 1954, p. 245.

[107] Cf. the prostate figure of the repentant Manasses in the Chloudov Psalter (Moscow, Hist. Mus. gr. 129, fol. 158[v]) inscribed H METANOIA TOY MANACH.

[108] Weitzmann, *Lectionary Morgan 639*, p. 372, pl. 306.

[109] *Il menologio*, p. 108.

[110] *Ibid.*, *loc.cit.*

[111] Representations of the first Ecumenical Council including the condemnation of Arios often appear in Byzantine art. See frescoes in the monasteries of Mt. Athos, reproduced in G. Millet, *Monuments de l'Athos. La peinture*, Paris 1927, pl. 140, 2. Cf. S. Salaville, "L'iconographie des 'sept conciles oecumeniques,'" *Echos d'Orient*, 25 (1926), pp. 144-76.

[112] *PG*, 36, 553.

rider brandishing a banner also seems to wear a crown. Although there is no name inscribed, one of the emperors was meant to be Valens;[113] the other may well be "the King of the Persians" mentioned in the succeeding forty-fifth paragraph of the homily.[114]

It follows, then, that the cited text explains the miniature and it seems reasonable to assume that the miniature was invented for it. Yet similar miniatures exist in chronicles, including, for example, the chronicle of Manasses in the Vatican (cod. Slav. II, fol. 136ᵛ),[115] and it is likely that the miniature came from the same chronicle as the other miniatures referring to the story.

D. THE BUCOLIC MINIATURES

In the homily on New Sunday, Gregory, having spoken of the reborn man and his soul that is born again in Christ, turns to the world of nature and speaks about the rebirth of nature in the spring. He describes the beauties of nature and the activities of man in these words:

"The Queen of the Hours conducts the Queen of the Days. . . . Now the sky is clearer; now the sun ascends higher; the circle of the moon is more golden and brighter and the choir of stars is clearer. . . . The valley brings forth a sweet fragrance; the plant blooms and the grass is mown; lambs leap in the fresh pastures. . . . A boat sails from a harbor and leaping dolphins . . . accompany the sailors joyfully. Now the farmer fixes his plough in the earth, looking upward, invoking the name of the Fruit-Giver; the farmer conducts the oxen under the yoke, and rejoices and hopes. . . . Now shepherd and herdsman tune their pipes and inspire a sweet melody, seated in the open, on airy rocks and among plants. . . . The gardener prunes the tree and the bird-catcher builds reed huts, glancing at the birds and investigating thoroughly the feather of a bird. . . . The fisherman sees clearly the bottom of the sea, lifts up the nets and sits on a rock.

"The labor-loving bee having freed her wings collects the honey from the flowers . . . and makes wax. . . . The bird builds a nest; one returns, the other remains; a bird flies around and fills the grove with its singing and speaks to man. . . . All animals rejoice now. And we enjoy ourselves with all our senses. Now the lordly horse trots in the valley and rejoices at the waters of the rivers. . . ."[116]

The manuscripts containing illustrations for this long passage are Jerusalem, Taphou 14; Athos, Panteleimon 6; Paris, Coislin 239; Paris gr. 533; Athos, Vatopedi 107; and Turin, Univ. Lib. C. I. 6. The last contains only a few historiated initials.

[113] The text of the homily is clear enough on this point. Commentators have taken this passage as referring to Valens. Cf. cod. Athos, Pantocrator 31, fol. 325ʳ, where, beside the relevant passage the scribe has written the word Οὐάλης.

[114] *PG*, 36, 553.

[115] B. D. Filov, *Les miniatures de la Chronique de Manassès* (cod. Vat. slav. II) (Codices e Vaticanis selecti, XVII), Sofia 1927, pl. XXVI, 1.

[116] *PG*, 36, 617ff.

"THE QUEEN OF THE HOURS CONDUCTS THE QUEEN OF THE DAYS"

The only manuscript illustrating this passage is the cod. Paris, Coislin 239. A column picture on fol. 26ʳ shows two figures standing frontally, dressed in the costume of the Byzantine empress, wearing crowns and holding globes (Fig. 197).

These two figures are identified by inscriptions as the Queen of the Hours and the Queen of the Days described in the text, and they certainly follow the tradition of personifying the Hours, which existed until late antiquity.[117] Personifications, Charity for example, in the attire of an empress are common in Byzantine art.[118]

"THE VALLEY BRINGS FORTH A SWEET FRAGRANCE . . . THE GRASS IS MOWN"

The cod. Athos, Panteleimon 6 illustrates the first passage with a column miniature on fol. 37ʳ consisting of a schematic mountainous landscape which encloses a valley in which there are five sheep (Fig. 140). In the upper corners the sun and the moon are represented. Within the sun a head appears in profile, a characteristic of Byzantine art which occurs in many Biblical representations. The rocky landscape is also typically Byzantine.

The cod. Jerusalem, Taphou 14, fol. 33ʳ has represented the two cited passages in one scene (Fig. 103). Upon a peaceful plain, where trees and grass grow, two lambs and a pair of goats are grazing. On the right a farmer cuts the luxuriant grass. Although these representations agree with the description given in the cited text, the possibility of the illustrator's use of older models must be considered.

Models for such a picture might be found in representations of the labors of the months. The illustrations of the months have been preserved in the Evangelarion in the Library of St. Mark's in Venice (cod. gr. DXL), in the cycle of the Octateuchs, and in a Typikon from Trebizond now in Vatopedi (cod. 1199), dated from A.D. 1346.[119] The scene most closely related to the Jerusalem miniature, although not identical, is the one personifying the month of June, as it is found in the manuscript of Venice.[120]

Webster, Levi, and Stern have shown that the cycle of the months may be traced back to Hellenistic sources.[121] Webster has emphasized "the constancy of devotion on

---

[117] Cf. R. Hinks, *Myth and Allegory in Ancient Art* (Studies of the Warburg Institute, 6), London 1939, pp. 43ff., fig. 2.

[118] See Chloudov Psalter (Moscow, Hist. Mus. 129), fol. 35ʳ, N. P. Kondakov, *Miniatiury Grecheskoi rukopisi IX veka iz sobraniia A. L. Khludova*, Moscow 1878, pl. XII, 4.

[119] J. C. Webster, *The Labors of the Months in Antique and Mediaeval Art*, Princeton 1938, p. 25, pl. X, 22; Strzygowski, *Rep. f. Kunst.* (1888), pp. 23ff. and figs.; *idem, Rep. f. Kunst.* (1890),

pp. 241ff. and figs.; K. Weitzmann, *Aus den Bibliotheken des Athos*, Hamburg 1963, pp. 109-12.

[120] Webster, *op.cit.*, pl. X, 22. Cf. the month of June in the Octateuchs (Strzygowski, *Rep. f. Kunst.* [1888], pp. 23ff.), and the month of July in the Typicon from Trebizond (*idem, Rep. f. Kunst.* [1890], pp. 257ff.).

[121] D. Levi, "The Allegories of the Months in Classical Art," *AB*, 23 (1941), pp. 241-91; H. Stern, *Le calendrier de 354*, Paris 1953. Cf. H.

the part of the Byzantine art to what was its own past."[122] It cannot be ascertained whether or not the artist of the Jerusalem manuscript or the artist of its model directly employed a classical model. If such a model was used, it has been entirely transformed into the Byzantine idiom.

The cod. Paris gr. 533 contains on fol. 34ʳ (top) a miniature showing a shepherd shearing a lamb, which was included in an earlier part of this study dealing with the scenes from the life of St. Mamas (Fig. 237). Since no explanation of this picture is offered by the text and since no pictorial parallel has been discovered[123] a conflation was suggested as a possible explanation. In the light of the bucolic scenes discussed so far it may be assumed that the artist borrowed elements from two miniatures: one portraying St. Mamas milking, and the other a shepherd mowing the grass. The conflation may have resulted from an attempt on the part of the artist to relate the milking scene to the text of the homily, or simply from mere confusion about the word κείρεται, which can be used for both grass and the wool of a lamb. Whatever the correct explanation, it must be admitted that neither the confusion nor the conflation would have occurred in such a manner had the artist known that the shepherd portrayed in one of the miniatures of his model was St. Mamas. If this explanation is not plausible, the picture must have another text as its source.

"A BOAT SAILS FROM A HARBOR"

All the manuscripts use a similar miniature, with slight variations in the number of crew members or the number of fish. The most complete miniature is found in the cod. Jerusalem, Taphou 14, fol. 33ʳ showing the boat sailing in the sea and fish swimming to and fro and depicting also a narrow, high building, representing the harbor from which the boat has set forth (Fig. 103).[124] No other miniature has indicated the harbor in this way. Naturally, compositions of sailing boats are rather conventional and, since they appear often in Byzantine and Classical art, their particular model need not be sought. The miniature of the cod. Paris gr. 533, fol. 34ʳ shows a similar boat crossing the water, enclosed by a schematic representation of a coast. An old man pulls the oars energetically, while two more sailors sit in the stern (Fig. 237). The three dolphins in the water are almost indistinguishable. In the miniature of the cod. Athos, Panteleimon 6, fol. 37ʳ, the crew of the sailing boat has been limited to two persons. One dolphin leaps from the water to the right of the boat (Fig. 140). Only a solitary figure, the oarsman, remains in the miniature of the cod. Paris, Coislin 239, fol. 26ᵛ, (Fig. 198). Finally the boat alone appears, sketched in a simple, primitive manner, in the cod. Athos, Vatopedi 107, fol. 27ᵛ (Fig. 318).

Stern, "Poésies et representations carolingiennes et byzantines des mois," *Revue archéologique*, 45 (1955), pp. 141-86.

[122] Webster, *op.cit.*, p. 26.

[123] A miniature of a different subject appears in the *Cynegetica* of Pseudo-Oppian (cod. Venice, Marc. 479, fol. 3ʳ). It shows a hunter catching a dog, and its similarities to the Gregory miniatures are only with regard to type.

[124] For the symbolism of dolphins and its usages by Gregory Nazianzenus, see E. Diez, "Dolphin," *Reallexikon für Antike und Christentum*, III (1956), pp. 667-82.

"THE FARMER FIXES HIS PLOUGH IN THE EARTH AND THANKS THE FRUIT-GIVER"

All the manuscripts under discussion illustrate this passage in a similar manner. The differences occur in the treatment of the landscape. The most beautiful miniature is that of the cod. Paris gr. 533, fol. 34ʳ, showing a farmer walking behind a plough pulled by two oxen (Fig. 237). He raises his left hand in a gesture of prayer and gazes up toward a bust of Christ in the upper right corner of the miniature. The farmer wears a short tunic which exposes his entire left leg. The treatment of line and the solidity of the design are as expressive as the lyrical rhythm of his hands, a rhythm which reinforces that conveyed by the hand of the blessing Christ appearing in the nuances of his aureola. The face of the farmer has a freshness that can be compared only to works of classical art.

Since ploughing scenes are common among representations of man's occupations in both ancient and Byzantine art, the Gregory illustration is clearly not a new invention. A ploughing scene appears, for instance, in the pastoral scenes of the floor mosaic in the house of the Laberii at Uthina.[125] In the Byzantine manuscripts such a scene is found in the *Cynegetica* of Pseudo-Oppian, cod. Marc. gr. 479, fol. 24ʳ, and in the eleventh-century cod. of John Climacus in the Vatican, cod. gr. 394, fol. 12ᵛ.[126] Of these two examples, the former is closer to the Paris miniature. Often this scene is found in calendar pictures as a representation of the month of November, as, for example, in the cod. Athos, Vatopedi 1199, fol. 76ʳ,[127] and it is probable that a calendar picture is the source of the miniature in question.

The miniature of the cod. Jerusalem, Taphou 14, fol. 33ʳ does not depict a bust of Christ but rather the hand of God at which a farmer, wearing a short tunic, is gazing (Fig. 103). Here the landscape is a green plain. The hand of God appears also in the miniatures of the codd. Athos, Panteleimon 6, fol. 37ʳ and Paris, Coislin 239, fol. 26ᵛ, which are very similar except that the mountainous landscape is seen in the former only (Figs. 140, 199). As in the other miniatures, the farmer, dressed in the Byzantine fashion and ploughing with two oxen, gives thanks to the Creator. This episode is also illustrated in the cod. Athos, Vatopedi 107, fol. 27ᵛ in the familiar primitive manner followed by the illustrator of this manuscript (Fig. 318).

An illuminated initial A in the cod. Turin, Univ. Lib. C. I. 6, fol. 20ʳ, referring to this particular passage does not seem to be a reduction of the more complete miniatures discussed above since it illustrates this passage with a man tilling (Fig. 33).

"SHEPHERD AND HERDSMAN TUNE THEIR PIPES AND INSPIRE A SWEET MELODY"

The cod. Athos, Panteleimon 6, fol. 37ᵛ, contains a miniature dominated by a hilly landscape (Fig. 141). A hill to the right seems to be in the background. Upon it a tree

---

[125] P. Gauckler, "Le domaine des Laberii à Uthina," E. Piot, *Monuments et mémoires*, 3 (1896), pp. 176ff., pl. XXII.

[126] Martin, *Ladder*, pl. XIC, 73.
[127] Strzygowski, *Rep. f. Kunst.* (1890), pp. 249 and figs.

and a few bushes grow. A shepherd, wearing a short tunic, sits on a hill to the left and plays a flute, while a dog watches over the flock of four lambs. Apparently this miniature refers to the ποιμήν (shepherd) of the text.

Bucolic scenes for their own sake are seldom found in Middle Byzantine art. This miniature of the Panteleimon codex, as well as the miniatures of the manuscripts discussed below, has an idyllic character which betrays the use of classical models. However, no precise parallels can be cited, because there is little comparative material extant. Yet similar iconographic motifs, and similar types of shepherds in bucolic representations, can be pointed out in late classical art or in Byzantine monuments of purely classical character. A similar type of seated shepherd, for example, appears among the pastoral scenes in the mosaic of the House of the Laberii at Uthina,[128] mentioned previously, and in the Nativity scene of the lectionary Athos, Panteleimon 2.[129]

A miniature similar to that of the Panteleimon manuscript of the homilies is found in the cod. Paris, Coislin 239, fol. 26ᵛ (Fig. 200). The framed miniature inserted in the column is almost completely flaked off, but the silhouette of the seated shepherd is still visible. He sits between two hills, playing a transverse flute. A shepherd playing a similar flute appears on the right side of the miniature in the cod. Jerusalem, Taphou 14, fol. 33ᵛ. On the left side, however, is another shepherd playing a syrinx (Fig. 107). Obviously the illustrator of the latter codex is more faithful to the text than the other illustrators inasmuch as he tries to distinguish the ποιμήν (shepherd) and the βουκόλος (herdsman) of the text. In fact, this distinction is shown also in the representations of the flocks they both tend. The shepherd on the left tends three lambs and a ram, a flock which identifies him as the ποιμήν of the text; but the flock of the shepherd on the right hill, consisting of a bull and a cow, suggests that he is the βουκόλος of the text. A similar differentiation of the two shepherds, and thus a further adherence to the text, occurs in the cod. Paris gr. 533, fol. 34ᵛ, illustrating the relevant sentence in two separate scenes (Fig. 240). In this instance the ποιμήν is making a pipe rather than playing one. This action may refer to the word ἁρμόζονται in the text, which means to make, as well as to fit in or to tune.

"THE GARDENER PRUNES THE TREE, THE BIRD-CATCHER"

Both occupations are fused into one scene in the cod. Athos, Panteleimon 6, fol. 37ᵛ (Fig. 141). A diagonal line on the hill of the landscape divides the miniature into two triangles, each devoted to a scene. In the upper triangle, a man dressed in a *tunica exomis* stands among a cluster of trees and trims one of them. The lower triangle contains a bird-catching scene. The bird-catcher sits in front of a hut pulling on a rope connected to his traps. The traps consist of the equipment for the hunt—in this case, cages. The enclosed birds serving as decoys and the bars of the cages are clearly indicated. The pruning of the tree illustrated in a similar manner is shown also in the

---

[128] Gauckler, *op.cit.*, *loc.cit.*　　　　　[129] Millet, *Recherches*, fig. 81.

cod. Paris, Coislin 239, fol. 27ʳ combined, however, with another scene which will be discussed later (Fig. 201).

Scenes illustrating the trimming of trees are rather unusual in Byzantine art. They appear in calendar pictures representing the occupation of the month of December.[130] A calendar, then, seems again to be the probable model of the Panteleimon miniature, which is very classical in style. As a matter of fact, the farmer in his *tunica exomis* cutting the branches suggests figures found in the pastoral scenes of the mosaic floor of the Great Palace in Constantinople.[131]

The method of depicting the hunting of birds shown in the Panteleimon manuscript was also known in antiquity and was described by Pseudo-Oppian, who wrote at the time of Caracalla (c. A.D. 200), and whose text offers a far better explanation for the details of the miniature than does Gregory's text. Actually a representation similar to that in the Gregory manuscript occurs in Pseudo-Oppian's illustrated *Cynegetica*.[132] The Pseudo-Oppian miniatures, however, have been traced to older models and this may be possible for the Gregory miniature. If so the artist of the Panteleimon miniature has transformed the style to such an extent that it does not betray the model.

Both episodes are illustrated in a single scene in the cod. Jerusalem, Taphou 14, fol. 33ᵛ (Fig. 107). On the left of the miniature a man is pruning a tree. The style and dress of the figure are typically Byzantine. On the right is a thatched hut in which the bird-catcher sits. He seems to be holding a bird, and is looking up at other birds flying overhead. In front of him are two cages placed on tripods with birds inside, which were used as decoys, according to Byzantine sources.[133] The hut of the bird-catcher recalls very similar huts in the illustrated manuscripts of Virgil's Eclogues.[134]

The illustration of the cod. Paris gr. 533, fol. 34ᵛ, has placed the two scenes one above the other (Fig. 240). The hunting scene presents some differences. The number of cages has been increased to six in two rows, and the hunter does not sit in a hut as the text specifies, but lies on a mattress under a tent. Because the miniature is flaked at this place, it cannot be discerned whether or not he is pulling a rope. Yet the posture and dress of the bird-catcher are similar to those found in the miniature of Pseudo-Oppian, referred to earlier.

The scene of the pruning of the tree in the historiated initial Δ of the cod. Turin, Univ. Lib. C. I. 6, fol. 20ʳ in the same homily, but beside a different passage, is too abbreviated to be related to the miniatures discussed above or to their models (Fig.

---

[130] Strzygowski, *Rep. f. Kunst.* (1890), p. 250 and figs. In western representations of the labors of the months this type often represents March.
[131] Brett, *The Great Palace*, pl. 30.
[132] Diehl, *Manuel*, II, p. 603, fig. 283. For the illustrated manuscripts of the *Cynegetica*, significance of their illustrations, and bibliography on the problems of authorship, see Weitzmann, *Mythology*, pp. 93ff. n. 1; *idem, Ancient Book Illumination*, Cambridge, Mass. 1959, pp. 26ff.

[133] Cf. Koukoules, *Bios*, v, 1952, pp. 401ff. Der Nersessian comparing the miniature of the cod. Jerusalem, Taphou 14 with a similar one in an illustrated manuscript of the romance of Barlaam interprets the cages as mirrors; see Der Nersessian, *Barlaam*, pp. 61, 62.
[134] See cod. Vat. lat. 3867, fol. 44ᵛ, *Picturae Ornamenta Codicis Vaticani 3867* (Codices e Vaticanis selecti, II) (facsimile), Rome 1902, fig. VIII.

34). If a relationship were postulated on the man's stance (if it was not dictated by the form of the letter), the assumption could be made that the miniature of the Turin manuscript is based on a different model.

"THE FISHERMAN SEES CLEARLY THE BOTTOM . . .
AND SITS ON A ROCK"

The cod. Athos, Panteleimon 6, fol. 37ᵛ illustrates the episodes by a marginal and a column miniature (Fig. 141). The former shows a fisherman sitting upon a stone and looking at his fishing rod, while the latter illustrates all the details that Gregory so vividly describes. In a boat bobbing on the waves a man is pulling on the oars, cutting a white wake through the black of the sea. At the stern a second man guides the boat to an area of gently rolling waves. In the middle of the boat a third fisherman stands, pulling in nets that sparkle with fish. A fourth figure bends far over the side of the boat, seeking to determine the depth of the sea with his immersed hands. In the flaked miniature of the cod. Paris, Coislin 239, fol. 27ʳ only the fisherman has been represented and can be recognized (Fig. 201). This scene has been conflated, however, with the episode of the pruning of the tree already discussed.

Fishing scenes are conventional and care should be taken in seeking models and making comparisons. Nevertheless, two somewhat similar scenes appear in the manuscript of Pseudo-Oppian in Venice, cod. Marc. 479, fols. 2ʳ and 59ʳ, one showing a fisherman similar to that in the Paris miniature,[135] and the other a fishing boat with a crew of three. The postures of the fisherman pulling the oars and the fisherman sitting at the stern are quite close to those of the corresponding persons in the miniature under discussion.

The miniature of the cod. Jerusalem, Taphou 14, fol. 33ᵛ, shows a fishing boat with three persons, of which only two—the helmsman and the netman—act as crew (Fig. 105). The third person, looking at his fishing rod, has just hooked a fish. There are two unusual things about this old fisherman. First, he wears a tunic that exposes his right shoulder, a trait found in classical art; and second, although he is in the boat, he sits on a rock! The latter can be explained by the miniature of the Panteleimon manuscript discussed above. There the fisherman is placed outside the main miniature and forms a separate scene. Also, taking into consideration the fact that Gregory describes the two episodes in different sentences, the obvious conclusion is that the miniature of the Jerusalem manuscript is an unmistakable example of conflation.

Although the relationship of this miniature to another cannot be supported on the basis of fishing equipment, it is worth noting that the fishing net in this case is the same as that represented in the miniature of Pseudo-Oppian. It should be pointed out, however, that this kind of net is described as ὑποχαὶ περιγέες (round bag net) by another Oppian (contemporary to Pseudo-Oppian), the writer of a didactic poem

---

[135] G. Muzzioli ed., *Mostra storica nazionale della miniatura, Palazzo di Venezia, Roma,* Florence 1954, p. 11, pl. IV; K. Weitzmann, *Ancient Book Illumination,* Cambridge, Mass. 1959, p. 27.

entitled *Halieutica*.[136] Therefore, the net of the Jerusalem miniature has to be differentiated from the net appearing in the Panteleimon miniature which, in all probability, is the kind of net described by Oppian as γρῖφοι (draw nets, drag nets).[137] The fisherman of the Jerusalem miniature is reminiscent of fishermen found in late antique or early Byzantine mosaics.[138]

A fusion of the two scenes appears in the cod. Paris gr. 533, fol. 34ʳ (Fig. 240). A fisherman sits on the shore leaning his head against his left hand. The two boats in front of him are now almost faded away but traces of nets are still visible, indicating that two separate scenes have undoubtedly been fused into one. The bending fisherman who seeks to determine the depth of the sea appears also in the cod. Athos, Vatopedi 107, fol. 27ʳ (Fig. 318). The manner of depiction of this conflated marginal miniature, as well as that of fol. 28ʳ (Fig. 319), does not permit a conclusion about whether or not the illustrator was in touch with any iconographic tradition.

"THE LABOR-LOVING BEE . . . COLLECTS THE HONEY OF THE FLOWERS"

Only two manuscripts, the codd. Jerusalem, Taphou 14, fol. 34ʳ and Paris gr. 533, fol. 34ᵛ illustrate this passage (Figs. 108, 240). These miniatures present trees, beehives, and flying bees—a highly conventional picture requiring no search for possible models.

"THE LORDLY HORSE TROTS IN THE VALLEY"

The two manuscripts just mentioned have in common another miniature illustrating the cited passage, which is the final line of Gregory's description of spring. A trotting horse is shown in both, fols. 34ᵛ, 35ʳ (Figs. 106, 238), but while the horse in the Jerusalem miniature is lordly, the one in the Paris miniature attempts to quench its thirst. Both types, one facing the other, appear in the illustrated Pseudo-Oppian of Venice, fol. 11ᵛ. Can this too be mere coincidence?

"A BIRD BUILDS A NEST. . . . WE ENJOY OURSELVES WITH ALL OUR SENSES"

The miniature of the cod. Jerusalem, Taphou 14, fol. 34ʳ illustrating the above passage presents—in a verdant, tree-dotted valley in which birds fly—a youth sleeping comfortably upon a red blanket, his head resting on his left arm (Fig. 108). Another young man, sitting beside him on a mattress placed on another red blanket,[139] seems to be eating from a bowl in front of him. Whether the bowl contains honey, as the text implies, or something else, can never be known. Both figures are placed by a stream

---

[136] *Halieutica*, III, ed. Loeb, p. 350, v. 81.
[137] *Ibid.*, v. 80.
[138] D. Levi, *Antioch Mosaic Pavements*, II, Princeton 1947, p. 53.

[139] There is no indication that one of the figures is a young woman and that her head is covered with a sheet, as has been suggested by Papadopoulos-Kerameus, I, p. 50.

which flows through the valley. At the top of the tree located near the head of the seated figure, there is a bird's nest in which a bird is hatching two eggs, while other birds fly nearby. This upper part of the miniature, appearing also in the manuscript of Paris cod. gr. 533, fol. 35ʳ (Fig. 239), is in accordance with the text. The text also implies the presence of men in the valley but by no means explains the main part of the miniature since no mention is made of sleeping and eating. It is possible that the idea of feasting, which the sentence πᾶσαν αἴσθησιν ἑστιώμεθα indicates, was interpreted by the artist as a feasting on the pleasures of sleeping and eating. This is not a satisfactory explanation, for it seems highly unlikely that the artists arbitrarily added important elements not found in the text. A curious detail is the arrangement of the mattress on top of the blanket, a strange device which suggests an attempt to adapt a model.

Since some parallels are found in the illustrated manuscript of Pseudo-Oppian, further parallels might be found there as well. On fol. 21ʳ of the *Cynegetica* in the Marcian Library in Venice there is a scene depicting a resting hunter. It differs, however, in many respects from the Jerusalem miniature; a boy waves a fan over the sleeping man, two standing hunters exchange bowls of food and another figure bathes in a stream to the right. The passage of Oppian illustrated by this picture is very revealing. It reads as follows (references to the episodes are made by number in the ensuing discussion):

(1) How sweet the sleep upon the flowers in spring time;
(2) How sweet in summer the low couch in some cave;
(3) What delight for hunters to break their fast amidst the rocks;
(4) The cold water flowing from a grotto;
(5) What a draft for a weary man;
(6) How sweet a bath.[140]

These lines offer an explanation for the Jerusalem miniature which is not supplied by the text of Gregory. The following careful comparison of the verses with the picture in Pseudo-Oppian and the miniature in Gregory's homily shows that occasionally each artist has chosen different episodes.

Episode 1 is illustrated in both Pseudo-Oppian and Gregory, episode 2 only in Gregory. The arrangement of mattress and blanket in the miniature of the Jerusalem codex may be explained as an adaptation of the cave which occurred when the picture was removed from its original context. Episode 3 is illustrated in both texts but the illustrations are different. Perhaps the difference is due to an attempt to depict the episode of eating in two phases, i.e. the preparation for eating, which is the exchange of bowls of food seen in the Pseudo-Oppian miniature, and the actual eating shown in the miniature of Gregory. Episode 4 is illustrated in both books, while episodes 5 and 6 appear only in the miniature of Pseudo-Oppian.

[140] *Cynegetica*, II, ed. Loeb, p. 57, v. 34-41. Translations of these verses and those that follow are taken from this edition and are by A. W. Mair.

Following this analysis the obvious question regarding the miniature of the Jerusalem manuscript arises: did this miniature originally come from a book of Oppian fully illustrated line by line? The question is answered later. Attention is now turned to clarification of the interrelationship of the bucolic miniatures contained in the discussed manuscripts. The Turin and Vatopedi miniatures, however, must not be taken into consideration since they cannot be related to the other miniatures with any degree of certainty. The historiated initials of the former are different or abbreviated, and the miniatures of the latter are too primitive to be used as evidence. The compositions referring to sailing, ploughing, pruning a tree, and fishing are similar in all four manuscripts which, in addition, have in common the scene that illustrated the passage referring to the shepherd. The remaining episodes do not appear in all manuscripts. But whenever scenes illustrating the same passage are found in more than one manuscript, they are similar from the point of view of iconography. Moreover, if a scene is found in only one manuscript, that scene illustrates a different passage of the text. Since the scenes which the manuscripts have in common are similar, the obvious conclusion is that all these bucolic miniatures are excerpts from a more complete cycle.

No textual justification at all could be found for two of the miniatures of this excerpted cycle in the homily of Gregory. One is the miniature of the cod. Paris gr. 533, fol. 34^r, representing the shearing of the lamb, and the other the miniature of the Jerusalem manuscript showing the resting shepherds or hunters (Figs. 237, 108). It was suggested earlier that the first might have been the result of a misunderstanding of the model by the artist, but the fact that another miniature also needs explanation casts doubt upon the validity of this proposal. Furthermore, Gregory's text, as has been pointed out, does not sufficiently explain all the details of the illustrations of the bird-catcher. These miniatures presuppose a text that describes the equipment and methods of bird-catching in detail. It is obvious, then, that the source of these illuminations must be sought elsewhere and, since they belong to the same cycle as other bucolic miniatures, the originality of the entire group must be questioned. Were the bucolic miniatures invented for Gregory's text or had they been invented previously for another text?

In the discussion of the iconography of these miniatures, some parallels were found in calendar books, some in Pseudo-Oppian or ancient pastoral representations, while for others no parallels were sought because of the rather conventional rendering of the scenes. In the light of this evidence it is possible to suggest that this cycle of miniatures was formed from two different sources: three of the scenes (mowing, ploughing, and pruning) may have come from an illustrated calendar book in which they represent the months of June, November, and December, respectively, whereas the remaining miniatures may have migrated from an illustrated classical bucolic book. The illustrations of this bucolic book could easily have been available to the artist illustrating Gregory's homilies. Consideration of the first of these suggested sources, however, must be held in abeyance until the second is examined more closely since a bucolic book may have contained the occupations of the months as well, in which case the artists would have had no need for the first source.

The assumption that the illustrations of a bucolic text might have been used by Gregory's illuminators is supported by the fact that the miniatures in question have an unusual freshness of conception; they are fully in the spirit of the familiar classical tradition to which they are related in theme and treatment. Furthermore, it should be borne in mind that, in addition to the pictorial parallels found within this tradition, the use of classical illustrations by Byzantine artists is not unusual.[141] Following this assumption, it could also be argued that this early bucolic book may have been one of the sources of Gregory's pastoral text as well, in which case the search for this early book might also be aided by an investigation of Gregory's literary sources.

A textual explanation for one of the miniatures has already been found in the *Cynegetica* of Pseudo-Oppian, among the illustrations of which were also found some pictorial parallels of the bucolic miniatures. Yet in discussing the fishing scenes appearing in Gregory's homily, it was pointed out that whereas a pictorial parallel was to be found in the *Cynegetica* a detailed description, especially with reference to the kinds of nets used, was provided by the text of the *Halieutica*, written by the other Oppian. This would mean that a search for the possible literary sources of the homily's bucolic miniatures should begin with both Pseudo-Oppian's and Oppian's texts. But since the matter of authorship was rather loosely treated in the Byzantine period (Suidas, the lexicographer, for example, attributed both *Cynegetica* and *Halieutica* to one Oppian), and since most of the extant manuscripts contain both treatises anyway,[142] it can be assumed that one such codex may have provided the literary model for the bucolic part of the homily. If this is so, the same may have been true for the illustrations. At least it would have been far more convenient for the artist to find as many as possible of the pictures he needed in one illustrated codex. It follows, then, that the distinction of authors in this case is immaterial. Thus, both texts will be considered together for the sake of clarity and convenience, and their authors referred to, jointly, as Oppian.

In fact, most of the episodes mentioned in Gregory's text are also found in Oppian, as the following passages show:

"Golden spring which puts to rout the chilly clouds; when the sea is navigable for seafaring men, who spread the white rigging of their canvas-winged ships, what time the earth rejoices in them that tend plants. . . . When the lily white combs fill the hives of the bees . . . when in the morning the countrymen with well-fashioned stilts guide the earth-cutting plough behind the steers beneath the pole; again in the evening when

[141] An example of the use of classical illustrations is provided by the panels of the Veroli casket in London, Victoria and Albert Museum; the scenes of the Rape of Europa were probably copied from illustrations for the poem *Europe*, written by the bucolic poet Moschus of Syracuse, second century B.C. See J. Beckwith, *The Veroli Casket*, London 1961; Weitzmann, *Mythology*, pp. 183-86, 194; idem, *Ancient Book Illumination*, Cambridge, Mass. 1959, passim.

[142] A. W. Mair, *Oppian*, ed. Loeb, London-New York 1928, pp. xiiiff.

the sun slopes . . . herdsmen command their herds what time they travel homeward to their folds . . . all leap about their beloved mothers, the bright-eyed cows, the lambs about their bleating horned ewes, the kids about the bleating goats. . . . A ship well-riveted, well-benched . . . and they feed infinite tribes of feasting fishes which Thy servants tend. . . . For straight way . . . the fish quickly meets and seizes the hook . . . for great delight is for the eye and mind to see the captive fish tossing and turning."[143]

"For their hunt the fowlers carry nor sword nor bill nor brazen spear . . . but long cord, and clammy yellow birdlines and the reeds that tread an airy path. . . ."[144]

"How sweet the sleep upon the flowers in spring time; how sweet in summer the low couch in some cave; what delight for hunters to break their fast amid the rocks. . . ."[145]

"Various are the tribes of horses . . . [that] gallop over the plains with swifter feet. . . ."[146]

The parallelism of the two texts indicates a literary relationship between the two and possibly a pictorial relationship as well. It may be that the artists who illustrated the homilies of Gregory borrowed their bucolic miniatures from an illustrated Oppian. Oppian seems a possible source for three reasons: There is proof that Oppian was illustrated, that it was known in the Middle Byzantine period and that it was used elsewhere in Middle Byzantine art.[147]

However, by comparing closely the texts of Gregory and Oppian, the following observations can be made: Oppian does not mention the shepherd's pipe-playing. This may be one of Gregory's own additions and consequently an adaptation of one of the relevant miniatures that appeared in Oppian. Moreover the phrase "tends plants" occurring in Oppian is not explicit enough to justify the two distinct scenes, mowing and pruning, occurring in both the text and the illustrations of Gregory. This observation strongly suggests that the artist could not find in Oppian, if he used it, two distinct scenes—mowing and pruning—mentioned in Gregory's text. Therefore, it is possible that he had to search elsewhere, and the earlier suggestion concerning the use of a calendar book now seems a very likely explanation. Finally, the episode of the shearing of the lambs was found in neither Gregory nor Oppian, a fact which raises the question whether or not Oppian is, after all, the basic text.

Most of the bucolic episodes also occur in other classical texts. Many episodes from Oppian referring to fishing occur in Aelian. Wellmann, who has studied the sources of Oppian and Aelian, regards Leonidas of Byzantium and Alexander of Myndos as the chief sources of the *Halieutica*.[148] Some of the pastoral episodes—the luxuriant

---

[143] *Cynegetica*, I, ed. Loeb, pp. 15-17, v. 117-46. *Halieutica*, I, ed. Loeb, p. 205, v. 58-72; p. 227, v. 189-213; III, pp. 351ff., v. 66-82.

[144] *Cynegetica*, I, ed. Loeb, p. 9, v. 62-67.

[145] *Ibid.*, II, p. 57, v. 34-38.

[146] *Ibid.*, I, pp. 19-39, v. 166-369.

[147] See Weitzmann, *Mythology*, pp. 150, 152, 153, 201ff.

[148] M. Wellmann, "Dorion," *Hermes*, 23 (1888), pp. 179-93; *idem*, "Alexander von Myndos," *Hermes*, 26 (1891), pp. 481-566; *idem*, "Juba, eine Quelle des Aelian," *Hermes*, 27 (1892), pp. 389-406; *idem*, "Leonidas von Byzanz und Demostratos," *Hermes*, 30 (1895), pp. 161-76; *idem*, "Pamphilos," *Hermes*, 51 (1916), pp. 1-64.

valleys, the leaping lambs, the bees, the singing birds, the fishing and sailing—also appear in the romance of Longus, *Daphnis and Chloe*.[149] Although it cannot be proved that this romance was illustrated, it is highly unlikely that it was not.[150] Therefore, Oppian was not necessarily the basic text of the miniatures, nor was it the only book of its type in antiquity. There is good reason, therefore, to assume the existence of a much older source, a Greek book of bucolic poetry, from which the text and illustrations migrated to later books of a similar type. Such a book may have included the shearing of the lambs.[151]

If Oppian is a possible source of the bucolic miniatures of Gregory's homilies, should it then be assumed that the miniatures migrated from the former to the latter directly, or is there another intermediary source? This question is raised because the pastoral paragraph of the homily on New Sunday is paralleled in a text which is earlier than the text of Gregory but later than that of Oppian. The text in question is an ἔκφρασις on spring by the sophist Libanius, possibly the teacher of Gregory. The similarity of the two texts was discovered by Sinko, who stated that the text of Libanius was a source of the pastoral paragraph in Gregory's homily.[152] Here both texts are presented for the sake of comparison.

Lib.: καὶ τότε δὴ φαιδρός τε ἥλιος	Greg.: νῦν ἥλιος ὑψηλότερος καὶ χρυσοειδέστερος
Lib.: ποιεῖ τὰ ἄστρα φαινόμενά τε καὶ οὐ κρυπτόμενα	Greg.: ἀστέρων χορὸς καθαρώτερος
Lib.: χλωρὰ τότε τὰ λήια γεωργοὺς εὐφραίνοντα ταῖς ἐλπίσιν	Greg.: γεωργός . . . ταῖς ἐλπίσιν εὐφραίνεται
Lib.: ἀνοίγονται τότε καὶ ἡ θάλαττα τοῖς πλωτῆρσιν	Greg.: ἄρτι μὲν ναῦς ἐκ λιμένων ἀνάγεται καὶ (δελφὶς) παραπέμπει πλωτῆρας
Lib.: ποταμοὶ δὲ καθαροὶ καὶ αἱ πηγαὶ δὲ πολὺ βελτίους ἢ τοῦ χειμῶνος	Greg.: νῦν πηγαὶ διαυγέστερον νάουσι νῦν δὲ ποταμοὶ δαψιλέστερον
Lib.: πρὸς ἔργον δ᾽ ἐπείγεται καὶ μελέτην ὁ ἱππεύς, ὁ τοξότης, ὁ κυνηγέτης	Greg.: ἄρτι δὲ ποιμὴν καὶ βουκόλος ἁρμοζονται σύριγγας . . . ἄρτι δὲ φυτὸν φυτουργὸς θεραπεύει καὶ ἰξευτὴς καλάμους οἰκοδομεῖ . . . καὶ ἁλιεὺς βυθοὺς διορᾷ

[149] Cf. Longus, *Daphnis and Chloe*, I, 9; II, 12; ed. Loeb.

[150] For illustrations of bucolic romances in Classical Antiquity, see K. Weitzmann, *Ancient Book Illumination*, Cambridge, Mass. 1959, pp. 107ff.

[151] The episode of the shearing of lambs occurs in Virgil's *Georgics*, where the other pastoral episodes of the group are found as well. Philologists agree that Virgil was under the influence of Greek bucolic poetry. Therefore, it is likely that the episode of the shearing of lambs, if it was not added by Virgil, harks back to an early Greek source. For the Greek sources of the *Georgics* see F. J. Deveau, *The Bucolics of Virgil*, New York 1935; cf. K. Buechner, "P. Vergilius Maro," *Paulys Realenzyclopädie der klassischen Altertumswissenschaft*, VIII, A, pp. 1180ff.

[152] Sinko, *Traditione*, p. 74.

to this text cited by Sinko two more passages which complete the cycle must be added:[153]

Lib.: χωροῦντες δὲ καὶ ἐπ' ἀγροὺς καὶ τρυφῶντες ἐν ὀρνίθων τε ᾠδαῖς καὶ ἀνθέων ὀσμαῖς

Greg.: Ἄρτι μὲν καλιὰν ὄρνις πήγνυται . . . ὁ δὲ περίπταται καὶ καταφωνεῖ τὸ ἄλσος

Lib.: ᾄδει μὲν χελιδὼν ἀλλὰ καὶ τὰ ἄλλα τῶν ὀρνίθων γένη φαίνεται πανταχοῦ πετόμενα

Lib.: Τὸ ἔαρ ἐξάγει τοὺς ἀνθρώπους καὶ κατακλίνει καὶ εὐωχεῖ

Greg.: καὶ πᾶσαν αἴσθησιν ἑστιώμεθα

The last passage (Lib. 90) explains the miniature of the Jerusalem manuscript, fol. 34[r] (resting shepherds), but it is too general to be compared with the detailed passage supplied by Oppian.

A comparison of the passages of both texts clearly reveals that the homily of Gregory contains the text of Libanius. This is not unusual in the case of ἐκφράσεις.[154] Gregory interrupts his discourse to describe the beauties of nature in spring, and for this purpose uses the text of Libanius. Libanius' text was written for teaching purposes and therefore was probably illustrated. It may well be that, just as Gregory borrowed the text from Libanius, so his illustrator borrowed the illustrations from the same source. After all, Libanius was well known and admired in the Middle Byzantine period.[155] It is possible, then, to consider the migrated illustrations of Libanius' ἔκφρασις as the intermediary source of the pastoral miniatures of Gregory's homilies.

In addition to these miniatures, others must be included here which do not illustrate the pastoral passage of the homily on New Sunday already discussed, but are related to some of its illustrations from the point of view of subject matter. In the eighth paragraph of the same homily is the sentence: "One year brings about four seasons."[156]

[153] The text is cited from the edition of Förster, VIII, pp. 479ff.

[154] An *ekphrasis* exists for its own sake in most cases and readily lends itself to transplantations from one text to another. This fact is verified especially by the practices of the Greek Fathers. When they wanted to create a vivid picture in the minds of the listeners, they could easily find it in an ekphrasis; having taken it into their texts, they attempted to relate it to general Christian themes. On the ekphrasis as a literary genre, see K. Krumbacher, *Geschichte der byzantinischen Literatur*, 2nd ed., Munich 1897, pp. 414, 454-56; for relations of ekphrasis to works of art, see A. Muñoz, "Alcune fonti letterarie per la storia dell'arte bizantina," *Nuovo Bull. di archeol. cristiana*, 10 (1904), pp. 221-32; idem, "Le ἐκφράσεις nella letteratura bizantina e i loro rapporti con l'arte figurata," *Recueil d'études dédiés à la mé-

moire de N. P. Kondakov, Seminarium Kondakovianum*, Prague 1926, pp. 138ff. For recent bibliography and more complete discussion, see G. Downey, "Ekphrasis," *Reallexikon für Antike und Christentum*, IV, pp. 921-44.

[155] On Libanius' life and works, see J. W. H. Walden, *The Universities of Ancient Greece*, New York 1909; P. Petit, *Libanius et la vie municipale à Antioche au IVe siècle après J. C.*, Paris 1955; idem, *Les étudiants de Libanius*, Paris 1957. Cf. G. Downey, "Libanius' Oration in Praise of Antioch (Oration XI)," *Proceedings of the American Philosophical Society*, 103 (1959), pp. 652-86; idem, *History of Antioch*, Princeton 1961, passim; G. Middleton, *Studies in the Orations of Libanius*, Part II, *Further Imitation of Classical Writers in Libanius' Orations*, Aberdeen 1928.

[156] *PG*, 36, 616.

The initial A of this phrase has been historiated in the cod. Turin, Univ. Lib. C. I. 6, fol. 19ᵛ, with the four seasons observed through the occupations of the months: ploughing, tree pruning, a man warming himself over a fire, and a flower-bearer (Fig. 32). The last scene is really too small for positive identification, but the general size of the object lifted by the figure and its position in relation to the figure suggests the baskets seen in some representations of the month of May.[157]

The first two scenes have been encountered in the discussion of the pastoral passage of the homily on New Sunday, and mention has been made of their occurrence in calendar books, where the two other scenes also appear: a man warming himself over a fire usually represents the month of February, and a flower-bearer, the month of May.[158]

Since seasons constitute the very essence of time, two more miniatures depicting their personification can be included here. One shows a month personification and appears in the cod. Paris, Coislin 239, fol. 13ʳ (Fig. 186). A warrior wearing a helmet, tunic, and chlamys, and holding a shield and a spear, has been depicted in the margin next to the following passage from the second sermon on Easter: "and yet the first month arrived; or rather the beginning of months. . . ."[159] An inscription identifies the warrior as the month of March and thus the miniature provides further clarification of the text, taking the place of a commentary.

The month of March represented as a warrior is a distinct mark of the developed Byzantine illustrations of the months as revealed by examples in the Octateuchs, or in the Gospel in the library of St. Mark's at Venice, cod. gr. DXL.[160] On the basis of the mosaic from Beisam, Webster and Levi have shown that this distinctly Byzantine theme goes back to Hellenistic sources.[161]

The other miniature is a personification of Night and historiates the initial N in the cod. Turin, Univ. Lib. C. I. 6, fol. 89ʳ (Fig. 59). This depiction is a direct reference to the sentence "Night was there, and the throne was ready,"[162] occurring in the funeral oration on St. Basil. Night, wearing a violet robe with a blue border and holding a flowing black mantle, stands by a throne decorated with red drapery. By adding the throne, the artist easily adapted a current classical personification to a new text. Night's stance reflects the creations of Hellenistic art and recalls similar personifications found in other works of Middle Byzantine art, such as the Night of the Paris Psalter, cod. gr. 139, fol. 435ᵛ.[163] Like them, the Turin miniature bears witness to the Classical trend which entered Byzantine art in the Macedonian Renaissance.[164]

---

[157] J. C. Webster, *The Labors of the Months*, Princeton 1938, pp. 14ff., pl. IX.

[158] Webster, *op.cit.*, pp. 25, 129, pl. X.

[159] *PG*, 36, 641.

[160] D. C. Hesseling, *Miniatures de l'octateuque grec de Smyrne* (Codices Graeci et Latini, suppl. VI) (facsimile), Leyden 1909, pl. 9, 27. Strzygowski, *Rep. f. Kunst.* (1888), p. 27 and figs.; Webster, *op.cit.*, p. 25, pls. IX, X, 22.

[161] Webster, *op.cit.*, p. 26; D. Levi, "The Allegories of the Months in Classical Art," *AB*, 22 (1941), pp. 280ff.

[162] *PG*, 36, 564.

[163] Bibl. Nat., *Byzance*, p. 8, pl. C (here complete bibliography).

[164] Weitzmann, *Mythology*, passim; *idem*, *Joshua*, pp. 64ff.

Finally, the Turin manuscript contains two more iconographically significant personifications forming the initial Ω, fol. 93ᵛ, in the funeral sermon on St. Basil and next to the following text: "He brought them [the active and contemplative life] together and united them, so that the contemplative spirit might not be cut off from society, or the active life be unaffected by the contemplative; but both might be united, just as sea and land are by an interchange of their several gifts, for the glory of God."[165] The miniature has not been completed, but the drawing shows a personification of the earth standing by a shore and a personification of the sea riding on a sea horse. A fisherman standing on the other side of the shore illustrates the last part of the cited sentence; through him the sea gives of her possessions to the earth (Fig. 60).

The sources of elements of this scene can be traced. An earlier Byzantine example showing the sea and her inhabitants is found in the Sacra Parallela, cod. Paris gr. 923, fol. 247ʳ,[166] but more particularly the sea and her charger can be traced in classical models, where the fisherman also appears.[167] Yet the adaptation and use of these borrowed elements as illustrations of the quoted passage show once again the great inventiveness and ingenuity of the Byzantine artist.

E. THE DECORATIVE MINIATURES

The miniatures included here constitute the final group of supplementary illustrations. They are found in the codd. Paris gr. 550; Turin, Univ. Lib. C. I. 6; Athos, Dionysiou 61; Vat. gr. 463; and they are mainly *decorative*. This term means that these miniatures are not direct illustrations of the narrative of Gregory's text, nor do they belong to any other basic text.

Some of these decorative miniatures are related only to the broader concept of a particular sermon rather than to any specific part of the text, such as a passage or a word. It is in this light that one should regard, for example, the two praying figures depicted on top of the main miniature in the Paris manuscript, fol. 5ʳ; the four busts, enclosed in medallions, which decorate the four corners of the same miniature (homily 1); and the cross and the dove before it, fol. 83ʳ, of the same manuscript (homily 8) (Figs. 401, 414). The praying figures express the concept of praising God for the glorious work of redemption achieved through Christ's Resurrection; the four medallions containing the busts may allude to the spreading of the redeeming message to the four corners of the earth; while the cross and the dove refer to the Incarnation and the Sacrifice of Christ, concepts found in the homily on the Nativity. A relationship can also be seen between the cross in the margin of fol. 153ʳ and the Baptism scene of the main miniature, probably intended to express the idea of Baptism as death and resurrection (Fig. 422).

[165] *PG*, 36, 577.
[166] Bibl. Nat., *Byzance*, p. 36.
[167] The motif of water personifications seated or carried by sea horses or tritons occurs often in late classical art, primarily on sarcophagi and mosaic pavements. For an example, see V. Lippold, *Die Skulpturen des Vaticanischen Museums*, III, 2, Berlin 1956, pl. 22.

In addition to these miniatures, there are others which are not related to the general ideas of the sermon, but illustrate instead a short phrase, or more often, a single word, taken out of its context. Such is the case of a number of miniatures found in the Turin manuscript. The tendency to illustrate just one word of the text reveals a desire on the part of the artist, not so much to interpret the text pictorially and preserve its narrative continuity, but to ornament the page. In other words the decorative effect of the page prevails. Finally, there are miniatures mostly in the form of historiated initials or marginal vignettes, for which no specific text at all can be cited, nor can any relationship to the ideas of the homily be suggested. Because of their special nature and great abundance—several are in the cod. Sinai 339—we are limited to the discussion of only a small fraction of these illustrations. I hope to be able to deal with them in a separate paper.

The miniatures that refer only to a short phrase or single word and those that appear to be quite independent of the written words serve a common purpose—the ornamentation of the page. In addition, they have a thematic affinity. In fact the majority of them are scenes that give intimate glimpses of the life of the time and reveal something more about the Byzantine artist and his approach to the written page. It is obvious, then, that all these miniatures should be grouped together and be given special consideration. They may be divided according to their subject matter into bird and animal representations, hunting scenes, and genre scenes.

1. BIRD AND ANIMAL REPRESENTATIONS

The cod. Paris gr. 550 displays a great variety of birds and animals represented in various activities. Birds resting in small branches (Fig. 410),[168] or at a fountain where some quench their thirst (Figs. 412, 423),[169] are alternated with birds eating the fruit of a tree (Fig. 401),[170] or pecking at the bark of a date tree (Fig. 425). In other instances an eagle displays its strong wings (Fig. 409), and peacocks their beautiful feathers (Figs. 402, 424),[171] charming rabbits drink water from an elaborate fountain (Fig. 424),[172] while griffins and leopards crouch on top of the miniatures (Figs. 423, 413).[173] Other animals, real and fantastic, rest on frames or form zoomorphic initials which are dispersed in the text and reveal the artist's fertile imagination, as for example the initial T on fol. 100ʳ (Fig. 419).

These birds and animals may or may not have symbolical significance. Kondakov

[168] Cf. E. Tsimas, S. Papachadjidakis, Ἱστορημένα Εὐαγγέλια τῆς Μονῆς Μεγάλου Σπηλαίου, Athens n.d., pl. 48.

[169] Cf. cod. Paris gr. 64, fol. 6ᵛ, Ebersolt, Miniature, pl. XLIII, 1; cod. Oxford, Bodl. Auct. T. infra 1, 10, fol. 21ʳ, O. Pächt, Byzantine Illumination, Oxford 1952, fig. 3; cod. Megaspelaion 8, Tsimas, Papachadjidakis, op.cit., pl. 51. Also cf. the rich ornamental decoration of the canon tables in the Gospels Parma, Pal. 5, fols. 7ʳ, 9ʳ, Lazarev, History, II, figs. 144, 145.

[170] Cf. A. Premerstein, K. Wessely and J. Mantuani, Dioscurides, cod. Aniciae Julianae picturis illustratus nunc vindob. Med. gr. I (Codices Graeci et Latini, x) (facsimile), Leyden 1906, p. 481.

[171] Cf. Ebersolt, Miniature, pl. XL, 1.

[172] Cf. A. Xyngopoulos, Ἱστορημένα Εὐαγγέλια τῆς Μονῆς Ἰβήρων τοῦ Ἁγίου Ὄρους, Athens 1952, pl. 16.

[173] Cf. Ebersolt, Miniature, pls. XLII, 1; LXX.

saw in them specific symbolism,[174] but in my opinion, a purely decorative, nonsymbolic function seems most likely. The parallelisms drawn indicate without any doubt that the source of these decorative representations are the decorative motifs of the Gospel canon tables. The ultimate source of the motifs in the canon tables and the means by which they were collected is a problem in itself, which cannot be solved here.

2. HUNTING SCENES

Inserted among the peaceful activities of the various animals depicted by the illustrator of the cod. Paris gr. 550 is one hunting scene on fol. 49[r] (Fig. 411). The hunter spears a deer which is leaping into a tree. Hunting, however, was not limited to deer but included ferocious animals as well, as the two leopards appearing on fol. 279[r] of the same manuscript may well indicate (Fig. 427). This is also true of the miniature of the cod. Turin, Univ. Lib. C. I. 6, fol. 4[r], depicting the slaying of a bear (not illustrated).

A treatise on hunting, Oppian's for example, provides a possible source of these hunting scenes, although no close parallels occur in Oppian's illustrated manuscripts. Moreover, it must be borne in mind that hunting was greatly favored by Byzantine emperors and that its depiction, which belonged to the cycle of imperial iconography, is often found in works of art and in a variety of media.[175] Accordingly, an intermediate rather than an ultimate possible source must be sought. The marginal illustration of the homilies with decorative hunting scenes recalls the embellishment of the canon tables of the Gospels and resembles similar episodes found there. One of the richest examples of this decoration is furnished by the cod. Paris gr. 64, which contains two hunting scenes on fols. 5[v] and 6[r].[176] Although they are not similar to the Gregory miniatures, the possibility that illustrated canons may have formed the intermediate source of the homilies' miniatures cannot be excluded.

3. GENRE SCENES

A series of scenes of everyday life that reveal another aspect of Byzantine art appear in the codd. Paris gr. 550, Turin, Univ. Lib. C. I. 6, Vat. gr. 463 and Athos, Dionysiou 61.

On fol. 30[r] of the Paris manuscript there is a marginal miniature showing a boy in a tree picking fruit (Fig. 409). Below, another boy is watching him or receiving the fruit, and a third boy carries the fruit in a basket. A similar episode occurs in the marginal miniature of fol. 204[r] (Fig. 416). One boy is helping another climb into a tree to pick its fruit, as the basket on the ground implies.

Scenes representing people picking fruit appear in the Oppian of Venice, fol. 21[r], and in the Dioscurides of the monastery of Lavra, cod. Ω 75, fol. 184[r]; the latter illustration has some similarities to the Paris miniatures but not enough to justify the assumption that a Dioscurides manuscript is their source.

---

[174] Kondakov, *Histoire*, pp. 97, 98.
[175] Grabar, *Empereur*, pp. 66ff.
[176] Ebersolt, *Miniature*, pl. XLII, 2.

On fol. 279ʳ of the Paris manuscript, two men are heraldically placed on either side of a tree (Fig. 427). They are preparing to tap the trunk for sap. This marginal miniature recalls similar ones appearing in botanical manuscripts, such as the previously mentioned Lavra Dioscurides, fol. 172ᵛ, in which the bark of some trees is being removed, while other trees are being tapped for medicinal purposes. The similarities existing between this example and the Paris miniature again do not permit the conclusion that a Dioscurides manuscript was the prototype of the Gregory miniature. Neither is it possible to determine a specific model for the beautiful figure of the shepherd forming the initial T on fol. 9ʳ of the Paris manuscript (Fig. 405). The shepherd, attended by his dog, carries a he-goat on his shoulders, and recalls the classical calfbearer or a shepherd with a lamb on his shoulders—a motif used to depict the month of April in Byzantine representations of the months.[177]

Shepherds appear in the Turin manuscript as well. Two of them, one young and one old, facing each other and leaning on their staffs, form the initial M on fol. 1ᵛ (Fig. 19). They are reminiscent of shepherds found in Nativity scenes, which have been imaginatively used by an inventive artist.

From the representations of occupations, the discussion moves into another, more charming sphere of genre scenes pertaining particularly to children's activities. In the sermon on St. Basil, Gregory, speaking of his friend's virtues and abilities, says that Basil could feed people ". . . with a longing for the Word which is life-giving, nourishing, and causes to grow to [spiritual] manhood him who is fully fed thereon. . . ."[178] It is the concept of growth that the artist of the Turin manuscript illustrates in the letter Δ which belongs to a word that follows the cited line, on fol. 83ʳ (Fig. 57). A woman teaches a child how to walk. This scene recalls the representation of the first steps of the Virgin in the mosaics of the monastery of Chora in Constantinople,[179] but a further relationship between the two should not be sought, for obviously the artist of the Turin manuscript, in order to decorate a page, has played with the meaning of the words and tried to imbue them with real life by making the intangible tangible. Once the child has taken his first steps, his world is widened.

In the initial Δ of fol. 100ʳ of the Paris manuscript, a nude boy plays with a dog; on fol. 6ʳ a boy lifts up a ball, another one waves a branch on fol. 9ᵛ, and on fol. 6ᵛ the initial Δ is formed by two naked boys who, perhaps playing a game, embrace each other while a third jumps over them (Figs. 420, 403, 406, 404). The same Paris manuscript on fol. 251ʳ contains a miniature depicting two children who gracefully push a third child in a swing suspended from a tree (Fig. 426). All three are barefooted and lightly dressed. They seem to be enjoying their own world. Two birds, undisturbed by the youngsters' voices, are busy pecking at the fruit of the tree.

Swinging has always been a favorite pastime. As early as the fifth century, Neilos

[177] J. C. Webster, *The Labors of the Months in Antique and Mediaeval Art*, Princeton 1938, p. 129, pl. x, 22.

[178] *PG*, 36, 548.

[179] P. A. Underwood, *The Kariye Djami*, I-III, New York 1966, II (The Mosaics), pl. 88. Cf. J. Lafontain-Dosogne, *Iconographie de la Vierge dans l'empire byzantin*, Brussels 1965.

the Ascetic mentions the popularity of this sport.[180] Its pictorial representation recalls the charming children who play with spoked wheels on the floor mosaics of the great palace of Constantinople.[181] These children, like those of the Gregory miniatures, are deeply absorbed in their activity.

As life goes on from childhood to adulthood, the world of games and of innocence is left behind. However, the upbringing that a child has received becomes a determining factor in what Gregory calls his spiritual growth. The role of the parents, then, is of primary importance. Gregory emphasizes this in his homily on Basil when he speaks about Basil's upbringing and his parents to whom great honor is due. He says: ". . . in my opinion the greatest claim to distinction and the most obvious one for parents is the excellence of their children (εὐτεκνία) . . . when the children are eminent, the honor is due to those who brought them up. . . ."[182] On fol. 69ᵛ of the Turin manuscript the sentence begins with the word περιφανέστατον followed by the word εὐτεκνία.

It is the latter word that the artist historiates in the initial of the former word (Fig. 52). How does the artist visualize the concept of successful parenthood? For him the greatest blessing that a parent can wish for is to have his eyes closed by the hands of his children and to be buried by them. Two children carrying a bed on their shoulders with their dead father lying on it introduce the word περιφανέστατον. In this historiated initial the artist has graphically rendered, with great simplicity and conviction, what was to him and to Gregory, the profound meaning of successful parenthood.

But life does not consist of the world of children only, nor of present duties and the demands for their fulfillment. Everyday trivialities also play their part.

In the fourteenth paragraph of the second sermon on Easter, Gregory, speaking of the sacrificial lamb, says: "The Victim, of whom I am speaking, purifies the five senses. . . ."[183] It is the idea of the cleansing of the senses that feeds the imagination of the artist in the historiated initial M, fol. 9ʳ, with which the paragraph opens (Fig. 22). The feet of a man, seated to the left on a faldstool, are being washed by a standing figure, probably a servant, who pours water over them into a basin. The master lifts his tunic a little above his knees. Certainly this miniature has preserved an intimate scene of everyday life, something that almost resembles a ritual, and something which no writer has recorded, probably because it was so common and ostensibly uninteresting an occurrence. The writers, theologians, and others could speak about the public baths of the Byzantines and equivalent matters,[184] but there was no reason to devote their attention to trivialities. Yet a painter, with innocence and simplicity, saw in this trivial ritual the tangible reflection of an idea.

Later in the same sermon the following phrase occurs: ". . . mine is the silver and

---

[180] PG, 79, 812; for children's games in the Byzantine period, see Koukoules, *Bios*, ɪ, 1, pp. 161-84.

[181] Brett, *The Great Palace*, pl. 29; for a more complete bibliography, see Beckwith, *Constantino-*

ple, p. 30 n. 42.

[182] PG, 36, 505. Cf. Koukoules, *Bios*, ɪᴠ, pp. 9ff.

[183] PG, 36, 641.

[184] For baths in Byzantine times in general, see Koukoules, *Bios*, ɪᴠ, pp. 419-67.

mine is the gold, and I give it to whom I wish."[185] On fol. 12[r] of the Turin manuscript the initial H is historiated by a figure giving a purse to another. One can easily imagine such a scene taking place in the streets of Constantinople (Fig. 24). More charming still is a miniature on fol. 47[v] forming the initial Π and illustrating the following words from the homily to Julian the Tax Collector: ". . . from both sides we are maltreated and torn into pieces. . . ."[186] The initial shows two women with arms outstretched tearing at each other's hair (Fig. 45). Such an illustration of the phrase makes this historiated initial timeless—here again a triviality of everyday life, depicted with great vividness. It would seem that the artist has used the phrase as an excuse to express his own feelings toward women. The artist's identification of quarrels and screams with women is shown by another initial in the same homily, fol. 48[r]. Alluding to his dispute with the Tax Collector, Gregory here speaks of a legal dispute having a good purpose, saying: "Oh, the good dispute. . . ."[187] The artist historiates the letter Ω with two slender women in blue chitons whose bare arms, extended and gesturing, clearly suggest the idea of a dispute (Fig. 47). However, between them the artist has placed an old man who forms the middle bar of the letter. He is seated in an attentive position and, like the disputing women, he too has been rendered with vividness and freshness. His left arm rests on his lap, while his right arm supports his head. Of course, the artist was concerned with the middle bar of the letter, but the choice clearly reveals how inventive and truly imaginative an artist he was. This figure of the old man is certainly meant to be the counsel or judge whose presence is necessary for the pictorial realization of the idea of a dispute.

In the same homily, on fol. 51[r], the historiated initial M shows two figures, a young man and an old one, carrying a bowl, illustrating Gregory's advice: "let no one be fruitless and empty. . . ."[188] The imagination of the artist is again revealed by his choices. It is not a desire for variety that obliges him to represent a young and an old man. It is in fact the concept of the word everyone that he attempts to illustrate. But life has its happy and joyful aspect as well. It is the marginal miniature of fol. 4[r] of the Turin manuscript that leads us to this aspect, for here women seem to be at peace with each other and dance gracefully. Dancing played a very important role in the life of the Byzantines,[189] and representations of this human activity are to be found in every art form. The obelisk of Theodosius II, a very early example, may be recalled,[190] or the dancing figures in the canon tables of the twelfth century Gospel book in Venice, cod. gr. Z. 540, fol. 3[v].[191] In the first of these two examples the dancing is related to the festivities that took place during the celebration of the emperor's triumph in the hippodrome; but one wonders whether the appearance of dancing scenes in the manuscripts of the homilies, among others, has any relation at all to the

[185] *PG*, 36, 652.
[186] *PG*, 35, 1045.
[187] *PG*, 35, 1048.
[188] *PG*, 35, 1053.
[189] Koukoules, *Bios*, v, pp. 206ff.

[190] L. Bréhier, *La sculpture et les arts mineurs byzantins*, Paris 1936, pl. v. Cf. A. Grabar, *Sculptures byzantines de Constantinople*, Paris 1963, pp. 26, 27.
[191] Lazarev, *History*, II, pl. 157a.

emperor and the hippodrome. Another dancing scene in the Turin manuscript, fol. 7ᵛ, is, in fact, related to the hippodrome.[192] In this miniature the dancers are acrobats, recalling the dancing and acrobatic shows that were performed in the hippodrome of Constantinople during the intermission of the main races or other athletic games, to amuse the spectators and calm the excitement of the various parties involved.[193] Perhaps such dancer-acrobats may have been in the mind of the artist of the Paris manuscript when he historiated the initial T of fol. 99ᵛ with a nude dancing figure who carries on his head a basket with a griffon on it (Fig. 418). Furthermore, a number of miniatures depict various scenes performed for the Byzantines in the hippodrome, in the theater, or in popular shows in the streets of the cities. The acrobats who form the initials Π and O in the cod. Turin manuscript, fols. 67ʳ, 72ᵛ, or the acrobat who balances himself on a ball in the historiated initial T, fol. 73ᵛ, probably reflect these entertainments (Fig. 54).

An interesting acrobatic game appears in the initial Φ of the cod. Vat. gr. 463, fol. 184ʳ, which is formed by a standing acrobat on whose head there is a boy sitting on a pole (Fig. 84). This feat, which must have often been performed in the presence of the emperor as its depiction in the frescoes of the church of St. Sophia at Kiev indicates,[194] corresponds exactly to the description of an acrobatic game given by John Chrysostom: "Holding poles on their foreheads, they [the acrobats] keep them immovable as if they were trees rooted on earth. And this is not their only achievement for one to wonder at, for small children stand on top of the pole and fight one against the other, and for all that the acrobats use neither their hands nor any other member of their body but only their forehead which seems to be the safest means of carrying and keeping the pole immobile. . . ."[195]

Other spectacles in the hippodrome mentioned by the texts include wrestling and the hunting of wild animals. These shows are also illustrated in the Turin and Paris manuscripts. In the former, on fol. 11ʳ, the historiated initial A consists of two wrestling figures that may reflect a relevant performance in the hippodrome,[196] although wrestling, especially between children, as Byzantine art demonstrates, is not unusual outside the arena (Fig. 23).[197]

The illustrator of the Paris manuscript has depicted in the margin of fol. 94ᵛ a

---

[192] Dancing and acrobatic shows related to the hippodrome appear in the frescoes of the church of Hagia Sophia in Kiev and elsewhere; see A. Grabar in *Seminarium Kondakovianum*, 8 (1935), pp. 102-17; O. Povstenko, "The Cathedral of St. Sophia in Kiev," *The Annals of the Ukrainian Academy of Arts and Sciences in the U.S.*, 3-4 (1954), pls. 170-96; A. Grabar, "Les fresques d'Ivanovo et l'art des paléologues," *Byzantion*, 25-27 (1955-1957) (Mélanges E. Dyggve), pp. 580-90. For the games in the hippodrome, see also E. Coche de la Ferté, *L'antiquité chrétienne au Musée du Louvre*, Paris 1958, pp. 31ff., 58, 60.

[193] Koukoules, *Bios*, II, p. 255.
[194] Grabar, *Empereur*, p. 64, fig. 4; Povstenko, *op.cit.*, pl. 185. Liudprand states (*Antapodosis*, VI, 9; J. Becker ed., *Die Werke Liudprandus von Cremona*, Scriptores rerum germanicarum, Hannover-Leipzig 1915, p. 157) that he saw acrobatic games performed in the Palace.
[195] *PG*, 49, 196.
[196] Cf. wrestlers in the frescoes of Hagia Sophia in Kiev, reproduced in Povstenko, *op.cit.*, pl. 182.
[197] See examples in Bordier, *Description*, p. 229; Millet, *Recherches*, p. 276, fig. 260.

hunter chasing a bear that tries to hide behind a tree (Fig. 415). The bear holds a round object painted yellow that seems to be a honeycomb, as has been suggested.[198] It may be that the composition represents a particular entertainment in the hippodrome where, according to the texts, shows with bears were often performed. Even the tree may not be a decorative element added by the illustrator, but may reflect the decor set up for such occasions in the hippodrome, where artificial trees were erected as setting for performances of hunting games. An example of this may be seen in the representations of the Ludus Gothicus in the frescoes of the church of St. Sophia at Kiev, and in the depiction of hunting scenes related to the arena on some fourteenth-century Byzantine vases.[199]

In addition to the bears, there were many other kinds of animals, including lions, leopards, tigers, panthers, and monkeys, that put on amusing performances in the arena or in the streets of the cities. Very often these shows took place under the auspices of the emperor[200] or formed part of the festivities that occurred during the celebration of the emperor's triumph. Perhaps the monkey playing a flute which forms the initial Δ on fol. 8ʳ of the Turin manuscript, or the monkey with a ball in the Paris manuscript, fol. 9ᵛ, reflect such entertainments (Fig. 406). Performances with monkeys were particularly favored by the Byzantines.

Among other spectacles in the hippodrome were those of jugglers and magicians, who on certain occasions also performed in the palace for the emperor.[201] The texts give details about the juggling performances. For example, they describe jugglers who, while walking on a tight rope, balanced jugs full of water on top of sticks that stood on their heads. In the light of such descriptions, it is possible to understand the miniatures of the historiated initial T, on fol. 6ᵛ of the Turin manuscript, showing a man who balances two censers on his forehead or his nose, and on fol. 12ᵛ depicting a juggler who performs a trick with a stick (Figs. 21, 25).

Jugglers and acrobats must often have displayed their skill to musical accompaniment. In fact the texts mention such instances[202] and a relevant illustration appears on fol. 72ʳ of the Turin manuscript (Fig. 53). In the initial T, a juggler-acrobat, standing on the shoulders of a musician, stretches a rope while heavy links hang from his arms. At the same time the musician, sitting cross-legged, plays a lute. The dark colors of their flesh suggest touring magician-acrobats from Africa or Asia, a point confirmed by the oriental headdress of the musician and the brilliant costumes that have blue, red, and gold as predominant colors. A charming lute-player, fol. 76ᵛ, who is on top of a column, is also in a similar position. His exotic headdress was probably dictated by the horizontal bar of the letter T which this musician decorates

[198] A. Grabar, *Byzance, L'art byzantin du moyen âge*, Paris 1963, pl. p. 145.

[199] Grabar, *Empereur*, p. 72; cf. Povstenko, *op.cit.*, pls. 184-85. A. Xyngopoulos, "Πρόσωπα τοῦ Ἱπποδρόμου ἐπὶ Βυζαντινῶν Ἀγγείων," E.E.B.S.,

20 (1950), pp. 3-16; V. Lazarev, *Old Russian Murals and Mosaics*, London 1966, pp. 56ff.

[200] Koukoules, *Bios*, I, 1, p. 251.

[201] *Ibid.*, p. 268.

[202] *Ibid.*, p. 256.

(Fig. 55). Shows in which exotic persons participated must have been a common occurrence in Byzantium, and Byzantine art represented them often.[203]

Another musician-dancer, who probably delighted the emperor like the musicians and dancers depicted in the frescoes of the church of St. Sophia at Kiev,[204] appears in the initial Γ on fol. 15ᵛ of the Turin manuscript (Fig. 26).

In popular shows the display of snakes was common and the Byzantines greatly enjoyed the various tricks of the snake charmers. This aspect, too, of their lives is represented pictorially in the manuscript of Gregory's homilies. A man holding two snakes is depicted on fol. 3ᵛ of the Turin manuscript and on fol. 67ʳ of the same manuscript the initial Π is formed by three acrobats who display skillfully their powers over a snake, while, on the same folio, a nude figure, illustrating the initial Δ, dances on the body of a snake to the accompaniment of a cymbal (Figs. 49, 50). On fol. 68ʳ, the initial M is formed by two snake charmers playing their pipes over a fire where presumably the snakes lie (Fig. 51). This miniature recalls the representation of a snake charmer in the Chloudov psalter, fol. 58ʳ, which differs from the Turin miniature. A snake charmer is also represented in the initial P of the Turin manuscript, fol. 67ᵛ. In this case the snake has wrapped itself around the body of the performer. Parallel descriptions of events similar to those represented in the miniatures are again found in Byzantine texts.[205]

Like the majority of the Byzantines, the illustrators of the homilies must have been particularly attracted by the various amusements and have recorded them lovingly in artistic form. It is a paradox indeed to find that the love of this particular aspect of secular life found a place in homilies whose author often ridiculed the various spectacles, or used them as examples of a lower, vulgar life.[206] For a moment one might think that Gregory's many efforts to direct attention to the life of Heaven met with no response from the people. Yet the Byzantines never lost sight of the life that was to come, of the mysteries of faith that pertain to the metaphysical side of man. The idea of a higher life was always there. Its presence was so real that one written word taken out of context would suffice to arouse memories and a feeling of piety in the mind of the illustrator, to bring forth the effect that the liturgy had on him.

It is to a glimpse of this higher aspect of life that the Turin illustrator leads the discussion now. In his homily on Basil, Gregory narrates the episode of Valens' visit in the church of Basil (paragraph 52), and at one point he says that Valens "had to offer the gifts at the Holy Table,"[207] probably referring to the customary donation of the emperors that had to be deposited on the Holy Altar. For the artist of the Turin manuscript, however, on fol. 88ᵛ the word gifts associated with the Holy Altar meant only one thing: the gifts of the Holy Eucharist. Hence he singles out the word δῶρα

---

[203] See, for example, the miniature on fol. 4ᵛ of the cod. Paris gr. 64 showing a Negro leading a camel and an elephant to a fountain, reproduced in Ebersolt, *Miniature*, pl. XLIII, 2. Cf. A. Grabar, "Le succès des arts orientaux à la cour byzantine sous les Macedoniens," *Münchner Jahrbuch*, 3rd series, 2 (1951), pp. 56ff.

[204] Grabar, *Empereur*, pp. 64, 72, fig. 3.

[205] Koukoules, *Bios*, I, 1, p. 262.

[206] Cf. *PG*, 37, 376, 627, 628.

[207] *PG*, 36, 564.

and historiates the letter P with a liturgical scene (Fig. 58). A deacon, dressed in a grey-white *sticharion* with black bands at the neck and hem, his *orarion* flowing behind, moves slowly along holding the Eucharistic chalice with a red napkin. The chalice is not empty. A figure of Christ Emmanuel with a cruciform nimbus and a blue mantle enters the chalice as if flying swiftly from above. The presence of Christ and the type of Christ give exceptional importance to this miniature. First, the specific moment during the celebration of the liturgy which this miniature represents must, if possible, be identified and discussed. The deacon who assists the officiating priest during the celebration of the sacrament of the Holy Eucharist plays an important part in it. However, in only one instance does he hold the chalice with the elements in it. It is the moment just before the communion of the faithful begins. The deacon opens the door of the sanctuary, receives the chalice with great reverence from the hands of the priest, and proceeds towards the Beautiful Gate. He lifts the chalice up and addressing the congregation, says: "In fear of God, faith and love, approach."[208] The communion of the faithful then begins, the mystery having been completed through the Epiclesis of the Holy Ghost. The Holy Ghost has changed the sacrificial elements, bread and wine, into the body and blood of Christ. Therefore, the presence of the figure of Christ in the chalice leaves no doubt that the miniature refers to that specific moment of the celebration, when the faithful are about to receive the body and blood of Christ, thus becoming participants in the redeeming results of his sacrifice and members of his mystic body.[209] Furthermore, as Theodore of Studios says, the Liturgy is a "recapitulation of the whole divine economy,"[210] and a visual recreation of the dogma of the Orthodox Church. The part that proceeds the sanctification of the elements refers to the epiphany of Christ on Earth, his Incarnation; the sanctification of the gifts refers to his sacrifice, and the part after the sanctification refers to the glory of Christ who fulfilled the economy of the Father.[211]

There is no doubt that the type of Christ Emmanuel chosen here by the illustrator of the Turin manuscript refers to both the Incarnation and the sacrifice of Christ since "Christ Emmanuel" means "God with us" and God the Sacrificial Lamb. The Eternal Logos, Child, and Victim are suggested by the adolescence of Emmanuel.[212] The location of representations of Christ Emmanuel on the apses or the vaults of the Prothesis of Byzantine churches,[213] where the preparation of the elements for the sacrifice takes place, proves this interpretation. Furthermore, Emmanuel is the Anointed of the Spirit who carries the sins of the world. "Heavens rejoice . . . for lo, Emmanuel

[208] For bibliography on Christian liturgies in general, see H. Beck, *Kirche und theologische Literatur im byzantinischen Reich*, Munich 1959, pp. 283ff. For the text of the so-called liturgy of St. John Chrysostom, see Brightman, *Liturgies*, pp. 353ff.

[209] J. Karmires, Τὰ δογματικὰ καὶ συμβολικὰ μνημεῖα τῆς Ὀρθοδόξου Καθολικῆς Ἐκκλησίας, 2nd ed., I, Athens 1960, pp. 284ff.

[210] *PG*, 93, 440.

[211] Nicholas Kabasilas, Ἑρμηνεία τῆς θείας Λειτουργίας, *PG*, 150, 396ff. For an English translation, consult *idem, A Commentary on the Divine Liturgy* (translated by J. M. Hussey and P. A. McNulty), London 1960.

[212] For a discussion of the significance of Emmanuel, see Millet, *Dalmatique*, pp. 69ff.

[213] For examples, see S. Pelekanides, Καστοριά, Thessalonica 1953, pl. 90a.

carries our sins," reads a hymn of the Greek Orthodox Church. The choice of the type may also suggest an awareness of its Platonic connotations. The youthfulness of the Emmanuel symbolizes the archetypal beauty which is the desire of every Christian. "To those who approach Thee"—another hymn says—"grant that they may dwell in Thy beauty and be participants of it."[214] Significant also is the fact that, after the sanctification of the elements and before the deacon invites the faithful to communion, the officiating priest, proceeding to receive communion, chants the following verses: "Christ, Thou hast attracted me with great desire and Thou hast changed me with Thy Divine Love."[215]

Like other liturgical miniatures which have been discussed in this study, this one is unique. A number of miniatures found in illustrated liturgical scrolls which refer to various phases of the liturgy are known.[216] In these miniatures whose importance cannot be sufficiently emphasized, representations of deacons assisting in the celebration of the liturgy are frequent, but in no one of them does the particular moment illustrated in the Gregory miniature appear. With regard to the presence and type of Christ and their significance, parallels can be seen in representations of the *melismos* in the protheses of Byzantine churches or in a miniature which illustrates one of the homilies of John Chrysostom in the cod. Athens, Nat. Lib. 211, fol. 56^r.[217] This latter example shows the Holy Altar, and on it the sacrificial elements: the bread on the left and the chalice on the right. Between them is the Gospel, the Word, and on it a Dove, the Holy Ghost, with a cross—all making clear the liturgical ideas of the Incarnation, the Sacrifice, and the Epiclesis of the Holy Ghost. Here, however, the ideas are expressed through a series of symbols, whereas in the Gregory miniature, the same ideas are more tangible. This is important because it suggests that, for the Turin artist, the Sacrament is not merely an assemblage of symbols, but a mystic reality; and since this artist was, after all, but one person among the many, an insight into the effect that the liturgy had on the people is gained. Herein lies the great importance of this miniature. It is significant not simply because it fills a gap in the pictorial reconstruction of the liturgy, but because it reveals something of a personal relationship between the individual Byzantine and the mystery of the Sacrament.

Liturgical mysticism and love for the exuberant side of life seem to form the two poles between which the Byzantines lived. One seems to oppose the other and this is the paradox of Byzantium, expressed in all manifestations of Byzantine life. One thinks of the Byzantine emperors and generals who, overwhelmed by the shouts in the hippodrome and worldly ambition, blinded each other, yet who knew, in the most

---

[214] Millet, *Dalmatique*, pp. 69ff.

[215] Karmires, *op.cit.*, p. 311.

[216] L. Bréhier, "Les peintures du rouleau liturgique no. 2 du monastère de Lavra," *Annales de l'Institut Kondakov (Seminarium Kondakovianum)*, 11 (1940), pp. 1-20; A. Grabar, "Un rouleau liturgique constantinopolitain et ses peintures," *Dumbarton Oaks Papers*, 8 (1954), pp.

161-99; G. Jacopi, "Le miniature dei codici di Patmo," *Clara Rhodos*, 6-7 (1932-1933), passim.

[217] For a reproduction of this miniature, see A. Grabar, "Miniatures gréco-orientales II. Un manuscrit des homélies de Saint Jean Chrysostome . . . ," *Seminarium Kondakovianum*, 5 (1932), p. 263, pl. XVII, 2.

symbolic way, how to kneel before an icon of the Virgin and ask forgiveness in the hour of the Lord's greatest wrath. Were the Byzantines ever redeemed from this paradox? Did the elements of the lower life enter the sphere of the higher life and remain there for eternity? Yes. This was accomplished by the hands of the painter, through whose language Byzantium speaks her best. It was the painter who redeemed the Byzantines, preserved the elements of triviality from their lower life and placed them in the realm of art. The painter exercised his "painterly" will, gave life to dead words, redeemed the soul of Byzantium, lifted up the lower life, and made the higher life more tangible. Perhaps he himself was not aware of all this, but he seemed to be fascinated by what he was doing, by his own profession; and in at least one case— that of the illustrator of the cod. Athos, Dionysiou 61—he hesitantly tried to record this fascination and reveal its secrets.

In the margin of fol. 35ʳ of the cod. Athos, Dionysiou 61, a painter works at an easel (Fig. 363). He is painting the portrait of a bishop, perhaps Gregory. Representations of painters in Byzantine art appear especially in connection with St. Luke who had painted the Virgin's icon, as is shown, for example, in a miniature in the homily on the Nativity previously attributed to John Damascenus, found in the cod. Jerusalem, Taphou 14, fol. 107ᵛ. The painter in the Athos miniature, however, has a pose and equipment similar to another representation of St. Luke in a drawing which reproduces an icon or a miniature of the fourteenth century or later.[218]

Despite the similarities, there is a fundamental difference between the two representations. While the representation of St. Luke reflects a theme of religious art in the strict sense of the term, the depiction of a common painter belongs to the sphere of secular art. This painter exists for his own sake. Such a fact is important, because a painter for his own sake rarely appears in Byzantine art. One recalls few instances indeed: perhaps only the painter found in the Dioscurides manuscript in Vienna[219] and another one appearing in the Sacra Parallela of John Damascenus, cod. Paris gr. 923, fol. 328ᵛ, fall into this category.[220] The latter illustrates a text of Basil the Great and shows the painter in the act of painting, but without easel or other implements. The rarity of examples of this kind gives added importance to the Dionysiou miniature.

In the course of this discussion it has been pointed out that decorative miniatures of genre scenes often adorn the canon tables of the Gospels. No precise parallels to the Gregory miniatures exist in the canon tables and no single source for all these miniatures has been found elsewhere. These miniatures, charming and graceful as they are, probably reflect the everyday life of the Byzantines. From the trivialities and the various aspects of a lower life, the artists have led the discussion with great fascination

---

[218] D. Klein, *St. Lukas als Maler der Maria*, Berlin 1933, pl. ii, 4.

[219] For the painter in the Dioscurides manuscript, see P. Capparoni, "Intorno ad una copia delle scene raffiguranti l'estrazione della mandragora . . . ," *Atti del V congr. inter. di studi bizantini Roma 1936*, ii, *Studi bizantini e neoellenici*, 6

(1940), pp. 64-69, pl. xviii, 2; V. Wylie Egbert, *The Mediaeval Artist at Work*, Princeton 1967, pp. 22, 23.

[220] For a brief description of the cod. Paris gr. 923 and bibliography, see Bibl. Nat., *Byzance*, pp. 34-37; for this particular miniature see Wylie Egbert, *op.cit.*, pp. 24, 25.

into the spheres of a higher life; they have allowed us to glimpse the mystic side of life; they have revealed their own world; they have represented the whole of life—life that moved on from generation to generation, then as now. The things that people have loved—their games, shows, dancing, and the eternal play of children—have changed little and there is no reason to assume that such activities should have been represented differently from one period to another. Nevertheless, some of these activities have been represented repeatedly, probably because of their thematic relationship to the imperial iconography. Their representations may have been disseminated and have persisted through manuscripts intended for the emperor, who was associated with many of them.

V. THE ARCHETYPE

A. THE RESULTS OF THE INVESTIGATION OF THE CYCLES

I T IS time to recapitulate briefly the results of the investigation of the cycles: the illustrations of the homilies of Gregory do not form a single cycle, but consist of several excerpted cycles which are so prevalent that the basic picture cycle,[1] i.e. the illustrations which were invented solely for the text of Gregory, constitute but a small fraction of the total illustration. The invented miniatures and those harking back to other cycles are as follows:

1. MINIATURES FOR THE GREGORY TEXT

- Cyprian bowing to Gregory
- Gregory and Cyprian conversing
- The Koimesis of St. Cyprian
- Cyprian revealing the location of his relics (?)
- Gregory and Julian the writers
- Julian collecting the taxes
- Gregory and the martyrs
- Julian giving the tax orders to the scribes
- The Koimesis of St. Basil, in two variants
- Gregory of Nazianzus and Gregory of Nyssa conversing
- Gregory of Nazianzus and Gregory of Nyssa in proskynesis
- Gregory of Nazianzus and Gregory of Nyssa in ecstatic meeting
- The Koimesis of St. Athanasius
- Gregory and the one hundred and fifty bishops
- Gregory bidding his last farewell
- Gregory and the poor
- The Almsgiving
- Gregory and his silent father
- The Fallen Heosphoros
- Scenes from St. Basil's life
- The Encaenia
- The liturgical scene of Baptism
- The author portrait
- The dedication page
- The teaching scene

[1] Cf. Weitzmann, *Roll*, pp. 193ff.

2. THE LECTIONARY GROUP

- Anastasis in three versions, including the miniature of the raising of the dead in cod. Paris gr. 543, fol. 27ᵛ
- Three Marys reporting to the Apostles
- The candle-bearers
- John the Baptist
- Simon of Cyrene carrying the cross of Christ
- Joseph of Arimathaea requesting the body of Christ from Pilate
- Two Marys at the tomb
- Figure of Christ
- Church and Synagogue
- The Incredulity of Thomas in two variants
- Pentecost
- Nativity in two variants
- Christ's Baptism
- John meeting Christ
- John preaching
- John baptizing

3. THE MENOLOGION GROUP

- St. Mamas scenes
- St. Justina's and St. Cyprian's scenes
- Scenes of the Maccabees
- A scene of Gregory's own life
- Figures of Church Fathers

4. THE OLD TESTAMENT GROUP

- Creation scenes
- Abraham
- Enos
- Enoch's metastasis
- Noah and his ark
- Moses, Aaron, Joshua
- Moses and the brazen serpent; seven lamps
- Samuel, David, Solomon
- Elijah, Three Holy Children, Joel
- Vision of Habakkuk

5. THE FOUR GOSPELS

- Isaiah and Christ

178

6. ACTS AND EPISTLES

– Stoning of Stephen
– Paul

7. HISTORICAL BOOK

– Scenes from Sozomenos, *Historia ecclesiastica*

8. MYTHOLOGICAL BOOK

9. BUCOLIC BOOK

10. CALENDAR BOOK

11. APOCRYPHAL ACTS OF PETER AND PAUL

12. A TREATISE ON HUNTING

13. ANIMAL TREATISE (?)

14. A THEOTOKARION (?)

Clearly, the miniatures of thirteen other groups have been intermingled with the miniatures invented for the text of Gregory, making the illustrated homilies of Gregory an outstanding example of a polycyclic manuscript. Since these groups ultimately derive from archetypes of different dates and localities, a discussion considering the relationship of the manuscripts, their possible origin in one archetype, and the date of that archetype has to be based on the invented miniatures that form the basic cycle.

The first question that must be answered is whether or not all the manuscripts stem from the same archetype and, if so, what the value of each manuscript in relation to this archetype is. An examination of the results of the investigation of the invented miniatures—whether title or supplementary—thus becomes necessary.

Of the title miniatures constituting the illustrations of the homily on New Sunday, only the *Encaenia* scene seems to have been invented for the text of Gregory. The miniature has been chosen by the illustrators of the codd. Paris gr. 543, Sinai 339, Moscow, Hist. Museum 146, and Turin, Univ. Lib. C. I. 6 (Figs. 457, 380, 4, 28). Since all four miniatures are iconographically the same, their derivation directly or indirectly from an archetypal miniature cannot be doubted. This assertion may well mean that the four manuscripts containing these miniatures depend directly or indirectly on the archetype which contained the Encaenia scene. Moreover, the fullest version of this miniature has been preserved in the latest of the manuscripts—the cod. Paris gr. 543; therefore, the Paris miniature is not a copy of the earlier ones.

The illustrations chosen for the homily on St. Cyprian are *St. Cyprian bowing to St. Gregory* (codd. Oxford, Canon. gr. 103; Sinai 346; Paris gr. 533; Milan, Ambros. G. 88 sup.; Figs. 279, 353, 243, 306), *A Discussion Group* (codd. Florence, Laur.

179

Plut. VII, 32; Oxford, Selden. B. 54; Figs. 265, 289), and *The Koimesis of St. Cyprian* (cod. Turin, Univ. Lib. C. I. 6; Fig. 44).

Whether these iconographically different scenes are related to one another, inasmuch as they may have stemmed from a common archetype, and which of the manuscripts now containing these scenes best reflects the archetypal miniatures, are questions that cannot be answered at this point, especially since the first two scenes are banal iconographic types and may be later substitutes for a more interesting composition, while the third illustration is inaccurate and inappropriate for a panegyric.

In the discussion of the illustrations of the homily to Julian the Tax Collector, four different scenes were distinguished: *Gregory and Julian the writers* (codd. Sinai 339; Jerusalem, Taphou 14; Florence, Laur. Plut. VII, 32; Oxford, Canon. gr. 103; Figs. 383, 112, 266, 280), *Julian Collecting the Taxes* (codd. Sinai 339; Paris gr. 543; Moscow, Hist. Museum 146; Turin, Univ. Lib. C. I. 6; Figs. 383, 460, 9, 46), *Julian Giving the Tax Orders* (codd. Paris gr. 550; Athos, Dionysiou 61; Figs. 413, 361), and *Gregory and the Martyrs* (codd. Paris gr. 543; Oxford, Roe 6; Figs. 460, 443). In addition to these distinct scenes, various conflations are apparent in the miniatures of the codd. Athos, Panteleimon 6; Paris gr. 533; Vat. gr. 1947; Oxford, Selden. B. 54; Paris, Coislin 239; Sinai 346; Athos, Dionysiou 61; Istanbul, Patr. 16; and Milan, Ambros. G. 88 sup.

Not only are the miniatures showing a particular scene related to each other and derived from an archetypal miniature, but different scenes are related to one another. All the manuscripts, therefore, go back to a common archetype. The chief evidence on which these conclusions are based is provided by the manuscripts which have used more than one scene, i.e. the codd. Sinai 339 and Paris gr. 543, and by the manuscripts which have conflated scenes.

The evidence of the illustrations of the homily to Julian the Tax Collector confirms the conclusions drawn in the discussion of the illustrations of the homily on New Sunday, and it relates the different scenes evidenced in the homily on St. Cyprian which could not be adequately related to each other on the basis of the evidence of that homily alone. In the homily on St. Cyprian, the codd. Oxford, Canon. gr. 103, Florence, Laur. Plut. VII, 32, and Jerusalem, Taphou 14 have each shown a different scene, but in the homily to Julian the Tax Collector, they have chosen the same scenes. Obviously, then, the conclusion suggested earlier, that all these manuscripts derived from a common archetype, is now firmly established.

Another question which must be answered concerns the number of illustrations in the homily to Julian. Did all four scenes exist in the archetype? Doubt must be raised about the scene of Gregory and the Martyrs because it appears only in the codd. Paris gr. 543, and Oxford, Roe 6, although this fact does not necessarily support the exclusion of the miniature from the archetype.

The pictorial evidence favors the existence in the archetype of the third scene, Julian Giving the Tax Orders. In addition to the codd. Paris gr. 550 and Athos,

Dionysiou 61 (the miniature of the latter has shown deviations already discussed) which have preserved this scene, the cod. Athos, Panteleimon 6 also suggests its existence. In fact, this picture is one of three that are found conflated in the miniature of the Panteleimon manuscript. Since these distinct scenes do not appear together in any other manuscript, the Panteleimon miniature cannot have depended on any of the extant related manuscripts. Moreover, the hypothesis that the illustrator has made use of three different models seems highly unlikely. Therefore, the assumption that the miniature of the Panteleimon manuscript has been derived from a fuller model is more plausible. If this fuller model were the archetype, or a direct copy of it, then the occurrence of the fourth scene in the archetype could be maintained.

Certainly there can be no doubt that the first and second scenes (Julian and Gregory the Writers and Julian Collecting the Taxes) existed in the archetype, whose miniatures in this case are best reflected in the miniatures of the codd. Sinai 339, Jerusalem, Taphou 14, Moscow, Hist. Museum 146, and Paris gr. 543.

A liturgical illustration of the homily on Baptism depicting the rite of the Sacrament of the Holy Baptism has been preserved in the codd. Milan, Ambros. G 88 sup., and Paris gr. 550 (Figs. 311, 408). Since both codices have thus far been related to the main body of manuscripts—the former especially has shown a constant relationship to the Jerusalem manuscript—and since no direct dependence on each other can be supported, it is reasonable to assume that their liturgical miniature was in the archetype.

The investigation of the illustrations of the homily to Gregory of Nyssa has revealed the existence of the following distinct scenes: *The two Bishops Conversing* (cod. Athos, Dionysiou 61; Fig. 366); *A Proskynesis scene* (codd. Jerusalem, Taphou 14; Vat. gr. 1947; Oxford, Selden. B. 54; Florence, Laur. Plut. VII, 32; Athos, Panteleimon 6; Paris, Coislin 239; Athos, Vatopedi 107; Athos, Dionysiou 61; Milan, Ambros. G. 88 sup.; Sinai 346; Istanbul, Patr. 16; Figs. 117, 133, 294, 271, 174, 229, 331, 367, 312, 350, 73); and *An Ecstatic Meeting* (cod. Paris gr. 550; Fig. 416, 421).

The first scene has already been encountered in another homily and may be considered a particular choice or addition made by the illustrator of the Dionysiou codex, which also contains a Proskynesis scene and is therefore related to the manuscripts that have depicted it. In addition to these, however, another episode, *The Sending of a Letter*, was observed among the conflated scenes (cod. Moscow, Hist. Museum 146; Fig. 14). In discussing its conflated state, the suggestion was made that it must originally have been a modification of, or a substitute for, a Proskynesis scene, either because such a type existed in the illustrations of other homilies and could therefore be applied to this one as well, or because one of the artists invented a new one. While the manuscripts which have chosen the first two scenes are related to each other, the cod. Paris gr. 550, which contains the third, cannot be related to them in this case. The evidence which might have been supplied by the codd. Sinai 339 and Paris gr. 543 is lacking because the illustrations of this homily have been cut out. Since in

181

previous homilies the cod. Paris gr. 550 has been related to the other manuscripts, an analogous relationship must be considered in this case as well, and it must be assumed that the episode of the Ecstatic Meeting either has been in the archetype, or is a later insertion by the artist of the Paris manuscript or of its model. Obviously, the only scene which undoubtedly existed in the archetype is the Proskynesis scene.

The study of the invented miniatures of the Farewell sermon has shown that all the manuscripts with title miniatures have depicted a *Council scene* (Figs. 119, 272, 296, 176, 231, 445, 135). This is all the more significant because the same scene appears even in manuscripts which have adapted the system of historiated initials, a fact that leaves no doubt concerning the derivation of all the manuscripts from a common archetype. However, the Council scene appearing in the cod. Paris gr. 550 is based on a different iconographic model (Fig. 425). It is unlikely that this version was the one depicted in the archetype. The cod. Jerusalem, Taphou 14, has introduced, in addition to the Council scene, a narrative one already used in the full edition of the homilies, representing the *Farewell* which is also adapted to the initial of the cod. Vat. gr. 463 (Figs. 120, 86). The fact that this scene was in the pictorial tradition of Gregory's homilies before the liturgical edition was made does not necessarily prove its existence in the archetype of the new edition. Since the Vatican codex does not depend directly on the Jerusalem manuscript, this scene must have been included among the illustrations of a model that both manuscripts had in common. It cannot be shown, however, whether this model was the archetype itself or simply a manuscript whose illustrator added the scene.

For the homily on the Love of the Poor, the following illustrations have been used: *Gregory and the Poor* (codd. Athos, Dionysiou 61; Sinai 339; and Paris gr. 543; Figs. 370, 391, 468) and *The Almsgiving*, by Gregory (cod. Paris gr. 550), by a monk (cod. Paris gr. 550), and by a layman (codd. Paris gr. 550; Moscow Hist. Museum 146; Figs. 426, 17). The Almsgiving scene occurs also in the cod. Athos, Vatopedi 107, but its miniature differs considerably (Fig. 337). The remaining manuscripts with illustrations for this homily, i.e. the codd. Jerusalem, Taphou 14; Milan, Ambros. G 88 sup.; Athos, Panteleimon 6; and Oxford, Selden. B. 54, contain conflated scenes, while the initial A's of the codd. Athos, Dionysiou 61; Sinai 339; Istanbul, Patr. 16; and Sinai 346, may be either compositional adaptations of the first scene, or reductions of the second. In addition to the general relationship of these manuscripts to each other, evidenced by this case as well—with the exception of the cod. Athos, Vatopedi 107 which differs in this respect—it should be noted that the Moscow manuscript, thus far closely related to the cod. Sinai 339, has in this case preserved a scene appearing also in the cod. Paris gr. 550. This scene, showing almsgiving by a layman, probably existed in the archetype which also contained the scene of almsgiving by Gregory. The existence of the latter scene in the archetype can be supported by considering the opinion, prevalent in the Middle Ages and already discussed, pertaining to the physical setting of the oration. There is no reason, however, to assume that almsgiving by a monk necessarily appeared in the archetype. It may have been added by the illustrator of the Paris manuscript. In addition to these, the archetype probably contained the first scene showing Gregory and the Poor as reflected in the codd. Athos, Dionysiou 61; Sinai 339; and Paris gr. 543. The first two miniatures seem to be the best, the most complete, and, most important, the closest to the Gospel models.

Two invented miniatures appear as illustrations of Gregory's homily to His Silent Father: *Gregory and His Father* (codd. Paris gr. 550; Jerusalem, Taphou 14; Paris gr. 543; Vat. gr. 1947; Athos, Dionysiou 61; Paris, Coislin 239; Oxford, Selden. B. 54; Athos, Panteleimon 6; Oxford, Canon. gr. 103; Sinai 346; Figs. 427, 122, 469, 125, 374, 233, 298, 180, 286, 354); and *The Sending of a Letter* (cod. Moscow, Hist. Museum 146; Fig. 18). Of the manuscripts which have included the first scene, only the miniature of the cod. Paris gr. 550 represents Gregory of Nazianzus paying respect to his father, an iconographic detail which differs from the interpretations of the text by the other miniaturists. The difference is probably a peculiarity of the artist of the Paris manuscript. The same is true for the second scene used by the illustrator of the Moscow manuscript for the formation of another illustration in another homily, and therefore its existence in the archetype cannot be maintained. The archetype must have contained only the first scene, and that as reflected in the miniature of the Jerusalem manuscript.

A discussion of the study of the illustrations for the two funeral orations, i.e. the homilies on St. Basil and St. Athanasius, is now in order. They have been left until the end because the nature of the subject permits the use of illustrations of similar iconography in both cases, a fact mentioned in the discussion of the illustrations of these homilies. The illustration chosen for the homily on St. Basil is a *Koimesis* scene, depicted in two variants. One variant includes among the mourners, in addition to Gregory of Nazianzus, Gregory of Nyssa (codd. Paris gr. 543; Florence, Laur. Plut. VII, 32; Jerusalem, Taphou 14; Vat. gr. 1947; Oxford, Canon. gr. 103; Milan, Ambros. G 88 sup.; a reduced form of this variant appears in the codd. Oxford, Roe 6; Athos, Panteleimon 6; Oxford, Selden. B. 54; Paris, Coislin 239; Figs. 461, 268, 114, 130, 282, 309, 441, 149, 291, 221). In the other variant, the principal mourner is Gregory of Nazianzus (codd. Athos, Dionysiou 61; Sinai 339; Sinai 346; Paris gr. 550; Moscow, Hist. Museum 146; and Athos, Vatopedi 107; Figs. 363, 388, 349, 415, 11, 328). Only the cod. Istanbul, Patr. 16 seems to have conflated the two variants (Fig. 70). Here again the choice of variants confirms the relationship of the manuscripts to each other and points to their derivation from the same archetype, which, as is shown shortly, had only one of the two variants of the Koimesis scene.

At this juncture it should be pointed out that, in addition to the Koimesis scenes, the codd. Athos, Panteleimon 6 and Paris, Coislin 239, have supplementary miniatures illustrating episodes from the life of St. Basil. Although a tradition for such narrative miniatures existed earlier, as the complete edition of the homilies in the cod. Paris gr. 510 shows, there is no reason to suppose that this tradition was followed by the creator of the archetype of the new edition, and therefore that these miniatures existed in this archetype. If the tradition of the full edition had been followed, the use of iconographically similar miniatures would have been expected. Yet the miniatures of the liturgical edition are different. Moreover, it must be admitted that the liturgical spirit of this new edition makes unlikely the existence of these narrative miniatures in the archetype.

In the discussion of the illustrations of the sermon on St. Athanasius, attention was drawn to the fact that some of the scribes had interpreted it as a funeral oration and others as a panegyric, and that the different interpretations resulted in the application of different illustrations. A *Koimesis* scene was used by the following codices: Paris gr. 550; Paris gr. 543; Moscow, Hist. Mus. 146; Vat. gr. 1947; Athos, Panteleimon 6; Paris, Coislin 239; Athos, Vatopedi 107 (Figs. 424, 466, 15, 134, 175, 230, 335). In fact, this Koimesis scene is an adaptation of the one used by the illustrators of these manuscripts for the funeral oration on St. Basil.

A *portrait of St. Athanasius* combined with that of Gregory or appearing by itself, and repeating iconographic schemes used in other homilies—especially in the homily on St. Cyprian—has been used by the illustrators of the manuscripts in which the sermon has been interpreted as a panegyric. These are the following: Jerusalem, Taphou 14; Istanbul, Patr. 16; Florence, Laur. Plut. VII, 32; Oxford, Canon. gr. 103; Paris gr. 533; Oxford, Roe 6; Milan, Ambros. G 88 sup.; Vat. gr. 463 (Figs. 118, 74, 263, 285, 251, 446, 313, 85).

In trying to define the scenes or, more particularly, the variants used in the archetype, as illustrations of the two funeral sermons, the illustrations of the homily on St. Cyprian should be considered as well, for, in addition to the miniatures of a panegyric character, a funeral scene not justified by the nature of the sermon was found.

A funeral scene must certainly be expected as an illustration of the homily on St. Basil, since this is unmistakably a funeral sermon. Concerning this scene, the following historical fact should be taken into consideration; St. Basil's funeral was attended by his brother, Gregory of Nyssa, and not by Gregory of Nazianzus, who delivered the funeral sermon for his departed friend two years after Basil's death. This fact was known to the illustrators of the sermon who apparently depicted the events in two distinct scenes: one scene showed the actual funeral with the figure of Gregory of Nyssa as an eminent mourner, and another scene portrayed Gregory of Nazianzus delivering the sermon to a congregation, over a sarcophagus; thus the historical fact concerning the delivery of the sermon over Basil's tomb was clearly suggested. In fact, this concept has been preserved in the cod. Paris gr. 543 and provides an explanation for the two variants now extant (Fig. 461). Probably an early conflation of the two scenes resulted in the transference of Gregory of Nazianzus from the sermon scene into the actual funeral scene—actually the most important one—which included Gregory of Nyssa as well. Therefore, one of the variants was formed, which naturally, from the point of view of composition, was based on iconographic models already discussed in the first part of this study. The second variant in which Gregory of Nyssa does not appear probably constitutes a further change made under the influence of the illustrations of the homily on St. Athanasius, where only Gregory of Nazianzus appeared with St. Athanasius.

Concerning the homily on St. Athanasius, since it is not known how the scribe of the archetype had interpreted the sermon and how he phrased the title, the miniature of the archetype cannot be specified. If it was a panegyric, as seems more logical, it may be assumed that the artist adapted an illustration already used for another panegyric sermon, that on St. Cyprian. If it was a funeral, the artist of the archetype adapted the miniatures which he had already used earlier for another funeral sermon, that on St. Basil. The adaptation consisted only in the omission of Gregory of Nyssa from St. Basil's funeral scene, while the scene showing Gregory of Nazianzus delivering the sermon was kept unaltered (cf. Fig. 461). In the course of subsequent condensations, either only one of the two scenes was retained, or the two scenes were conflated. In the former case the miniature did not undergo any changes and therefore it did not contain the figure of Gregory of Nazianzus; the miniature of the cod. Paris gr. 550 illustrates this arrangement (Fig. 424). In the latter case the figure of Gregory of Nazianzus was moved from the scene depicting the delivering of the sermon into that showing the actual funeral, and thus another "anachronistic" picture was created like the one of the cod. Athos, Panteleimon 6 (Fig. 175).

Finally, in order to complete the discussion of the invented miniatures, the supplementary miniature depicting the Fallen Heosphoros in the Jerusalem manuscript must be mentioned (Fig. 101). Since it does not appear in any other codex, there is no reason to suggest its existence in the archetype. In all probability, like the migrated, supplementary miniatures that occur in the Jerusalem manuscript which are discussed below, the Heosphoros miniature is a later addition.

The foregoing discussion has established the common recension of the manuscripts, and the proposal of the scenes of the archetype has prepared the way for a separate evaluation of each manuscript and a determination of its actual position in a stemma. It has become clear that the archetype contained more than one scene for each homily, a feature for which there was apparently an older tradition, as the cod. Paris gr. 510 proves. Not all the scenes of each homily, however, were copied in the new offshoots of the archetype; instead, choices of different scenes were made. Moreover, some scenes, such as the Koimesis of St. Cyprian, Gregory bowing to Cyprian, the Sending of a Letter, Gregory mourning for St. Athanasius, the priest giving alms, Christ blessing the almsgiving, Gregory paying respect to his father, and the concept of Julian as a ruler, are in all probability later additions or deviations.

The largest number of scenes was chosen by the illustrator of the cod. Sinai 339, the great importance of which is therefore obvious. Not only does this codex contribute to the clarification of the interrelationship of the manuscripts, but it furnishes the greatest number of scenes, all iconographically accurate, for the reconstruction of the archetype.

A similar choice of scenes was followed by the illustrators of the codd. Moscow, Hist. Museum 146, and Paris gr. 543. Both are of great importance, for they do not depend on each other or on the Sinai manuscript. The Moscow codex, which is the earliest of the three, includes scenes that appear in both the other manuscripts, scenes found only in the Paris manuscript, and scenes found in other manuscripts, like the Almsgiving, which appears in the cod. Paris gr. 550, and the Sending of a Letter found in the cod. Paris gr. 533. The same observations apply to the cod. Paris gr. 543, which, in some instances, has preserved miniatures iconographically better than the miniatures of the other two manuscripts, such as, for example, the illustration for the homily on St. Basil which probably has best preserved the tradition of the archetype. This means that all three manuscripts depend on the same model, which may well be the archetype itself. Of special interest is the relationship between the codd. Moscow and Paris, i.e. between the earliest and the latest of the three manuscripts. This relationship, which in certain instances applies to the format as well, proves that a late copy can be as close to the archetype as an early one.

The cod. Turin, Univ. Lib. C. I. 6, has three invented title miniatures: Encaenia, Julian Collecting the Taxes, and the Koimesis of St. Cyprian (Figs. 28, 46, 44). The first two scenes are similar to those contained in the Moscow and Sinai manuscripts and, since the presence of the third scene has been adequately explained, the derivation of the Turin codex from the earlier Moscow manuscript can be suggested.

In the eight invented miniatures of the cod. Paris gr. 550, deviations from the miniatures of the manuscripts mentioned so far, or additions of elements not existing in the archetype, have been observed. There is, for instance, an iconographic novelty in the presentation of Gregory bowing to his father in the miniature of the homily addressed to Gregory the Elder, and a probable addition may be the composition of the lower part of the miniature illustrating the homily on the Love of the Poor (Fig. 426). Yet as long as deviations and additions are sufficiently explained, there is no need to propose an intermediary model for this codex, which may well stem directly from the archetype from which the manuscripts mentioned thus far are derived.

Closely related to these manuscripts, and more particularly to the codex Paris gr. 550, is the cod. Athos, Dionysiou 61, which cannot be derived from any of them for the following reasons: Its illustrator knew the Proskynesis scene which he applied to the homily addressed to Gregory of Nyssa, assuming, of course, that the scene in this case was not accidentally formed by the shape of the initial Φ which it decorated. Moreover the conflated illustration of the homily on St. Cyprian can be explained neither through the cod. Paris gr. 550, nor through the cod. Sinai 339, but presupposes a fuller model. Lastly, the miniature of the homily addressed to Gregory the Elder is closely related to the miniatures of the codd. Paris gr. 543, and Paris, Coislin 239. All these observations indicate that the cod. Athos, Dionysiou 61 must also depend

186

on the archetype and that none of the extant manuscripts can serve as an intermediary model.

If it were possible to prove that the Dionysiou manuscript was of an earlier date, the likelihood of its having served as model for the eleventh-century codex Sinai 346 could have been suggested. But since an earlier manuscript obviously cannot depend on a later one, the six invented and extremely minute miniatures of the Sinai codex, all but one illustrating initials and therefore either condensed or conflated, must have been derived from another model similar to the Dionysiou manuscript, perhaps the archetype itself.

The remaining manuscripts, however, do not seem to have been derived directly from the archetype, but from one of its offshoots, no longer extant. These manuscripts are Jerusalem, Taphou 14; Florence, Laur. Plut. VII, 32; Oxford, Canon. gr. 103; Milan, Ambros. G 88 sup.; Oxford, Selden. B. 54; Vat. gr. 1947; Athos, Panteleimon 6; Paris, Coislin 239; Oxford, Roe 6; Istanbul, Patr. 16; and Vat. gr. 463.

All these manuscripts contain the same selection of miniatures. Therefore, they must have been derived from a model that had made this choice from the archetype. The selection in itself, then, is sufficient evidence for establishing this branch, indicated in the stemma by the letter Y. Furthermore, it must be pointed out that all the manuscripts of branch Y have used the same conflated scene, the Koimesis of St. Basil, derived from a more complete illustration, as was shown in the discussion of the illustrations of the homily on St. Basil. This is significant evidence since it seems unlikely that each of the artists produced the same conflation by independently consulting the complete version of the illustration that presumably existed in the archetype. The conflation must have been initiated by one manuscript and then copied by others. Therefore, the postulation of a model on which these manuscripts depend is essential.

The main characteristic of this branch is that it contains fewer miniatures from the archetype than the number chosen by the manuscripts that depend directly on the archetype. Excluding scenes that are deviations or additions in particular manuscripts, there is only one scene, the traces of which cannot be found in those directly related to the archetype: Gregory Bidding Farewell. The question arising from this evidence is whether branch Y is not, in fact, an offshoot of one of the directly related manuscripts. This does not seem to be the case, however, because some of the conflated miniatures of branch Y cannot be explained by the miniatures of any one of those stemming directly from the archetype. Also, in certain instances, such as the scenes depicting the two Gregorys in Proskynesis, or Gregory and his Silent Father, the manuscripts of branch Y have preserved more closely the tradition of the archetype, on which, therefore, their lost model must have directly depended. It cannot be ascertained, however, whether this model added the Farewell scene or took it from the archetype.

The cod. Jerusalem, Taphou 14 contains an extensive cycle of invented miniatures which are similar to the miniatures of the cod. Florence, Laur. Plut. VII, 32. The latter parallels the former in iconographic accuracy, and, in some instances, reflects better the tradition of the archetype. For example, the miniature of Basil's Koimesis, although derived from two distinct miniatures, has preserved the angels carrying Basil's soul, an element required by the text of the homily (Fig. 268). This element may well be a later improvement of the original miniature and does not necessarily mean that the manuscript of Florence is derived from a more fully illustrated model, which may have also served as model for the Jerusalem manuscript. Yet there is one more miniature, the Council scene, which also presents a better version of the subject than the relevant miniature of the Jerusalem manuscript. It seems, then, that the suggestion of a common source for these two manuscripts is more plausible than that of the derivation of one from the other.

Two more manuscripts, the codd. Oxford, Canon. gr. 103, and Milan, Ambros. G 88 sup., contain miniatures very similar to those appearing in the Jerusalem manuscript. Whereas the first of the two manuscripts contains no miniature which cannot be sufficiently explained by the miniatures of the Jerusalem manuscript, the second codex contains one such miniature, a Baptismal scene. It was shown earlier that this Baptismal scene must have existed in the archetype and therefore the direct dependence of the Milan codex on the Jerusalem manuscript cannot be suggested; probably both these manuscripts have a common source.

The cod. Oxford, Selden. B. 54 is closely related to the Jerusalem and Florence manuscripts. Its miniatures are smaller but iconographically accurate, and present important iconographic details, such as the veiled hands of the two Gregorys in the Proskynesis Scene (Fig. 294). Although it cannot be ascertained whether the Oxford artist added the element or retained it from the archetype, it must be pointed out that he was aware of its liturgical significance. Despite the close similarities of this Oxford manuscript to the Jerusalem and Florence manuscripts, its direct dependence on either of them seems rather unlikely. The scene depicting Gregory the Elder Keeping Silence presupposes a fuller model than the codex in Florence. The frequent use of the writing table with the seated Gregory may, however, reflect a mode of illustration in which the author portrait appeared in every homily; such a mode of illustration is not used in the Jerusalem manuscript. For these reasons the dependence of the Oxford manuscript on the model of the two manuscripts seems plausible.

By the same token, although it contains miniatures similar to those of the Jerusalem manuscript, the cod. Vat. gr. 1947 does not depend on it but on its model. The combined iconographic traditions of the miniatures in the homilies on Cyprian and to Julian the Tax Collector, and in the Farewell sermon establish this relationship.

The miniatures of the codd. Athos, Panteleimon 6, and Paris, Coislin 239, are very similar to each other and Millet has suggested that from the point of view of style they might have been products of the same hand. The stylistic similarities can be explained by the style of a common model which the artists did not personalize. Although most of these miniatures are conflated, they contain elements indicating that the two manuscripts depend neither on each other nor on the Jerusalem codex, but that they are derived from a more fully illustrated model. A case in point is the miniature of the Panteleimon cod. fol. 77ʳ (Fig. 147), illustrating the homily to Julian the Tax Collector, in which three distinct scenes that do not appear together in any single manuscript have been conflated. Since it seems unlikely that the painter has used three separate models for the composition of the conflated scene, it is most probable that he found these scenes in one model, which must also have been the model for the Jerusalem manuscript.

Two other manuscripts decorated with historiated initials can be assigned to this branch: the codd. Istanbul, Patr. 16, and Vat. gr. 463. The initials of the Patriarchal manuscript, among which there are only three invented for the text of the homilies, could have been derived from the miniatures of the cod. Athos, Panteleimon 6, had the latter been of an earlier date. It is only for reasons of date that the Patriarchal manuscript must be assigned to an earlier model, probably the cod. Y itself. Among the initials of the Vatican manuscript, only one is invented and that in a conflated form (combination of Teaching and Farewell scenes) which does not make possible an accurate assignment of this manuscript. If the initials of this manuscript and its date (1062) are considered, its dependence on the Patriarchal codex can be suggested. The initials of the Vatican manuscript could, in fact, be explained by those of the Patriarchal codex, while its date excludes the possibility of its derivation from other manuscripts of this branch produced after 1062.

Finally, the cod. Oxford, Roe 6 can also be assigned to this branch since two of its three invented miniatures, the Council scene and the Koimesis of St. Basil, find their closest parallels here. Its third invented miniature, however, that of Gregory and the Martyrs in the homily to Julian the Tax Collector, relates this manuscript to the cod. Paris gr. 543 whose direct dependence on the archetype has been suggested. The possibility that the Oxford miniaturist was familiar with two models cannot be ignored. Yet the suggestion that this miniature existed in branch Y and that, among the manuscripts of this branch, only the Oxford codex copied it, seems more plausible. The real value of this manuscript lies in the Teaching scene and in the number of examples of format adaptation which this codex provides.

It is difficult to find a place in the stemma for the codex Athos, Vatopedi 107, the only manuscript with a cycle of illustrations which has not been discussed so far. Of its four invented miniatures, which are banal iconographic types, only the Proskynesis scene suggests that the miniaturist was acquainted with the iconographic tradition of the illustrated homilies. But any attempt to define further the relationship between the iconographic tradition of the homilies and the Vatopedi manuscript would only be arbitrary. The interest of the illustrator of this codex, or of its model, in depicting cities mentioned in the homilies must be pointed out as a special feature of the manuscript.

This relationship among the main manuscripts has been based on the study of the invented miniatures. The question that can now be raised is whether or not the arguments for such a relationship can be strengthened by the results of the study of the migrated miniatures.

Regarding the codd. Moscow, Hist. Museum 146, Sinai 339, Paris gr. 543, and Turin, Univ. Lib. C. I. 6, the migrated miniatures confirm the relationship established by the invented miniatures. These four manuscripts have the following miniatures of the migrated cycle in common: the Anastasis (missing in the Turin manuscript); the Incredulity of Thomas (of which a separate type was used in the Paris codex, a departure which was probably made within the same iconographic tradition however); and scenes of Cyprian's life (the great number of scenes in the Paris manuscript is probably an indication of a larger cycle existing in the model of these manuscripts) (Figs. 1, 378, 454, 3, 380, 457, 29, 8, 397, 459, 43). In addition to these, the Sinai and the Paris manuscripts have in common a migrated miniature showing women worshiping the Panagia Blachernitissa, while the Sinai and the Moscow manuscripts have in common the migrated miniatures of the Vision of Habakkuk, the Pentecost, and the Milking scene from the life of St. Mamas (Figs. 385, 463, 379, 382, 381, 2, 6, 5). The cod. Paris gr. 550 (derived from the archetype as well) has the following migrated miniatures in common with the cod. Sinai 339: the portraits of the Maccabees and of Cyprian and Justina, and the Nativity scene (Figs. 411, 412, 414, 392, 395, 396, 384).

Another miniature of interest in the cod. Paris gr. 550 is the one showing the Church and Synagogue (Fig. 407). A similar miniature exists in the codd. Brit. Museum, Add. 24381 (which has a further miniature, the figures of the Maccabees, in common with the cod. Paris gr. 550); Athos, Panteleimon 6; Paris, Coislin 239; and Athos, Dionysiou 61 (Figs. 94, 139, 195, 358). In all probability, therefore, the representation of the Church and Synagogue existed in the common archetype from which ultimately all the manuscripts are derived. The codd. Florence, Laur. Plut. VII, 32; Jerusalem, Taphou 14 and Vat. gr. 1947 are related with regard to their migrated miniatures as well. The first two have a similar Nativity scene, while all three have similar conflated scenes of the Maccabees, although the Jerusalem codex contains more conflated scenes of the Maccabees' martyrdom than the other two (Figs. 267, 113, 264, 110, 126). Finally, the Jerusalem manuscript and the cod. Vat. gr. 1947 have in common a scene from the life of St. Mamas (Figs. 104, 123).

The remaining manuscripts display greater diversity in their migrated miniatures, and in any attempt to relate them one is on less sure ground.

There is, however, another distinction to be made on the basis of the migrated miniatures. A case in point is the supplementary illustrations, mainly the mythological and the bucolic miniatures. The mythological miniatures, that is, the Pseudo-Nonnos scenes, appear in the codd. Vat. gr. 1947; Jerusalem, Taphou 14; Paris, Coislin 239; and Athos, Panteleimon 6. The last three manuscripts and the cod. Paris gr. 533 contain also bucolic miniatures which belong to the same iconographic tradition. Since there is no manuscript so complete that it includes the scenes of all others, it is obvious that they all must belong together and be derived from a model that contained those supplementary scenes. This model, however, may very well have been the same cod. Y from which all the manuscripts of this branch were derived; its supplementary miniatures were taken over only by some of its offshoots.

Did the supplementary narrative illustrations exist in the archetype from which the cod. Y might have taken them, or were they added later? It is most probable that these miniatures did not exist in the archetype, but were added shortly thereafter, as may be concluded from the following reasoning. If the illustrator of the archetype had indeed added narrative miniatures to those homilies which gave scope to additional detailed, narrative illustration, one would have expected to find traces of them in manuscripts of excellent iconographic tradition, such as the cod. Sinai 339, which selected such a large number of miniatures in order to make use of its margins. Moreover, it has been proved that the mythological miniatures had existed independently outside the tradition of the illustrations of the homilies of Gregory. There is also proof that a similar later addition occurred in the marginal psalters.[2] For instance, the Theodore Psalter in London, Brit. Mus. Add. 19352, dated 1066, contains a larger number of miniatures than the ninth-century psalters of the same family.

What was the date of that assumed archetype from which the manuscripts sprang? Comparisons made throughout this study have indicated—where they are applicable— that no essential iconographic relationship exists between the liturgical edition and the earlier full editions of the homilies, save the Teaching Scene. This conclusion applies particularly to the archetype of the new edition, for there is no proof that among its invented miniatures it contained the narrative scene, Gregory's Farewell, for which there was a pictorial tradition in the cod. Paris gr. 510. Even if that scene existed in the archetype, the fact remains that a new set of miniatures not deriving from the earlier editions was especially made for the new one. Moreover, all other miniatures which migrated into the archetype from various sources show that the artist who first undertook to illustrate the selected homilies did not follow his earlier colleagues in his choice of illustrations.

However, the fundamental and most important difference between the two editions lies in the character of the illustrations and the spirit that prompted their choice. The two best representatives of the full edition, the codd. Milan Ambros. E. 49-50 inf. and Paris gr. 510 differ from each other and from the abridged edition. The illustrator of the Milan manuscript applied what in general may be termed a banal type of illustration. But the cod. Paris gr. 510 is unique in more than one way. Der Nersessian has shown that its illustrations have a theological and imperial character, are sym-

[2] J. J. Tikkanen, *Die Psalter-Illustration im Mittelalter*, Helsingfors 1895, pp. 12ff.; L. Marriès, "L'irruption des saints dans l'illustration du psautier byzantin," *Analecta Bollandiana*, 68 (Mélanges P. Peeters, II), (1950), pp. 153-62. For another view, see L. H. Grondijs, "La datation des psautiers byzantins," *Byzantion*, 25-27, (Mélanges E. Dyggve), (1955-1957), pp. 591-616.

bolical, and interpretive of Gregory's thoughts.[3] The illustrations of the liturgical edition lack on the whole a speculative spirit and do not stress an interpretive one. If its illustrator had followed such a trend he would have betrayed the purpose of the new edition. The task set to him was not to pursue the arguments and speculate on particular thoughts of Gregory but to present pictorially the essence of the sermon within the frame of the liturgy and the Church feasts with which these homilies had come to be associated. Therefore he chose to emphasize the principal subject of each homily, thus serving the spirit of the new book, and to illustrate the subject in a way that revealed the character of the new edition. In the choice and manner of illustration emphasis was placed upon the liturgical aspect of the homilies.

Naturally when copies of the archetype began to be made and more manuscripts produced, the personality of each illustrator left its impact on the illustrations as well. For example, some artists produced variations of the same theme by choosing different iconographic types, or by using different models. Of course their choices to a certain extent depended on what was available to them, but on many occasions they were the result of the artist's own preference, and very often suggest a personal interpretive spirit. Others were fascinated by Gregory the storyteller, or Gregory the landscape-poet, and came to add a series of narrative illustrations. Still others in adding new illustrations remained faithful to the liturgical aspect of the book and thus stressed the essential character of the archetype even more.

The prevalence of the liturgical spirit in the new edition points to a later date than that of the cod. Paris gr. 510, but the earliest extant manuscript of the liturgical edition cannot be dated earlier than the first half of the eleventh century. A tenth-century date seems the most likely. The relationship of the various copies to their archetype is indicated graphically in the stemma presented in the chart below (text fig. 2). Concerning the physical appearance of this archetype, the discussion of the invented miniatures has shown that there must have been more than one illustration in each homily. Since these illustrations are in most cases title illustrations, it seems very likely that they were all placed on one page preceding the text of each homily. The codd. Paris gr. 543 and Moscow, Hist. Museum 146 give the best idea of the arrangement of the miniatures and indicate that on each page there were superimposed strip miniatures. This arrangement was not an innovation, for it had been utilized in the illustrations of the homilies before the liturgical edition was made, as the cod. Paris gr. 510 shows.

B. STYLE

This section deals with form, movement, composition, background, and other artistic expressions evident in the manuscripts. Since the stylistic characteristics of

---

[3] S. Der Nersessian, "The Illustrations of the Homilies of Gregory of Nazianzus, Paris gr. 510," *Dumbarton Oaks Papers*, 16 (1962), p. 225.

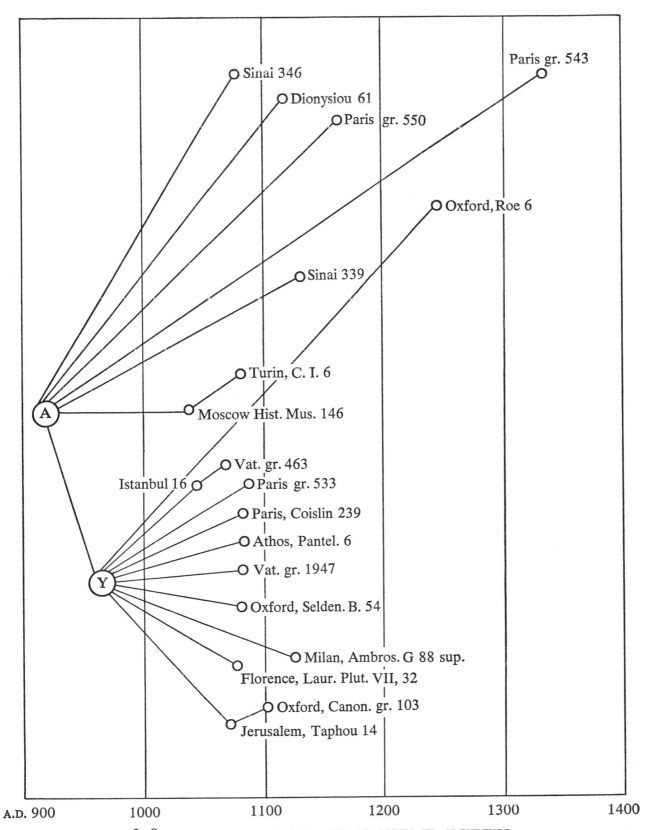

2. STEMMA SHOWING RELATIONSHIP OF COPIES TO ARCHETYPE

each manuscript are described in the Catalogue, the manuscripts as a whole are discussed here within the artistic movements of the chronological periods they represent, i.e. the eleventh-twelfth, thirteenth, and fourteenth-fifteenth centuries.

The style of the figures in the manuscripts of the eleventh and twelfth centuries displays the characteristics of the contemporary Constantinopolitan school: oval face with planes of delicate modeling; large, expressive eyes; narrow nose; small mouth; thin, pointed feet that are not strong enough to bear the weight of the body; delicately attenuated silhouettes. (Only the cod. Oxford, Selden. B. 54 contains figures of somewhat squat proportions.) In some instances and often within the same manuscripts that picture the most predominant Constantinopolitan characteristics of this period, the figures are rounded and show sculpturesque effects achieved by the careful modeling that recalls good models of the Macedonian Renaissance. This observation applies primarily to the earlier manuscripts of this period, such as the cod. Moscow, Hist. Museum 146, or some of the miniatures of the codd. Jerusalem, Taphou 14, and Athos, Panteleimon 6 (Figs. 1, 100, 141). However, other figures, such as some of Gregory's audience in the miniatures of the Jerusalem manuscript, resemble stiffly moving little puppets, recalling similar ones in Oppian's *Cynegetica* (cod. Venice, Marc. gr. 479). Still other figures are treated very austerely, for example, the figures in the cod. Florence, Laur. Plut. VII, 32, or the portrait of Gregory in the cod. Oxford, Canon. gr. 103 (Figs. 272, 275). In such figures modeling has given place to sharp contrasts of shadow and light, a feature more pronounced in the twelfth-century manuscripts, such as the codd. Sinai 339 and Athos, Dionysiou 61 (Figs. 377, 370). Here the forms have become relatively disembodied; the figures are more reserved and ethereal, hovering in space; the stance of the body is more conceptualized than naturalistic. Other Constantinopolitan manuscripts of the period, such as the homilies of James of Kokkinobaphos, or the cod. Vat. Urb. 2, reveal a similar figure style.[4]

In addition to compositions whose figures belong to either the *classicizing* or the *monastic* style, which are also called conventionally the *court* and the *popular*, there are other miniatures with what may be termed the *Byzantinized classicizing* figures. Some of the mythological or bucolic miniatures betraying classical models, but disguised by a current style, may be included in this category.[5]

The flatness and the sharp contrasts of light and shade remain in the thirteenth-century manuscript, while a new emphasis on line appears. The sharp brush strokes on Gregory's forehead and the separate treatment of the hair announce the fourteenth-century figure style, exemplified by the cod. Paris gr. 543. The heads become too elongated; the large, expressive eyes of the earlier periods give way to beadlike eyes, recalling particular Constantinopolitan manuscripts of the period, such as the cod.

[4] Bibl. Nat., *Byzance*, no. 36; Stornajolo, *Giacomo monaco*; Beckwith, *Constantinople*, pp. 121, 122, 127.

[5] For the change of the style of classical figures into the Byzantine idiom, see Beckwith, *Constantinople*, pp. 75ff.

Paris gr. 1242.[6] The linear treatment of the figure reaches its peak in the early fifteenth-century cod. Moscow, State Hist. Museum 155.

The draperies accentuate both the rotundity in some instances, and in others the discmbodiment of the figures combined with a conceptualized rendering of the human body in the manuscripts of the eleventh and twelfth centuries, and the dynamic use of line in the manuscripts of the thirteenth and fourteenth centuries. The draperies often consist of flat areas of color which contribute to a disembodiment of the figures, exemplified by the codd. Oxford, Canon. gr. 103; Moscow, Hist. Museum 146; and Paris gr. 550 (Figs. 280, 2, 427). This dematerialization is intensified at times by narrow, parallel lines of gold, for example, the initials in the cod. Istanbul, Patr. 16, or in the cod. Vat. gr. 463. In these cases, the gold lines and the sharp juxtaposition of color suggest the artist's indebtedness to the craftsmen of the enamel technique. These characteristics also recall illuminations made in the monastery of John of Studios in the second half of the eleventh century, such as the Theodore Psalter (cod. London, Brit. Mus. Add. 19352), or the Paris Gospel cod. gr. 74.[7]

Beside this kind of drapery are found draperies with delicate naturalistic folds (Moscow, Hist. Museum 146, fig. 3), which suggest the volume of the body without pressing against it, thus not emphasizing its full plastic value. Nevertheless, the folds of the garments even in these cases are indicated by sharp, angular lines, as though the fabric were crumpled. In the thirteenth-century manuscript the lines are clear and the drapery simple, falling heavily over the bodies. In the fourteenth-century cod. Paris gr. 543, the drapery is either simple (Fig. 457), or exaggerated and agitated in order to intensify the movement and rhythm of the figures (Fig. 454). Similar agitation appears in the only miniature of the cod. Moscow, Hist. Museum 155 (Fig. 473).

Movement and rhythm are not confined to the fourteenth-century manuscript. They appear in almost all manuscripts, but in varying degree. With the exception of the thirteenth-century manuscript, cod. Oxford, Roe 6, where monotony of stance prevails, the figures of the manuscripts show a wide variety of attitudes. They are depicted in full profile, three-quarter profile, or frontally. Quite often all three manners occur in the same miniature, as for example, on fol. 61^v of the cod. Moscow, Hist. Museum 146 (Fig. 9). Unconventional postures showing the actual turning from one position to another have occasionally been depicted in manuscripts of the earlier period (Figs. 100, 138). The walking posture also has its place and is found in the twelfth- and fourteenth-century manuscripts. Two examples are the codd. Paris gr. 550, and Paris gr. 543 (Figs. 402, 457).

Often the unconventional posture creates dramatic tensions, as seen in Heosphoros falling, his arms paralleling his wings, set against a neutral background next to a rigid

[6] For bibliography and discussions, see Bibl. Nat., *Byzance*, no. 50; Talbot Rice, *Byzantium*, pl. xxxix, 190; Beckwith, *Constantinople*, pp. 147ff.

[7] For bibliography and discussion, see Bibl. Nat., *Byzance*, no. 21; Beckwith, *Constantinople*, p. 114.

vertical figure of Gregory, or the Baptism of the People in the Moscow manuscript, or even the miniatures of the Vision of Habakkuk. The Dionysiou miniature with the Vision of Habakkuk is particularly notable (Fig. 357). It is clearly a true work of art in its own right. The startled movement of Habakkuk opposite a rigid Gregory and against an extraordinary landscape, the sky filled with the heavenly apparition, the marvelous colors, the sense of proportion—all reveal the hand of a real artist. Nor can the elegant and ethereal figure of the Christos-Angelos in white draperies, in the Moscow miniature of the same subject, be forgotten (Fig. 2). Moreover, the miniatures depicting the Vision of Habakkuk are important for another reason: they show that style can be a means of expressing different psychological situations. The agitated figure is Habakkuk, while Gregory who witnesses the event, but does not participate in it, is rigid and flat. This tension has been lost in the fourteenth-century miniature, where the representation has been patternized (Fig. 455).

In contrast with such daring and dynamic figures, others have been deprived of any real movement or luxury of form. Figures such as the portrait of Gregory in the cod. Paris gr. 550, or in Oxford, Canon. gr. 103, placed against undefined backgrounds, removed from "reality," become manifestations of divine reality (Figs. 400, 275). They recall figures of solemn saints depicted in eleventh-century menologia or in illustrated monastic treatises such as the Heavenly Ladder of John Climacus. In such cases the Platonic quality of Byzantine painting is revealed.[8] The artist, by means of style and the use of earthly matter, expresses the incorporeal quality of things. A particular gesture of the hand, a turn of the glance, an exaggeration of the eyebrow, an emphasis on the contours of the face, a chromatic juxtaposition, all can be used effectively to suggest the inward beauty of spirituality and to reveal the form of the divine.

As well as the figures, the compositions, too, can express rhythms suitable to the depicted subject matter. The artist becomes aware of the potentialities of geometric shapes as means of expression. He realizes the ceremonial aspects of balanced, symmetrical compositions, and the dramatic effect of a diagonal line in an otherwise balanced composition. Such an effect is gained by the use of the diagonal hill in the extraordinary miniature of the Turin manuscript, which depicts the scene of the collection of taxes (Fig. 46). The sloping hill pierces the center of the composition like a spear, as if it were meant to disturb the calmness of the tax collector and intensify the tension of the taxpayers whose bodies form repeated curved lines. The artist becomes aware of the dynamic use of the circle and applies it to suitable subjects, such as the scenes of heavenly visions in the codd. Athos, Dionysiou 61, and Paris gr. 543 (Figs. 357, 455).

In most cases, regardless of chronological limits, the compositions have been constructed on one plane. In some instances attempts to create depth have caused individual heads or even scenes to be placed one above the other (Figs. 467, 426).

---

[8] For this problem see G. Mathew, *Byzantine Aesthetics*, London 1963 (here the older bibliography).

There are compositions, however, in which the position of figures or objects in two different planes has been attempted. For example, in the cod. Jerusalem, Taphou 14, fol. 224^v, a feeling of space is created by the placement of the architectural backgrounds in two different planes (Fig. 118). Such devices are common in Byzantine painting.[9]

The backgrounds—neutral, architectural, or landscape—serve to unify the compositions. Neutral backgrounds appear in almost all manuscripts, but they are more common in the eleventh- and twelfth-century manuscripts. In the architectural backgrounds, the buildings are rectangular constructions seen from one side, from one angle, or in full view (Figs. 265, 46, 369). At times the door of the building is depicted with a tympanum (Figs. 263, 459, 395) or with a drapery hanging over it that recalls the draperies found in the Bible of Leo the Wise, the Vatican Menologion, or in Palaeologan manuscripts (Figs. 117, 457). In rare instances, views of interiors or even views of cities are shown (Figs. 44, 8). Whatever the architectural backgrounds, the manuscripts of the eleventh and twelfth centuries have the clarity and simplicity found in other contemporary manuscripts.[10] This clarity and simplicity has been lost in the buildings of the thirteenth- and fourteenth-century manuscripts. The buildings have now become ornamental rather than functional structures, a tendency evident in other Palaeologan manuscripts.[11]

The compositions of almost all the title miniatures are enclosed within ornamental frames. These frames are either very rich or very simple narrow bands ending at the corners in anthemia or palmettes. In some manuscripts the richness of the ornamentation is consistent throughout, while in others it is confined to the first folios. The former case is exemplified by the cod. Athos, Dionysiou 61, the latter by cod. Oxford, Roe 6. In cases where the miniatures are not enclosed in decorative bands or where they historiate initials only (Fig. 81), a large ornamental band heads the title (Fig. 313).

The ornament of these frames was created in the Byzantine capital about the middle of the tenth century and, in the eleventh century, it replaced all other decoration in the manuscripts of the Constantinople school.[12] Although the motifs used in the manuscripts of one or another period are similar, none, in fact, duplicates or even copies any other. The development of the Constantinopolitan ornament can be followed in the manuscripts of Gregory's homilies. It evolves from the clarity of the flower-petal and the geometric motifs of, for example, the codd. Athos, Panteleimon 6, Paris, Coislin 239 and Moscow, Hist. Museum 146, which recall the ornament of other Constantinopolitan manuscripts, to the more complicated floral motifs and imaginary birds of the cod. Oxford, Canon. gr. 103 (Figs. 137, 195, 3, 276). It proceeds from

---

[9] Cf. *ibid.*, pp. 31-34 and passim.

[10] See, for example, the cod. Oxford Auct. T. infra 1. 10, fol. 231^v, reproduced in O. Pächt, *Byzantine Illumination*, Oxford 1952, fig. 8.

[11] See cod. Leningrad, Publ. Lib. gr. 101, fol.

76^v, reproduced in Lazarev, *History*, II, pl. 258, dating from the thirteenth century, and the cod. Vienna, Theol. gr. 300, fol. 88^r, *ibid.*, pl. 313, dating from the fourteenth century.

[12] Weitzmann, *Buchmalerei*.

the simple and delicate bands of the cod. Jerusalem, Taphou 14 to the most intricate geometric designs (Figs. 99, 384), recalling the best Constantinopolitan manuscripts of the time. The academic geometric precision that reaches a point of dryness can be studied in the cod. Paris gr. 550 and its development can be followed in a rather wiry, repetitious, and totally flattened ornament in the cod. Paris gr. 543 (Figs. 426, 469). The flower-petal motif can still be recognized even in the fifteenth-century manuscript cod. Moscow, Hist. Museum 155 (fols. 5^r, 260^r, 332^r, 406^r), although it has been transformed (Fig. 474). The enamel subtleties in color have disappeared; the animals tend to be more naturalistic; and palmettes have been substituted for the long, spiny leaves which faintly recall the plant known as *agave*, grown in warmer climates.

The differences and the changes in the ornament that can be studied in the manuscripts of Gregory during the course of five centuries testify to a constant renewal of artistic expression, which is evident in the development of the figure style as well. These expressions, regardless of their differences from one period to another, can be summarized and contrasted in the following terms: court and popular traditions; classicizing and monastic style; elegant sophistication and simplicity; dramatic tension and hieratic aloofness. True, these terms can be applied to the whole of Byzantine painting from the tenth century on. They can be applied above all, however, to Constantinopolitan manuscripts no matter whether they originated in the palace or in the monasteries of the capital; the parallels which have been drawn in many instances leave no doubt that almost all the manuscripts of this edition are products of that area. The few exceptions are found in the catalogue.

This conclusion is significant because it infers that the common archetype from which the manuscripts sprang—as the study of the iconography has shown—was made in Constantinople. In addition to its iconography, can the stylistic quality of this archetype be established? It should not be assumed that all the stylistic varieties noted in this study are necessarily reflections of the style of the archetype. However, since the manuscripts belong to the school of a particular area, the archetype must have shown the trends of that school in the period of its creation, i.e. tenth-century Constantinople. The two main traditions of this period, i.e. "the classicizing" and the "monastic," must have existed in the archetype not only side by side, but often mingled in the same miniature. This assertion alone underlines the difficulties and dangers of attempting to draw a line between the two and to define their boundaries.[13]

C. CHRONOLOGICAL LIMITS OF THE RECENSION

The assertions that the archetype was made in Constantinople and that the majority of its copies were made within the Constantinopolitan area, coupled with the time-

[13] The dangers of making such a distinction have been pointed out by Beckwith, *Constantinople*, pp. 115, 116. Cf. also K. Weitzmann, "Eleventh Century Miniature and Icon Painting," *Proceedings of the XIIIth Inter. Congress of Byzantine Studies, Oxford 1966*, London 1967, pp. 211ff.

limits of the recension (which do not go beyond the fifteenth century), raise two more questions: why did the recension not become popular in the provinces and why was it no longer illustrated after the fifteenth century? These questions become more urgent when one considers the history of the illustrations of a popular romance, *Barlaam and Joasaph*, and of a monastic treatise, *The Heavenly Ladder* by John Climacus, both mentioned several times in this study. Their illustrations were disseminated over great distances and many years: they became popular in the provinces and outlived the fall of the Empire. The first of the two books certainly owed its popularity to the fact that it was a romance, the "best-seller" of its time. The second had an edifying purpose and so is more akin to the text of Gregory. Therefore it seems only fair to use the *Heavenly Ladder* both for comparison and as evidence in order to answer the foregoing questions. The *Heavenly Ladder* was illustrated in the provinces and continued to be so until the seventeenth century. Its persistence and obvious popularity in the monastic world can be explained by the nature of its text. The treatise of John Climacus is a re-creation of eleventh-century monasticism; it refers directly to monks and their lives in the cloisters. Despite its mystic and lofty character, it is a practical book, and it became the daily reading for the monk. As long as true monasticism lived, the monks needed pictures to explain the meaning of the book that narrated their life, and this is why the illustrations spread over distance and time.

In the light of this observation, the nature of the text of Gregory's homilies should be considered. It was pointed out at the beginning of this study that the liturgical edition of the homilies was created as a supplement to the readings of the Gospel, and that it formed part of the Byzantine liturgy as formulated in the Middle Byzantine period. In addition, the text itself reveals Gregory as a great orator following the method of the rhetoricians of antiquity, a profound theologian explaining the doctrines in lofty terms and defending the true faith, a bishop suffering and struggling for the souls of his flock, an aristocrat of the spirit and, at the same time, the possessor of a warm, sensitive, tender heart that embraced the natural as well as the supernatural, and as a humanist of this world and an ascetic struggling to reconcile in himself secular culture and religious convictions. Fleury says: "Pas plus que le chrétien n'avait étouffé l'humaniste, l'ascète en lui n'avait anéanti l'homme . . . nous ne l'entrevoyons jamais au sommet d'une tour d'ivoire, jamais il ne se cache derrière la grille d'un cloître, les murs d'une école, les portes d'un palais. Nous le trouvons à nos côtés. Loin de mépriser nos tâtonnements et nos faiblesses d'intellectuels fatigués, il se propose pour nous conduire à sa suite sur les hautes sereines où se réalise l'accord du naturel et du surnaturel."[14] This Gregory does throughout his sermons. The following conclusions can therefore be drawn: Gregory's sermons are directly related to the liturgy of the Church and not to the life and deeds of monks within the walls of monasteries; Gregory appeals above all to the intellectuals who, like him, have attempted the difficult fusion of Gospel and antiquity. Men like Constantine Porphyro-

[14] Fleury, *Hellenism*, p. 374.

genitus, and others from the palace circle later, admired the beauty of Gregory's words and often referred to his texts as well as to those of the other Cappadocians in their theological discussions. These reasons are sufficient to explain why the illustrated recension of the liturgical edition of his homilies did not spread geographically far or survive the fall of the Empire.[15]

When the intellectuals turned their attention to the monastic, mystic theology of Symeon the New Theologian and later to the proponents of the doctrine of Light, Gregory was no longer in the foreground of intellectual life. Although undue emphasis should not be placed on the fact that most of the manuscripts belong to the first period—the case of other works is analogous—it can be assumed that the turn from classical intellectualism to monastic ideas in the eleventh century was the cause of the reduction in the number of illustrated copies in the subsequent centuries.

Being thus directly related to the liturgy of the Church, Gregory followed it into the monasteries after the fall of Constantinople. There the readings of the homilies continued in the same way as before; they remained, however, a part of the liturgy and not of the monastic life proper. There were no longer any theological controversies, nor precepts of a Christian life for newly converted Christians, nor panegyrics of martyrs. There was no longer a struggle in the world, but a struggle for the world outside the world, and a struggle to attain the beauty of the "Beloved" in the cloister. There was no nature or beauty of nature, but the beauty of the "Beloved," which the monk could reach by following certain prescribed rules and by ascending the well-defined steps of the Heavenly Ladder.

Gregory and Hellenism gave place to patristic literature that appealed to the monks: the Mystics of Light, the Fathers of the Desert, and John Climacus. The illustrated recension of Gregory's homilies stopped producing new offspring. The thinking of the period that had created the archetype of this recension had already reached its geographic limits. When thinking changed in the course of time, the chronological limits were also set.

[15] It should not be concluded, however, that the interest in Gregory declined completely in post-Byzantine times; see Sajdak, *Scholia*, pp. 198ff.

VI. EPILOGUE

IN THE preceding chapters, proceeding from one group of miniatures to another, I have unfolded the history of the illustrations of Gregory's homilies of the liturgical edition. In telling the story of their illustrations, I have attempted to define the character of the archetype from which the copies studied have stemmed.

The period of the creation of this archetype, the Macedonian Renaissance, is of great importance in the history of Byzantine book illumination. My final task is to place the illustrations of Gregory within the framework of this period.

After the iconoclasm, "les cycles iconographiques," writes Bréhier, "ne servirent plus seulement à l'instruction du peuple, mais prirent une valeur mystique. . . ."[1] Art becomes a symbol of liturgy. The Christian story is not told in narrative fashion. The iconography changes, and the liturgical cycle comes to the fore. The elements of liturgy—rites, prayers, litanies, and hymns—are illustrated.[2] The liturgical Gospel divided in *pericopes* replaces the narrative Gospel, and becomes not only the most important book of the holy altar, but also a prototype for other liturgical books. The edition of Gregory's selected homilies follows the sequence of the lectionary and the liturgical aspect of its illustrations. The homilies, however, emphasize the liturgical aspect of Middle Byzantine art, not only in the miniatures borrowed from the lectionary, but even in those made especially for the text of Gregory. Pictures such as the two Gregorys in Proskynesis, the Encaenia, the Baptism, and the Eucharistic scenes were conceived in the spirit of the liturgy and contribute to our knowledge of liturgical art. The liturgical illustrations of Gregory make it clear that the purpose of liturgical art is not to please, but to create a mystical response in the soul of the beholder. It is, in other words, a true spiritual art, lacking what Paul calls "fleshly mind."[3]

Besides the liturgical, there is another trend in the Macedonian period: classicism.[4] A revival movement, primarily a book renaissance, is evident, expressed in the copying of classical texts and the illustration of secular manuscripts, such as the Pseudo-Nonnos, the Pseudo-Oppian, and the Theriaca of Nicander.

The illustrations of Gregory's homilies are an important contribution to this aspect of Middle Byzantine art. The supplementary illustrations, added, I believe, shortly after the archetype was created, are unique in including bucolic scenes. The bucolic scenes are an undeniable expression of the renaissance movement and contribute to our knowledge of illustrations of classical bucolic poetry. Weitzmann has observed that in the Macedonian Renaissance there is a kind of absorption of classical elements,

[1] L. Bréhier, *L'art byzantin*, Paris 1924, p. 41.

[2] J. D. Stefănescu, *L'illustration des liturgies dans l'art de Byzance et de l'Orient*, Brussels 1936.

[3] Col. 2: 18.

[4] Cf. Bréhier, "L'enseignement classique et l'enseignement religieux à Byzance," *Revue d'histoire de philosophie religieuse*, 1941, pp. 34-61; Weitzmann, *Joshua*, passim; *idem, Mythology*, passim; *idem*, "The Classical in Byzantine Art as a Mode of Individual Expression," *Byzantine Art—An European Art, Lectures*, Athens 1966, pp. 151-77.

affecting the inner substance of Biblical pictures.[5] The Heosphoros miniature confirms this observation.

In this important period of Byzantine art, there is a third, equally significant, trend: monastic art. Activities in monasteries and advances in asceticism did not fail to create a new iconography with "emphasis on monks and monkish deeds," as Martin says.[6] The illustrations of *The Heavenly Ladder*, the illustrations of *Barlaam and Joasaph*, and the mosaics of St. Luke are examples of this trend, and the illustrations of Gregory are further evidence of it. Although his sermons were not delivered particularly to monks, Gregory appears in the illustrations in monk's dress, teaching monks. He and his audience of monks and other clerics bear testimony to the trend towards monasticism, which is also conveyed by a greater austerity and spirituality. The type of ascetic saint that was to become the norm in Byzantine art of the eleventh and twelfth centuries is prominent in the illustrations of Gregory. To support this idea, I remind the reader of the standing portrait of Gregory in the cod. Paris gr. 550 and the portrait of Gregory writing in cod. Oxford, Canon. gr. 103 (Figs. 400, 275).

In addition to these three trends in the art of the Macedonian period, there is another one which has probably always existed in Byzantine art: the representation of scenes from everyday life. The illustrations of Gregory's homilies have shed light on this aspect of Byzantine art, and have revealed that the Byzantine artist must have believed that life in heaven and on earth reflected one another, and that one of his natural tasks was to discover the garb of glory given to all that was related to man's earthly existence. The painter's interest in the events of everyday life is significant for it indicates that to him man remains an inexhaustible source of inspiration. This is humanism. In fact this humanism is more important than that pursued by literary figures throughout Byzantium, and it is more important than the copying of miniatures from ancient models, for it is an authentic humanism related directly to life.

The illustrations of Gregory's homilies reflect and combine all these trends, and herein lies their importance. At the beginning of this study, I asked if the diversity of the text was reflected in the illustrations. The answer has been strongly affirmative. Only one other manuscript, the romance of Barlaam and Joasaph, can be compared to Gregory in its diversity of artistic trends. Although this romance is a glorification of monastic life, the nature of the subject has permitted a secular trend in its illustrations to exist side by side with monastic art.

We have studied the copies of an archetype, the prestige of which must have been great. This is all the more natural since the text is sacred, and its images are sacred also. From this attitude derives the traditionalism that Weitzmann has called "an art of reverence towards a picture,"[7] a traditionalism which becomes even more evident

---

[5] Weitzmann, *Mythology*, p. 206; *idem*, "The Survivals of Mythological Representations in Early Christian and Byzantine Art and their Impact on Christian Iconography," *Dumbarton Oaks Papers*, 14 (1961), pp. 45-68.

[6] Martin, *Ladder*, p. 163.

[7] K. Weitzmann, "Narration in Early Christendom," *American Journal of Archaeology*, 61 (1957), p. 91.

in the individual religious pictures. Gregory said that the duty of the faithful Christian was to keep, word for word, the tradition received at the knees of his mother.[8] The duty of the artist is to revere a created image like a remembrance of those who had existed before. But it is more than that. The artist who is to render a religious image pictorially should live with it. Once it is given reality by pigment, it is a being that no one dares change. Yet the artist opposes his own inventiveness to this conservatism. Between the ephemeral world of men and the absolute world of God, a third world is created, the world of the artist. Of this the illustrations of Gregory have offered ample proof. We have seen that the artist added pictures not occurring in the archetype. The artist deviated from the pictorial tradition of the archetype and expressed his own understanding of the text. He combined elements, which produced new pictures that revealed talents of improvisation and inventiveness. The composite scenes of the Gregory manuscripts suffice to answer those who would claim that Byzantine art was dry and uncreative.

Gregory has spoken to us through the illustrations of his homilies. He has spoken about liturgical art, about the art of our ephemeral world which the Byzantines knew, about the ascetic ideals of an art born in secluded monasteries, and about the world of the artist who is "delivered from the bondage of corruption into the glorious liberty of the children of God."[9]

[8] *PG*, 35, 840.   [9] Rom. 8: 21.

VII. CATALOGUE OF ILLUSTRATED
MANUSCRIPTS

THE following catalogue lists all the extant illustrated manuscripts of the homilies of the liturgical edition known to me. The physical characteristics, contents, and system of illustration of each codex are briefly indicated, and the style and date discussed. No attempt has been made to edit inscriptions.

1. ATHENS, NATIONAL LIBRARY, COD. 213. 220 folios, 34 x 24 cm., parchment. XI century

Contents:

Fifteen homilies of the liturgical edition.

Decoration:

fol. 1ʳ. Christ raising Adam and Eve, in initial A (homily 1).

The remaining homilies are decorated with ornamental bands, in most cases of the typical flower-petal style ornament.

Style and Date:

The manuscript has no colophon. The following lines are in the right column of fol. 220ᵛ: Τάρξγχης μου γράψε—" Ὁ Θεός νά μοῦ συγχωρέση—ἐλεεινόν καὶ τὸν ἁμαρτω-λόν—καὶ πρεσβεία τῆς Παναγίας." Sakellion believed the manuscript to be tenth century, but, because of the ornament, it must be dated in the second half of the eleventh century. The flower-petal style of the ornamental bands recalls the style that appears in the eleventh-century manuscripts of the Constantinopolitan school.[1] The treatment of the ornament shows a tendency toward a decorative effect that is more evident on fols. 15ʳ and 151ᵛ where the ornamental bands are formed by semicircles and zigzag lines. The richness of the enamel-like color and the refined technique suggest that the manuscript was made in Constantinople.

Bibliography:

J. Sakellion, Κατάλογος τῶν Χειρογράφων τῆς Ἐθνικῆς Βιβλιοθήκης τῆς Ἑλλάδος, Athens 1892, p. 41.

2. ATHENS, NATIONAL LIBRARY, COD. 2554. 158 folios, 32.3 x 23.5 cm., parchment. XI century. (Figs. 257-60)

Contents:

The codex in its present state contains only twelve homilies of the liturgical edition. The text of the twelfth homily stops on fol. 158ᵛ; the remaining part of the codex has been cut out. Five folios containing a musical piece " Ἀπόστολοι πανεύφημοι οἱ τοῦ κόσμου πρεσβευταὶ ἀσθενούντων ἰατροί. . . ." are a later insertion.

---

[1] Cf. fol. 38ᵛ with fol. 371ʳ of the cod. Vat. gr.463; see infra no. 31.

Decoration:

fol. 1ʳ.   Christ and Adam in initial A (homily 1).

fol. 3ʳ.   A saint, probably Habakkuk, in initial E, almost totally flaked (homily 2).

fol. 25ᵛ.   Pentecost in initial Π (homily 4).

fol. 60ᵛ.   Nativity, including the Bathing of the Child, in initial X (homily 8).

fol. 69ᵛ.   Gregory and the dead Basil in initial E (homily 9).

Style and Date:

The historiated initials are flaked to such an extent that a discussion of the figure style is not possible. Most of the ornamental bands are painted in the typical eleventh-century flower-petal style, but other motifs have also been used. For example, on fol. 60ᵛ there is a band of intersecting circles like those occurring in the cod. Oxford, Selden. B. 54, fol. 88ᵛ, which can be dated in the second half of the eleventh century. Furthermore, the initials resemble those found in the cod. Vat. gr. 463, dating from the year 1062.[2] The preserved colors are quite bright and the combination of blue, red, and gold is very successful. Occasionally a meager quality appears in the treatment of the ornament and in the script itself, which raises doubts about the Constantinopolitan origin of the manuscript. Perhaps it was made in one of the provinces that were under the influence of the capital. The codex found its way to the National Library of Athens from Serrae, but it is difficult to know whether it was written in Serrae. In the margin of fol. 41ᵛ the monogram for the monastery Ἰωάννου Προδρόμου has been inscribed in red ink:

Δ I

ΜΩ

Bibliography:

Germanos, "Κατάλογος χειρογράφων τῆς παρὰ τὰς Σέρρας Μονῆς Ἰωάννου Προδρόμου," Νέος Ποιμήν, 2 (1920), pp. 338, 339.

3. Athos, Monastery of Dionysiou, cod. 61. 180 folios, 21.2 x 15.4 cm., parchment. XI-XII century. (Figs. 355-76)

Contents:

The sixteen homilies of the liturgical edition. The last homily is incomplete.

Decoration:

fol. 1ᵛ.   Dedication page. Gregory of Nazianzus offers a book to a prince.
            ὁ ἅ(γιο)ς Γρηγ(όριος) ὁ Θεολόγ(ο)ς
            Above, a bust of Christ.

fol. 2ʳ.   Anastasis- ἡ ἀνάστασ(ι)ς. The same in initial A (homily 1).

fol. 4ʳ.   The so-called vision of Habakkuk- Ὁ ἅγι(ο)ς Ἀμβακούμ, ὁ ἅγιος Γρη(γόριος) ὁ Θεολόγος, Ἰ(ησοῦ)ς Χ(ριστό)ς. Gregory, Habakkuk and a bust of Christ in initial E (homily 2).

---

[2] Infra, no. 31.

fol. 17ʳ. Mamas standing frontally- ὁ ἅ(γιο)ς μάμ(ας), Mamas milking a hind; Church and Synagogue. Gregory teaching, in initial E (homily 3).

fol. 21ᵛ. Pentecost- ἡ Πεντηκοστή. The same in initial Π (homily 4).

fol. 28ᵛ. Julian the Tax Collector and scribes- ὁ ἐξισωτὴς Ἰουλιανός. Gregory and a scribe in initial T (homily 7).

fol. 35ʳ. The Koimesis of Basil the Great- Ἡ κοίμησις τοῦ ἁ(γίου) Βασιλεί(ου). A painter painting an icon of a bishop, in the right margin of the second column. Gregory teaching in initial E (homily 9).

fol. 70ʳ. The Nativity, including the Bathing of the Child- Ἡ γέ(ννησις) τοῦ Χ(ριστ)οῦ.
The same in initial X (homily 8).

fol. 77ʳ. The Baptism of Christ- Ἡ Χ(ριστ)οῦ Βάπτισις.
John baptizing Christ in initial Π (homily 10).

fol. 113ʳ. Gregory of Nyssa and Gregory of Nazianzus conversing- Ὁ ἅγ(ιο)ς Γρηγ(όριος) ὁ Νύ(σσης). Ὁ ἅγ(ιος) Γρηγ(όριος) ὁ Θεολόγ(ος).
The two Gregorys and Christ in initial Φ (homily 12).

fol. 130ʳ. Gregory teaching two groups of bishops- Ὁ ἅ(γιος) Γρηγ(όριος) ὁ Θεολόγ(ο)ς, οἱ ἐπίσκοποι.
Gregory addressing one bishop in initial Π (homily 14).

fol. 142ʳ. Gregory and the poor- Ὁ ἅ(γιος) Γρηγ(όριος) ὁ Θεολόγ(ος), οἱ ἐν Χ(ριστ)ῶ ἀδελφοί.
Gregory giving alms to two cripples in initial A (homily 15).

fol. 165ʳ. Gregory pointing out Cyprian to a group of people- Ὁ Θεολ(ό)γ(ος), ὁ μάρ(τυς) Κυπριανός.
Justina, Christ-Emmanuel, and Cyprian in initial M (homily 6).

fol. 172ᵛ. Gregory pointing out his father to a group of people- Ὁ τοῦ Θεολόγ(ου) π(ατ)ήρ, ὁ Θεολόγος.
Gregory teaching, in initial T (homily 16).

Style and Date:

On the evidence of the palaeography of the text, Lambros assigned the codex to the thirteenth century. This is not supported by the style, on the basis of which Weitzmann proposed a late eleventh-century date. Although this date cannot be excluded, the ornamentation and particular features in the rendering of the figures point rather to the following century. The ornament—large bands in flower-petal style, defined by a fillet of an S-dotted motif—finds analogies in the codd. Paris, suppl. gr. 27 and Istanbul, Patr. 2, for which a twelfth-century date has been proposed on stylistic grounds.[3] Likewise, the treatment of the hair in separate strokes and the sharp contrasts of light and shadow on the face recall the cod. Vat. Urb. gr. 2, which can be

---

[3] Frantz, *AB* (1934), pl. XII, 22. Cf. Athos, Dionysiou 61, fol. 4ʳ (Fig. 357) with Istanbul, Patr. 2, fol. 133ʳ reproduced in Soteriou (1937), pl. 54.

dated between the years 1119 and 1143 because of the portraits of the Comnenian emperors.[4] Another characteristic common to both manuscripts is an emphasis on the chin when figures are portrayed in profile, and the flame-like edges of the rocks in the landscape.[5] These details, however, appear with greater emphasis in the Vatican codex than in the Athos manuscript, a fact that may suggest a slightly earlier date for the latter.

There is no reason to assume that the codex was originally incomplete, and a colophon including the names of the scribe and the prince depicted on the dedication page may have existed at the end of the missing folios. Constantinople was without doubt the place of origin. The high quality of the miniatures, the subtlety of the colors, and the presence of the unknown prince support this conclusion.

Bibliography:

Lambros, I, p. 323.

O. Wulff, *Altchristliche und byzantinische Kunst*, II, Berlin 1924, p. 538, fig. 473.

A. Marava-Chatzinikolaou, 'Ο ῞Αγιος Μάμας, Athens 1953, pp. 88, 89.

K. Weitzmann, *Aus den Bibliotheken des Athos*, Hamburg 1963, pp. 97, 98, fig. p. 99.

4. ATHOS, MONASTERY OF IVIRON, COD. 271. 314 folios, 25 x 19.5 cm., parchment. XI century (Fig. 178)

Contents:

The sixteen homilies of the liturgical edition.

Decoration:

The codex once contained sixteen title miniatures extending over both columns of the text, all of which have been cut out. In addition to the title miniatures, the manuscript had supplementary illustrations, one in the twelfth homily and two in the fourteenth. The first one on fol. 118ʳ has been cut out, but its place between the words Θαλάμῳ χρυσῷ κίονας may suggest the possibility of a miniature depicting Gregory and Basil flanking a ciborium, such as that in the cod. Athos, Panteleimon 6. Of the two other supplementary illustrations, the one on fol. 252ᵛ (bottom of left column) has been cut out. On the basis of the text and the miniature illustrating the same text in the cod. Athos, Panteleimon 6, a small representation of the murder of Julian the Apostate may be suggested. The second supplementary illustration of the same codex, on fol. 272ᵛ (right column), is the only one left in the whole manuscript. It shows the Emperor Valens—Οὐάλης ὁ ᾿Αρειανός—in anathema. The word κῦφος is above the prostrate emperor.

Style and Date:

Only on the bases of the palaeography and the style of that single figure of the emperor can an eleventh-century date be suggested for the codex.

---

[4] Stornajolo, *Giacomo monaco*, pls. 84, 91.

[5] Cf. cod. Vat. Urb. gr. 2, fols. 20ᵛ and 260ᵛ, Stornajolo, *Giacomo monaco*, pls. 84, 90.

Bibliography:
Lambros, II, p. 69.

5. ATHOS, MONASTERY OF KARAKALOU, COD. 24. 276 folios, 24 x 16.9 cm., parchment. XIII-XIV century. (Figs. 452-53)

Contents:
The sixteen homilies of the liturgical edition.

Decoration:
     fol. 3ᵛ.   The author portrait- ὁ ἅ(γιος) Γρηγόριος ὁ Θεολόγος.
     fol. 6ᵛ.   Gregory and his vision of Christos-Angelos in the margins (homily 1).

Style and Date:
The ornamental bands decorating the beginning of each sermon consist of flower-petal ornaments, zigzag patterns, and floral motifs. The ornament in flower-petal style is meager and the design is not solid. It is somewhat similar to the ornament appearing in the cod. London, Add. 11870, assigned on stylistic grounds to the thirteenth century.[6]

The figures have all the characteristics of late Byzantine art: protruding foreheads, wavy hair, and beards executed by separate strokes. Most pronounced are the zigzag edges of both Christ's and Gregory's garments and the large successive pleats, which find analogies in fourteenth-century manuscripts such as the cod. Oxford, gr. th. f. 1 dated, on internal evidence, in the mid-fourteenth century.[7] Gregory's figure, however, lacks the elegant movement, the impression of a momentary pose, which the figures of the Oxford manuscript possess, and resembles more the figures appearing in the *Typicon* of Lincoln College, cod. gr. 35, dating, on internal evidence, from the first half of the fourteenth century,[8] a date which I would suggest for the miniatures of the Karakalou manuscript.

Lambros has proposed a thirteenth-century date on the basis of the palaeography of the text. This date can be maintained for the ornament only, not for the miniatures, which, as closer observation reveals, were added later. The color washes are bright and their combinations very subtle. The blues and light reds of the garments have been successfully combined with brown and greenish colors. The use of the color nuances suggests Constantinople as the place of the manuscript's origin.

Bibliography:
Lambros, I, p. 131.

6. ATHOS, MONASTERY OF GRAND LAVRA, COD. B 111. 398 folios, 32.5 x 24.6 cm., parchment. XII century. (Fig. 430).

Contents:
    1) The sixteen homilies of the liturgical edition.

[6] Frantz, *AB* (1934), pl. XII, 17.
[7] O. Pächt, *Byzantine Illumination*, Oxford 1952, p. 8, fig. 16.
[8] *Ibid.*, p. 5, fig. 21.

2) Two homilies of John Chrysostom: μή πλησιάζειν θεάτροις καὶ εἰς τὸν ᾿Αβραάμ, fols. 338ᵛ-367ᵛ (*PG*, 56, 541-54), and εἰς Μακάριον Φιλογόνιον, fols. 368ʳ-381ᵛ (*PG*, 48, 742-56).

3) Basil the Great's homily on Baptism, fols. 382ʳ-397ʳ (*PG*, 31, 1429-1437).

Decoration:

    fol. 1ᵛ.   The author portrait- ὁ ἅγιος Γρηγόριος ὁ Θεολόγος.

Style and Date:

The miniature of the author portrait is badly flaked. A detail of the beard still visible in the original manuscript shows a moderate use of highlights, whereas the treatment of the body has a flattened quality. Both details suggest a twelfth-century date. This dating, based on style, is supported by the ornaments used. The flower-petal ornament, with its exquisite Constantinopolitan colors and love of detail, has become more stylized and less naturalistic here. It finds parallels in another manuscript of Gregory's homilies, the cod. Paris gr. 550, which is generally dated in the twelfth century.[9]

Bibliography:

Spyridon-Eustratiades, *Catalogue Lavra*, pp. 28, 29.

7. ATHOS, MONASTERY OF ST. PANTELEIMON, COD. 6. 293 folios, 24.5 x 20 cm., parchment. XI century. (Figs. 137-77, 179-80)

Contents:

The sixteen homilies of the liturgical edition. The last homily is incomplete as the text breaks off on fol. 293ᵛ. Two pages from another text have been sewn in upside down at the end.

Decoration:

    fol. 2ʳ.   Anastasis (homily 1).

    fol. 5ᵛ.   The so-called vision of Habakkuk- ὁ προφήτης ᾿Αββακούμ (homily 2).

    fol. 30ʳ.   Gregory teaching a group of people- ὁ ἅ(γιος) Γρηγόριος ὁ Θεολόγος Church and Synagogue (homily 3).

The illustrations of fols. 37ʳ-38ᵛ listed below belong to the same homily.

    fol. 37ʳ.   Three miniatures of occupations: a) Sheep grazing. b) Sailing. c) Ploughing.

    fol. 37ᵛ.   Three miniatures of occupations: a) Shepherds playing the flute. b) Pruning and hunting. c) Fishing.

    fol. 38ᵛ.   Mamas as shepherd- ὁ ἅ(γιος) Μάμας -column picture.

    fol. 39ᵛ.   Pentecost- ἡ πεντηκοστή (homily 4).

    fol. 53ʳ.   The seven Maccabees standing (homily 5).

---

[9] Infra, no. 27.

fol. 63ᵛ. Gregory teaching- ὁ ἅγιος Γρηγόριος ὁ Θεολόγος -in the margin (homily 5).

fol. 64ʳ. Cyprian standing- ὁ ἅγιος Κυπριανός (homily 6).

fol. 77ᵛ. Julian the Tax Collector and Gregory as writers. One scribe and another standing figure (homily 7).

fol. 89ᵛ. Nativity, including the Bathing of the Child and the Adoration of the Magi- ἡ Χ(ριστο)ῦ γέννησις (homily 8).

fol. 90ᵛ. John the Baptist standing- ἅ(γιος) Ἰω(άννης) ὁ Πρόδρομ(ος) -in the margin (homily 8).

fol. 100ʳ. The Koimesis of Basil the Great (homily 9).

The illustrations of fols. 105ʳ-155ᵛ listed below belong to the same homily.

fol. 105ʳ. Three hinds, in the margin.

fol. 115ʳ. Basil and Gregory at either side of a baldachin- ὁ ἅγιος Βασίλειος, ὁ ἅγιος Γρηγόριος ὁ Θεο(λόγος) -in the column.

The miniatures contained within fols. 116ʳ-132ʳ are marginal.

fol. 116ʳ. Midas.

fol. 119ʳ. Gregory standing- ὁ ἅ(γιος) Γρηγόριος ὁ Θεολό(γος).

fol. 123ʳ. Arios- ὁ Ἄρειος.

fol. 132ʳ. Riders.

fol. 134ᵛ. First trial of Basil, in the column- ὁ ἅ(γιος) Βασίλειος ἐρωτόμενος.

fol. 135ʳ. The same in the column.

fol. 138ʳ. Two scenes superimposed within the column: a) Basil with other ecclesiastics in a boat. b) Basil healing the emperor's son.

fol. 138ᵛ. Basil healing the prefect, in the margin.

fol. 140ʳ. Basil before the prefect, second trial, in the column. Instruments of torture, in the margin.

fol. 140ᵛ. The prefect seated between two groups of protesting people, in the column.

fols. 151ᵛ-155ᵛ contain only marginal miniatures.

fol. 151ᵛ. a) Adam in Paradise- ὁ Ἀδάμ. b) Enos standing- Ἐνώς.

fol. 152ʳ. a) The Translation of Enoch- ἡ μετάθεσις τοῦ Ἐνώχ.

b) Noah and the ark- ὁ Νῶε, ἡ κιβωτός.

c) The Sacrifice of Abraham- Ἀβραάμ, Ἰσαακ΄.

d) Isaac carrying the sacrificial wood.

fol. 152ᵛ. Jacob and the ladder- ὁ Ἰακώβ, ἡ κλίμαξ.

fol. 153ʳ. a) Joseph and his brothers- Ἰωσήφ. b) Moses- Μωυσής. c) Aaron- Ἀαρών.

fol. 153ᵛ. Joshua- Ἰησοῦς τοῦ Ναυῆ.

fol. 154ʳ. a) Samuel- Σαμουήλ. b) David- ὁ προφήτης Δα(υί)δ. c) Solomon-
ὁ προφήτης Σολομ(ών).

fol. 154ᵛ. a) The Ascension of Elijah- ὁ προφήτης Ἠλίας, ὁ προφήτης Ἐλισσαῖος.
b) The three holy children in the fire- οἱ ἅγιοι τρεῖς παῖδες.

fol. 155ʳ. John the Baptist- ὁ ἅ(γιος) Ἰω(άννης) ὁ Πρόδρομ(ος).

fol. 155ᵛ. The stoning of Stephen- ὁ Σαῦλος, ὁ ἅ(γιος) Στέφανος ὁ Πρωτομάρ-
(τυς).

Only the preliminary drawing of this miniature has been preserved.

fol. 161ʳ. The Baptism of Christ (homily 10).

fols. 162ᵛ-165ᵛ contain the Pseudo-Nonnos's illustrations (homily 10).

fol. 162ᵛ. The birth of Zeus (Cronos swallowing the stone)- ὁ κρόνος, ἡ ῥέα.

fol. 163ʳ. a) The birth of Zeus (the child Zeus surrounded by the Couretes).
b) The cult of Rhea- ἡ ῥέα.

fol. 163ᵛ. a) The birth of Dionysos- Ζεύς, διόνυσος.
b) The cult of Semele- ἡ σεμέλη.

fol. 164ʳ. a) The cult of Aphrodite- ἡ ἀφροδίτη.
b) The cult of Artemis- ἡ ἄρτεμις.

fol. 164ᵛ. a) The butchery of Pelops- ὁ Ζεύς, ἡ ἀθήνα, ἡ ἀφρο(δίτη), ἡ δημήτηρ,
ὁ ἑρμῆς, ἄρης, καὶ ἡ ἄρτεμις, ὁ τάνταλο(ς), πέλωψ.
b) The Egyptian gods- οἱ Δελφῖνες.

fol. 165ʳ. a) The astrology of the Chaldeans.
b) Orpheus playing his harp- ὁ Ὀρφεύς.

fol. 165ᵛ. a) The worship of the sun of Mithras- οἱ θρησκεύοντες τὸν ἥλιον.
b) The goat of Mendes- οἱ θρησκεύοντες τοὺς τράγους.

fol. 173ʳ. John the Baptist, in the margin. The outer margin has been cut out
and surely contained more illustrations (homily 10).

fol. 178ʳ. Gregory teaching (homily 11).

fol. 214ʳ. Gregory of Nazianzus and Gregory of Nyssa in proskynesis (homily
12).

fol. 219ʳ. The Koimesis of Athanasius of Alexandria (homily 13).

fol. 240ᵛ. Gregory among four seated bishops (homily 14).

fol. 242ᵛ. a) Mercurius killing Julian the Apostate- Ἰουλιανὸς ὁ ἀποστάτης.
b) Valens- Οὐάλης ὁ ἀρειανός -preliminary drawing.

fol. 257ʳ. Gregory and the poor (homily 15).

fol. 262ʳ. The margin has been cut out. It probably contained miniatures
(homily 15).

fol. 281ʳ. Gregory pointing out his father to a group of people (homily 16).

Style and Date:

The text is written in one column, and the date that it was read is indicated at the
beginning of each homily. The quality of the miniatures is very high and their state
of preservation excellent. The title miniatures are within a richly decorated frame of

flower-petal ornament. Each large ornamental band is defined by a smaller one, imitating the silver or gold borders that often appear on enamels.

A comparative study of the ornament applied in this codex points to a late eleventh-century date. The flower-petal ornament is similar to that appearing in cod. Paris, Coislin 79, dating from the period 1078 to 1081.[10] The two manuscripts have also in common their richness of color, and even a similar use of palmettes.[11]

The figure style finds analogies in late eleventh-century manuscripts. The same kind of fiery, wide-open, ecstatic eyes appear in the title miniatures of the lectionary of the Morgan Library, cod. 639, dating from the end of the eleventh century. Both manuscripts reflect the use of a good Macedonian Renaissance model; in both there is the same certainty in the stance of the figures, the same elaboration of detail, and the same miniature-like style.[12] Although such comparisons are of only relative value, it should be noticed that the treatment of the garment in the Athos codex is clearer than that in the Morgan manuscript.[13] This detail indicates an earlier date for the Athos manuscript, still, however, within the latter part of the eleventh century.

The richness and perfection of color, the elegance of design, the wealth of ornament, the use of gold script for entire pages—all characteristics of the school of the capital—support the assignment of the manuscript to Constantinople.

Bibliography:

Schlumberger, *Epopée*, I, p. 497.

D. Ainalov, "Vizantiiskije pamiatniki Afona," *Vizantiiskii Vremennik*, 6 (1899), pp. 87-95.

Lambros, II, p. 282.

N. P. Kondakov, *Pamiatniki Khristianskogo iskusstva na Afone*, St. Petersburg 1902, p. 295.

Pokrovskii, *Evangelie*, pl. XLIX, 60, figs. 17, 18, 47.

Idem, Ocherki pamiatnikov Khristianskogo iskusstva i ikonografii, St. Petersburg 1910, p. 168, figs. 123-25.

Millet, *Recherches*, fig. 133, pp. 134 n. 3, 176 n. 8.

Diehl, *Manuel*, II, figs. 304, 305.

H. Brockhaus, *Die Kunst in den Athos-Klöstern*, 2nd ed., Leipzig 1924, pp. 194, 230.

Ebersolt, *Miniature*, p. 38 n. 3.

F. Dölger, *Mönchsland Athos*, Munich 1943, p. 188, fig. 107.

Lazarev, *History*, I, pp. 128, 326 n. 100, 354 n. 136.

Weitzmann, *Roll*, pp. 146ff, 199, figs. 135, 136.

Idem, Mythology, see index.

---

[10] Frantz, *AB* (1934), pl. VIII, 4, 5. Cf. Weitzmann, *Buchmalerei*, pp. 2ff.

[11] Frantz, *AB* (1934), pl. XXII, 3.

[12] Cf., for instance, fol. 178r of the Panteleimon manuscript (Fig. 172) with fol. 294r of the Morgan codex; see Weitzmann, *Lectionary Morgan 639*, fig. 319.

[13] Cf. cod. Morgan 639, fol. 294r with Panteleimon, fols. 240v and 100r (Figs. 176, 149); see Weitzmann, *Lectionary Morgan 639*, fig. 319.

8. ATHOS, MONASTERY OF PANTOCRATOR, COD. 31. 402 folios,[14] 28 x 19 cm., parchment. XII century. (Fig. 428)

Contents:

The sixteen homilies of the liturgical edition. It also contains one of the homilies of the complete edition, i.e. ἀπολογητικὸς τῆς εἰς τὸν Πόντον φυγῆς ἕνεκεν, fol. 8ᵛ (*PG*, 35, 407-514).

Decoration:

fol. 4ᵛ.   The author portrait- ὁ ἅ(γιος) Γρηγόριος ὁ Θεολόγος, Ἰ(ησοῦ)ς Χ(ριστό)ς.

On the book is written 'Αναστάσεως ἡμέρα.

Style and Date:

The ornament forming the frame of the frontispiece bears some resemblance to the ornament of the cod. Athos, Dionysiou 8, dating from the year 1135.[15] Moreover, the flower-petal ornament of the decorative headpiece, which is given a linear and patternized treatment, is typical of the twelfth century, and recalls the style of a similar ornament appearing in the cod. Paris gr. 550.[16] Unfortunately, the figures of the frontispiece are so flaked that a stylistic analysis is impossible. Gregory's mantle, however, shows a linear treatment with simple parallel lines, which finds analogies in such works of the twelfth century as the Sinai manuscript of the *Heavenly Ladder* by John Climacus, cod. gr. 418.[17] In addition, a miniature in the Athens psalter, cod. gr. 7, showing John Chrysostom receiving inspiration from Paul, assigned by Xyngopoulos to the twelfth century, must be taken into consideration since it is quite similar in style and iconography to the codex under discussion.[18]

On the basis of these comparisons, a twelfth-century date can be suggested for the manuscript, with Constantinople as its place of origin. This location is indicated by the notices on fols. 3ʳ, 399ʳ, 2ᵛ, and on the back of the cover. On fol. 3ʳ the following notice written in uncial, gold script appears: Κ(ύρι)ε βοήθ(ει) τῷ σῷ δούλ(ῳ) σου Λέοντι τῷ πρ(ωτο)βέστῃ πραι(πο)σίτῳ κ(αὶ) ἐπὶ τοῦ κοιτῶνος τοῦ Κορώνη. 'Αμήν. On fol. 399ʳ, at the bottom of the page there is the following text: 'Εγράφη ἡ παροῦσα βίβλος ὑπὲρ μνήμης σωτηρίας τε καὶ ἀφέσεως τῶν ἁμαρτιῶν Λέοντος τοῦ Χριστιανικωτάτου πρωτοβέστου πραιποσίτου καὶ ἐπὶ τοῦ κοιτῶνος τοῦ Κορώνη. Κ(ύριο)ς δὲ ὁ Χ(ριστὸ)ς καὶ Θ(εὸ)ς ἡμῶν διαφυλάξαι αὐτὸν καὶ ἐλεῆσαι καὶ καταξιῶσαι τῆς ἐπουρανίου αὐτοῦ βασιλείας πάντοτε νῦν καὶ ἀεὶ καὶ εἰς τοὺς αἰῶνας τῶν αἰώνων ἀμήν.

The codex was dedicated to the monastery of Pantocrator by the patriarch of

[14] The figure of 399 folios quoted by Lambros is not correct. A careful examination of the manuscript showed that number 226 was repeated twice and that two pages, one between folios 228 and 229, and another between folios 316 and 317, were left unnumbered.

[15] Frantz, *AB* (1934), pl. xv, 12.

[16] Cf. ornamental headpiece of the cod. Paris gr. 550, fol. 4ᵛ (Fig. 400) with ornament on fol. 97ʳ of the Pantocrator manuscript.

[17] Martin, *Ladder*, pl. LVII, 175.

[18] A. Xyngopoulos, "'Ιωάννης ὁ Χρυσόστομος, Πηγὴ Σοφίας," 'Αρχαιολογικὴ 'Εφημερίς, 81-83 (1942-1944), 17, fig. 5.

Constantinople Νήφων. The relevant text, fol. 2ʳ, reads as follows: Ἡ θεία αὕτη καὶ ἱερὰ βίβλος ἀφιερώθη εἰς τὴν εὐγενεστάτην ἱερὰν βασιλικὴν καὶ πατριαρχικὴν μονὴν τοῦ παντοκράτορος σ(ωτῆ)ρ(ο)ς Χ(ριστ)οῦ τὴν ὄν(?) ἐν τῷ ἄθῳ ὄρει κειμένην παρὰ τοῦ ἐν εὐσεβεῖ τῇ λήξει γενομένου ἀοιδήμου πατριάρχου Κωνσταντινουπόλεως κυρίου Νήφωνος καὶ ὁ θεὸς φυλάξει αὐτὸν ἐν τῇ βασιλείᾳ αὐτοῦ, ἀμήν.

A similar text appears on the inside of the cover. Although there is no indication whether he is Nephon I (1311-1314) or Nephon II (1486-1489, 1497-1498),[19] there can be no doubt that the donor was the latter patriarch since reliable sources make special mention of him as καλλιγράφος and as one who liked to transcribe manuscripts. These sources also state that he was associated with the monastery of Pantocrator, to which he had retreated after spending some time in the monastery of Vatopedi.[20]

Bibliography:
Lambros, I, p. 96.
Vogel-Gardthausen, p. 261.

9. ATHOS, MONASTERY OF STAVRONIKETA, COD. 15. 293 folios, 35.8 x 26 cm., parchment. XII century. (Figs. 431-34)

Contents:
The sixteen homilies of the liturgical edition.

Decoration:

fol. 1ʳ. Within a decorative frame enclosing the title are medallions representing:
the Deesis- Μ(ήτ)ηρ Θ(ε)οῦ, Ἰ(ησοῦ)ς Χ(ριστό)ς, Ἰω(άννης), top bar; Gregory the Theologian- ὁ ἅ(γιος) Γρηγόριος ὁ Θεολόγος left bar; Gregory Thaumaturgos- Γρηγόριος Θαυματουργός, John Chrysostom, Gregory of Nyssa- Γρηγόριος, bottom bar; Basil the Great (?) totally flaked, right bar. Anastasis in initial A; figures of Adam and Eve are flaked (homily 1).

fol. 87ʳ. Nativity in initial X. Scene of the Bathing of the Child flaked (homily 8).

fol. 98ᵛ. Gregory teaching, in initial E (homily 9).

fol. 205ʳ. Bust of Gregory in initial Φ (homily 12).

Style and Date:
The flower-petal ornament, being in a very elegant style, points to the Constantinopolitan school of the twelfth century. A somewhat similar ornament appears in cod. Rome, Barberini gr. 449, dating from the year 1153.[21] The doubling of the ornamental bands, which often appears in the ornament of the Stavroniketa manuscript, is also indicative of a twelfth-century date.

[19] M. Gedeon, Πατριαρχικοὶ Πίνακες, Constantinople 1890, pp. 411, 481ff.

[20] *Ibid.*, p. 489.

[21] Frantz, *AB* (1934), pl. VIII, 11.

The figures are badly flaked, but, since it is in a better state of preservation, the figure of Gregory shows the use of strong highlights on the eyebrows, very like that appearing in twelfth-century manuscripts such as the Homilies on the Virgin by the monk James of Kokkinobaphos.

The Constantinopolitan origin of the manuscript, suggested by the ornament and the color combinations, is confirmed by the closing lines of the codex: ἡ παροῦσα βίβλος ἐτελειώθη ἐν τῇ σεβασμίᾳ βασιλικῇ μονῇ τοῦ ἁγίου Γεωργίου Μαγγάνων παρ᾽ ἐμοῦ τῶν ἱεροδιακόνοις ἐλαχίστου Λουκᾶ μοναχοῦ. As a product of the scriptorium of that famous monastery of the Byzantine capital,[22] the codex is of special importance.

Bibliography:
Lambros, I, p. 76.
Vogel-Gardhausen, p. 268.

10. ATHOS, MONASTERY OF VATOPEDI, COD. 107. 278 folios, 30 x 21 cm., parchment. XI-XII century. (Figs. 316-40)

Contents:
The sixteen homilies of the liturgical edition.

Decoration:
All the miniatures listed below occupy the margins of the manuscript and bear explanatory legends added later.

fol. 1ᵛ. a) A cross and two angels above- ἅγια πάθη του Κ(υρίο)υ π(ατρὸς) ὑμ(ῶν) Ἰ(ησο)ῦ Χ(ριστο)ῦ.

b) Gregory teaching- ὁ ἅγ(ιος) Γρηγόριος ὁ Θεολόγος κηρύττων τὴν οἰκονομίαν τῆς θεότητος τῆς ἐνσάρκου ἐνανθρωπήσεως -on the table of contents.

fol. 4ᵛ. Anastasis- Ἡ ἀνάστασις, ὁ Ἀδάμ, ἡ Ἐβα -(homily 1).

fol. 27ᵛ. a) The Incredulity of Thomas- ἡ ψηλάφησις τοῦ Θωμᾶ ὁ ἅ(γιος) Θωμᾶς, Ἰ(ησοῦ)ς Χ(ριστό)ς. Three unidentified saints.

b) Four spring occupations (birds, sailing, fishing, ploughing) (homily 3).

fol. 28ʳ. Sheep, birds, Mamas seated- ὁ ἅγιος μάμας -(homily 3).

fol. 35ʳ. Pentecost- ἡ πεντηκοστὴ -(homily 4).

fol. 47ᵛ. The city of Zion- πόλις σιών ἱερουσαλήμ -(homily 4).

fol. 48ʳ. The seven Maccabees, Eleazar, Solomone- οἱ ἅγιοι ἑπτὰ παῖδες μακκαβαίοις κ(αὶ) ἡ μ(ήτ)ηρ αὐτ(ῶν) σολομονή κ(αὶ) Ἐλεάζαρ ὁ διδάσκαλος αὐτῶν -(homily 5).

fol. 59ᵛ. Gregory, Cyprian and Justina- ὁ ἅγιος Γρηγόριος ὁ Θεολόγιος χαίρων κ(αὶ) δοξάζων κ(αὶ) μεγαλύνων τ(ὸν) Θεόν ἐπὶ τὸ μαρτύριον τῆς αποτιτος

[22] For the monastery of Μαγγάνων, see R. Janin, *La géographie ecclésiastique de l'empire byzantin,* III (les églises et les monastères), Paris 1953, pp. 75-81.

(?) κ(αὶ) ἀθλήσε(ω)ς τοῦ ἁγίου ἱερομάρτυρ(ο)ς Κυπριανοῦ, ὁ ἅγιος Κυπριανός, κ(αὶ) ἡ ἁγία Ἰουστίνα -(homily 6).

fol. 72ʳ.   The three holy children in the fire, bust of Christ, the prophet Daniel, the fire, the city of Babylon- οἱ ἅγιοι τρεῖς παῖδες κ(αὶ) ὁ προφήτης Δανιήλ, ἡ κάμινος, ἡ Βαβυλών -(homily 7).

fol. 82ᵛ.   The Virgin seated, Christ-Emmanuel, two angels, the city of Nazareth- Μ(ήτη)ρ Θ(εο)ῦ ἡ ὁδηγήτρια. Ἐν κλίνη κατακοιμε τῇ ἁμαρτία, εἰς ἄδην βυθίζομαι κολαστηρίως ἀλλά σύ τῇ κραταιά δίδου μοι χεῖρα. καὶ τάχους βοῶ λύτρωσον Παναγία. ἁμαρτωλοῦ ἀλεξίου τοῦ τάχατε μοναχοῦ τοῦ νομάτη τοῦ δουκαίτη. Ἰ(ησοῦ)ς Χ(ριστὸ)ς ὁ ἐμανουήλ.

Θεογενές βλάστιμα ἐκ τῆς παρθένου Κύριος ὁ Θεός ὢν ὁ Κτίστης τῶν πάντων θέλων σαρκοφόρον μορφήν . . . τὸν πάλαι πτώσει πτωθέντα ἀδάμ σώσαι.

Between the angels: οἱ ἄγγελοι τρέμουσιν βρέφος κράτιτε προβλέπει μόνον μητρικαῖς ἐναγγάλαις -(end of homily 8).

fol. 93ᵛ.   The Baptism of Christ- Βάπτησις τοῦ Κ(υρί)ου ἡμῶν Ἰησοῦ Χριστοῦ- (homily 10).

fol. 105ᵛ.   Christ baptizing Peter. Two other saints below- ἐβαπτίζετο ὁ Πέτρος ὑπὸ τοῦ Κυρίου ἡμῶν Ἰ(ησοῦ) Χ(ριστοῦ) -(homily 11).

fol. 135ᵛ.   The Koimesis of Basil the Great- (ἐ)ξώδιον ἀστικοῦ ὕμνου ἐνταφιάζετε ὁ μέγας Βασίλειος παρά τοῦ Ἁγίου Γρηγορίου Θεολόγου- (end of homily 11).

fol. 136ʳ.   The city of Caesarea- Πόλις Καισάρεια -(homily 9).

fol. 188ᵛ.   Gregory and two groups of people (homily 9).

fol. 189ʳ.   Gregory, his father and the city of Nazianzus- ὁ π(ατ)ὴρ τοῦ Θεολόγου. Ἡ πόλις ναζιανζοῦ -(homily 15).

fol. 203ᵛ.   Gregory of Nazianzus and Gregory of Nyssa in proskynesis, the city of Nyssa- Ἰ(ησοῦ)ς Χ(ριστό)ς, πνευματικῆς ὁμιλίας προσφέρει ὁ ἅγιος Γρηγόριος ὁ Θεολόγος μετὰ τοῦ ἁγίου Γρηγορίου τῆς νίσης ἀδελφοῦ τοῦ ἁγίου Βασιλείου. Πόλις νισαέων -(homily 12).

fol. 208ᵛ.   Gregory teaching- (Δια)λεχθείς ὁ μέγας Γρηγόριος ὁ Θεολόγος μὲ τούς ρν̅ ἐπισκόπους παρετούμενος τόν θρόνον τοῦ πατριάρχου Κωνσταντινουπόλεως ἐκβάς ἔξω τοῦ κάστρου πρὸς ἀναχώρησιν ἀπέρχεται κλαίοντες καὶ θρηνοῦντες οἱ τῆς πόλεως. This legend was written by a different hand (homily 14).

fol. 209ʳ.   The patriarchal throne, the city of Constantinople- Κων(σταντινού)-πολις. Ὁ Θρόνος, ὁ πατριαρχικός -(homily 14).

fol. 226ᵛ.   The Koimesis of Athanasius of Alexandria- ἐνταφιάζετε ὁ ἅγιος ἀθανάσιος παρά τοῦ ἁγίου Γρηγορίου τοῦ Θεολόγου, ἐξώδιον ὕμνον. Ἅγ(ιος) Ἀθανάσιος -(homily 13).

216

fol. 227ʳ.   The city of Alexandria- ᾿Αλεξάνδρεια -(homily 13).

fol. 248ᵛ.   Christ blesses the distribution of bread to the poor- ᾿Ι(ησοῦ)ς Χ(ριστὸ)ς ὁ φοβερός κριτής ὁ κρίνων δικαιοσύνην καὶ καλῶν τούς ἐλεήμονας
εἰς τὸν κλῆρον τῶν δικαίων τῆς βασιλείας οὐρανῶν.

Then follows Matt. 25: 34-36, 40 and these lines:

φιλόχριστοι οἱ τοὺς ἄρτους προσφέροντες (εἰς) τράπεζαν ἐλεημοσύνης
προστεθέντες βαστάζοντες τούς κοφίνους. Χειροδηγούμενοι οἱ τυφλοί καὶ
οἱ τῆς ἱερᾶς νοσουσῶν ἀδελφοί καὶ ἀδελφαί ἡμῶν λαμβάνοντες ἐλεημοσύ-
νην παρά τῶν φιλοχρίστων -(end of homily 13).

fol. 277ʳ.   St. Demetrius, St. George, and two other saints, drawn in ink by a
later hand.

fol. 277ᵛ.   The Virgin of Blachernae- ἡ Παναγία, ᾿Ι(ησοῦ)ς Χ(ριστό)ς.

fol. 278ʳ.   Christ, a half figure of a saint and a standing bishop, drawn by a
later hand.

Style and Date:

The codex was not originally intended to be illustrated. This explains the extensive
use of the margins and misplacements in the sequence of the miniatures. The illustrations are composed of black contours tinted with pale greenish and brownish washes.

The earlier miniatures (by far the largest group) are the work of an artist so
primitive that stylistic analysis is extremely difficult. There are two illustrations,
fols. 4ᵛ and 227ᵛ, which have some stylistic merit, probably due to their model. A
characteristic detail is the zigzag edge of the garments which conveys the impression
of hard material. This finds parallels in works of Palaeologan times.[23] But such a date
cannot be proposed on this criterion alone. Palaeographically, the codex can be
assigned to the eleventh or twelfth century. How much later this set of miniatures
was added we do not know. Perhaps the addition was made in the twelfth century.

The inscriptions for these earlier miniatures were written by one hand, which con-
sistently used red capitals and repeated the same errors in spelling. The pictures on
fols. 277ʳ and 278ʳ are drawn in ink, evidently by another hand and at a much later
date. The iconography of the saints on fol. 277ʳ points to the same conclusion. The
miniature of St. Demetrius with his armor hanging from his left shoulder could date
from a period no earlier than the fifteenth century. In fact, it is of a much later date,
for it is reminiscent of the military saints depicted on the walls of the Athos monasteries, such as those of Lavra painted by Theophanes in 1535.[24] A seventeenth-century
date, however, seems the most probable for these two miniatures since the motif of
the shield hanging from the shoulder finds its closest analogies in works, chiefly icons,
of the seventeenth century.[25]

[23] Cf. cod. Paris gr. 543, infra, no. 26.

[24] G. Millet, *Les monuments de l'Athos. La
Peinture*, Paris 1927, pl. 139, 3-4. For the motif
of the saint with the shield on his left shoulder
after the fourteenth century, see A. Protich, "Un

model des maîtres bulgares du xv et du xvi
siècles," *Recueil N. P. Kondakov, Seminarium
Kondakovianum*, Prague 1926, p. 101.

[25] D. Talbot Rice, G. Millet, *The Icons of Cyprus*, Oxford 1937, p. 238, pl. xxxii, 79.

Bibliography:

Eustratiades-Arcadios, *Catalogue Vatopedi*, p. 29.

R. L. McGrath, "The Martyrdom of the Maccabees on the Brescia Casket," *AB*, 47 (1965), pp. 259, 260, fig. 5.

11. FLORENCE, BIBLIOTECA LAURENZIANA, COD. PLUT. VII, 24. 265 folios, 19.8 x 14.5 cm., parchment. *Anno* 1091. (Fig. 97)

Contents:

The sixteen homilies of the liturgical edition.

Decoration:

> fol. 3ᵛ.   The author portrait- ὁ ἅγιος Γρηγόριος ὁ Θεολόγος.

Style and Date:

The quality of the only miniature in this codex is high indeed. The skillful use of highlights adds to the figure an otherworldly quality, which is intensified by the successful combination of colors and the rhythm of line. The saint has a very expressive face. His eyes are deeply set, his forehead made prominent by the use of highlights, and the elongation of his nose is intensified by the unbroken line of light and the dark contour which defines it, while the face is rendered "concave" by the same technique. The hand of the artist seems to be very steady. He likes details, but not mannerisms. He probably copied a good model of the Macedonian Renaissance, although the miniature has lost part of the corporeality of the original. The manuscript was written in the year 1091, as the following colophon indicates: Ἐγράφη ἡ βίβλος αὕτη τοῦ Θεολόγου μηνὶ Ἀπριλίῳ ἰνδικτιῶνος τεσσαρεσκαιδεκάτης, ἔτους ἑξακισ-χιλιοστοῦ πεντακοσιοστοῦ ἐνενηκοστοῦ ἐνάτου, χειρὶ Εὐθυμίου μοναχοῦ ἁμαρτωλοῦ τοῦ Ξιφιλίνου οὗ ταῖς πολλαῖς ἁμαρτίαις ἵλεων γενέσθαι τὸν φιλάνθρωπον ἡμῶν Κύριον καὶ Θεὸν Ἰησοῦν τὸν Χριστόν, οἱ ἀναγινώσκοντες εὔξασθαι μὴ ὀκνήσετε· δώη δὲ καὶ ὑμῖν αὐτὸς ἄφεσιν τῶν πταισμάτων ὑμῶν, ἀμήν. Although in this colophon there is no indication of the scriptorium which produced the manuscript, the highly artistic quality of the execution and the skillful subtlety of colors point once again to Constantinople.

Bibliography:

Bandini, I, pp. 275, 276.

L. S. Lefort, J. Cochen, *Palaeographisches Album*, Leuven 1932, pl. 93.

12. FLORENCE, BIBLIOTECA LAURENZIANA, COD. PLUT. VII, 32. 191 folios, 22.4 x 18.8 cm., parchment. XI-XII century. (Figs. 261-74)

Contents:

The sixteen homilies of the liturgical edition.

Decoration:

The positioning of the miniatures within each homily varies. Some are of one-column width while others extend to two columns, and they are placed at either the top or the bottom of the column. Their exact position is indicated in the list below.

fol. 1ʳ.　A later page dated after the fifteenth century, the original beginning of the codex being lost.

fol. 2ᵛ.　Completely flaked figure bowing, bottom of left column (homily 1).

fol. 14ᵛ.　Mamas standing between lambs; Mamas milking, top of left column (homily 3).

fol. 18ᵛ.　Pentecost, in the right column (homily 4).

fol. 26ʳ.　Athanasius of Alexandria- ὁ ῞Αγιος ᾿Αθανάσιος, bottom left column (homily 13).

fol. 40ʳ.　Seven Maccabees, Solomone and Eleazar before Antiochus, in the right column (homily 5).

fol. 48ʳ.　Gregory of Nazianzus and St. Cyprian holding a discussion, top of left column (homily 6).

fol. 56ʳ.　Gregory of Nazianzus and Julian the Tax Collector as writers, top of right column (homily 7).

fol. 63ʳ.　Nativity, including the Bathing of the Child, top of left column. Below, within the decorative frame enclosing the title, Gregory teaching a group of people, top of left column (homily 8).

fol. 70ʳ.　The Koimesis of Basil the Great, over both columns (homily 9).

fol. 110ᵛ.　Gregory teaching, the Baptism of Christ, over both columns (homily 10).

fol. 120ʳ.　Teaching scene, over both columns (homily 11).

fol. 145ʳ.　Gregory of Nazianzus and Gregory of Nyssa in proskynesis, over both columns (homily 12).

fol. 149ʳ.　Gregory addressing two groups of seated bishops, over both columns (homily 14).

fol. 162ʳ.　Teaching scene, over both columns (homily 15).

fol. 181ʳ.　Gregory teaching, top of right column (homily 16).

Style and Date:

The manuscript contains no textual indication of its provenance, but the artistic quality of the miniatures and the clarity of the colors suggest the area of Constantinople. Although parts of some miniatures are flaked, the golden backgrounds still reflect their own light on the pale blue, violet, brown, and red of the garments. In several instances the gold of the background is repeated on the gold covers of the books that the saints hold. The bright red tiles of roofs and the vivid blue curtains hanging from the doors of narrow buildings give an earthly touch to the eternity of the backgrounds. Such a combination of colors and the skillful transition from one nuance to another are traits of Constantinopolitan manuscripts.

The title of each homily, which is sometimes repeated at the end of the sermon, is in gold and is very decorative, and it seems that to a certain extent these titles are substitutions for the real ornament. Yet, in addition to the blue palmettes placed in the corners of the miniatures' frames, there is a flower-petal style ornament in some of the decorative frames which enclose the titles. This ornament is typical of the late eleventh century. A similar one may be found in cod. Moscow, Bibl. Univ. 2, dating from the year 1092.[26] The palmettes of the Florence manuscript are like those appearing in another Constantinopolitan manuscript, the cod. Paris Coislin 79, dated between the years 1078 and 1081.[27] Moreover, some stylistic observations may help us to be more precise. In the garments of the figures of the Florence manuscript, there is an apparent schematization which at times achieves a decorative effect. In almost all the miniatures the folds of the garment of the seated and standing figures form a pronounced spiral motif on the upper part of the leg. This is most pronounced on folios 110^v and 149^r. This motif appears, but with less decorative effect, in the Athos psalter Pantocrator 49, the Easter tables of which begin with the year 1084.[28] If, on the other hand, one compares the miniatures of the Florence codex with those of the Gospel book in the Vatican, cod. Urb. gr. 2, which can be dated between the years 1119 and 1143, one realizes that the schematization of the garments in the latter has been increased.[29] This means that the Florence manuscript must be dated either in the last years of the eleventh century or the very beginning of the twelfth.

Bibliography:

Bandini, I, p. 293, pl. IV, 5.

F. Buslaiev, *Obscisja ponjatija o russkom ikonopisie*, 1866, p. 98.

Kondakov, *Histoire*, pp. 98, 99.

Millet, *Recherches*, pp. 176 n. 8, 205 n. 3, 207 n. 8.

Ebersolt, *Miniature*, p. 38 n. 3.

Tikkanen, *Farbengebung*, p. 128.

T. Lodi, S. Vagaggini eds., *Mostra della Biblioteca di Lorenzo nella Biblioteca Medicea Laurenziana 1949*, Florence 1949, No. 13.

K. Weitzmann, "Zur byzantinischen Quelle des Wolfenbüttler Musterbuches," *Festschrift Hans R. Hahnloser*, Basel-Stuttgart 1961, p. 248, fig. 23.

13. ISTANBUL, LIBRARY OF THE ECUMENICAL PATRIARCHATE, COD. 16. 274 folios, 31.5 x 24 cm., parchment. XI century. (Figs. 61-77)

Contents:

The sixteen homilies of the liturgical edition.

Decoration:

      fol. 2^v.   The author portrait- ὁ ἅγιος Γρηγόριος ὁ Θεολόγος.

      fol. 3^r.   Anastasis in initial A (homily 1).

      fol. 5^v.   The author portrait and hand of God in initial E (homily 2).

[26] Frantz, *AB* (1934), pl. VIII, 2.

[27] *Ibid.*, pl. XXI, 16.

[28] Weitzmann, *Lectionary Morgan 639*, p. 359; cf. *idem, Joshua*, pp. 75ff.

[29] Stornajolo, *Giacomo monaco*, pls. 83-93.

fol. 27ʳ.   Gregory seated, Mamas standing, hand of God, all in initial E (homily 3).

fol. 33ʳ.   Pentecost in initial Π (homily 4).

fol. 45ʳ.   Medallions containing the seven Maccabees, Solomone, and Eleazar in initial T (homily 5).

fol. 56ʳ.   Cyprian and Justina holding scrolls over fire (homily 6).

fol. 68ʳ.   Gregory teaching, Julian standing, in initial T (homily 7).

fol. 78ᵛ.   Nativity, including the Bathing of the Child, in initial X (homily 8).

fol. 89ᵛ.   Gregory reading sermon over the body of Basil, in initial E (homily 9).

fol. 144ᵛ. The Baptism of Christ in initial Π (homily 10).

fol. 156ᵛ. The Baptism of Christ in initial X (homily 11).

fol. 189ᵛ. Gregory of Nazianzus and Gregory of Nyssa in proskynesis in initial Φ (homily 12).

fol. 194ᵛ. Athanasius of Alexandria as writer, Gregory teaching, in initial A (homily 13).

fol. 234ᵛ. Gregory addressing the bishops in initial Π (homily 14).

fol. 243ᵛ. Gregory giving alms, in initial A (homily 15).

fol. 261ʳ. Gregory teaching, in initial T (homily 16).

Style and Date:

The manuscript contains only figured initials and ornamental headpieces. These initials present stylistic affinities with those of the cod. Vat. gr. 463, dating from the year 1062.[30] A common trait of both manuscripts is the flattened look of the figures and an emphasis on line with a tendency toward a certain patternizing effect, which is apparent to a lesser degree in the Patriarchal manuscript.[31] The patterned and incorporeal effect comes to the fore in both manuscripts, particularly because of the constant use of gold highlights in the drapery. This use of highlights was a characteristic of the scriptorium of the monastery of Studios. Today, however, it is assumed that other Constantinopolitan scriptoria might have had the same characteristic and this manuscript cannot therefore be ascribed to that particular scriptorium.[32]

The similarities between both manuscripts do not end here since the range of colors is common to both codices. One distinction should be made however: at times the Patriarchal codex shows a tendency toward dark colors, especially ranges of brown, for the drapery. In the portrait of the author the color reaches the point of being somber. In other cases the illustrator of the Patriarchal codex chooses ranges of blue against which the gold highlights are very effective. There are miniatures, such as the initial of the homily of New Sunday, in which the color plays a symphony of light blue and violet.

In the ornament the colors become very vivid and gay. The pattern and the freshness of color is similar in both manuscripts, but the ornament of the Patriarchal codex

---

[30] Infra, no. 31.

[31] Cf. cod. Istanbul, Patr. 16, fol. 144ᵛ (Fig. 71),

with cod. Vat. gr. 463, fol. 107ʳ (Fig. 82).

[32] Infra, no. 31.

is simpler and points to a slightly earlier date, perhaps in the middle of the eleventh century. This slightly earlier date agrees with the evidence of the style—already discussed—and with that of the palaeography. I cannot, therefore, accept the tenth-century date proposed by Tsakopoulos.

Bibliography:

A. Tsakopoulos, "Περιγραφικὸς κατάλογος τῶν χειρογράφων τῆς Βιβλιοθήκης τοῦ Οἰκουμενικοῦ Πατριαρχείου," Ὀρθοδοξία, 25 (1950), pp. 225ff, and figs.

A. Marava-Chatzinikolaou, Ὁ Ἅγιος Μάμας, Athens 1953, p. 91.

14. JERUSALEM, GREEK PATRIARCHAL LIBRARY, COD. SABAS 258. 243 folios, 25.6 x 18.9 cm., parchment. XII century. (Fig. 429)

Contents:

The codex in its present state contains:

1) fourteen of the homilies of the liturgical edition (homilies 6 and 16 are missing, and homily 15 is incomplete);

2) one of the homilies of the complete edition, i.e. Ἀπολογητικὸς τῆς εἰς τὸν Πόντον φυγῆς fols. 4ʳ-38ʳ (*PG*, 35, 407-514);

3) grammatical exercises in fols. 234-243 which were added much later as substitutes for the original folios.

Decoration:

     fol. 1ᵛ.   The author portrait.

Style and Date:

No colophon has been preserved and the only miniature is badly flaked. The flatness of the figure, the linear treatment of the drapery, the repetitious motifs in the background buildings, and even the iconographic motif of the inspiring figure find analogies in another codex of Gregory's homilies, the cod. Athos, Pantocrator 31.[33] The twelfth-century date suggested for the Athos codex can be proposed for the Sabas codex too.

The codex does not have the richness of the Constantinopolitan manuscripts, yet the few ornamental bands which appear at the head of some of the homilies suggest, from the point of view of both pattern and color, Constantinople or its artistic area as the place of origin.

Bibliography:

Papadopoulos-Kerameus, II, pp. 383, 384.

15. JERUSALEM, GREEK PATRIARCHAL LIBRARY COD. TAPHOU, 14. 314 folios, 31.8-32.0 x 23.8-25.5 cm., parchment. XI century. (Figs. 98-122)

Contents:

1) The sixteen homilies of the liturgical edition, fols. 1-91ᵛ, 114ʳ-306ᵛ.

[33] Supra, no. 8.

2) One homily on the Birth of Christ, inserted between the eighth and ninth homilies of Gregory, fols. 92ʳ-113ᵛ, formerly ascribed to St. John of Damascus, but now ascribed by most scholars to John of Euboea (*PG*, 96, 1435-50).³⁴

3) The commentary of Pseudo-Nonnos, fols. 307ʳ-313ᵛ.

Decoration:

fol. 2ᵛ.	The author portrait.
fol. 3ʳ.	Anastasis (homily 1).
fol. 6ʳ.	The so-called vision of Habakkuk (homily 2).
fol. 9ʳ.	The fallen Heosphoros, in the margin (homily 2).
fol. 11ʳ.	a) Adam in Paradise. b) The death of the first man. Both in the margin (homily 2).
fol. 27ʳ.	Mamas, milking, sought by a soldier (homily 3).

fols. 33ʳ-34ᵛ have supplementary marginal illustrations for homily 3.

fol. 33ʳ.	a) Sheep grazing, mowing of grass. b) Sailing boat. c) Ploughing.
fol. 33ᵛ.	a) Fishing scene. b) A shepherd and a herdsman playing their pipes. c) Man pruning a tree, bird hunter.
fol. 34ʳ.	a) Two trees and three beehives from which bees are emerging. b) In a landscape setting with trees and birds, one figure sleeping and another eating.
fol. 34ᵛ.	A trotting horse.
fol. 35ʳ.	Pentecost (homily 4).
fol. 47ʳ.	King Antiochus seated, two executioners pulling a wheel bearing one of the Maccabees, another Maccabee prone beneath it, Solomone, Eleazar, and the five other Maccabees (homily 5).
fol. 58ʳ.	Gregory pointing out Cyprian to a group of people (homily 6).
fol. 70ʳ.	Gregory and Julian the Tax Collector as writers (homily 7).
fol. 81ʳ.	Nativity, including the Bathing of the Child and the Adoration of the Magi (homily 8).

fols. 92ʳ-112ᵛ contain 56 illustrations for the homily on the Nativity by John of Euboea.

fol. 92ʳ.	John of Damascus writing, and a group of monks.
fol. 96ʳ.	The Flight into Egypt.
fol. 97ᵛ.	Nativity.
fol. 98ᵛ.	a) The Journey of the Magi. b) The Adoration of the Magi. c) The Lacedaemonian Attalus and Dorias.
fol. 99ʳ.	Dorias killing Attalus.
fol. 99ᵛ.	a) The Achaeans and the priestess Euopia. b) The Castalian spring.
fol. 100ʳ.	Priestess of Athena.
fol. 101ʳ.	The Tripod of Delphi.

³⁴ O. Bardenhewer, *Geschichte der altkirchlichen Literatur*, V, Freiburg in Breisgau 1932, p. 142.

fol. 101ᵛ. Kyrus consulting the gods.

fol. 103ʳ. The destruction of the idols.

fol. 104ᵛ. a) Herodes and the Magi. b) The Journey of the Magi. c) The Arrival of the Magi at Jerusalem.

fol. 105ʳ. The Magi conversing with the Israelites, in three scenes.

fol. 106ʳ. The Adoration of the Magi.

fol. 106ᵛ. a) Luke painting the Virgin. b) The Magi, a Persian and the icon of the Virgin. c) The Virgin and the Magi holding Jesus.

fol. 107ʳ. a) The Virgin seated, and the Magi, one of them holding Jesus. b) The Virgin holding Jesus and speaking to the Magi.

fol. 107ᵛ. a) The angel telling the Magi to depart. b) The departure of the Magi.

fol. 108ʳ. a) The journey of the Levite and the youth. b) The city Gibeon. c) The Levite and the youth entering the city and meeting the concubine.

fol. 109ᵛ. a) A house and a group of people. b) The same house and its owner sending out the concubine.

fol. 110ʳ. a) The dead concubine lying outside the house. b) The Levite and the youth mourning the concubine. c) The transference of her body.

fol. 110ᵛ. a) The body of the concubine on a table and a youth with a spear. b) Council of Israelites against the tribe of Benjamin. c) Gibeonites pursuing the Israelites.

fol. 111ʳ. a) The Israelites preparing for a new attack. b) The mourning of the Israelites in Bethel.

fol. 111ᵛ. a) Attack of the Israelites against the Sabeonites. b) The destruction of the city.

fol. 112ʳ. The Massacre of the Innocents.

fol. 112ᵛ. a) Angels worshiping Mary and Child. b) Five shepherds. c) The Magi adoring the Virgin.

fol. 114ʳ. The Koimesis of Basil the Great (homily 9).

fol. 173ʳ. The Baptism of Christ (homily 10).

fol. 186ʳ. Teaching scene (homily 11).

fol. 219ᵛ. Gregory of Nazianzus and Gregory of Nyssa in proskynesis (homily 12).

fol. 224ᵛ. Gregory pointing out Athanasius of Alexandria to a group of people (homily 12).

fol. 247ʳ. Gregory addressing the bishops (homily 14).

fol. 265ʳ. Gregory taking leave, in the margin (homily 14).

fol. 265ᵛ. Gregory and the poor (homily 15).

fol. 292ʳ. Gregory pointing out his father to a group of people (homily 16).

fol. 307ᵛ-313ʳ contain 17 miniatures illustrating the text of Pseudo-Nonnos.

fol. 307ᵛ. Pelops and Oenomaos.

fol. 308ʳ. a) Artemis and Actaeon. b) Chiron and Achilles.

fol. 308ᵛ. Gyges and Candales.

fol. 309ʳ. Midas.

fol. 309ᵛ. a) Bellerophon. b) Alpheus and Arethusa.

fol. 310ʳ. a) Orestes and Pylades. b) Minos and Rhadamanthys.

fol. 310ᵛ. The birth of Zeus.

fol. 311ʳ. The birth of Dionysus.

fol. 311ᵛ. Mausolus of Caria and the Colossus of Rhodes.

fol. 312ʳ. a) The birth of Athena. b) Hecate.

fol. 312ᵛ. Oak of Dodona.

fol. 313ʳ. a) The goat of Mendes. b) Egyptian gods.

Style and Date:

The ornament is very simple, consisting primarily of narrow bands which form the rectangular frames of the title miniatures. The palmettes which decorate these frames are of typical Constantinopolitan style.

There is no colophon to indicate the manuscript's date and provenance. A note once existing on fol. 306ᵛ is no longer visible, but the nature of the applied ornament and the excellent quality of the miniatures suggest a Constantinopolitan origin. The style of the miniatures is homogeneous. A hieratic spirit is reflected in all scenes. More specifically, the miniatures have the dry elegance of the late eleventh century art of the capital. The bodies, with a few exceptions, are thin, without volume or firm stance. The faces are elongated, having a vivid expression which in most cases is the same. The modeling of the faces is achieved by a subtle gradation of tones and by the brightness of color that is typical of Constantinopolitan school. The classical combinations of blue and red are preferred here. The feet are disproportionately small. An emphasis on lines is evident, especially in the folds of the garments, which do not show the fullness of the body underneath. These characteristics began to appear in the second half of the eleventh century, and indeed the Jerusalem manuscript presents stylistic similarities to the Princeton Climax, Univ. Lib., Garrett cod. 16, which is dated 1081.[35]

A comparison of the two, however, shows that in the Jerusalem codex the figures reveal a feeling for corporeality and some of them better reflect their classical models of the Macedonian Renaissance.[36] Thus a slightly earlier date for the Jerusalem manuscript is justifiable and becomes all the more likely when one compares its miniatures to those in the Theodore Psalter (British Museum, cod. Add. 19352) dating from the year 1066. Although in the latter codex one can detect the styles of various models, some of the better preserved miniatures show features in common with the miniatures of the Jerusalem codex. For example, a comparison of the miniatures on fol. 187ᵛ of the psalter, and more particularly of the group showing the youth and the virgins,

---

[35] Martin, *Ladder*, p. 175.

[36] Cf., for example, the angels in cod. Jerusalem, Taphou 14, fols. 6ʳ and 81ʳ (Figs. 100, 113), with those of the Climax manuscript, fols. 76ʳ, 63ᵛ, and 94ʳ, reproduced in Martin, *Ladder*, pls. xi, 36, 38; xii, 45.

with the group of listeners in the miniature on fol. 58^r of the Jerusalem manuscript, shows the same slenderness in the figures, and a similarity in the prominent necks, treatment of hair, and arrangement of figures. The relationship of the drapery to the body seems to be more successful in the Jerusalem miniature. Moreover, a comparison of any of the apostles in the Pentecost scene in the Jerusalem codex (fol. 35^r) with the figure of David in the London psalter (fol. 65^v) demonstrates that the latter figure, both in stance and treatment of drapery, is less sophisticated and has greater clarity and simplicity. Although the touch of different artists may account for some of these details, such details nevertheless suggest that the two manuscripts should be dated not far from each other. Therefore the chronological termini of the Jerusalem manuscript can be set at A.D. 1066 and 1081.

Bibliography:

Papadopoulos-Kerameus, I, pp. 45-65, pls. 2, 3.

N. P. Kondakov, *Arkheologicheskoe puteshestvie po Sirii i Palestine*, St. Petersburg 1904, pp. 281-83, 296.

Schlumberger, *Epopée*, III, figs. pp. 32, 33, 37, 117, 125.

Diehl, *Manuel*, II, p. 626, figs. 300-3.

W. H. P. Hatch, *Greek and Syrian Miniatures in Jerusalem*, Cambridge, Mass. 1931, pp. 58-75, pls. I-XVIII.

Der Nersessian, *Barlaam*, p. 62.

Millet. *Dalmatique*, pp. 51ff.

Lazarev, *History*, I, pp. 108, 312, 313; II, pls. 123, 130.

Weitzmann, *Roll*, p. 147.

Idem, the Fresco Cycle of S. Maria di Castelseprio, Princeton 1951, pp. 38, 39.

Idem, Mythology, see index.

A. Marava-Chatzinikolaou, Ὁ Ἅγιος Μάμας, Athens 1953, pp. 88, 89.

K. Weitzmann, *Ancient Book Illumination*, Cambridge, Mass. 1959, pp. 58, 96ff; pls. XXX, 67; XLIX, 103.

Idem, "Zur byzantinischen Quelle des Wolfenbüttler Musterbuches," *Festschrift Hans R. Hahnloser*, Basel-Stuttgart 1961, p. 232, fig. 9.

Idem, "The Survival of Mythological Representations in Early Christian and Byzantine Art . . . ," *Dumbarton Oaks Papers*, 14 (1960), pp. 52, 53, fig. 13.

S. Der Nersessian, "The Homilies of Gregory of Nazianzus, Paris gr. 510," *Dumbarton Oaks Papers*, 16 (1962), pp. 202 n. 22, 215 n. 89, n. 90, 226 n. 139.

K. Weitzmann, *Geistige Grundlagen und Wesen der Makedonischen Renaissance*, Köln-Opladen 1963, pp. 17, 18, pl. 8.

Byzantine Art, an European Art, 9th Exhibition of the Council of Europe, 2nd ed., Athens 1964, p. 334.

M. Chatzidakis, A. Grabar, *Byzantine and Early Medieval Painting*, London 1965, p. 18, fig. 94.

K. Weitzmann, "Byzantine Miniature and Icon Painting in the Eleventh Century," *Proceedings of the XIIIth Inter. Congress of Byzantine Studies, Oxford 1966*, London 1967, p. 217, pl. 27.

16. LONDON, BRITISH MUSEUM, COD. ADD. 24381. 236 folios, 17.7 x 12.9 cm.,[37] parchment. *Anno* 1088. (Figs. 94-96)

Contents:

This codex, which once contained the sixteen homilies of the liturgical edition, is now imperfect and incomplete. The beginnings of most of the orations have been torn out, probably for the sake of the miniatures.

Decoration:

fol. 2ʳ.   Church and Synagogue- Κυριακὴ τῶν ἐγκαινίων -(homily 3).

fol. 41ᵛ.   The seven Maccabees between Solomone and Eleazar- οἱ ἅγιοι Μακκα-βαῖοι σὺν Ἐλεαζάρῳ καὶ τῇ μητρὶ αὐτῶν -(homily 5).

fol. 52ʳ.   Christ enthroned, flanked by Gregory and Cyprian; Justina in prayer- ὁ ἅγιος Γρηγόριος, Ἰ(ησοῦ)ς Χ(ριστό)ς, ὁ ἅγιος Κυπριαν(ός), ἡ ἁγία (Ἰουστίνα) -(homily 6).

Style and Date:

A colophon was on the original wooden cover and was copied by the officials of the British Museum as follows: τὸ παρόν βιβλιον υπαρχει τῆς μονης του αγιου πρωτο-μαρτυρος και αρχιδιακονου στεφάνου εἰς την πογωνιανη(ν), και ειναι αφόυ της εγράφι ἕως τὴν σήμερον χρόνοι πεντακόσιοι ὀγδόη(κο)ντα και εινε του ἁγίου Γρηγοριου του Θεολογου διδαχαις πανυ αρχαιες (?), εγραψα (ταυ)την (?) σημ(ερ)ον αχξη (1088) εγω ο εντελης σφαντζος (?) διὰ νὰ φαίνεται εἰς δόξαν Θεοῦ. ἀμήν. The copyist, who was attempting to reproduce an ancient handwriting, may have made some palaeographical errors. Nevertheless, the figure style of the manuscript agrees with the date of the colophon and therefore the given date may well be the correct one.

The date given in the colophon can also be confirmed by the ornament. That of fol. 2ʳ, for instance is similar to that of fol. 1ʳ of the cod. Paris, Coislin 79, dated between the years 1078 and 1087.[38] The monastery of St. Stephen in Pogoniane (province of Τροιζήν in Argolis), mentioned in the colophon, is not necessarily the place of origin of the codex.

Bibliography:

Catalogue of additions to the manuscripts in the British Museum in the years MDCCCLIV-MDCCCLXXV, II, London 1877, p. 61.

K. and S. Lake eds., *Dated Greek Minuscule Manuscripts to the Year 1200*, II, Boston 1934, p. 16, pl. 132.

---

[37] The margins have been restored so that the original height and width can no longer be determined.

[38] Omont, *Min. gr.* (1929), pl. LXI.

17. MILAN, BIBLIOTECA AMBROSIANA, COD. G 88 SUP. (GR. 416). 292 folios, 30.8 x 22 cm., parchment. XII century. (Figs. 299-315)

Contents:

The sixteen homilies of the liturgical edition.

Decoration:

fol. 3ᵛ.   Teaching scene.

fol. 4ʳ.   Anastasis in initial A (homily 1).

fol. 7ʳ.   Habakkuk in initial E, angel and labarum- ἀββακοὺμ ὁ προφήτης- (homily 2).

fol. 29ʳ.   Gregory in initial E (homily 3).

fol. 36ᵛ.   Pentecost (homily 4).

fol. 48ʳ.   Gregory in initial T (homily 16).

fol. 63ʳ.   The seven Maccabees, Eleazar, and Solomone, in initial T (homily 5).

fol. 73ʳ.   Gregory and Cyprian in initial M (homily 6).

fol. 85ʳ.   Gregory in initial T (homily 7).

fol. 95ʳ.   Nativity, including the Bathing of the Child, in initial X (homily 8).

fol. 105ʳ.   Gregory of Nazianzus and Gregory of Nyssa mourning Basil the Great, in initial E (homily 9).

fol. 163ʳ.   The Baptism of Christ in initial Π (homily 10).

fol. 176ᵛ.   Baptism, liturgical scene (homily 11).

fol. 213ʳ.   Christ, Gregory of Nazianzus and Gregory of Nyssa, in initial Φ (homily 12).

fol. 220ʳ.   Gregory of Nazianzus giving a book to Athanasius of Alexandria- Ὁ ἅγιος Γρηγόριος ὁ Θεολόγος. Ὁ ἅγιος Ἀθανάσιος- (homily 13).

fol. 245ʳ.   Gregory addressing the bishops in initial Π (homily 14).

fol. 264ᵛ.   Gregory discoursing on the poor (homily 15).

Style and Date:

The ornament of the manuscript finds analogies in that of twelfth-century manuscripts such as the cod. Athos, Vatopedi 960, dated in A.D. 1128 and that of the Sinai Climax cod. 418, for which a twelfth-century date has been postulated on stylistic grounds.[39] The main characteristic of the miniatures of the Gregory codex is a softness of modeling which contrasts with the use of highlights in other cases. Despite the soft modeling, the human figures have an uncertainty of stance which is the more pronounced because of the unlifelike feet and flattened drapery. These traits find parallels in twelfth-century manuscripts such as the Sinai Climax quoted above.[40] The mannered treatment of the chair on which Gregory sits on fol. 3ᵛ should also be noted. This kind

---

[39] K. and S. Lake eds., *Dated Greek Minuscule Manuscripts to the year 1200*, III, Boston 1935, pp. 14, 15, pl. 196; Martin, *Ladder*, pl. LXXIV,

210, 212.

[40] Cf. Martin, *Ladder*, pls. LXVI, 192; LXXVI, 214.

of treatment appears in twelfth-century manuscripts and recalls a somewhat similarly mannered chair in the miniature of the author portrait in the cod. Oxford, Canon. gr. 103. The twelfth-century date which I propose on the basis of these observations agrees also with the palaeography of the text, for which the same date seems most probable. The color is dark and muddy, but at times it shows the delicacy of the capital (cf. fol. 213ʳ), near which the codex was probably written.

Bibliography:
Martini-Bassi, I, pp. 496, 497.
Lazarev, *History*, I, p. 342 n. 43.

18. MILAN, BIBLIOTECA AMBROSIANA, COD. I 120 SUP. (GR. 470). 277 folios, 30 x 23 cm., parchment. XIII century. (Fig. 451)

Contents:
The sixteen homilies of the liturgical edition. Part of the sixteenth homily is missing.

Decoration:
   fol. 1ʳ.   The author portrait. Anastasis in initial A (homily 1).

Style and Date:
Although the miniatures are flaked, the underdrawing reveals the depiction of large foreheads and the use of an agitated line, traits that recall another manuscript of Gregory's homilies, the cod. Oxford, Roe 6, for which a thirteenth-century date has been suggested. This same date is supported for the Milan codex by both the palaeography of the text and the linear treatment of the ornament consisting of geometric patterns, stylized palmettes, and crosses, all of poor quality and dark colors. The same applies to the rendering of the titles, for which only red ink has been used. These particular features of the manuscript suggest a province, rather than the capital of the empire, as the place of provenance.

Bibliography:
Martini-Bassi, I, pp. 564, 565.
Lazarev, *History*, I, p. 342 n. 43.

19. MOSCOW, STATE HISTORICAL MUSEUM, COD. VLAD. 146 (SABBA 61). 260 folios, 19.4 x 14.9 cm., parchment, XI century. (Figs. 1-18)

Contents:
The sixteen homilies of the liturgical edition.

Decoration:
   fol. 1ᵛ.   a) Anastasis. b) Gregory teaching (homily 1).
   fol. 4ᵛ.   The so-called vision of Habakkuk, bust of Christ blessing, in the left margin (homily 2).

fol. 23ᵛ. a) The Incredulity of Thomas. b) Consecration of a church. Both in the left margin (homily 3).

fol. 29ᵛ. a) Mamas milking, in the left margin (homily 3). b) Pentecost, at the bottom of the page (homily 4).

fol. 40ᵛ. The martyrdom of the seven Maccabees in six scenes (homily 5).

fol. 50ᵛ. The martyrdom of Cyprian, at the bottom of the page (homily 6).

fol. 61ᵛ. Julian as money changer, at the bottom of the page (homily 7).

fol. 71ʳ. Nativity, including the Bathing of the Child, Adoration, and Annunciation to the Shepherds, in the right margin (homily 8).

fol. 81ʳ. The Koimesis of Basil the Great, at the bottom of the page (homily 9).

fol. 133ᵛ. The Baptism of Christ, in the left margin (homily 10).

fol. 145ʳ. John baptizing the people, at the bottom of the left column (homily 11).

fol. 177ʳ. Gregory of Nazianzus and Gregory of Nyssa, at the bottom of the left column (homily 12).

fol. 181ᵛ. The Koimesis of Athanasius (homily 13).

fol. 202ᵛ. Gregory addressing the bishops, at the bottom of the right column (homily 14).

fol. 219ᵛ. The Almsgiving, in the left margin (homily 15).

fol. 244ᵛ. Gregory of Nazianzus receiving a scroll from his seated father, in the left margin (homily 16).

Style and Date:

This richly decorated manuscript presents a variety of ornaments—with *Laubsäge* and the flower-petal style predominating—which find parallels in late tenth- and early eleventh-century Constantinopolitan manuscripts. The flower-petal ornament, for example, on fol. 1ᵛ resembles that of the cod. Paris gr. 519 dated 1007 while other patterns are similar to those in the cod. Athens 56, fol. 219ʳ, which Weitzmann dates in the third quarter of the tenth century.[41] The Moscow ornament, however, is less clear and more complex in design, which characteristics point to a later date and make more probable a chronological proximity to cod. Paris gr. 519.

The figure style shows great simplicity, a sensitive treatment of line, and a knowledge of anatomical details. The elegant, slender, but warmly fleshed figures, as, for example, the figure of the angel on fol. 4ᵛ, the flowing garments, and, in St. Cyprian's death scene, a classical city gate with the walls and the delicate trees behind it conveying the impression of depth, are all good indications of an art familiar with the classical prototypes that the Macedonian dynasty had revived. However, in contrast to this calm and flowing style, there are here and there figures which show a mannered treatment—an agitated use of line, and a flattening effect on the bodies. The figure of Gregory in the vision scene (fol. 4ᵛ) is an example of this effect's being stressed

[41] Frantz, *AB* (1934), pl. VII, 11, 12; Weitzmann, *Buchmalerei*, pl. XXVII, 149.

by the application of purple and white colors side by side, as is the figure of Gregory kneeling before the altar on fol. 23ᵛ. In the latter instance one should note the geometric rendering of the feet, a characteristic which appears at the end of the tenth century and becomes dominant in the eleventh. The most agitated treatment of line appears in the scenes of the martyrdom of the Maccabees. Here the gold lines of the garments create an incorporeal effect, and the characteristic spiral ornamental motif on the thigh, which appears in eleventh-century manuscripts, is present also. In other instances, as in the miniature of the homily to Julian the Tax Collector, the tendency toward patternization is stressed by the treatment of the folds as well as by the use of pattern motifs. There is no need to suggest the collaboration of different artists, each with a different artistic style, since both tendencies often occur in the same miniature. It is more plausible to suggest that the manuscript was produced at a time when an established classical art had begun to yield to a more austere, more spiritual art, the so-called monastic art. A most probable date, which agrees also with the comparative study of the ornament, is c. 1000.

Bibliography:

Copies photographiques des miniatures des manuscrits grecs conservés à la Bibliothèque Synodale autrefois Patriarchal de Moscou, III, Moscow 1865, pl. 1.

Kondakov, *Histoire*, II, p. 99.

Pokrovskii, *Evangelie*, pp. 169, 402, 404, 427, pl. XLVIII.

Archimandrite Vladimir, *Sistematicheskoe opisanie rukopisei Moskovskoi Sinodal'noi Biblioteki*, I, *Rukopisi grecheskiia*, Moscow 1894, pp. 151, 152.

Millet, *Recherches*, p. 205.

Lazarev, *History*, I, pp. 109, 314 n. 23, pl. 135 B, C.

20. MOSCOW, STATE HISTORICAL MUSEUM, COD. VLAD. 155 (SABBA 66; MATTH. LXVII). 464 folios, 14.2 x 11.3 cm., parchment. XV century. (Figs. 473-74)

Contents:

1) The sixteen homilies of the liturgical edition, with a commentary by Nicetas of Heraclea, fols. 1-403ᵛ.

2) The Apocalypse with commentary (incomplete) by Andrew of Caesarea, fols. 404ʳ-463ᵛ (*PG*, 106, 499-786).

Decoration:

fol. 4ʳ.   The author portrait.

Style and Date:

Lazarev suggested a fourteenth-century date. The opinion of Vladimir, who assigned the codex to the fifteenth century, seems to be more plausible. Stylistically most striking about the single miniature is the rendering of the beard by unbroken, wavy lines. This is too linear a treatment and has lost the Palaeologan expressiveness. Something resembling this rendering can be seen in some post-Byzantine icons assigned by authorities to the fifteenth and sixteenth centuries.[42] The palaeography of the text points to the same date.

According to a notice on fols. 3ʳ, 463ᵛ and 464ʳ, the manuscript was written in the monastery of the Grand Lavra of St. Athanasius on Mt. Athos. Unfortunately no date is given. The notice containing the name of the scribe reads as follows: Παροῦσα θεία καὶ ἱερὰ βίβλος ἐγεγόνει παρ' ἐμοῦ ἐλαχίστου ἐν ἱερομονάχοις Συμεὼν τοῦ Μαλεσηνοῦ· καὶ ὡς αὐτὴ μαρτυρεῖ, ἐπιμελῶς πάνυ καὶ λυσικαλῶς· ἐπεὶ οὖν οὕτω κεκοπίακα, καὶ οὕτως ἐπεμελησάμην, θέλω καὶ σφόδρα ἀποδέχομαι, ἵνα καὶ μετὰ θάνατόν μου εὑρίσκηται εἰς τὴν καθ' ἡμᾶς σεβασμίαν καὶ ἱερὰν βασιλικὴν μεγάλην λαύραν τοῦ ἁγίου πατρὸς ἡμῶν ᾿Αθανασίου.

Bibliography:

Vladimir, *op.cit.*, pp. 156-58.

Lazarev, *History*, I, p. 370.

21. OXFORD, BODLEIAN LIBRARY, COD. CANON. GR. 103. 282 folios, 33 x 26 cm., parchment. XI-XII century. (Figs. 275-86)

Contents:

1) The sixteen liturgical homilies of Gregory of Nazianzus, fols. 1ʳ-279ᵛ.

2) Gregory's epigram on the tomb of Basil the Great interpreted by Nicetas of Paphlagonia, fols. 280-282 (*PG*, 38, 72-75); these folios are of paper and were added later.

Decoration:

fol. 2ᵛ.	The author portrait- ὁ ἅγιος Γρηγόριος ὁ Θεολόγος.
fol. 3ʳ.	Anastasis in initial Α (homily 1).
fol. 35ʳ.	Pentecost (homily 4).
fol. 47ʳ.	Eleazar, Christ, ᾿Ι(ησοῦ)ς Χ(ριστό)ς, Solomone, and the seven Maccabees (homily 5).
fol. 57ʳ.	Gregory and Cyprian standing, in the right column (homily 6).
fol. 69ʳ.	Gregory and Julian as writers, in the right column (homily 7).
fol. 79ᵛ.	Nativity arranged around the title, beginning from the left: three Magi, the Bathing of the Child, Nativity proper, Annunciation to the Shepherds, in the left column (homily 8).
fol. 90ᵛ.	The Koimesis of Basil the Great, in the right column (homily 9).
fol. 146ʳ.	The Baptism of Christ in initial Π (homily 10).
fol. 192ʳ.	Gregory of Nazianzus addressing Gregory of Nyssa, in the left column (homily 12).
fol. 197ʳ.	Gregory addressing Athanasius of Alexandria, in the left column (homily 13).
fol. 264ʳ.	Teaching scene, in the left column (homily 16).

[42] G. Soteriou, *Guide du Musée byzantin d'Athénes*, Athens 1955, pl. XXVIII; M. Chatzidakis, *L'icône byzantine*, Venice 1959, fig. 27.

Style and Date:

The flower-petal style ornament finds parallels in the ornaments of eleventh- and twelfth-century manuscripts such as the codd. Paris, suppl. gr. 27; Paris, Coislin 239; and Paris gr. 519.[43]

The ornament, the very high quality of the miniatures, and the subtleties and brilliance of the color all point to Constantinople as the place of origin.

The frontispiece, fol. 2ʳ, shows a mannered treatment of the drapery and over-ornamented furniture which has lost the classical qualities of the Macedonian Renaissance. However, in the decoration of the other folios, neither mannerisms nor the characteristic highlights around the eyes, which became a constant feature in the twelfth century, are as apparent. A comparison with the miniatures of the cod. Paris, Coislin 239, reveals characteristics common to both manuscripts: narrow foreheads, the treatment of the hair, the prominence given to the neck in an attempt at articulation, the rendering of line, and the slenderness of the figures. Yet in the cod. Canon 103, the linear system which controls body and drapery alike has a more marked dematerializing effect. This indicates that the Oxford manuscript is later in date, and belongs either to the last decade of the eleventh century or to the first years of the twelfth. A date c. 1100, already suggested by Pächt, seems more probable.

Bibliography:

Coxe, III, p. 95.

O. Pächt, *Byzantine Illumination*, Oxford 1952, pls. 7, 25, 26, 29.

Masterpieces of Byzantine Art, Edinburgh Inter. Festival 1958, no. 204.

Byzantine Art, an European Art, 9th Exhibition of the Council of Europe, 2nd ed., Athens 1964, pp. 335, 336, pl. 347.

22. OXFORD, BODLEIAN LIBRARY, COD. ROE 6. 186 folios, 20 x 14.8 cm., parchment. XIII century. (Figs. 435-50)

Contents:

1) A homily on Christ's Resurrection by John Chrysostom, fol. 1ʳ (*PG*, 50, 821-24).

2) The sixteen homilies of the liturgical edition, folios 2ʳ-184ʳ. A text on Sunday of Orthodoxy begins on fol. 185ʳ.

Decoration:

The text occupies the whole width of each page and the miniatures are either title miniatures or frontispieces.

fol. 1ᵛ.   The author portrait.

fol. 2ʳ.   Anastasis (homily 1).

fol. 4ʳ.   The so-called vision of Habakkuk (homily 2). Gregory teaching, in initial E.

[43] Omont, *Min. gr.* (1929), pl. XCVII. Frantz, *AB* (1934), pl. XII, 5, 8. Weitzmann, *Buchmalerei*, p. 27, pl. XXXVII, 206. For the cod. Paris, Coislin 239, see infra, no. 28.

fol. 18ʳ.   Mamas standing- Μά(μα)s -(homily 3).

fol. 22ᵛ.   Pentecost- ἡ Πεν(τηκοσ)τή -(homily 4).

fol. 30ᵛ.   Nativity, including the Bathing of the Child, Adoration, and Annunciation to the Shepherds (homily 8).

fol. 38ʳ.   The Koimesis of Basil the Great- Κοίμησις τοῦ ῾Αγίου Βασιλείου- (homily 9).

fol. 73ᵛ.   The Baptism of Christ- ἡ βάπτισις, Ἰ(ησοῦ)s Χ(ριστό)s -(homily 10).

fol. 103ᵛ.   Group of martyrs (homily 7).

fol. 110ᵛ.   Teaching scene (homily 12).

fol. 115ᵛ.   Teaching scene (homily 14).

fol. 128ʳ.   Bust of Athanasius of Alexandria- ὁ ἅγιος ᾿Αθανάσιος -(homily 13).

fol. 143ᵛ.   Teaching scene (homily 15).

fol. 159ᵛ.   Eleazar, Solomone, and the seven Maccabees (homily 5).

fol. 167ᵛ.   Cyprian standing (homily 6).

fol. 175ᵛ.   Teaching scene (homily 16).

Style and Date:

Only one miniature, that on fol. 2ʳ, has an ornamental border and this is of the typical flower-petal style. All the other miniatures, including the frontispiece, are without any ornament, save small plain bands of ropelike motif, in imitation of the silver borders of enamels.

Most of the miniatures are badly flaked and only the under-drawing remains. In cases where the painting has been preserved, as on Joseph's mantle in the Nativity miniature, the bold treatment of line and the extreme simplicity of the garment are the main characteristics. Another important feature is the bent knee of the assisting maid in the Nativity scene, demonstrating her quick walk. This rapid motion of the body is in contrast to the statuesque poses of other figures, such as Gregory's audience in the teaching scenes. All these characteristics find analogies in the manuscripts of the so-called family 2400.[44] Comparing, for instance, the miniatures of the Oxford codex with those of the Karahissar gospels, cod. Lenin. State Lib. gr. 105, one sees that both codices have in common the flaked pigment and the absence of ornamental bands around the miniatures.[45] In addition, the posture of the assisting maid in the Oxford manuscript finds analogies in several figures in the Karahissar gospels. Moreover, the relationship between these manuscripts extends also to iconography, such as the iconography of the Anastasis and Nativity miniatures, which is the same in both, while the half-figures of the Oxford Gregory recall those in the McCormick New Testament. For example, the figure of St. Athanasius in the homilies is so like that of

[44] For discussion and bibliography of the cod. Chicago, Rockefeller McCormick Collection 2400, and its family, see H. R. Willoughby, *Codex 2400 and its Miniatures*, Chicago 1933; E. J. Goodspeed, D. W. Riddle, H. R. Willoughby, *The*

Rockefeller McCormick New Testament, I-III, Chicago 1932.

[45] E. C. Colwell, H. R. Willoughby, *The Four Gospels of Karahissar*, II, Chicago 1936, pls. XLII, XLVII, XLIX.

St. James in the McCormick New Testament that there can be no doubt about the inclusion of the Oxford manuscript in the same family.[46] Like the codices of this family, the Oxford one claims a thirteenth-century date. Trebizond has been suggested as the place of origin for the Karahissar gospels, and the Oxford Gregory may also have come from there.

Bibliography:

Coxe, I, p. 462.

O. Pächt, *Byzantine Illumination*, Oxford 1952, pl. 23.

Byzantine Art, an European Art, 9th Exhibition of the Council of Europe, 2nd ed., Athens 1964, p. 336, pl. 348.

23. OXFORD, BODLEIAN LIBRARY, COD. SELDEN. B. 54. 217 folios, 26.7 x 20.6 cm., parchment. XI-XII century. (Figs. 287-98)

Contents:

1) The sixteen homilies of the liturgical edition. The text of the codex begins in the middle of the second homily, thus the illustrations of the first and second homilies are missing. There are no illustrations for the third homily.

2) Three homilies of the full edition, namely, the homilies: εἰς ἑαυτὸν καὶ τούς λέγοντας, fols. 129ᵛ-133ᵛ, (*PG*, 36, 205-80); εἰς ἑαυτὸν καὶ λαόν, fols. 133ᵛ-140ʳ, (*PG*, 35, 1228-52); ἀπολογητικὸς τῆς εἰς τὸν Πόντον φυγῆς, fols. 140ʳ-154ᵛ (*PG*, 35, 407-526). These three homilies have no illustrations.

3) Selections from an evangelarium, fols. 155ʳ-217ᵛ, of a later date.

Decoration:

fol. 8ᵛ.   Pentecost, in the left column (homily 4).

fol. 14ᵛ.   The seven Maccabees, Eleazar, and Solomone standing, in the left column (homily 5).

fol. 19ᵛ.   Gregory and Cyprian seated, in the right column (homily 6).

fol. 25ᵛ.   Gregory and Julian as writers, in the right column (homily 7).

fol. 36ʳ.   The Koimesis of Basil the Great, in the left column- Ἡ κιδία τοῦ ἁγίου βασιλείου- (homily 9).

fol. 62ʳ.   Gregory, Christ, and John the Baptist, in the right column (homily 10).

fol. 67ᵛ.   Gregory teaching, in the right column (homily 11).

fol. 85ᵛ.   Gregory of Nazianzus and Gregory of Nyssa in proskynesis, in the right column (homily 12).

fol. 88ᵛ.   Athanasius of Alexandria, on top of initial A- ἅγιος ἀθανάσιος- in the left column (homily 13).

[46] E. J. Goodspeed, D. W. Riddle, H. R. Willoughby, *The Rockefeller McCormick New Testament*, I, Chicago 1932, fol. 138ʳ.

fol. 99ʳ.   Gregory addressing bishops, in the right column (homily 14).

fol. 108ʳ.   Gregory teaching, in the right column (homily 15).

fol. 121ʳ.   Gregory of Nazianzus, his silent father and a group of people, in the right column (homily 16).

Style and Date:

The ornament, which consists of a floral motif, of either flower-petal style or rectilinear patterns, finds parallels in the manuscripts of the late eleventh century.

A zigzag ornament, somewhat similar to the one appearing on fol. 8ᵛ, can be seen in the cod. Paris gr. 81 dated in A.D. 1092.[47] But the ornament of the Oxford manuscript is more patternized, has less plasticity, and seems to be more provincial. The floral motif finds parallels among manuscripts that Weitzmann has classified in the "ägyptisch-palästinensische Gruppe," as for instance the Vatican cod. Ottob. gr. 457, which is dated in the year 1039.[48] The stylization of the Oxford manuscript, however, points to a later date.

As the ornament seems provincial, so does the style. The figures do not have the slenderness that characterizes the school of the capital, their heads are large and their eyes glassy. The treatment of line is at times very meager. The colors are in most cases dark and muddy, having none of the brilliance of Constantinopolitan colors.

These static, stiff, and heavily drawn figures, with gloomy faces and staring eyes, seemingly withdrawn from this world and frozen by an unknown vision that inspires them with awe, find stylistic analogies in the manuscript of the *Heavenly Ladder* in the Vatican, cod. Ross. 251, dated in the eleventh or twelfth century.[49] The figure of Cyprian on fol. 19ᵛ, for example, presents similarities to that of John Climacus on fol. 2ᵛ in the Climax manuscript for which Martin has proposed a Palestinian origin.[50] Perhaps the same region may be suggested for the miniature of the Oxford codex.

Bibliography:

Coxe, I, pp. 610, 611.

24. PARIS, BIBLIOTHÈQUE NATIONALE, COD. GR. 533. 311 folios, 37 x 26.5 cm., parchment. XI century. (Figs. 234-55)

Contents:

1) The sixteen homilies of the liturgical edition, fols. 1ʳ-276ᵛ.

2) Life of Gregory Nazianzenus written by Gregory the Presbyter, fols. 276ʳ-307ᵛ, (*PG*, 35, 243-304).

3) Testament of Gregory of Nazianzus, fols. 308ʳ-311ʳ, (*PG*, 37, 389-95).

Decoration:

fol. 3ᵛ.   Teaching scene.

fol. 4ʳ.   Anastasis in initial A (homily 1).

[47] Frantz, *AB* (1934), pl. I, 7.

[48] Weitzmann, *Buchmalerei*, pp. 72ff., pl. LXXXI, 502.

[49] Martin, *Ladder*, pl. LXXXI, 226.

[50] *Ibid.*, p. 185.

fol. 7ʳ. The so-called vision of Habakkuk- ὁ προφή(της) Ἀμβακοὺμ -(homily 2).

fol. 34ʳ. a) Shepherd shearing a lamb. b) Boat sailing. c) Ploughing. All three in the second column of the text (homily 3).

fol. 34ᵛ. a) Shepherd playing the flute. b) Herdsman making a pipe. c) The pruning of a tree. d) Hunting. e) Fishing. f) Trees and beehives (homily 3).

fol. 35ʳ. a) Birds flying over a cluster of trees, between the columns. b) A horse about to drink water, in the margin (homily 3).

fol. 35ᵛ. Gregory teaching, in initial Π. Group of people, in the opposite margin (homily 4).

fol. 47ᵛ. Gregory teaching, in initial T. Group of people, in the opposite margin (homily 5).

fol. 58ʳ. Gregory and Cyprian holding scroll, in initial M (homily 6).

fol. 70ʳ. Gregory teaching, in initial T. Group of people, in the opposite margin (homily 7).

fol. 77ᵛ. Gregory teaching, in the left margin. Julian writing, in the right margin- ὁ ἐξισωτὴς Ἰουλιανός -(homily 7).

fol. 91ʳ. Gregory of Nazianzus and Basil the Great (homily 9).

fol. 146ʳ. a) Christ meets John the Baptist. b) Gregory teaching, in the margin (homily 10).

fol. 154ʳ. a) The Baptism of Christ. b) Gregory teaching. Both in the margins (homily 10).

fol. 158ᵛ. Gregory teaching, below initial X. Group of people, in the margin (homily 11).

fol. 192ʳ. Gregory of Nazianzus, in the left margin. Gregory of Nyssa, in the right margin (homily 12).

fol. 196ᵛ. Gregory of Nazianzus, in the left margin. Athanasius, in the right margin (homily 13).

fol. 218ᵛ. Gregory addressing a group of bishops, below initial Π (homily 14).

fol. 236ʳ. Gregory teaching, in initial T. Group of people, in the right margin (homily 16).

fol. 251ʳ. Gregory teaching, below initial A. Group of people, in the right margin (homily 15).

fol. 276ᵛ. Gregory the Presbyter teaching a group of people, in the left margin. Gregory of Nazianzus teaching, in the right margin (beginning of the life of Gregory).

Style and Date:

There is no colophon and no definite indication of the provenance of this manuscript. The ornament and the style of the miniatures, however, point to the area of Constantinople. Similar flower-petal style ornaments appear in cod. Paris, Coislin 79, which is dated between the years 1078 and 1081.[51] The standing figures of the teaching scenes have all the stylistic characteristics of late eleventh-century Byzantine art. The dry elegance and the slender figures poised as if deprived of bodily weight find close stylistic similarities in the Princeton illustrated manuscript of the *Heavenly Ladder*, cod. Garrett 16, dated in A.D. 1081. These similarities have already been pointed out by Martin.[52] A different style with a very pronounced sense of corporeality appears in the bucolic scenes; it is due not to different hands, but to the influence of classical models.

In the fourteenth century the following text was added on fol. 1[r]: Ἠγοράσθη τὸ παρ(ὸ)ν βηβλίον παρὰ τοῦ μοναχοῦ Μεθοδίου, ὅς ἔθηκεν τοῦτο ἐν τῇ ἁγίᾳ μονῇ τοῦ Ἀγροῦ ὑπὲρ ἀφέσεως ἁμαρτιῶν αὐτοῦ καὶ τῶν γοναίων αὐτοῦ, εὔχεσθαι . . . (καὶ) οὐκ ἔξ(εστ)η αὐτο ξενόσε ἐκ τὴν ἁγίαν μονήν τοῦ Ἀγροῦ· εἰ δὲ τις τολμήσει τοῦτο ξενόσε αὐτό ἐκ τῆς μονῆς αὐτῆς ἔστω ἀφωρισμ(έν)ο(ς) ἔξω πάσης ἐκκλησίας. Ὁ ταπεινὸς Ἰακὼβ (καὶ) π(ατ)ὴρ πνευ(ματ)ικὸς τοῦ Ἀργοῦ καὶ τοῦ Στύλ(ου).

This monastery, also mentioned in other notes added by other hands, perhaps in the fifteenth and seventeenth centuries, was probably in Cyprus.[53]

Below the miniature of fol. 3[v] we read the following verses written in gold uncial letters.

> Πάλαι σε δῶρον ἐκ Θεοῦ, θεηγόρε,
>
> Πλουτοῦντες ἐν γῇ σῶν μετείχομεν λόγων.
>
> Καὶ νῦν σε πλουτήσειεν αὖθις προστάτην
>
> Ἐκλιπαροῦμεν πάντες οἱ συνηγμένοι
>
> Ὁ τοὺς δὲ τοὺς σοὺς ἐν βίβλω χρυσοὺς λόγους,
>
> Ἄριστε Νικόλαε, ἐνθεὶς ἐνθέως.

The Ἄριστε Νικόλαε of the text has been correctly interpreted by Bordier as the name of the man who ordered the manuscript.

Bibliography:

Bordier, *Description*, pp. 140-44, fig. 67.

Omont, *Inventaire sommaire*, I, p. 76.

Pokrovskii, *Evangelie*, pp. 169, 179, 180, 187, 402; pl. XLVIII.

Schlumberger, *Epopée*, I, pp. 513-17.

Millet, *Recherches*, see index.

Omont, *Min. gr.* (1929), pp. 51, 52, pls. CIII-CV.

Tikkanen, *Farbengebung*, pp. 136, 153, 164.

C. Diehl, *La peinture byzantine*, Paris 1933, p. 91, pl. LXXV.

Frantz, *AB* (1934), pl. II, 19.

Der Nersessian, Barlaam, p. 62.

P. Lemerle, *Le style byzantin*, Paris 1943, p. 98.

Lazarev, *History*, I, pp. 112, 314 n. 33.

[51] Omont, *Min. gr.* (1929), pl. LXIV.
[52] Martin, *Ladder*, pp. 176, 177.

[53] J. Darrouzès, "Notes pour servir à l'histoire de Chypre," Κυπριακαὶ Σπουδαί, 20 (1956), 49.

A. Marava-Chatzinikolaou, Ὁ Ἅγιος Μάμας, Athens 1953, p. 90.

Schweinfurth (1954), pp. 80, 147; figs. 44b, 45a, b.

J. Darrouzès, "Notes pour servir à l'histoire de Chypre," Κυπριακαὶ Σπουδαί, 20 (1956), p. 49.

Bibl. Nat., *Byzance*, pp. 15, 16, pl. XIII.

S. Der Nersessian, "The Homilies of Gregory of Nazianzus, Paris gr. 510," *Dumbarton Oaks Papers*, 16 (1962), p. 226 n. 139.

D. Talbot Rice, *The Byzantines*, London 1962, pl. 37.

Byzantine Art, an European Art, 9th Exhibition of the Council of Europe, 2nd ed., Athens 1964, pp. 941, 942.

25. PARIS, BIBLIOTHÈQUE NATIONALE, COD. GR. 541. 427 folios, 27.8 x 19.4 cm., parchment. XIV century.

Contents:

The sixteen homilies of the liturgical edition with a commentary by Nicetas of Serrae.

Decoration:

fol. 0ᵛ.   The author portrait.

fol. 9ᵛ.   Anastasis (homily 1).

fol. 85ᵛ.   Pentecost (homily 4).

fol. 163ᵛ.   Nativity (homily 8).

The remaining homilies are decorated by simple ornamental bands.

Style and Date:

Since the miniatures are badly flaked, a stylistic analysis for the purposes of dating has to be based on the ornament, which, consisting primarily of ivy leaves, is extremely decorative and patternized. So are the interlace designs ornamenting some of the titles which find their best parallels in very late fourteenth-century Constantinopolitan manuscripts.[54] An examination of the palaeography of the text also points to this late date.

Bibliography:

Bordier, *Description*, p. 185.

Omont, *Inventaire sommaire*, I, p. 80.

Ebersolt, *Miniature*, pp. 55 n. 1, 56 n. 5, 60 n. 1, 61 n. 2, pl. LXVII.

Tikkanen, *Farbengebung*, p. 182.

Frantz, *AB* (1934), pl. VI, 11.

Lazarev, *History*, I, p. 370 n. 78.

---

[54] A somewhat similar ornament is to be seen in the codd. Moscow gr. 182, dating from 1335, and Paris gr. 2243, dating from 1339. Cf. Ebersolt, *Miniature*, pls. LXVII, 2, LXIX, 1; and Frantz, *AB* (1934), pls. V, 6, XXII, 25.

26. PARIS, BIBLIOTHÈQUE NATIONALE, COD. GR. 543. 357 folios, 25.7 x 19.8 cm., parchment. XIV century. (Figs. 454-69)

Contents:

1) Hypotheses of the sixteen homilies, fols. 1ʳ-9ᵛ.
2) Anonymous commentary on homilies 6, 9 and 10, fols. 10ʳ-23ʳ.
3) The sixteen homilies of the liturgical edition, fols. 23ᵛ-357ʳ.

Decoration:

The illustrations are full-page miniatures which precede each homily. Each illustrated page is divided into two registers, each of which contains one or more scenes. The manuscript includes only fourteen illustrated pages because the illustrations of the homilies on Pentecost (fol. 59ᵛ) and to Gregory of Nyssa (fol. 237ᵛ) have been cut out. At the beginning of every homily there is an ornamental headpiece in flower-petal style. At the bottom of the pages with headpieces are found the calendar directions for each homily. The first twenty-two folios are beautifully decorated with initials and floral bands.

fol. 23ᵛ. a) Anastasis. b) Gregory, his father, and a group of monks (homily 1).

fol. 24ʳ. Anastasis in initial A (homily 1).

fol. 27ᵛ. a) The so-called vision of Habakkuk. b) The raising of the dead, an angel ties Satan (homily 2).

fol. 28ʳ. Gregory, bust of Christ and a figure of Habakkuk, in initial E (homily 2).

fol. 51ᵛ. a) The Incredulity of Thomas. b) Consecration of a church (homily 3).

fol. 59ᵛ. Miniature cut out (homily 4).

fol. 74ᵛ. The martyrdom of the seven Maccabees, Eleazar, and Solomone (homily 5).

fol. 87ᵛ. a) Cyprian conversing with devils; Justina appearing at the window of a house. b) Gregory seated; the martyrdom of Cyprian (homily 6).

fol. 102ᵛ. a) Julian as money changer. b) Gregory writing before a group of martyrs (homily 7).

fol. 116ᵛ a) Nativity. b) Adam and Eve in Paradise called for by the Creator-Logos; the quickening of Adam. c) Adam and Eve, in the margin (homily 8).

fol. 117ᵛ. The Virgin Blachernitissa in initial X, two worshiping women, in lower left margin (homily 8).

fol. 130ᵛ. a) The Koimesis of Basil the Great. b) Gregory teaching (homily 9).

fol. 197ᵛ. a) The Baptism of Christ. b) John meets Christ; John preaching (homily 10).

fol. 213ᵛ. a) John baptizes the people. b) Gregory reading his sermon to a group of standing clerics; another seated cleric blessing a group of monks (homily 11).

fol. 237ᵛ. Miniature cut out (homily 12).

fols. 238-250 are by a later hand.

fol. 260ᵛ. a) The Koimesis of Athanasius of Alexandria. b) Gregory teaching (homily 13).

fol. 288ᵛ. a) Gregory in front of a group of monks receiving a staff from the Emperor Theodosius behind whom are two groups of court officials. b) Gregory standing between two groups of bishops (homily 14).

fol. 310ᵛ. a) Gregory holding a scroll and standing between two groups of clerics and laymen. b) Gregory and the poor (homily 15).

fol. 342ᵛ. a) Gregory between his seated father and a group of people. b) Gregory teaching (homily 16).

fols. 351ʳ-357ʳ are by a later hand.

Style and Date:

The artist of this richly illustrated manuscript has succeeded in creating a homogeneous style, although some details reveal the use of different models. The style of the miniature on fol. 260ᵛ, for instance, shows strong modeling and a softness in the treatment of line, whereas the modeling of the figures in the miniature on fol. 51ᵛ (upper register) is different. Here the contours are stressed by a distinct line—in some cases black—which is a general characteristic of mosaic work.

The main stylistic characteristics of the manuscript are elongation of the figures, disproportion in the bodies, ascetic appearance, vivid gestures and attitudes, bold foreheads, and emphasized highlights. Not all these characteristics find parallels in manuscripts of the twelfth century, which date is assigned to this one by Bordier and by the author of the Catalogue of the 1958 Paris Exhibition of the Bibliothèque Nationale. On the contrary, these are the general characteristics of Palaeologan art. More particularly they are reminiscent of the menologion in Oxford, cod. gr. th. f. 1, dated on internal evidence in the mid-fourteenth century.[55] Moreover, the beadlike rendering of the eyes—another particular feature of the Paris manuscript—recalls a similar treatment occurring in the cod. Paris gr. 1242 (a copy of the theological works of the Emperor John VI Cantacuzene) executed at Constantinople between 1370 and 1375.[56] The correct date, therefore, is that given by Omont.

The elegance of the style and the clarity of colors—light ones with a great variety of nuances predominating—lead to the supposition that the manuscript was in all probability made at one of the Constantinopolitan scriptoria. The combinations of contrasting colors in the buildings are remarkable. Use of olive green against blue is

[55] O. Pächt, *Byzantine Illumination*, Oxford 1952, p. 8, fig. 16.

[56] Omont, *Min. gr.* (1929), pl. CXXVI; for bibliography and discussion, see Bibl. Nat., *Byzance*, no. 50; Talbot Rice, *Byzantium*, pl. XXXIX, 190; Beckwith, *Constantinople*, pp. 147ff.

made. The olive green is also used for the hills, which are successfully set against gold backgrounds.

The manuscript remained in Constantinople until the eighteenth century when, according to a note in the manuscript, it was given by Chrysanthos Notaras, patriarch of Jerusalem (1707-1731), to Louis XV, king of France.

Bibliography:

Bordier, *Description*, pp. 186-92, fig. 92.

Kondakov, *Histoire*, p. 92.

Pokrovskii, *Evangelie*, see index.

Schlumberger, *Epopée*, I, p. 477.

Omont, *Inventaire sommaire*, I, p. 80.

H. L. Kehrer, *Die heiligen drei Könige in Literatur und Kunst*, II, Leipzig 1909, fig. 88.

Millet, *Recherches*, p. 746, figs. 43, 167, 168.

Ebersolt, *Miniature*, pp. 56 n. 5, 60 n. 3, 5, 6, 61 n. 7, 62 n. 1, 2; pls. LXX, LXXI.

C. Couderc, *Les enluminures des manuscrits du moyen âge de la Bibliothèque Nationale*, Paris 1927, p. 46, pl. XII.

Omont, *Min. gr.* (1929), pp. 56, 57, pls. CXIX-CXXV.

Tikkanen, *Farbengebung*, pp. 128, 168, 170, 201, 203-5, 209-10.

Frantz, *AB* (1934), pls. II, 18, 25; III, 22.

E. C. Colwell, H. R. Willoughby, *The Four Gospels of Karahissar*, Chicago 1936, II, p. 465.

Lazarev, *History*, I, pp. 222, 362 n. 32.

Schweinfurth (1934), p. 81, fig. 58.

Grabar, *Min. Byz.*, fig. 56.

Martin, *Ladder*, p. 180.

Bibl. Nat., *Byzance*, p. 23.

S. Der Nersessian, "The Homilies of Gregory of Nazianzus, Paris gr. 510," *Dumbarton Oaks Papers* 16 (1962), p. 215 n. 89.

27. PARIS, BIBLIOTHÈQUE NATIONALE, COD. GR. 550. 294 folios, 27 x 19.5 cm., parchment. XII century. (Figs. 398-427)

Contents:

The sixteen homilies of the liturgical edition.

Decoration:

fol. 3ᵛ. Crucifixion.

fol. 4ʳ. A medallion with a bust of Basil the Great on the intersection of a cross; above, two smaller medallions with busts of John Chrysostom and Nicolas of Myra.

fol. 4ᵛ. The author portrait.

fol. 5ʳ. A large square frame enclosing Anastasis flanked by the episode of the three Marys reporting to the apostles. In the upper register, four half figures of flying angels and four archangels bearing the symbols of the Passion. In the lower register, the dead rising, in the center, flanked by people bearing candles. Initial A is formed by a figure of Gregory writing. In the right margin, four birds picking the fruit of a tree (homily 1).

fol. 6ʳ. A boy standing on a rabbit and holding a ball forms initial K (homily 1).

fol. 6ᵛ. Two naked boys standing on two birds and embracing each other with a third boy flying above form initial Δ (homily 1).

fol. 8ᵛ. The so-called vision of Habakkuk. Figures of Gregory and Habakkuk in initial E. A peacock, in the left margin (homily 2).

fol. 9ʳ. Shepherd with a dog, in initial T (homily 2).

fol. 9ᵛ. Nude man with gold branch in initial K (homily 2).

fol. 30ʳ. Mamas praying to a bust of Christ. Mamas milking, in initial E. Three boys picking and carrying the fruit of a tree, in the right margin (homily 3).

fol. 30ᵛ. Gregory teaching a group of people and Church and Synagogue, in initial E (homily 3).

fol. 34ᵛ. Bishop baptizing a youth in a font, in the left margin (homily 3).

fol. 37ʳ. Pentecost. The same with the addition of a bust of Christ, in initial Π. Birds eating the fruit of a tree, in the left margin (homily 4).

fol. 49ʳ. Eleazar, the seven Maccabees, Solomone. Busts of the seven Maccabees in initial T. A hunter piercing a deer, in the left margin (homily 5).

fol. 59ᵛ. Cyprian and Justina standing. The same in initial M, holding a cross. Two birds at a fountain, in the left margin (homily 6).

fol. 72ʳ. Julian the Tax Collector giving the tax orders. Bust of Gregory in initial T. Two parrots flanking a fig tree, in the right margin (homily 7).

fol. 83ʳ. Nativity, including the Bathing of the Child, the Adoration, and the Annunciation to the Shepherds. Nativity in initial X. A shepherd, in the right margin (homily 8).

fol. 94ᵛ. The Koimesis of Basil the Great. Gregory censing over the body of Basil, in initial E. A hunter and a bear, in the left margin (homily 9).

fol. 99ᵛ. A dancing young man holding a griffon over his head, in initial T (homily 9).

fol. 100ʳ. A nude boy playing with a dog and a bird, in initial Δ (homily 9).

fol. 153ʳ. The Baptism of Christ. The same in initial Π. A cross, in the right margin (homily 10).

fol. 166ᵛ. John baptizing the people. The same in initial X. Two birds at a fountain, in the left margin (homily 11).

fol. 204ʳ. Gregory of Nazianzus and Gregory of Nyssa in an ecstatic meeting. The same in initial Φ. One boy helping another to climb a tree, in the left margin (homily 12).

fol. 209ᵛ. The Koimesis of Athanasius of Alexandria. The figures of Gregory and Athanasius in initial A. Two rabbits at a fountain, in the left margin (homily 13).

fol. 232ʳ. Gregory of Nazianzus and four bishops, all seated. The same in initial Π. Four birds picking fruit from a date tree, in the right margin (homily 14).

fol. 251ʳ. Gregory giving alms; below, a monk and a young layman, both giving alms. Gregory and a group of people, in initial A. A child being swung by two others, in the right margin (homily 15).

fol. 279ʳ. Gregory of Nazianzus between his father and a group of people on whom hail is falling. Below, another group of people. A bust of Gregory in initial T. Two people sapping a palm tree, in the right margin (homily 16).

Style and Date:

This richly illustrated codex dates from the twelfth century. The illustrations are set in a broad frame, usually rectangular on the outside, and on the inside either rectangular or in the shape of a quatrefoil. It is thus evident that great stress was placed on ornament. The flower-petal ornament in a rather linear design finds analogies in twelfth-century manuscripts of the Constantinopolitan school, as in the manuscript of the Homilies on the Virgin by James of Kokkinobaphos,[57] although its brush technique is not always very fine. The style of the miniatures argues also for this date and locality. A quality of grandeur, achieved by the remarkable simplicity of the composition, the austere symmetry, the use of gold backgrounds, and the complete absence of landscape or architectural setting (with the exception of the Nativity scene) is apparent in most scenes. An emphasis on line is evident in the faces of the rather wiry figures and in the treatment of the hair and garments, the folds of which are indicated by fine dark lines. Martin has pointed out its close similarities in style and in method of decoration to the Sinai Climax cod. gr. 418, which can be dated in the twelfth century.[58] The master of the Paris Gregory is superior, showing better understanding in the treatment of ornament and in the use of fantastic animals within the foliage, which do not appear in the Sinai codex. Often the figures are very expressive, and at times—as the figure of Habakkuk, fol. 8ᵛ—they reflect a good Macedonian Renaissance model. Martin has suggested Sinai as the origin of the Climax codex. The master of the Paris Gregory was, however, trained in Constantinople,

[57] Cod. Paris gr. 1208, fol. 110ʳ, Ebersolt, *Miniature*, pl. LII, 1.

[58] Martin, *Ladder*, pp. 188, 189.

although the colors of the manuscript are not brilliant and cannot equal the colors of the best Constantinopolitan manuscripts.

According to a note on fol. 1ʳ, the manuscript was bound in the fourteenth century (1363) by the hieromonk and later Archimandrite Νεόφυτος of the monastery of St. Nicholas Καλαμιτζίων, τὴν κλῆσιν ἔχοντος τοῦ Φιλοκάμνου, which was perhaps in Chalkidike. In 1585 it was in the hands of John Raoult, archdeacon of the diocese of Rodez (Aveyron).

Bibliography:

Bordier, *Description*, pp. 198-203, fig. 95.

Omont, *Inventaire sommaire*, I, p. 84.

Kondakov, *Histoire*, pp. 93, 94.

Pokrovskii, *Evangelie*, pp. 60, 169, 332, 402, 404, 451; pl. XLVIII.

H. L. Kehrer, *Die heiligen drei Könige in Literatur und Kunst*, II, Leipzig 1909, p. 83.

Millet, *Recherches*, p. 746, figs. 41, 134.

Ebersolt, *Miniature*, pp. 38 n. 3, 43 n. 5, 47 n. 7, 50 n. 4, pl. XXXIV, 2.

C. Couderc, *Les enluminures des manuscrits du moyen âge de la Bibliothèque Nationale*, Paris 1927, p. 47, pl. XIII.

G. Millet, "La scène pastorale de Doura et l'annonce aux bergers," *Syria*, VII (1926), p. 149, fig. 5.

Omont, *Min. gr.* (1929), pp. 52-54, pls. CVI-CXV.

Tikkanen, *Farbengebung*, see index.

W. Volbach, *L'art byzantin*, Paris 1933, pp. 70, 71, pl. 79A.

Frantz, *AB* (1934), pls. X, 13, 21; XI, 4; XII, 16; XVI, 14-17; XVII, 10.

E. C. Colwell, H. R. Willoughby, *The Four Gospels of Karahissar*, II, Chicago 1936, pp. 62, 65, 465.

Grabar, *Min. Byz.*, figs. 53-55.

Lazarev, *History*, I, pp. 114, 317 n. 41, 323, 360; II, pl. 155a.

Schweinfurth (1943), p. 81, figs. 54, 55.

A. Marava-Chatzinikolaou, Ὁ Ἅγιος Μάμας, Athens 1953, pp. 89, 90, pl. II.

A. Grabar, "Un rouleau liturgique Constantinopolitain et ses peintures," *Dumbarton Oaks Papers*, 8 (1954), p. 196 n. 47.

Martin, *Ladder*, p. 189.

H. Buchthal, *Miniature Painting in the Latin Kingdom of Jerusalem*, Oxford 1957, p. 29.

Bibl. Nat., *Byzance*, pp. 24-26, pl. XVIII.

Beckwith, *Constantinople*, p. 126, fig. 167.

S. Der Nersessian, "The Homilies of Gregory of Nazianzus, Paris gr. 510," *Dumbarton Oaks Papers*, 16 (1962), p. 202.

A. Grabar, *Byzance, L'art byzantin du moyen âge*, Paris 1963, p. 142, pl. p. 145.

Byzantine Art, an European Art, 9th Exhibition of the Council of Europe, 2nd ed., Athens 1964, p. 335.

28. PARIS, BIBLIOTHÈQUE NATIONALE, COD. COISLIN 239. 295 folios, 26.2 x 21 cm., parchment. XI century. (Figs. 181-233)

Contents:

1) The sixteen homilies of the liturgical edition, fols. 1ʳ-228ᵛ.

2) Life of Gregory Nazianzenus, written by Gregory the Presbyter, fols. 229ʳ-155ᵛ (*PG*, 35, 243-304).

3) Ἀπολογητικὸς τῆς εἰς τὸν Πόντον φυγῆς, fols. 256ʳ-295ᵛ (*PG*, 35, 407-514).

Decoration:

The text is written in two columns and the miniatures extend over one of them. The original folios 3 and 5 are missing and have been replaced by paper folios in modern script. The illustration begins on fol. 6ʳ.

fol. 6ʳ. The so-called vision of Habakkuk. Habakkuk in initial E (homily 2). The illustrations of fols. 8ʳ-19ᵛ belong to the same homily.

fol. 8ʳ. Athanasius of Alexandria, in the outer right margin- ἀθανάσιον λέγει ἐπίσκοπον Ἀλεξανδρείας.

fol. 11ᵛ. Moses, in the left margin- Μωσῆς.

fol. 13ʳ. Isaiah, in the left margin- Ἡσαίας. Personification of March, in the right margin- Μὴν Μάρτιος.

fol. 15ʳ. Lot's wife, in the right margin- τοῦ Λώτ ἡ γυνή.

fol. 15ᵛ. John the Baptist, between the two columns- Ἰωάννης ὁ Πρόδρομος.

fol. 16ʳ. Paul, between the columns- ὁ Παῦλος.

fol. 18ʳ. Moses raising the brazen serpent, in the first column.

fol. 18ᵛ. a) Simon of Cyrene carrying the cross of Christ, in the left margin- Σί(μων) ὁ Κυρηναῖος. b) Joseph of Arimathaea asking Pilate for permission to remove the body of Christ from the cross, in the right column.

fol. 19ʳ. The two Marys at the tomb, in the left column.

fol. 19ᵛ. Isaiah pointing to Christ, in the margins at either side of the first column- Ἡσαίας, Ἰ(ησοῦ)ς Χ(ριστό)ς.

fol. 22ʳ. Church and Synagogue. Gregory standing, in the margin of the first column- ὁ Ἅγιος Γρηγόριος ὁ Θεο(λόγος) -(homily 3).

The miniatures of fols. 26ʳ-27ᵛ, all placed within the text-column, belong to the same homily.

fol. 26ʳ. Two personifications of the Hours- ἡ βασίλισσα τῶν ὡρῶν. Τὸ ἔαρ, ἡ καινὴ Κυριακή.

fol. 26ᵛ. a) Sailing, in the left column. b) Ploughing. c) Shepherd playing the flute, in the right column.

fol. 27ʳ. The pruning of a tree and fishing, in the left column.

fol. 27ᵛ. Mamas as shepherd, in the left column- ὁ ἅ(γιος) Μάμας.

fol. 28ʳ. Pentecost (homily 4).

fol. 30ʳ. Seven-branched candlestick, in the margin of the left column (homily 4).

fol. 34ᵛ. Joel, in the left margin, left column- Ἰωήλ ὁ Προφήτης (homily 4).

fol. 37ᵛ. Gregory, Solomone, Eleazar, the seven Maccabees, all in medallions (homily 5).

Illustrations of fols. 38ʳ-45ᵛ are within the written columns of the same homily.

fol. 38ʳ. Eleazar brought to Antiochus, in the right column.

fol. 39ᵛ. The scourging of Eleazar, in the right column.

fol. 40ʳ. The seven Maccabees before Antiochus, in the right column.

fol. 41ᵛ. Antiochus ordering the eldest Maccabee to be brought forward, in the right column.

fol. 43ᵛ. Solomone exhorting her sons, in the left column.

fol. 44ᵛ. Solomone in the furnace, in the right column.

fol. 45ᵛ. Antiochus and a group of Israelites, in the right column.

fol. 46ᵛ. Gregory pointing out Cyprian to a group of people (homily 6).

The illustrations on fols. 50ʳ-55ʳ are column pictures and belong to the same homily.

fol. 50ʳ. Gregory pointing out Justina to a group of people, in the left column.

fol. 53ʳ. Cyprian before Decius, in the left column.

fol. 54ʳ. The martyrdom of Cyprian, in the right column.

fol. 55ʳ. Cyprian appearing in a woman's dream, in the left column.

fol. 57ʳ. Gregory and Julian seated (homily 7).

fol. 65ᵛ. Nativity, including the Bathing of the Child and the Adoration (homily).

fol. 74ʳ. The Koimesis of Basil the Great (homily 9).

fols. 100ᵛ-105ʳ have illustrations inserted in the written columns and belong to the same homily.

fol. 100ᵛ. Basil before the prefect of Caesarea, in two scenes, in the left and right columns.

fol. 101ᵛ. The prefect reports to the Emperor Valens, in the left column.

fol. 104ᵛ. Second trial of Basil, in the left column.

fol. 105ʳ. The inhabitants of Caesarea protesting to the prefect, in the right column.

fol. 120ʳ. The Baptism of Christ (homily 10).

fols. 121ʳ-122ᵛ contain miniatures illustrating the text of Pseudo-Nonnos.

fol. 121ʳ. a) The birth of Zeus in two episodes (Cronos swallowing the stone, the infant Zeus and the priest). b) Rhea.

fol. 121ᵛ. a) The rape of Persephone. b) The birth of Dionysus. c) The birth of Aphrodite.

fol. 122ʳ. a) Tantalus and Pelops. b) Hecate. c) The Magi.

fol. 122ᵛ. a) Orpheus. b) Isis. Both in the left column.

fol. 130ᵛ. Teaching scene (homily 11).

fol. 158ᵛ. Gregory of Nazianzus and Gregory of Nyssa in proskynesis (homily 12).

fol. 163ʳ. The Koimesis of Athanasius of Alexandria (homily 13).

fol. 182ʳ. Gregory and bishops, all seated (homily 14).

fol. 196ᵛ. Teaching scene (homily 15).

fol. 217ʳ. Gregory, his father and a group of people (homily 16).

fol. 299ʳ begins the life of Gregory. A blank space has been left at the beginning, probably for a miniature which was never executed.

Style and Date:

The title miniatures have frames richly decorated with flower-petal style ornament, typical of late eleventh-century Constantinopolitan manuscripts. Bordier dated the manuscript in the twelfth or thirteenth century but the latter is too late a date for the style of the miniatures. Omont suggested a twelfth-century date, while Weitzmann dates it in the late eleventh century. Weitzmann's dating seems the most plausible in the light of stylistic comparisons with the cod. Athos, Panteleimon 6.[59] The miniatures of the Paris manuscript are smaller than those of the Athos codex, but are stylistically related. In both manuscripts appear the same expressive heads (in the Coislin, however, the expressions become monotonous at times), the same small feet that seem unable to support the body, the same narrow foreheads, the same rhythm in the stance—characteristics which suggest an approximately contemporary date for both manuscripts.

Bibliography:

B. de Montfaucon, *Bibliotheca Coisliniana*, Paris 1715, p. 297.

Bordier, *Description*, pp. 205-14, figs. 97-106.

Omont, *Inventaire sommaire*, III, p. 160.

Pokrovskii, *Evangelie*, pp. 170, 386, pl. XLVIII.

A. Heisenberg, *Grabeskirche und Apostelkirche*, II, Leipzig 1908, p. 252.

Millet, *Recherches*, pp. xviii, 134 n. 3, 176 n. 8, 205 n. 3, 466.

Ebersolt, *Miniature*, pp. 38 n. 3, 47 nn. 6, 7.

Omont, *Min. gr.* (1929), pp. 54-56, pls. CXVI-CXVIII.

E. Panofsky, F. Saxl, "Classical Mythology in Medieval Art," *Metropolitan Museum Studies*, 4 (1933), p. 248 n. 26, fig. 3.

Tikkanen, *Farbengebung*, pp. 104 n. 1, 128, 160, 166.

Frantz, *AB* (1934), pls. II, 10, 14; III, 19; IX, 18; XI, 3; XVII, 13; XVIII, 4.

E. C. Colwell, H. R. Willoughby, *The Four Gospels of Karahissar*, Chicago 1938, II, p. 461.

H. Buchthal, *The Miniatures of the Paris Psalter*, London 1938, p. 15, pl. XVI, 24.

[59] Supra, no. 7.

248

R. Devreesse, *Paris, Bibl. Nationale, Catalogue de manuscrits grecs*, ii, *Les fonds Coislin*, Paris 1945, p. 219.

Lazarev, *History*, i, pp. 128, 326 n. 99.

Weitzmann, *Mythology*, see index.

Bibl. Nat., *Byzance*, pp. 28, 29.

S. Der Nersessian, "The Homilies of Gregory of Nazianzus, Paris gr. 510," *Dumbarton Oaks Papers*, 16 (1962), p. 226 n. 141.

29. PATMOS, MONASTERY OF ST. JOHN THE EVANGELIST, COD. 45. 302 folios, 33.5 x 25 cm., parchment. XI or XII century. (Figs. 341-42)

Contents:

The sixteen homilies of the liturgical edition.

Decoration:

fol. 1ᵛ.   Anastasis (homily 1).

Style and Date:

The ornament of the title miniature and the ornamental headpieces on fol. 33ᵛ, floral motifs in zigzag patterns and flower-petal style, is typical of the late eleventh century. A parallel ornament is found in cod. Paris, Coislin 79, fol. 1ʳ, dated between 1078 and 1087.[60] A late eleventh-century date is also indicated by the style of the figures. If the Patmos miniature is compared to the cod. Paris gr. 1208, a twelfth-century manuscript, one sees that the use of highlights in the former is rather reserved and the mannerisms are not as pronounced as in the latter.[61] A comparison with two late eleventh-century manuscripts, however, i.e. the codd. Athos, Panteleimon 6 and Paris Coislin 239, shows that the Patmos miniature must be slightly later because of the rather increased schematization in the treatment of the drapery. It is on the basis of such comparisons that I propose a late eleventh- or early twelfth-century date. Perhaps the date 1100 is the most plausible.

A prayer to Christ, written in uncial letters on fol. 1ʳ, contained originally the names of the donor and the monastery to which the codex was offered. If a tracing of some of the flaked letters by a later hand is correct, the monastery's name may be restored as follows: $\theta(\epsilon\acute{\iota}\alpha\nu)$ $\mu(ον\acute{η}\nu)$ . . . $\acute{ο}σ\acute{\iota}ου$ $π(\alpha\tau\rho\grave{ο})$ς $\acute{η}\mu(\hat{\omega})\nu$ $\Sigma\acute{α}\beta\alpha$. Could it be that the manuscript was written in the monastery of St. Sabas in Jerusalem? If so it should be included among other known codices produced in that monastery, such as the illustrated Gospels in Princeton University Library, Garrett MS 3.

Bibliography:

J. Sakkelion, Πατμιακὴ Βιβλιοθήκη, Athens 1863, pp. 34, 35.

G. Jacopi, "Le miniature dei codici di Patmo," *Clara Rhodos*, VI-VII, 3 (1932-1933), p. 580, pl. v.

[60] Omont, *Min. gr.* (1929), pl. LXI.   [61] Ebersolt, *Miniature*, pl. XXXVI, 1.

30. PRINCETON UNIVERSITY, THE ART MUSEUM, COD. 2. 230 folios, 34 x 25 cm., parchment. XI century. (Fig. 256)

Contents:

1) The sixteen homilies of the liturgical edition, fols. 1ʳ-188ᵛ.
2) The Pseudo-Nonnos commentaries, fols. 189ʳ-227ᵛ.
3) The testament of Gregory of Nazianzus, fols. 228ʳ-230ʳ (*PG*, 37, 389-96).

Decoration:

In the Princeton codex each homily was originally headed by a miniature, but unfortunately all have been cut out. What is left is the lower part of a standing Gregory in the initial E on fol. 18ʳ and four ornamental headpieces at the beginning of the Pseudo-Nonnos commentaries.

The full-page miniature with the author portrait—ὁ ἅγιος Γρηγόριος ὁ Θεολόγος— preceding the text of the homilies was inserted at a later period.

Style and Date:

No colophon is preserved. On the basis of the flower-petal ornament, Weitzmann has dated the manuscript in the beginning of the eleventh century, a date which also agrees with the palaeography, and he has suggested Constantinople as the place of origin because of the brilliant technique and colors of the decoration. Thus the Princeton codex is probably one of the earliest of the extant illustrated manuscripts of the homilies of the liturgical edition.

For the inserted full-page miniature Weitzmann has suggested a late eleventh- or early twelfth-century date.

Bibliography:

S. de Ricci, W. J. Wilson, *Census of Medieval and Renaissance Manuscripts in the U.S.A. and Canada*, I, New York 1935, p. 693.

K. Weitzmann, "A Codex with the Homilies of Gregory of Nazianzus," *Record of the Museum of Historic Art, Princeton University*, 1 (1942), 14-17, figs. 1-3.

Idem, Mythology, see index.

31. ROME, BIBLIOTECA VATICANA, COD. GR. 463. 469 folios, 41.4 x 30.6 cm., parchment. *Anno* 1062. (Figs. 78-93)

Contents:

1) The sixteen homilies of the liturgical edition, fols. 1ʳ-443ᵛ.

2) The homily εἰς ἑαυτὸν καὶ εἰς τὸν γέροντα πατέρα by Gregory of Nazianzus, fols. 444ʳ-449ᵛ, (*PG*, 35, 844-49).

3) John Chrysostom's homily addressed to Philogonios, fols. 450ʳ-457ʳ, (*PG*, 48, 747-56).

4) The testament of Gregory of Nazianzus, fols. 457ᵛ-460ʳ, (*PG*, 37, 389-96).

5) Epitaphs of Gregory for Basil, ἑρμηνεία Νικήτα τοῦ φιλοσόφου, and λόγος εὐχαρι-
στήριος, fols. 460ʳ-462ᵛ, (*PG*, 38, 72-75 and *PG*, 37, 511-14).

6) Commentaries of Pseudo-Nonnos, fols. 463ʳ-469ᵛ.

Decoration:

fol. 3ᵛ.	The author portrait- ὁ ἅγιος Γρηγόριος ὁ Θεολόγος.
fol. 4ʳ.	Nativity, including the Bathing of the Child, in initial X (homily 8).
fol. 21ᵛ.	Within a quatrefoil, a cross on three steps in gold, full-page miniature (homily 8). The following cipher is between the arms of the cross: Α, Π, Μ, C (ἀρχὴ πίστεως μυστηρίου σταυρός.)
fol. 22ʳ.	Basil in initial E (homily 9).
fol. 107ʳ.	The Baptism of Christ in initial Π (homily 10).
fol. 127ʳ.	The same in initial X (homily 11).
fol. 184ʳ.	Acrobat with child on his head, in initial Φ (homily 12).
fol. 192ʳ.	Athanasius of Alexandria in initial Α (homily 13).
fol. 229ᵛ.	Full-page ornament like that of fol. 21ᵛ, in gold (homily 13). The following inscription is between the arms of the cross: Φ(ῶ)ς Ζ(ω)ή.
fol. 230ʳ.	Gregory taking leave of a group of bishops, in initial Π (homily 14).
fol. 295ʳ.	Gregory standing, in initial T (homily 16).
fol. 319ʳ.	Anastasis in initial Α (homily 1).
fol. 323ᵛ.	Full-page ornament like that on fol. 21ᵛ, a cross on four steps— IC-XC; two birds above the arms of the cross (homily 1).
fol. 324ʳ.	Habakkuk in initial E (homily 2).
fol. 358ᵛ.	Full-page ornament and cipher as on fol. 21ᵛ (homily 2).
fol. 359ʳ.	Christ seated frontally, in initial E (homily 3).
fol. 370ᵛ.	Full-page ornament like that on fol. 21ᵛ (homily 3). The following inscription is between the arms of the cross: Φ(ῶ)ς Χ(ριστοῦ) Φ(αίνει) Π(ᾶσι).
fol. 371ʳ.	Pentecost in initial Π (homily 4).
fol. 390ᵛ.	Full-page ornament and inscription as on fol. 370ᵛ.
fol. 391ʳ.	Gregory standing, in initial M (homily 6).
fol. 411ʳ.	The seven Maccabees in the fire and an angel modeled after the three holy children, in initial T (homily 5).

Style and Date:

A colophon has been preserved on fol. 469ᵛ giving the exact date and the name of the scribe, and suggesting the place of origin. The text reads as follows: αὕτη ἡ βίβλος πέφυκε Θεοδώρου (μον)αχ(οῦ) πρεσβυτέρου καὶ προεστῶτος τῆς τῶν Γαλακρηνῶν μονῆς πόθῳ πολλῷ καὶ ἐπιμελείᾳ ἐξ οἰκείων αὐτοῦ. Μᾶλλον δὲ τῶν τοῦ Θ(εο)ῦ δωρεῶν κατασκευ- ασθεῖσα καὶ κοσμηθεῖσα, γραφεῖσα δὲ τῇ αὐτοῦ προτροπῇ χειρὶ Συμεών (μον)αχ(οῦ) τοῦ αὐτοῦ μαθητοῦ καὶ τελειωθεῖσα μη(νὶ) δεκεμβρίῳ ἰνδ(ικτιῶνος) πρώτης ἐν ἔτει τῷ ϛφοά

(1062), βασιλεύοντος τοῦ εὐσεβεστάτου Κωνσταντίνου τοῦ Δούκα καὶ Ἐβδοκίας τῆς Αὐγούστης.

Each homily is headed by an ornamental headpiece of flower-petal style ornament and other floral motifs enclosed in circles and trapezoids of great richness. Birds are placed in the foliage at times, while animals that evidently excited the artist's imagination rest on pillars outside the frames, as occasional substitutes for the usual palmettes. The color of the ornament is extremely rich and brilliant.

The same brilliance and finesse in execution are observed in the small figured initials, which give evidence of the artist's imagination. The illustrator liked detail, had a feeling for balancing masses, a sense of rhythm in the use of line, and an academic elegance in his drawing of the figures. At times he showed his love of color by alternating olive green with pink for the flesh, as on fol. 107^r where the nude body of Christ is pink. Another distinct characteristic of the artist, and probably of his scriptorium, is the use of gold highlights in the drapery, which has a dematerializing effect. Heretofore to the best of our knowledge of Constantinopolitan scriptoria, such highlights were used only by the scriptorium of St. John of Studios.[62] The present manuscript, however, proves that this particular feature should now be ascribed to other Constantinopolitan scriptoria as well, among them the monastery of Galakrenon.[63]

Bibliography:

J. B. Seroux d'Agincourt, *Histoire de l'art par les monuments*, V, Paris 1823, pl. XLIX, 3.

Kondakov, *Histoire*, pp. 99ff.

Pokrovskii, *Evangelie*, p. 402, pl. XLVIII.

Schlumberger, *Epopée*, II, p. 561.

Vogel-Gardthausen, p. 410.

H. Peirce, R. Tyler, *Byzantine Art*, London 1926, pp. 42, 43, pl. 57.

K. and S. Lake eds., *Dated Greek Minuscule Manuscripts to the Year 1200*, VIII, Boston 1937, pls. 528-30.

R. Devreesse, *Codices Vaticani graeci*, II, Vatican 1937, pp. 231-33.

Lazarev, *History*, I, pp. 109, 314 n. 21.

32. ROME, BIBLIOTECA VATICANA, COD. GR. 464. 168 folios, 29 x 21.8 cm., paper. *Anno* 1359. (Figs. 470-72)

Contents:

1) The sixteen homilies of the liturgical edition, fols. 1^r-160^r.

2) Commentaries of Pseudo-Nonnos, fols. 160^v-166^v.

[62] Weitzmann, *Lectionary Morgan 639*, p. 360; N. Eleopoulos, Ἡ Βιβλιοθήκη καὶ τὸ Βιβλιογραφικὸν Ἐργαστήριον τῆς Μονῆς τῶν Στουδίου, Athens 1967.

[63] For sources, discussion and bibliography on the monastery of Γαλακρηνῶν, see R. Janin, *Constantinople byzantin*, Paris 1950, p. 453.

Decoration:

fol. 1ᵛ.   The author portrait—'Ο ἅγιος Γρηγόριος ὁ Θεολόγος.

fol. 44ᵛ.   The author portrait (homily 9).

fol. 76ᵛ.   The author portrait (homily 8).

Style and Date:

A colophon has been preserved on fol. 167ᵛ which reads as follows: Τέλο(ς) ἔλα(βεν) τὸ παρόν οὗτον βιβλ(ί)ον ἐν μηνὶ αὐγούστω ιέ π(ερι) π(α)το(ῦν)το(ς) ἰνδι-κτ(ο)υ τῆς . . . ἔτος ἄγοντ(ο)ς ἐξακισχιλιάδ(ο)ς καὶ δύς τετράκ(ι)ς ἐξήκοντ(α) σὺν ζ' ἡμέρ(ας) έ τὸ τέλο(ς) ἐγεγόνει. ἐγράφ(η) ἐξ ἐμοῦ ἱερέ(ω)ς 'Αλεξί(ου) τοῦ ἁμαρτωλοῦ (καὶ) ξένου.

The colophon contains no indication of the manuscript's place of origin. The minia-tures are done in a crude drawing technique with slight color-washes. However, an interesting feature appears: the figure of Gregory is placed within an architectural setting. The tower-like structures, which resemble columns and support arches, the comparatively high footstool, and the way the cushion is depicted so that much of it is visible, all present similarities to the portrait of Matthew in a Gospel book in Athens, cod. 74, fol. 59ʳ, which Weitzmann has classified among the south Italian manuscripts.[64] Perhaps this Gregory manuscript was written in the same region.

Bibliography:

Vogel-Gardthausen, p. 14.

R. Devreesse, *Codices Vaticani graeci*, ii, Vatican 1937, p. 233.

33. ROME, BIBLIOTECA VATICANA, COD. GR. 1947. 152 folios, 29.5 x 23 cm., parch-ment. XI century. (Figs. 123-36)

Contents:

1) The sixteen homilies of the liturgical edition, fols. 1ʳ-141ᵛ.

2) The commentaries of Pseudo-Nonnos, fols. 142ʳ-150ᵛ.

Decoration:

fol. 1ʳ.   Miniature totally flaked (homily 1).

fol. 2ᵛ.   The so-called vision of Habakkuk (?) almost totally flaked (homily 2).

fol. 13ʳ.   Mamas milking, sought by a soldier (homily 3).

fol. 16ᵛ.   Pentecost (homily 4).

fol. 22ᵛ.   Gregory teaching a group of people; his silent father sitting at the left (homily 16).

fol. 30ʳ.   The seven Maccabees, Eleazar, and Solomone before Antiochus (homily 5).

fol. 35ᵛ.   Gregory addressing a group of people and Cyprian (homily 6).

fol. 41ᵛ.   Gregory and Julian the Tax Collector, both seated (homily 7).

[64] Weitzmann, *Buchmalerei*, p. 85, pl. XCI, 580.

fol. 47ʳ.   Nativity, including the Bathing of the Child and the Annunciation to the Shepherds (homily 8).

fol. 52ᵛ.   The Koimesis of Basil the Great (homily 9).

fol. 81ʳ.   A teaching scene, miniature almost totally flaked (homily 10).

fol. 87ᵛ.   The Baptism of Christ (homily 11).

fol. 104ʳ.   Gregory of Nazianzus and Gregory of Nyssa in proskynesis (homily 12).

fol. 106ᵛ.   The Koimesis of Athanasius of Alexandria (homily 13).

fol. 119ʳ.   Gregory addressing a group of bishops, all seated (homily 14).

fol. 128ʳ.   Teaching scene (homily 15).

fols. 142ʳ-150ᵛ contain 23 miniatures illustrating the Pseudo-Nonnos commentaries.

fol. 142ᵛ.   Pelops and Oenomaus.

fol. 143ᵛ.   a) Artemis and Actaeon. b) Chiron and Achilles.

fol. 144ʳ.   a) Gyges and Candales. b) Midas.

fol. 144ᵛ.   a) Bellerophon. b) Alpheus and Arethusa.

fol. 145ʳ.   a) Space left for a miniature which was to depict the Molionides, but was never executed. b) Minos and Rhadamanthys.

fol. 146ʳ.   a) The birth of Zeus. b) The cult of Rhea.

fol. 146ᵛ.   Persephone.

fol. 147ʳ.   The birth of Dionysus.

fol. 147ᵛ.   The birth of Aphrodite.

fol. 148ʳ.   The scourges of the Lacedaemonians.

fol. 148ᵛ.   Hecate.

fol. 149ʳ.   Oak of Dodona and tripod of Delphi.

fol. 149ᵛ.   a) The Magi and the Chaldeans. b) Orpheus.

fol. 150ᵛ.   a) The goat of Mendes. b) Apis.

Style and Date:

The state of preservation is poor, the miniatures in most cases being flaked. The codex is sparsely ornamented. Plain blue bands frame the pictures, and ivy leaves decorate the frame corners. The flaked miniature on fol. 1ʳ is the only one that has the finials and palmettes typical of the late eleventh century. The style of the miniatures—wherever the state of preservation permits stylistic observations—also points to the last years of the eleventh century. The heads of the figures are comparatively high, the foreheads very narrow, the feet tiny—all characteristics found in late eleventh-century manuscripts, such as the codd. Athos, Panteleimon 6 and Paris, Coislin 239. Indeed, the Vatican manuscript has many affinities with those manuscripts. A closer examination reveals that in this manuscript the figures are flatter than in the cod. Paris, Coislin 239, the stance of the figures has a greater monotony, and at times the figures seem dead and not well related to each other. Such observations point to a slightly later date, still in the latter years of the eleventh century.

Bibliography:

T. Sinko, "De expositione Pseudo-Nonniana historiarum, quae in orationibus Gregorii Nazianzeni commemorantur," *Charisteria Casimiro de Morawski oblata*, Krakow 1922, p. 126 n. 1.

Weitzmann, *Mythology*, see index.

34. SINAI, MONASTERY OF ST. CATHERINE, COD. GR. 339. 437 folios, 32.3 x 25.4 cm., parchment. XII century. (Figs. 377-97)

Contents:

The sixteen homilies of the liturgical edition.

Decoration:

The illustrations begin on fol. 4ᵛ. The preceding folios are devoted to the following: fol. 2, table of contents; fol. 3ʳ, dedication written in uncial script; fol. 4ʳ, a later note.

fol. 4ᵛ.	The author portrait.
fol. 5ʳ.	Anastasis. The same in initial A (homily 1).
fol. 9ᵛ.	a) The so-called vision of Habakkuk. Christ and the four *zodia*, title miniature. b) The vision of Habakkuk and Gregory: Christos-Angelos and host of angels, in the left margin. c) Gregory seated, Habakkuk and a bust of Christ blessing, in initial E (homily 2).
fol. 42ᵛ.	a) Gregory teaching, Mamas as shepherd, title miniature. b) The Incredulity of Thomas. c) Consecration of a church. The latter two in the left margin. d) Gregory teaching and a bust of Christ, in initial E (homily 3).
fol. 53ʳ.	Mamas milking, in the right margin of the right written column (homily 3).
fol. 54ʳ.	Pentecost. The same in initial Π (homily 4).
fol. 73ᵛ.	a) Gregory and Julian as authors, title miniature. b) Julian as money changer, in the right margin. c) Gregory and the scribes in initial T (homily 7).
fol. 91ʳ.	Nativity, including the Bathing of the Child, Adoration, and the Annunciation to the Shepherds. Nativity in initial X (homily 8).[65]
fol. 91ᵛ.	Five women worshiping the Virgin Blachernitissa, in initial X (homily 8).
fol. 109ʳ.	The Koimesis of Basil the Great. Gregory teaching, in initial E (homily 9).
fol. 197ᵛ.	The Baptism of Christ. The same in initial Π (homily 10).
fol. 217ʳ.	Teaching scene. The Baptism of Christ in initial X (homily 11).
fol. 270ʳ.	The original folio has been cut out; a new page was added, perhaps sometime in the fourteenth century, to complete the missing text. On

[65] From here on the folios have been numbered incorrectly. The given numbers are the correct ones.

the verso side space has been left for a miniature never executed but intended to replace the one cut out (homily 12). Precisely the same procedure of cutting the folio, replacing it, and leaving space for a new miniature occurs on fols. 278, 313, and 415 (homilies 13, 14, and 16).

fol. 341ᵛ. Gregory and the poor. Gregory giving alms, in initial A (homily 15).

fol. 381ᵛ. The martyrdom of the seven Maccabees and Eleazar in six scenes. Figures of Maccabees, Eleazar, and Solomone in initial T (homily 5).

fol. 397ʳ. a) Gregory, Cyprian, and Justina standing. The same in initial M.
b) The martyrdom of Cyprian, in the right margin (homily 6).

Style and Date:

The richness of the illustration and the beauty of the miniatures make this manuscript an outstanding monument of Middle Byzantine book illumination. The ornament in flower-petal style, rendered in a great variety of imaginative versions, can find analogies only in the best Constantinopolitan manuscripts, such as the canon tables of the Vatican cod. Urb. gr. 2, or the lectionary of the Morgan Library, cod. 639.[66]

The subtlety and brilliance of the colors and the range of tones add to the beauty of the illustrations. The brightness of yellow-gold broken by enamel-blue is enriched by the freshness of the gracefully arranged green leaves and is intensified by reddish-purplish tones. All these features are the more intriguing because the origin of the manuscript is known. On fol. 3ʳ there is the following dedication in uncial gold letters: ἀφιερώθη ἡ παροῦσα βίβλος τῇ μονῇ τῆς Παντανάσσης, Ἁγίας Θ(εοτό)κου τῇ ἐν τῇ νήσῳ τῆς ἁγίας Γλυκερίας παρὰ τοῦ καθηγουμένου τῆς βασιλικῆς μονῆς τοῦ Παντοκράτορος τοῦ μοναχοῦ Κυρ(οῦ) Ἰωσὴφ τοῦ Ἁγιογλυκερίτου. Kondakov thought that the manuscript came from Lemnos, the island of St. Glykeria.[67] There is no reason to accept his suggestion because neither in the dedication note nor in the other note on fol. 437ᵛ is it stated that the manuscript was written in Lemnos. On the contrary, in the second note it is clearly written that τὴν βίβλον . . . τεῦξεν μοναστὴς Ἰωσὴφ ἀρχηγέτης μονῆς μοναστῶν Παντοκράτορος. . . . Although it is not explicitly stated that the manuscript originated in the monastery of Pantocrator, that is the obvious conclusion since the man who executed it was abbot in the monastery.

This conclusion also gives a *terminus post quem* in the early part of the twelfth century, because the monastery of Pantocrator was established in Constantinople by Irene, the wife of the Emperor John Comnenos (1118-1143)—probably soon after her husband's ascension to the throne, since the typikon of the monastery was granted in the year 1136.[68] The twelfth century is also the *terminus ante quem*, because

[66] Weitzmann, *Lectionary Morgan 639*, fig. 290.
[67] Kondakov, *Histoire*, p. 98. Cf. Gardthausen, *Codices sinaitici*, p. 22. M. Gedeon (Βυζαντινὸν Ἑορτολόγιον, Constantinople 1899, p. 104) locates

the monastery of St. Glykeria in the bay of Nicomedia.
[68] A. van Millingen, *Byzantine Churches in Constantinople*, London 1912, p. 220. R. Janin, *La*

stylistically the illustrations cannot belong to any other century. A general characteristic of the miniatures is the radiating highlights on the knees. A somewhat similar treatment is found in the cod. Laur. Plut. VII, 32, for which I propose an eleventh- or early twelfth-century date.[69] A comparison of the two, however, shows that in the cod. Sinai 339 the mannered treatment is intensified. At times, as on fol. 53^r, the brush strokes are broad, and it seems that the artist has played with lines and shapes. Another particular stylistic feature is the application of gold highlights on the garments, which tends to flatten the bodies. Apparently the systematic application of such highlights to give an incorporeal effect was current in Constantinople. The scriptorium of the monastery of Pantocrator, which makes its first appearance in Constantinopolitan book illumination with the cod. Sinai 339, must now be included among the scriptoria of Studios and Galakrenon which used this system of gold highlights.[70]

It is not known when the codex was taken from Lemnos to Mt. Sinai. Another later note on fol. 4^r states that by July 1758 the manuscript was in the monastery of St. Catherine and that at that date it was repaired by the monk Γερμανὸς οἰκονόμος τῆς Κρήτης.

Bibliography:

Kondakov, *Histoire*, pp. 97ff.

Idem, Puteshestvie na Sinai v 1881 godu, Odessa 1882, pp. 147ff., pl. LXXIX.

Pokrovskii, *Evangelie*, pl. XLVIII.

N. P. Kondakov, *Initiales zoomorphiques des manuscrits grecs et glagolitiques du X et du XI s., dans la bibliothèque du monastère du Sinai*, St. Petersburg 1909, pl. I.

Gardthausen, *Codices Sinaitici*, p. 72.

Vogel-Gardthausen, p. 220.

Bénéchévitch, *Catalogus*, p. 199.

H. L. Kehrer, *Die heiligen drei Könige in Literatur und Kunst*, II, Leipzig 1909, fig. 79.

O. Dalton, *Byzantine Art and Archaeology*, Oxford 1911, fig. 296.

Millet, *Recherches*, pp. 103 n. 5, 154, 176 n. 8, 178 n. 4, 183, 190, 207 n. 7.

H. Glück, *Die Christliche Kunst des Ostens*, Berlin 1923, p. 4, fig. 3.

V. Bénéchévitch, *Monumenta sinaitica*, St. Petersburg 1925, pl. 32.

Ebersolt, *Miniature*, pp. 38 n. 3, 43 n. 4, 47 n. 7, 50 n. 3, 63 n. 3.

M. Nekrasov, "Les frontispices architecturaux dans les manuscrits russes . . . ," *L'art byzantin chez les Slaves, Recueil T. Uspenskij*, II, Paris 1932, pp. 253, 254, pl. XXXVIII.

A. Xyngopoulos, "Ἡ μικρογραφία ἐν ἀρχῇ τοῦ Σιναϊτικοῦ κώδικος 339," *E.E.B.S.*, 16 (1940), pp. 128-37.

Lazarev, *History*, I, p. 115.

---

géographie ecclésiastique de l'empire byzantin, III (Les églises et les monastères), Paris 1953, pp. 529ff.

[69] Supra, no. 12.

[70] Supra, no. 31. Cf. Weitzmann, *Lectionary Morgan 639*, p. 360.

H. Stern, "Nouvelles recherches sur les images des conciles dans l'église de la nativité à Bethléem," *Cahiers archéologiques*, 3 (1948), p. 104.

A. Grabar, "Un rouleau liturgique Constantinopolitain et ses peintures," *Dumbarton Oaks Papers*, 8 (1954), pp. 179 n. 21, 196 n. 47.

S. Der Nersessian, "The Homilies of Gregory of Nazianzus, Paris gr. 510," *Dumbarton Oaks Papers*, 16 (1962), p. 202 n. 22.

K. Weitzmann, "Mount Sinai's Holy Treasures," *The National Geographic Magazine*, January 1964, pp. 124, 125.

35. SINAI, MONASTERY OF ST. CATHERINE, COD. GR. 346. 250 folios, 11 x 9.3 cm., parchment. XI century. (Figs. 343-54)

Contents:

Fifteen homilies of the liturgical edition.

Decoration:

fol. 27^r.	Gregory teaching, Mamas standing, and a bust of Christ, in initial E (homily 3).
fol. 32^r.	Pentecost with bust of Christ in initial Π (homily 4).
fol. 42^v.	Julian the Tax Collector writing and Gregory standing, in initial T (homily 7).
fol. 51^r.	Nativity in initial X (homily 8).
fol. 61^r.	The Koimesis of Basil the Great. A cleric (Gregory of Nazianzus ?) in initial E (homily 9).
fol. 112^v.	The Baptism of Christ, in initial Π (homily 10).
fol. 123^r.	The same initial X (homily 11).
fol. 152^v.	Basil, Gregory of Nazianzus, Gregory of Nyssa, in initial Φ (homily 12).
fol. 180^r.	Gregory teaching, in initial Π (homily 14).
fol. 194^v.	Gregory giving alms to the poor, in initial A (homily 15).
fol. 227^r.	Gregory of Nazianzus and Cyprian, in initial M (homily 6).
fol. 237^r.	Gregory of Nazianzus and his father (badly flaked) in initial T (homily 16).

Style and Date:

The ornament, consisting of rectilinear patterns and floral motifs (flower-petal style and ivy leaves), is rather meager and sketchy. The manuscript was probably made in Constantinople, but its miniatures cannot parallel the high quality of the best Constantinopolitan manuscripts although the patterns of its ornament find parallels in them. The miniatures are extraordinarily minute, which is the main characteristic of the manuscript. This minuteness and the poor state of preservation prevent careful stylistic analysis. However, just as the ornament points to a late eleventh-century date, so also do the figures. Both the absence of strong highlights and the smooth painterly quality of modeling indicate the eleventh century.

Bibliography:

N. P. Kondakov, *Puteshestvie na Sinai v 1881 godu*, Odessa 1882, pp. 152, 153.
Idem, Histoire, p. 100.
Gardthausen, *Codices sinaitici*, p. 75.

36. TURIN, UNIVERSITY LIBRARY, COD. C. I. 6. 199 folios, 34 x 23 cm., parchment. XI century. (Figs. 19-60)

Contents:

The sixteen homilies of the liturgical edition.

Decoration:

Apart from three extant title miniatures, the decoration of this richly illustrated manuscript consists of literally hundreds of historiated initials, of which only those related directly to the main theme of each homily have been indicated below.

fol. 1ʳ.   Anastasis (only Christ and the gates of Hell preserved) in initial A (homily 1).

fol. 1ᵛ.   Two shepherds in initial M (homily 1).

fol. 2ʳ.   Page cut out and restored, modern writing. Probably scenes from Christ's life cut out.

fol. 3ʳ.   The author portrait in initial E (homily 2).

fol. 16ʳ.   Consecration of a church, in the margin. Gregory teaching, in initial K (homily 3).

fol. 18ʳ.   Incredulity of Thomas, in the margin. David playing the lyre, in initial A (homily 3).

fol. 18ᵛ.   Temptation of Eve in initial Z (homily 3).

fol. 19ᵛ.   The four seasons in initial A (homily 3).

fol. 20ʳ.   Man stepping on a hook, in initial A. Pruning of a tree, in initial Δ (homily 3).

fol. 21ᵛ.   Abraham in initial T (homily 3).

fol. 22ʳ.   The Prophet Elijah in initial K (homily 3).

fol. 29ʳ.   The martyrdom of the seven Maccabees. The decapitation of Eleazar, in initial X (homily 5).

fol. 30ʳ.   Eleazar and Solomone in initial Θ (homily 5).

fols. 30ᵛ, 31ᵛ. Solomone and one of her sons, in initials Ω and Λ (homily 5).

fol. 34ᵛ.   Eleazar in initial T (homily 5).

fol. 37ᵛ.   The Koimesis of Cyprian (homily 6).

Illustrations on fols. 38ʳ-43ʳ belong to the same homily.

fol. 38ʳ.   The author portrait in initial E.

fol. 39ʳ.   Cyprian teaching, in initial E.

fol. 39ᵛ. Cyprian in initial K.

fol. 43ʳ. Cyprian with a devil, in initial Σ.

fol. 47ʳ. Julian the Tax Collector as money changer (homily 7).

fol. 55ᵛ. Title miniature cut out except initial X, formed by four angels holding medallion with Christ (homily 8).

fol. 82ᵛ. Peter and Paul in an ecstatic meeting, in initial E (homily 9).

fols. 84ᵛ-91ᵛ contain historiated initials illustrating single words or phrases in
the same homily.

fol. 94ᵛ. Pencil and pen drawings begin.

Style and Date:

Fols. 1ʳ and 3ʳ have large ornamental headpieces of flower-petal style, in the foliage of which fantastic animals have at times been included. Palmettes and cypress trees stand on the lower corners of the frames of the miniatures. A similar arrangement of the flower-petal style ornament in spirals appears in another Gregory manuscript, the cod. Vat. gr. 463, fol. 324ʳ, dated in the year 1062.[71] In addition to the ornament the two manuscripts have affinities in the extensive use of figured initials and in the rhythm of the line. Their affinities, however, stop there and the differences between them suggest a later date for the Turin manuscript. Quite often in the Turin manuscript the treatment of the drapery is unclear, as in the scene of the martyrdom of the Macca-bees, or the drapery is sketched in a few general lines, as in the miniature of Julian. The relationship of the architectural backgrounds is also unclear. Occasionally stronger highlights appear on the foreheads, as on fol. 3ʳ, and the hair is represented in distinct locks. In the light of these observations, a late eleventh-century date seems the most probable.

The manuscript was probably made in Constantinople. At least this is suggested by the color and richness of the ornament, although it does not have the aristocratic elegance or the academic perfection of the best Constantinopolitan manuscripts. A spirit of excitement moves through the miniatures. It seems that everything works toward intensifying that excitement: the sweeping lines, the broad brush technique, the mantles that flutter in the air, and at times the iconography. Can it be suggested that the art of the eastern provinces of the Empire influenced the unknown illustrator of the Turin manuscript?

Bibliography:

G. Pasini ed., *Codices manuscripti Bibliothecae Regii Taurinensis Athenaei*, I, Turin
(Biblioteca nazionale) 1749, p. 90.

W. Volbach, *L'art byzantin*, Paris 1933, p. 71.

Lazarev, *History*, I, p. 316 n. 36.

[71] Supra, no. 31.

INDEX

PLATES

1. Fol. 1ᵛ: Anastasis; Gregory Teaching

MOSCOW, STATE HIST. MUSEUM. COD. 146

2. Fol. 4ᵛ: Vision of Habakkuk

3. Fol. 23ᵛ: Doubting Thomas

4. Fol. 23ᵛ: Encaenia

5. Fol. 29ᵛ: St. Mamas Milking

6. Fol. 29ᵛ: Pentecost

MOSCOW, STATE HIST. MUSEUM. COD. 146

7. Fol. 40^v: Martyrdom of Maccabees

8. Fol. 50^v: Martyrdom of Cyprian

9. Fol. 61^v: Julian as Money Changer

10. Fol. 71^r: Nativity

MOSCOW, STATE HIST. MUSEUM. COD. 146

11. Fol. 81ʳ: Koimesis of Basil

12. Fol. 133ᵛ: Baptism of Christ

13. Fol. 145ʳ: John Baptizing

14. Fol. 177ʳ: Gregory of Nazianzus and Gregory of Nyssa

MOSCOW, STATE HIST. MUSEUM. COD. 146

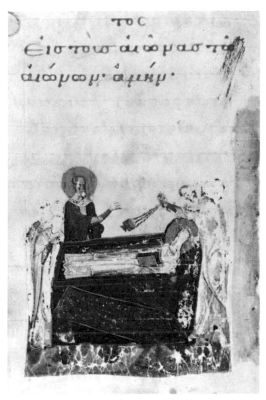

15. Fol. 181ᵛ: Koimesis of Athanasius

16. Fol. 202ᵛ: Gregory Addressing Bishops

17. Fol. 219ᵛ: Almsgiving

18. Fol. 244ᵛ: Gregory and His Father

MOSCOW, STATE HIST. MUSEUM. COD. 146

19. Fol. 1ᵛ: Shepherds

20. Fol. 3ʳ: Author Portrait

21. Fol. 6ᵛ: Juggler

22. Fol. 9ʳ: Genre Scene

23. Fol. 11ʳ: Wrestling

24. Fol. 12ʳ: Genre Scene

25. Fol. 12ᵛ: Juggler

26. Fol. 15ᵛ: Musician

27. Fol. 16ʳ: Author Portrait

28. Fol. 16ʳ: Encaenia

TURIN, UNIV. LIB. COD. C.I.6

29. Fol. 18ʳ: Doubting Thomas

30. Fol. 18ʳ: David

31. Fol. 18ᵛ: Eve Tempted

32. Fol. 19ᵛ: Four Seasons

33. Fol. 20ʳ: Tilling

34. Fol. 20ʳ: Pruning

35. Fol. 21ᵛ: Abraham

36. Fol. 22ʳ: Elijah

38. Fol. 29ʳ: Martyrdom of Eleazar

37. Fol. 29ʳ: Martyrdom of Maccabees

39. Fol. 30ʳ: Eleazar and Solomone

TURIN, UNIV. LIB. COD. C.I.6

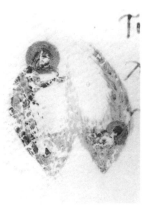

40-41. Fols. 30ᵛ, 31ᵛ: Solomone and Son

42. Fol. 34ᵛ: Eleazar

43. Fol. 37ᵛ: Martyrdom of Cyprian

44. Fol. 37ᵛ: Koimesis of Cyprian

45. Fol. 47ᵛ: Genre Scene

46. Fol. 47ʳ: Julian as Money Changer

47. Fol. 48ʳ: Genre Scene

48. Fol. 55ᵛ: Christ and Angels

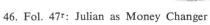

TURIN, UNIV. LIB. COD. C.I.6

49. Fol. 67ʳ: Acrobats

50. Fol. 67ʳ: Snake Dance

51. Fol. 68ʳ: Snake Charmers

52. Fol. 69ᵛ: Genre Scene

53. Fol. 72ʳ: Jugglers and Musician

54. Fol. 73ᵛ: Acrobat

55. Fol. 76ᵛ: Musician

56. Fol. 82ᵛ: Peter and Paul
Meeting

57. Fol. 83ʳ: Genre Scene

58. Fol. 88ᵛ: Liturgical Scene

59. Fol. 89ʳ: Night

60. Fol. 93ᵛ: Earth and Sea

TURIN, UNIV. LIB. COD. C.I.6

61. Fol. 2ᵛ: Author Portrait

62. Fol. 3ʳ: Anastasis

63. Fol. 5ᵛ: Author Portrait

64. Fol. 27ʳ: Gregory and
St. Mamas

65. Fol. 33ʳ: Pentecost

66. Fol. 45ʳ: Maccabees,
Solomone, Eleazar

67. Fol. 56ʳ: Cyprian and Justina

68. Fol. 68ʳ: Gregory and Julian

69. Fol. 78ᵛ: Nativity

70. Fol. 89ᵛ: Koimesis of Basil

71. Fol. 144ᵛ: Baptism of Christ

72. Fol. 156ᵛ: Baptism of Christ

73. Fol. 189ᵛ: Gregorys in
Proskynesis

ISTANBUL, PATR. LIB. COD. 16

74. Fol. 194ᵛ: Gregory and
Athanasius

75. Fol. 234ᵛ: Gregory and
Bishops

76. Fol. 243ᵛ: Gregory
Giving Alms

77. Fol. 261ʳ: Gregory Teaching

ISTANBUL, PATR. LIB. COD. 16

78. Fol. 3ᵛ: Author Portrait

79. Fol. 21ᵛ: Cross

80. Fol. 4ʳ: Nativity

81. Fol. 22ʳ: Basil the Great

82. Fol. 107ʳ: Baptism of
Christ

ROME, VATICAN. COD. GR. 463

83. Fol. 127ʳ: Baptism of
Christ

84. Fol. 184ʳ: Acrobat

85. Fol. 192ʳ: Athanasius of
Alexandria

87. Fol. 295ʳ: Gregory of
Nazianzus

88. Fol. 319ʳ: Anastasis

89. Fol. 324ʳ: Habakkuk

90. Fol. 359ʳ: Christ

91. Fol. 371ʳ: Pentecost

92. Fol. 391ʳ: Gregory of
Nazianzus

ROME, VATICAN. COD. GR. 463

86. Fol. 230r: Gregory
Taking Leave

94. Fol. 2r: Church and Synagogue

93. Fol. 411r: Martyrdom of
Maccabees

95. Fol. 41v: Maccabees, Solomone, Eleazar

LONDON, BRIT. MUS. COD. ADD. 24381

96. Fol. 52ʳ: Deesis Scene

97. Fol. 3ᵛ: Author Portrait

98. Fol. 2ᵛ: Author Portrait

FLORENCE, BIBL. LAUR. COD. PLUT. VII, 24   JERUSALEM, PATR. LIB. COD. TAPHOU 14

99. Fol. 3ʳ: Anastasis

100. Fol. 6ʳ: Vision of Habakkuk

101. Fol. 9ʳ: Fallen Heosphoros

JERUSALEM, PATR. LIB. COD. TAPHOU 14

102. Fol. 11ʳ: Adam; Death of
First Man

103. Fol. 33ʳ: Bucolic Scenes

104. Fol. 27ʳ: St. Mamas Milking

JERUSALEM, PATR. LIB. COD. TAPHOU 14

105. Fol. 33ᵛ: Bucolic Scenes

106. Fol. 34ᵛ: Trotting Horse

107. Fol. 33ᵛ: Bucolic Scenes

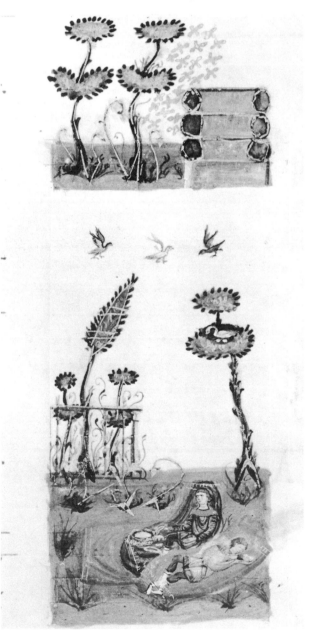

108. Fol. 34ʳ: Bucolic Scenes

JERUSALEM, PATR. LIB. COD. TAPHOU 14

109. Fol. 35ʳ: Pentecost

110. Fol. 47ʳ: Martyrdom of Maccabees

111. Fol. 58ʳ: Teaching Scene with Cyprian

112. Fol. 70ʳ: Gregory and Julian

113. Fol. 81ʳ: Nativity

114. Fol. 114ʳ: Koimesis of Basil

JERUSALEM, PATR. LIB. COD. TAPHOU 14

115. Fol. 173r: Baptism of Christ

116. Fol. 186r: Gregory Teaching

117. Fol. 219v: Gregorys in Proskynesis

118. Fol. 224ᵛ: Teaching Scene with Athanasius

119. Fol. 247ʳ: Gregory Addressing Bishops

120. Fol. 265ʳ: Gregory Taking Leave

JERUSALEM, PATR. LIB. COD. TAPHOU 14

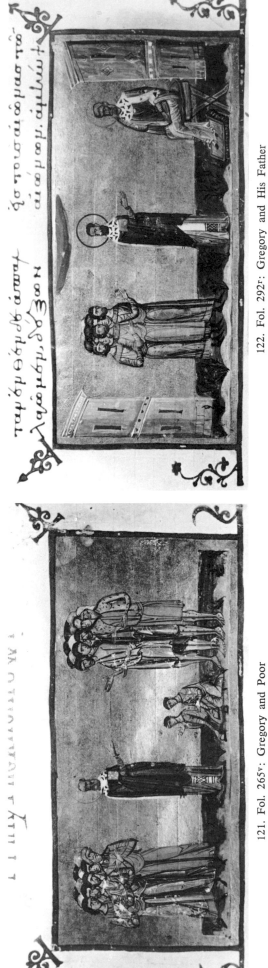

121. Fol. 265v: Gregory and Poor

122. Fol. 292r: Gregory and His Father

JERUSALEM, PATR. LIB. COD. TAPHOU 14

124. Fol. 16v: Pentecost

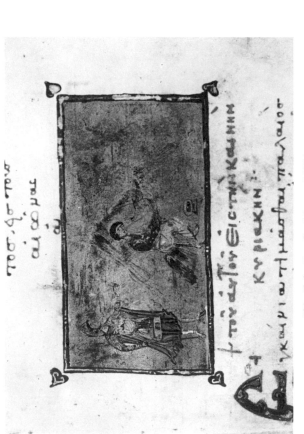

123. Fol. 13r: St. Mamas Milking

126. Fol. 30r: Maccabees, Eleazar, and Solomone before Antiochus

128. Fol. 41v: Gregory and Julian

125. Fol. 22v: Gregory and His Father

127. Fol. 35v: Teaching Scene with Cyprian

ROME, VATICAN. COD. GR. 1947

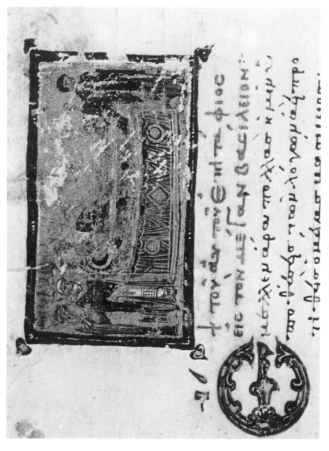

130. Fol. 52ᵛ: Koimesis of Basil

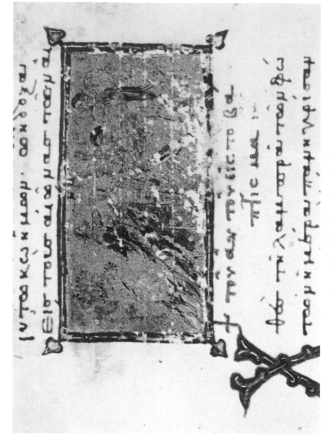

132. Fol. 87ᵛ: Baptism of Christ

129. Fol. 47ʳ: Nativity

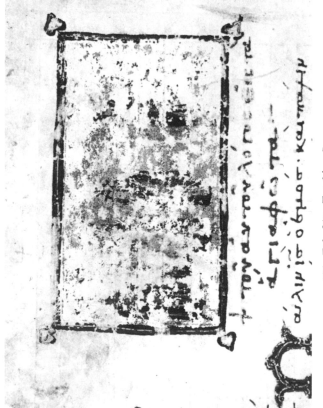

131. Fol. 81ʳ: Teaching Scene

134. Fol. 106v: Koimesis of Atanasius

136. Fol. 128r: Teaching Scene

133. Fol. 104r: Gregorys in Proskynesis

135. Fol. 119r: Gregory Addressing the Bishops

ROME, VATICAN. COD. GR. 1947

139. Fol. 30ʳ: Church and Synagogue

137. Fol. 2ʳ: Anastasis

138. Fol. 5ᵛ: Vision of Habakkuk

141. Fol. 37v: Bucolic Scenes

140. Fol. 37r: Bucolic Scenes

ATHOS, PANTELEIMON. COD. 6

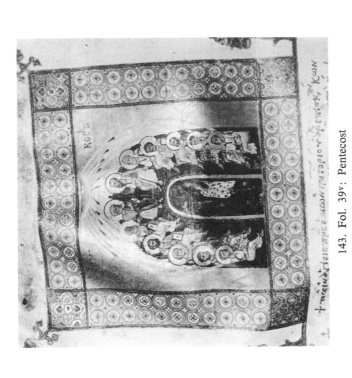

143. Fol. 39v: Pentecost

145. Fol. 63v: Gregory Teaching

142. Fol. 38v: St. Mamas

144. Fol. 53r: Maccabees

147. Fol. 77ᵛ: Gregory and Julian

149. Fol. 100ʳ: Koimesis of Basil

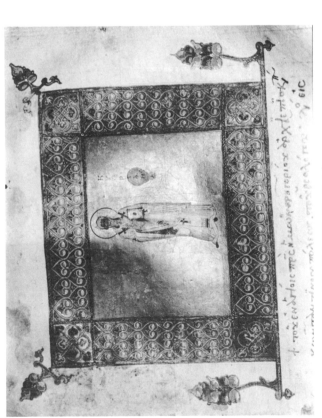

146. Fol. 64ʳ: St. Cyprian

148. Fol. 89ᵛ: Nativity

ATHOS, PANTELEIMON. COD. 6

153. Fol. 134ᵛ: First Trial of Basil

157. Fol. 135ʳ: First Trial of Basil

152. Fol. 115ʳ: Basil and Gregory

156. Fol. 132ʳ: Riders

151. Fol. 105ʳ: Hinds

155. Fol. 123ʳ: Arios

150. Fol. 90ᵛ: John the Baptist

154. Fol. 119ʳ: Gregory

162. Fol. 151ᵛ: Adam in Paradise; Enos

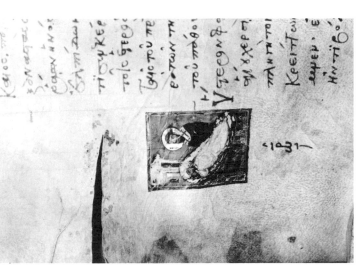

160. Fol. 140ᵛ: Second Trial of Basil

159. Fol. 138ᵛ: Basil Healing Prefect

158. Fol. 138ʳ: Basil's Exile; Basil Healing Emperor's Son

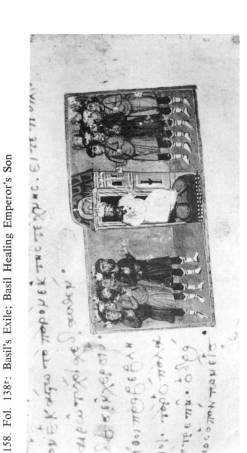

161. Fol. 140ᵛ: People Protesting to Prefect

ATHOS, PANTELEIMON. COD. 6

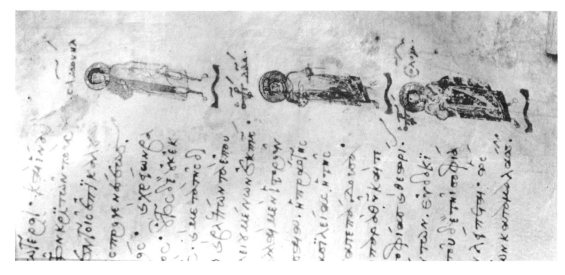

167. Fol. 154ʳ: Samuel, David, Solomon

165. Fol. 153ʳ: Joseph with Brothers; Moses; Aaron

164. Fol. 152ᵛ: Jacob and Ladder

166. Fol. 153ᵛ: Joshua

163. Fol. 152ʳ: Old Testament Scenes

171. Fol. 173ʳ: John the Baptist

173. Fol. 161ʳ: Baptism of Christ

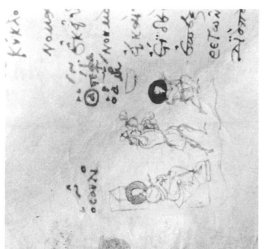

170. Fol. 155ᵛ: Stoning of Stephen

169. Fol. 155ʳ: John the Baptist

168. Fol. 154ᵛ: Ascension of Elijah;
Three Holy Children

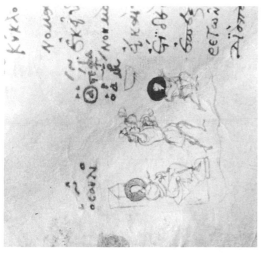

172. Fol. 178ʳ: Teaching Scene

ATHOS, PANTELEIMON. COD. 6

175. Fol. 219r: Koimesis of Athanasius

178. Fol. 272v: Valens

ATHOS, IVIRON. COD. 271

177. Fol. 242v: Mercurius Killing Julian; Valens

174. Fol. 214r: Gregorys in Proskynesis

176. Fol. 240v: Gregory and Bishops

ATHOS, PANTELEIMON. COD. 6

186. Fol. 13^r: March

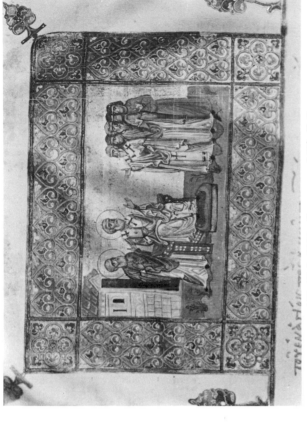

180. Fol. 281^r: Gregory and His Father

185. Fol. 15^r: Isaiah

134. Fol. 11^v: Moses

ATHOS, PANTELEIMON. COD. 6

183. Fol. 8^r: Athanasius

182. Fol. 6^r: Habakkuk

179. Fol. 257^r: Gregory and Poor

181. Fol. 6^r: Vision of Habakkuk

PARIS, BIBL. NAT. COD. COISLIN 239

187. Fol. 15ʳ:
Lot's Wife

188. Fol. 15ᵛ: John
the Baptist

189. Fol. 16ʳ:
Paul

190. Fol. 18ʳ: Moses Raising Brazen Serpent

191. Fol. 18ᵛ: Joseph of
Arimathea and Pilate

192. Fol. 18ᵛ:
Simon of Cyrene

193. Fol. 19ʳ: Two Marys at Tomb

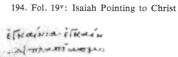

194. Fol. 19ᵛ: Isaiah Pointing to Christ

195. Fol. 22ʳ: Church and Synagogue

196. Fol. 22ʳ:
Gregory

197. Fol. 26ʳ: The Hours

198. Fol. 26ᵛ: Sailing

PARIS, BIBL. NAT. COD. COISLIN 239

199. Fol. 26ᵛ: Bucolic Scene

200. Fol. 26ᵛ: Bucolic Scene

201. Fol. 27ʳ: Bucolic Scenes

202. Fol. 27ᵛ: St. Mamas

203. Fol. 28ʳ: Pentecost

204. Fol. 30ʳ: Seven-Branched Candlestick

205. Fol. 34ᵛ: Joel

206. Fol. 37ᵛ: Gregory, Solomone, Eleazar, Maccabees

207. Fol. 38ʳ: Eleazar Brought to Antiochus

208. Fol. 39ᵛ: Scourging of Eleazar

209. Fol. 40ʳ: Maccabees before Antiochus

210. Fol. 41ᵛ: Antiochus and Eldest Maccabee

211. Fol. 43ᵛ: Solomone Exhorting Sons

212. Fol. 44ᵛ: Solomone in Furnace

213. Fol. 45ᵛ: Antiochus and Israelites

214. Fol. 46ᵛ: Gregory and Cyprian

PARIS, BIBL. NAT. COD. COISLIN 239

215. Fol. 50ʳ: Gregory and Justina

217. Fol. 57ʳ: Gregory and Julian

216. Fol. 53ʳ: Cyprian before Decius

218. Fol. 54ʳ: Martyrdom of Cyprian

219. Fol. 65ᵛ: The Nativity

220. Fol. 55ʳ: Cyprian Revealing His Relics

221. Fol. 74ʳ: Koimesis of Basil

PARIS, BIBL. NAT. COD. COISLIN 239

222. Fol. 100ᵛ: Basil before Prefect

223. Fol. 105ʳ: Caesareans Protesting

224. Fol. 100ᵛ: Basil before Prefect

226. Fol. 120ʳ: Baptism of Christ

225. Fol. 101ᵛ: Prefect Reporting to Valens

227. Fol. 104ᵛ: Second Trial of Basil

228. Fol. 130ᵛ: Teaching Scene

PARIS, BIBL. NAT. COD. COISLIN 239

229. Fol. 158ᵛ: Gregorys in Proskynesis

230. Fol. 163ʳ: Koimesis of Athanasius

231. Fol. 182ʳ: Gregory Addressing Bishops

232. Fol. 196ᵛ: Teaching Scene

233. Fol. 217ʳ: Gregory and His Father

PARIS, BIBL. NAT. COD. COISLIN 239

235. Fol. 4r: Anastasis

236. Fol. 7r: Vision of Habakkuk

234. Fol. 3v: Teaching Scene

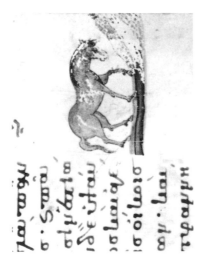

238. Fol. 35r: Bucolic Scene

239. Fol. 35r: Bucolic Scene

PARIS, BIBL. NAT. COD. GR. 533

237. Fol. 34r: Bucolic Scenes

240. Fol. 34ᵛ: Bucolic Scenes
PARIS, BIBL. NAT. COD. GR. 533

241. Fol. 35ᵛ: Gregory Teaching

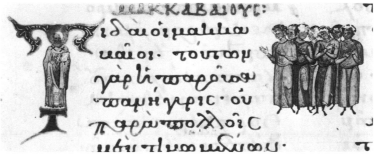

242. Fol. 47ᵛ: Gregory Teaching

243. Fol. 58ʳ: Gregory and Cyprian

244. Fol. 70ʳ: Gregory Teaching

245. Fol. 77ᵛ: Gregory and Julian

PARIS, BIBL. NAT. COD. GR. 533

247. Fol. 154ʳ: Baptism of Christ; Gregory Teaching

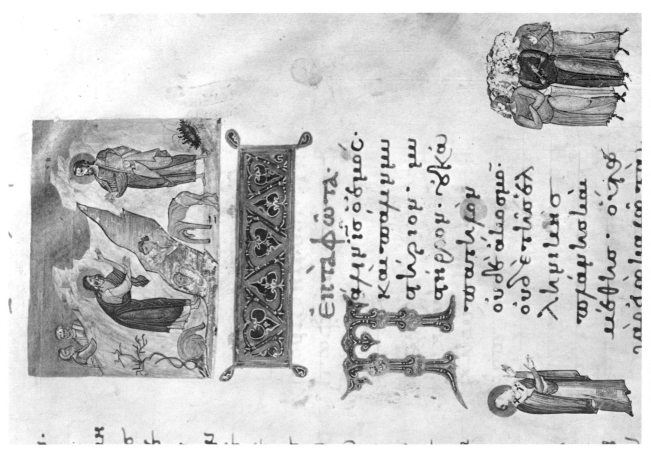

246. Fol. 146ʳ: Christ Meets John the Baptist; Gregory Teaching

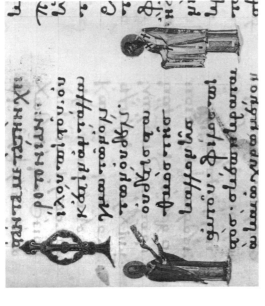

250. Fol. 192r: Gregory of Nazianzus and Gregory of Nyssa

253. Fol. 236r: Gregory Teaching

249. Fol. 158v: Gregory Teaching

252. Fol. 218v: Gregory Addressing Bishops

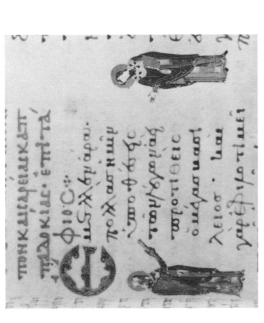

248. Fol. 91r: Gregory and Basil the Great

251. Fol. 196v: Gregory of Nazianzus and Athanasius

PARIS, BIBL. NAT. COD. GR. 533

254. Fol. 251ʳ: Gregory Teaching

255. Fol. 276ᵛ: Gregory the Presbyter and Gregory of Nazianzus Teaching

PARIS, BIBL. NAT. COD. GR. 533

256. Fol. O: Author Portrait

PRINCETON, THE ART MUSEUM. COD. 2

257. Fol. 3ʳ: Habakkuk   258. Fol. 25ᵛ: Pentecost   259. Fol. 60ᵛ: Nativity   260. Fol. 69ᵛ: Koimesis of Basil

ATHENS, NAT. LIB. COD. 2554

261. Fol. 14ᵛ: St. Mamas

262. Fol. 18ᵛ: Pentecost

FLORENCE, BIB. LAUR. COD. PLUT. VII, 32

L

264. Fol. 40ʳ: Maccabees, Solomone, Eleazar before Antiochus

266. Fol. 56ʳ: Gregory and Julian

263. Fol. 26ʳ: Athanasius of Alexandria

265. Fol. 48ʳ: Gregory and Cyprian

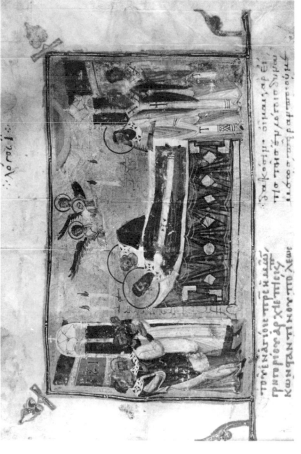

267. Fol. 63ʳ: Nativity; Gregory Teaching

268. Fol. 70ʳ: Koimesis of Basil

270. Fol. 110ᵛ: Gregory Teaching Baptism of Christ

269. Fol. 120ʳ: Teaching Scene

FLORENCE, BIB. LAUR. COD. PLUT. VII, 32

272. Fol. 149ʳ: Gregory Addressing Bishops

274. Fol. 181ʳ: Gregory Teaching

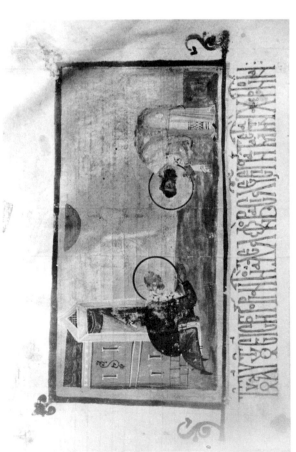

271. Fol. 145ʳ: Gregorys in Proskynesis

273. Fol. 162ʳ: Teaching Scene

FLORENCE, BIB. LAUR. COD. PLUT. VII, 32

275. Fol. 2ᵛ: Author Portrait

OXFORD, BODL. LIB. COD. CANON. GR. 103

276. Fol. 3ʳ: Anastasis

277. Fol. 35ʳ: Pentecost

278. Fol. 47ʳ: Eleazar, Christ, Solomone
and Maccabees

279. Fol. 57ʳ. Gregory and Cyprian

280. Fol. 69ʳ: Gregory and Julian

281. Fol. 79ᵛ: Nativity

282. Fol. 90ᵛ: Koimesis of Basil

283. Fol. 146ʳ: Baptism of Christ

284. Fol. 192ʳ: Gregory of Nazianzus and Gregory of Nyssa

285. Fol. 197ʳ: Gregory and Athanasius of Alexandria

286. Fol. 264ʳ: Teaching Scene

287. Fol. 8ᵛ: Pentecost

288. Fol. 14ᵛ: Eleazar, Solomone, and Maccabees

289. Fol. 19ᵛ: Gregory and Cyprian

290. Fol. 25ᵛ: Gregory and Julian

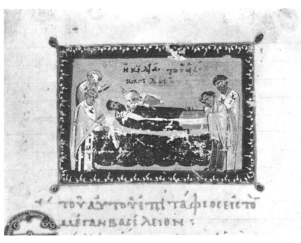

291. Fol. 36ʳ: Koimesis of Basil

292. Fol. 62ʳ: Gregory, Christ, and John the Baptist

OXFORD, BODL. LIB. COD. SELDEN. B. 54

293. Fol. 67ᵛ: Gregory Teaching

294. Fol. 85ᵛ: Gregorys in Proskynesis

295. Fol. 88ᵛ: Athanasius of Alexandria

296. Fol. 99ʳ: Gregory Addressing Bishops

297. Fol. 108ʳ: Gregory Teaching

298. Fol. 121ʳ: Gregory and His Father

OXFORD, BODL. LIB. COD. SELDEN. B. 54

299. Fol. 3ᵛ: Teaching Scene

300. Fol. 4ʳ: Anastasis

301. Fol. 7ʳ: Vision
of Habakkuk

302. Fol. 29ʳ: Gregory

303. Fol. 36ᵛ: Pentecost

304. Fol. 48ʳ: Gregory

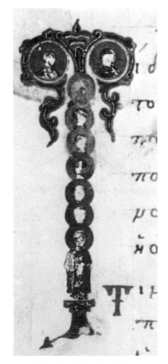

305. Fol. 63ʳ: Maccabees,
Eleazar, and Solomone

306. Fol. 73ʳ: Gregory
and Cyprian

307. Fol. 85ʳ: Gregory

MILAN, BIBL. AMBROSIANA. COD. G 88 SUP. (GR. 416)

308. Fol. 95ʳ: Nativity

309. Fol. 105ʳ: Koimesis of Basil

310. Fol. 163ʳ: Baptism of Christ

311. Fol. 176ᵛ: Sacrament of Baptism

312. Fol. 213ʳ: Christ
and Gregorys

313. Fol. 220ʳ: Gregory Giving Book to Athanasius

314. Fol. 245ʳ: Gregory Addressing
Bishops

315. Fol. 264ᵛ: Gregory and Poor

MILAN, BIBL. AMBROSIANA. COD. G 88 SUP. (GR. 416)

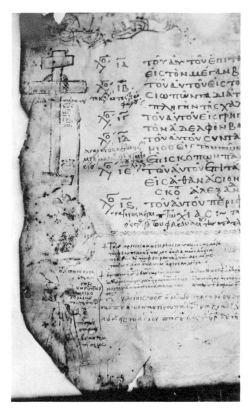

316. Fol. 1ᵛ: Table of Contents;
Gregory Teaching

317. Fol. 4ᵛ: Anastasis

318. Fol. 27ᵛ: Doubting Thomas; Saints;
Bucolic Scenes

319. Fol. 28ʳ: St. Mamas

320. Fol. 35ʳ: Pentecost

321. Fol. 47ᵛ: City of Zion

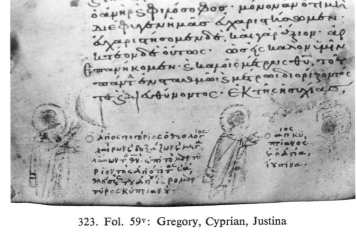

322. Fol. 48ʳ: Maccabees, Eleazar, Solomone

323. Fol. 59ᵛ: Gregory, Cyprian, Justina

324. Fol. 72ʳ: Three Holy Children and Daniel

325. Fol. 82ᵛ: Virgin, Christ, Angels, Nazareth

326. Fol. 93ᵛ: Baptism of Christ

327: Fol. 105ᵛ: Christ Baptizing Peter; Saints

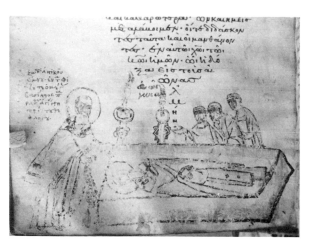

328. Fol. 135ᵛ: Koimesis of Basil

329. Fol. 136ʳ: Caesarea

330. Fol. 188ᵛ; Teaching Scene

331. Fol. 203ᵛ: Gregorys in Proskynesis; Nyssa

332. Fol. 189ʳ: Gregory and Father; Nazianzus

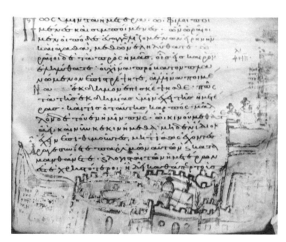

333. Fol. 209ʳ: Patriarchal Throne; Constantinople

334. Fol. 208ᵛ: Gregory Teaching

ATHOS, VATOPEDI. COD. 107

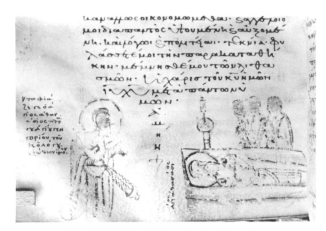

335. Fol. 226ᵛ: Koimesis of Athanasius

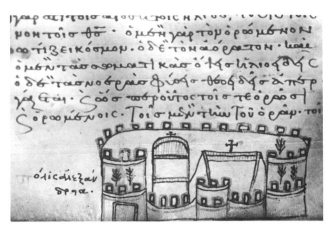

336. Fol. 227ʳ: Alexandria

337. Fol. 248ᵛ: Christ Blesses Feeding of Poor

338. Fol. 277ʳ: SS. Demetrius, George, and Other Saints

339. Fol. 277ᵛ: Virgin of Blachernae

340. Fol. 278ʳ: Christ and Saints

ATHOS, VATOPEDI. COD. 107

341. Fol. 1ᵛ: Anastasis

342. Fol. 33ᵛ

PATMOS. COD. 45

343. Fol. 27ʳ: Teaching Scene
with St. Mamas

344. Fol. 32ʳ: Pentecost

345. Fol. 42ᵛ: Gregory and Julian

346. Fol. 51ʳ: Nativity

347. Fol. 112ᵛ: Baptism of Christ

348. Fol. 123ʳ: Baptism of Christ

349. Fol. 61ʳ: Koimesis of Basil

350. Fol. 152ᵛ: Basil, Gregorys

351. Fol. 180ʳ: Gregory Teaching

352. Fol. 194ᵛ: Almsgiving

353. Fol. 227ʳ: Gregory and Cyprian

354. Fol. 237ʳ: Gregory and Father

SINAI. COD. GR. 346

355. Fol. 1ᵛ: Gregory of Nazianzus Offering Book to a Prince

ATHOS, DIONYSIOU. COD. 61

357. Fol. 4r: Vision of Habakkuk

356. Fol. 2r: Anastasis

359. Fol. 21v: Pentecost

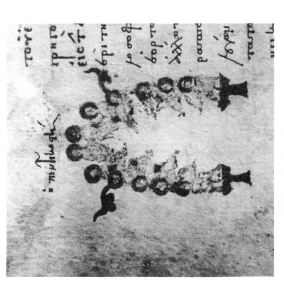

360. Fol. 21r: Pentecost

358. Fol. 17r: St. Mamas; Church and Synagogue

ATHOS, DIONYSIOU. COD. 61

363. Fol. 35ʳ: Koimesis of Basil; Painter at Work

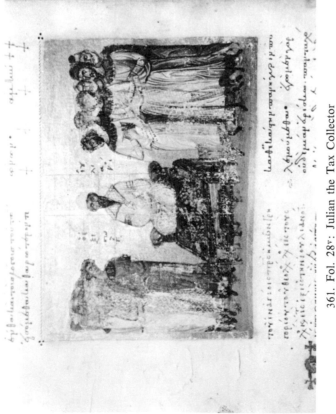

361. Fol. 28ᵛ: Julian the Tax Collector

362. Fol. 28ᵛ: Gregory and Scribe

365. Fol. 77r: Baptism of Christ

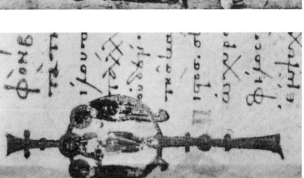

368. Fol. 77v: Baptism of Christ

367. Fol. 113r: Proskynesis

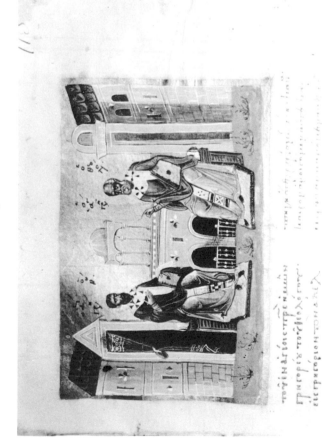

364. Fol. 70r: Nativity

366. Fol. 113r: Gregory of Nyssa and Gregory of Nazianzus

ATHOS, DIONYSIOU. COD. 61

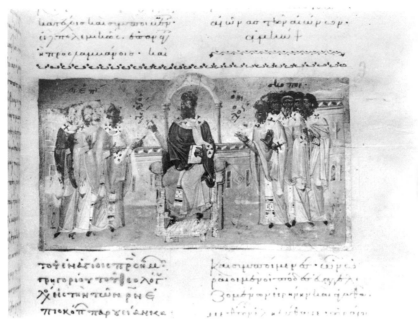

369. Fol. 130ʳ: Gregory Addressing Bishops

370. Fol. 142ʳ: Gregory and Poor

371. Fol. 130ʳ: Gregory
and Bishops

372. Fol. 142ʳ: Almsgiving

373. Fol. 165ʳ· Teaching Scene with Cyprian

374. Fol. 172ᵛ: Gregory and His Father

375. Fol. 165ʳ: Justina,
Cyprian, Christ

376. Fol. 172ᵛ: Gregory Teaching

ATHOS, DIONYSIOU. COD. 61

377. Fol. 4ᵛ: Author Portrait

SINAI. COD. GR. 339

378. Fol. 5ʳ: Anastasis

SINAI. COD. GR. 339

379. Fol. 9ᵛ: Vision of Habakkuk

SINAI. COD. GR. 339

380. Fol. 42ᵛ: Teaching Scene with St. Mamas; Doubting Thomas; Encaenia

381. Fol. 53ʳ: St. Mamas Milking

SINAI. COD. GR. 339

382. Fol. 54ʳ: Pentecost

SINAI. COD. GR. 339

383. Fol. 73ᵛ: Gregory and Julian the Tax Collector; Julian as Money Changer

SINAI. COD. GR. 339

εἰς Τὴν Γενεθλϊον Ημεραν Τ̅ κ̅υ̅ η̅μ̅ϊν ι̅υ̅ χ̅υ̅

Ὕ γράμματα·
Δόξα σ̅ο̅υ̅·
χ̅υ̅ ὁ λόγος ου,
ἀναση̣κ το ου
το· χ̅υ̅ ἑ οι γ̅η̅ς,
ὑφαθηι το αίσα

τὸ τω λϊῶ τωῦ
σαι η λϊωϊ ϊμ
ἁμφότερα ου
μελαμ έσω, ἅ
φραι μέσθω σαμ
οἱ ὀμωϊ ωϊᾱ ω

384. Fol. 91ʳ: Nativity

385. Fol. 91ᵛ: Worship of Virgin

386. Fol. 109ʳ: Gregory Teaching

387. Fol. 197ᵛ: Baptism of Christ

SINAI. COD. GR. 339

388. Fol. 109ʳ: Koimesis of Basil

389. Fol. 197ᵛ: Baptism of Christ

SINAI. COD. GR. 339

390. Fol. 217ʳ: Teaching Scene

391. Fol. 341ᵛ: Gregory and Poor

SINAI. COD. GR. 339

392. Fol. 381ᵛ: Martyrdom of Maccabees

393. Fol. 217ʳ: Baptism of Christ

394. Fol. 341ᵛ: Almsgiving

SINAI. COD. GR. 339

395. Fol. 397ʳ: Gregory, Cyprian, Justina

396. Fol. 397ʳ: Gregory, Cyprian, Justina

397. Fol. 397ʳ: Martyrdom of Cyprian

SINAI. COD. GR. 339

398. Fol. 3ᵛ: Crucifixion

PARIS, BIBL. NAT. COD. GR. 550

400. Fol. 4v: Author Portrait

399. Fol. 4r: Basil, John Chrysostom, Nicholas of Myra

PARIS, BIBL. NAT. COD. GR. 550

401. Fol. 5ʳ: Anastasis; Author Portrait

PARIS, BIBL. NAT. COD. GR. 550

405. Fol. 9ʳ: Shepherd

408. Fol. 34ᵛ: Bishop Baptizing Youth

404. Fol. 6ᵛ: Boys at Play

407. Fol. 30ᵛ: Gregory Teaching Church and Synagogue

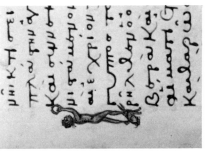

403. Fol. 6ʳ: Boy on Rabbit

406. Fol. 9ᵛ: Boy and Monkey

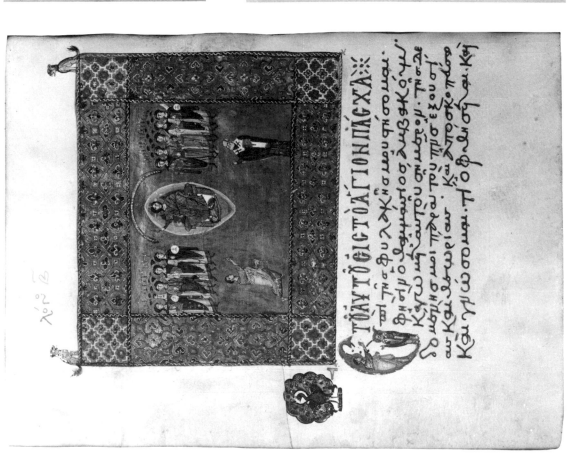

402. Fol. 8ᵛ: Vision of Habakkuk

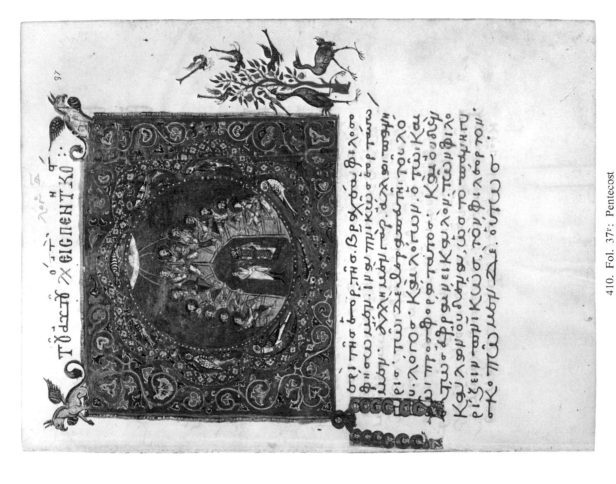

410. Fol. 37r: Pentecost

405. Fol. 30r: St. Mamas Praying and Milking; Boys Picking Fruit

PARIS, BIBL. NAT. COD. GR. 550

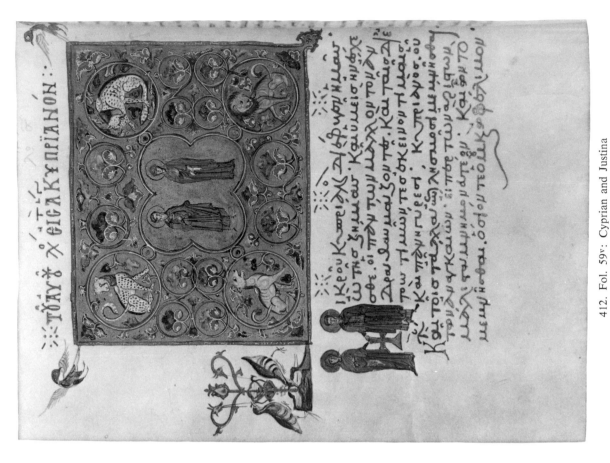

412. Fol. 59v: Cyprian and Justina

411. Fol. 49r: Eleazar, Solomone, and Maccabees; Hunting Scene

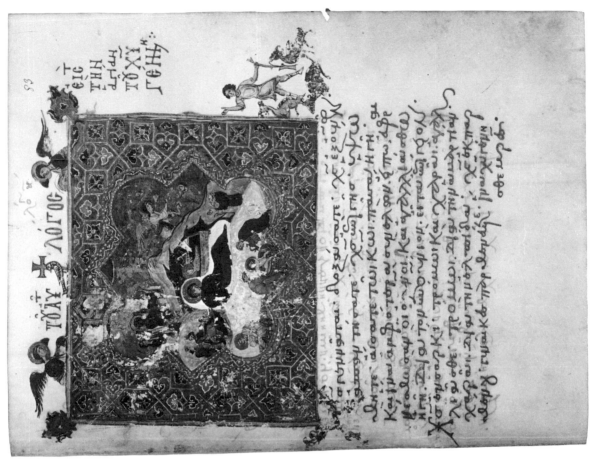

414. Fol. 83r: Nativity

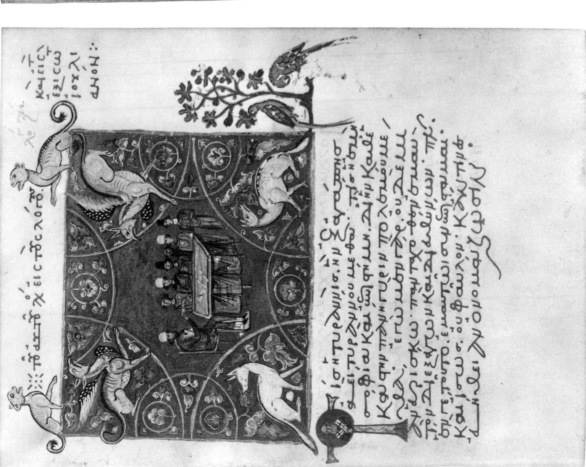

413. Fol. 72r: Julian Giving Tax Orders; Gregory of Nazianzus

PARIS, BIBL. NAT. COD. GR. 550

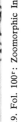

415. Fol. 94ʳ: Koimesis of Basil; Hunter and Bear

416. Fol. 204ʳ: Gregorys Meeting; Genre Scene

417. Fol. 94ᵛ: Koimesis of Basil

418. Fol. 99ᵛ: Dancing(?) Youth

419. Fol. 100ʳ: Zoomorphic Initial

420. Fol. 100ʳ: Genre Scene

421. Fol. 204ʳ: Gregorys Meeting

423. Fol. 166v: John Baptizing People

422. Fol. 153r: Baptism of Christ

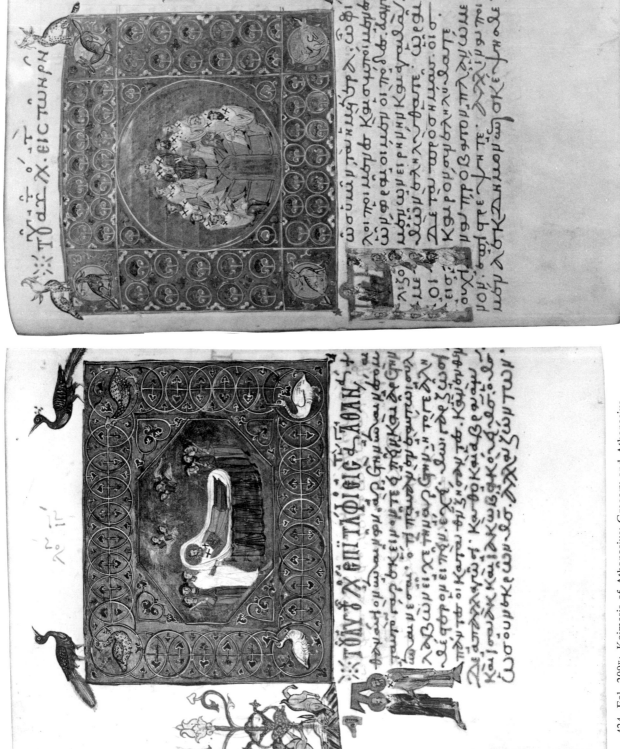

425. Fol. 232r: Gregory Addressing Bishops

424. Fol. 209v: Koimesis of Athanasius; Gregory and Athanasius

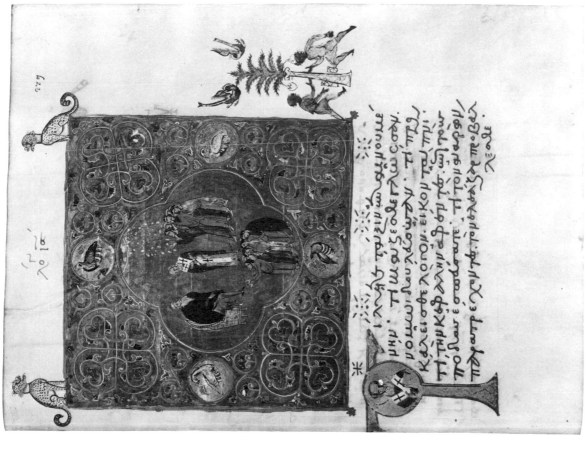

427. Fol. 279r: Gregory and His Father; Sapping Palm; Gregory Teaching

426. Fol. 251r: Almsgiving; Teaching Scene; Children at Play

PARIS, BIBL. NAT. COD. GR. 550

429. Fol. 1v: Author Portrait

JERUSALEM, PATR. LIB. COD. SABAS 258

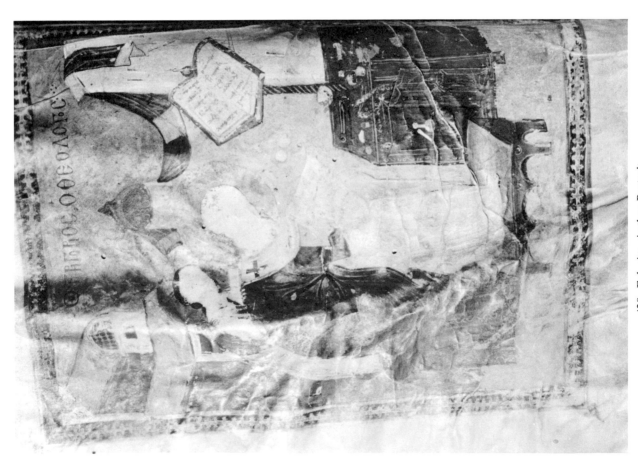

428. Fol. 4v: Author Portrait

ATHOS, PANTOCRATOR. COD. 31

434. Fol. 87ʳ: Nativity

431. Fol. 1ʳ: Deesis Scene

432-33. Fols. 98ᵛ, 205ʳ: Gregory of Nazianzus

ATHOS, STAVRONIKETA. COD. 15

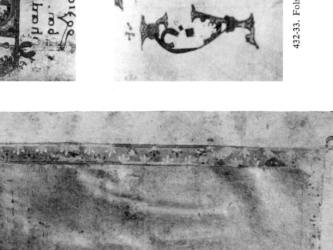

430. Fol. 1ᵛ: Author Portrait

ATHOS, LAVRA. COD. B. 111

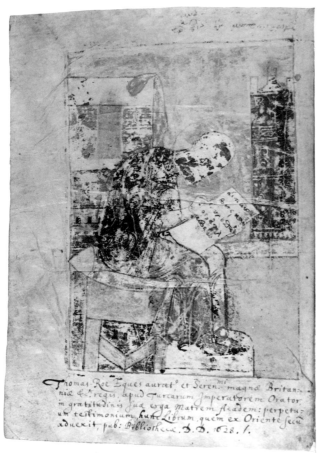

435. Fol. 1ᵛ: Author Portrait

436. Fol. 2ʳ: Anastasis

437. Fol. 4ʳ: Vision of Habakkuk; Gregory Teaching

438. Fol. 18ʳ: St. Mamas

OXFORD, BODL. LIB. COD. ROE 6

439. Fol. 22ᵛ: Pentecost

440. Fol. 30ᵛ: Nativity

441. Fol. 38ʳ: Koimesis of Basil

442. Fol. 73ᵛ: Baptism of Christ

OXFORD, BODL. LIB. COD. ROE 6

443. Fol. 103ᵛ: Group of Martyrs

444. Fol. 110ᵛ: Teaching Scene

445. Fol. 115ᵛ: Gregory Addressing Bishops

446. Fol. 128ʳ: Athanasius of Alexandria

OXFORD, BODL. LIB. COD. ROE 6

447. Fol. 143ᵛ: Teaching Scene

448. Fol. 159ᵛ: Eleazar, Solomone, and Maccabees

449. Fol. 167ᵛ: St. Cyprian

450. Fol. 175ᵛ: Teaching Scene

OXFORD, BODL. LIB. COD. ROE 6

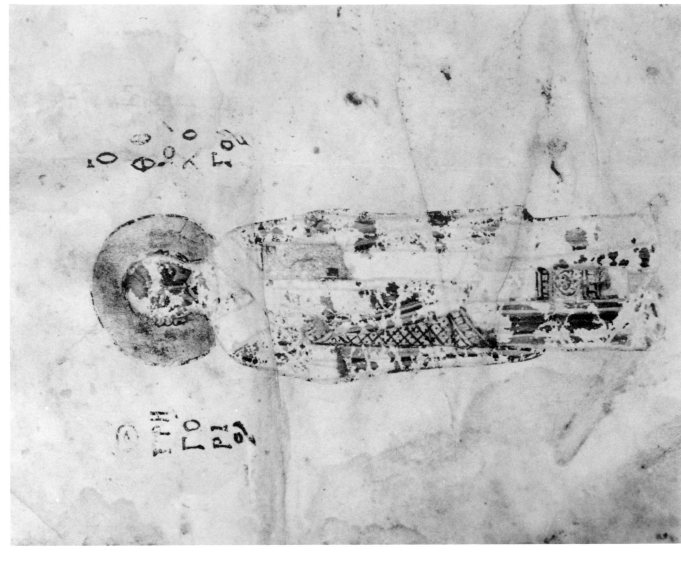

452. Fol. 3ᵛ: Author Portrait

ATHOS, KARAKALOU. COD. 24

451. Fol. 1ʳ: Author Portrait

MILAN, BIBL. AMBROS. COD. I 120 SUP. (GR. 470)

453. Fol. 6ᵛ: Vision of Gregory

455. Fcl. 27ᵛ: Vision of Habakkuk; Raising of Dead

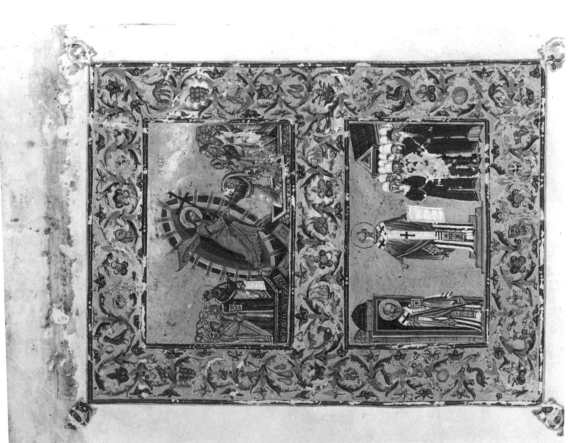

454. Fol. 23ᵛ: Anastasis; Gregory Teaching

PARIS, BIBL. NAT. COD. GR. 543

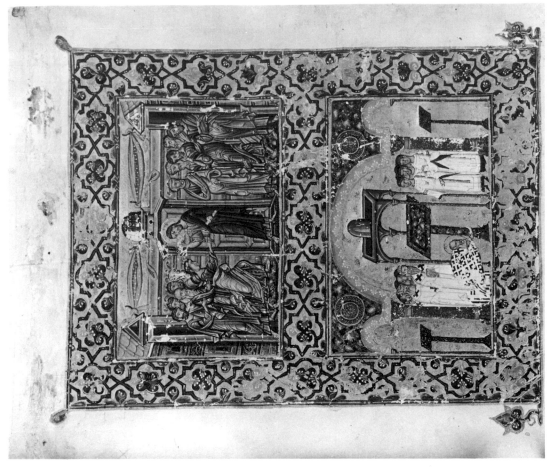

457. Fol. 51v: Doubting Thomas; Encaenia

456. Fol. 28r: Vision of Habakkuk

459. Fol. 87ᵛ: Cyprian Conversing with Devil; Author Portrait;
Martyrdom of Cypriar

458. Fol. 74ᵛ: Martyrdom of Maccabees

PARIS, BIBL. NAT. COD. GR. 543

461. Fol. 130ᵛ: Koimesis of Basil; Gregory Teaching

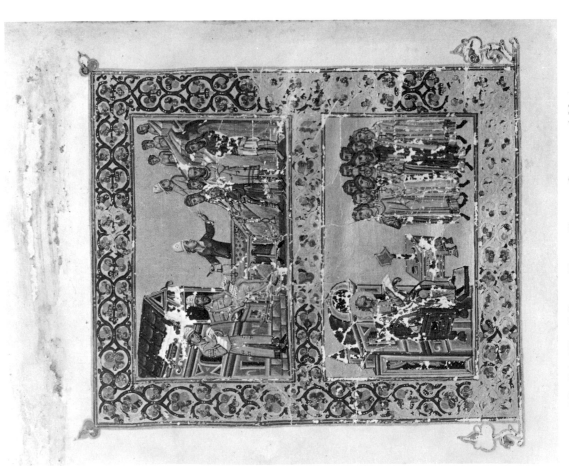

460. Fol. 102ᵛ: Julian as Money Changer; Gregory and Martyrs

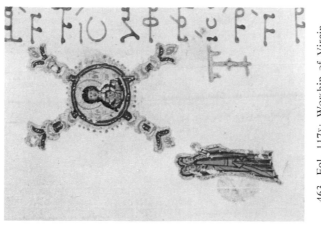

463. Fol. 117v: Worship of Virgin

462. Fol. 116v: Nativity; Genesis Scenes

PARIS, BIBL. NAT. COD. GR. 543

465. Fol. 213^v: John Baptizing; Teaching Scene

464. Fol. 197^v: Baptism of Christ; John Meets Christ; John Preaching

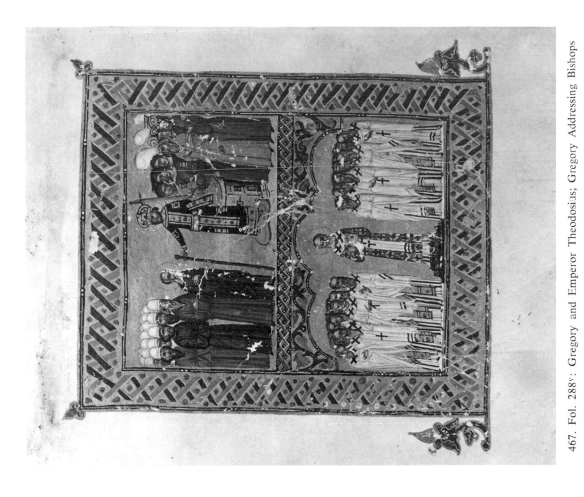

467. Fol. 288ᵛ: Gregory and Emperor Theodosius; Gregory Addressing Bishops

466. Fol. 260ᵛ: Koimesis of Athanasius; Gregory Teaching

PARIS, BIBL. NAT. COD. GR. 543

469. Fol. 342ᵛ: Gregory and His Father; Gregory Teaching

468. Fol. 310ᵛ: Gregory Teaching; Gregory and Poor

PARIS, BIBL. NAT. COD. GR. 543

471. Fol. 44ᵛ: Author Portrait

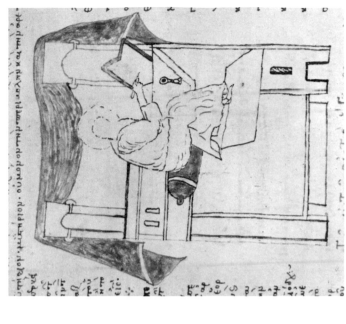

472. Fol. 76ᵛ: Author Portrait

470. Fol. 1ᵛ: Author Portrait

ROME, VATICAN. COD. GR. 464

473. Fol. 4ʳ: Author Portrait

474. Fol. 5ʳ

MOSCOW, STATE HIST. MUSEUM. COD. 155